MW00593896

NBC

NBC
America's Network

MICHELE HILMES, Editor

MICHAEL HENRY
Library of American Broadcasting, Photo Editor

UNIVERSITY OF CALIFORNIA PRESS
Berkeley   Los Angeles   London

University of California Press, one of the most distinguished university
presses in the United States, enriches lives around the world by advancing
scholarship in the humanities, social sciences, and natural sciences. Its
activities are supported by the UC Press Foundation and by philanthropic
contributions from individuals and institutions. For more information, visit
www.ucpress.edu.

University of California Press
Berkeley and Los Angeles, California

University of California Press, Ltd.
London, England

Library of Congress Cataloging-in-Publication Data

NBC : America's network / Michele Hilmes, editor ; Michael Henry,
Library of American Broadcasting, photo editor.
    p.   cm.
  Includes bibliographical references and index.
  ISBN-13: 978-0-520-25079-6 (cloth : alk. paper)
  ISBN-13: 978-0-520-25081-9 (pbk. : alk. paper)
    1. National Broadcasting Company, inc.   I. Hilmes, Michele, 1953–
II. Henry, Michael (Michael Lowell)
PN1992.92.N37N33 2007
384.55'06573—dc22   2006027331

Manufactured in the United States of America

15 14 13 12 11 10 09 08 07 06
10 9 8 7 6 5 4 3 2 1

This book is printed on New Leaf EcoBook 50, a 100% recycled fiber
of which 50% is de-inked post-consumer waste, processed chlorine-
free. EcoBook 50 is acid-free and meets the minimum requirements
of ANSI/ASTM D5634–01 (*Permanence of Paper*).

Contents

Illustrations

Acknowledgments

This book is a joint effort of its contributors. My thanks as editor go first of all to the authors of the chapters, whose expertise, hard work, determined research, brilliant insights, patience, and persistence made this volume what it is. I am very proud to bring their work together into a first attempt to sketch out a cultural history of one of the major social institutions of the twentieth century, the National Broadcasting Company.

Special thanks must go to Michael Henry of the Library of American Broadcasting (LAB) for serving as photo editor for the volume. Thanks, too, to Douglas Gomery, resident scholar at the LAB, for his assistance in this project.

Mary Francis at the University of California Press provided steady support and encouragement throughout the process of bringing this book to publication. I am grateful to the anonymous reviewers for their insightful comments on the volume in its early stages, and for their words of praise for the admittedly large and complex undertaking of comprising the history of a network in one small volume.

Thanks also to those within the NBC establishment who supported this project from the beginning, especially Horst Stipp, senior vice president for primary and strategic research, who coauthored a chapter with Karen Hill-Scott, a frequent consultant to NBC in the field of children's programming. William Bartlett, vice president of executive communications at NBC, took notice of the project early on and sent me copies of the recent NBC publications *Brought to You in Living Color* and *Connections: Reflections on 60 Years of Broadcasting*, both valuable histories undertaken by the network itself, along with many helpful comments.

Finally, thanks must go to the archivists of the Wisconsin Historical Society, the Wisconsin Center for Film and Theater Research, and the Library of Congress (as well as all of those mentioned in the book's final chapter); without their efforts of collecting, organizing, and preserving the important documents of NBC history, most of these chapters could not have been written. In particular, I would like to mention Peter Gottlieb, Harry Miller, Maxine Flexner-Ducey, and Dorinda Hart-mann as those whose assistance and support over the years have contributed greatly to historical scholarship both here and in many other publications.

It is my fondest hope that the publication of this volume on NBC's history will inspire those who have in their keeping the still-inaccessible papers of the other two major U.S. networks, ABC and CBS, to take steps to make those vitally important documents available to the public and to future generations of historians.

PART ONE

Broadcasting Begins
1919–38

Introduction to Part One

Broadcasting Begins, 1919–38

MICHELE HILMES

The late 1910s and early 1920s were a period of immense social and political up-
heaval in the United States, and indeed across the globe. Immigration, nativism, World
War I, the newfound power of women, migration from farms to cities, the growth
and problems of urban life, and a growing popular culture challenged nineteenth-
century Progressive notions of assimilation and control. Entertainment industries
like publishing, advertising, sports, movies, and vaudeville rose up to amuse, inform,
cajole, and educate the increasingly polyglot breed of Americans. A new kind of
popular culture developed at the grassroots level that many, especially the established elites, feared and resisted. Mass communication began to be recognized as
a powerful new social phenomenon in an atmosphere of expanding democracy and
social instability.

The advent of radio drew on and affected all these trends. Far from arriving as
a finished, uncontroversial technology that could be easily adopted by existing structures and hierarchies, radio stirred up conflicts, offered competing uses, provoked
struggles over whose interests would prevail, and raised fears about the dangerous
cultural forces that might be unleashed by this invisible medium of connection and
communication. Out of these many forces radio broadcasting arose as a vital and
necessary participant in the American experience. In chapter 1, "NBC and the Network Idea: Defining the 'American System,'" Michele Hilmes places NBC in the
context of these large social, political, and cultural forces and shows the role played
by America's first network in building up the United States' unique system of commercial network broadcasting.

In the period between the formation of RCA in 1919 and the founding of NBC
in 1926, radio broadcasting emerged from its previous domain in the garages and
attics of the amateurs and became a truly American social practice. Joining the social upheavals and disturbances of the Jazz Age, a time of rising affluence, increasing
social tensions, technological advancement, and cultural experimentation, radio

added its own unique voice to the mix. New institutions arose to address and control the growing business of radio. Though many U.S. governmental structures were similar to those in other nations, the United States, significantly alone among the major nations of the world, chose to entrust its rapidly growing broadcasting system to major private corporations rather than to the state. The rise of the commercial network represented America's major contribution to broadcast industry and culture. As it became important in people's everyday lives, radio also attracted serious debate. How should such a powerful new medium be controlled and shaped to best serve the public interest of all Americans? How could its threatening aspects be contained and its promises be developed? Over the next decade, Americans would strive to provide answers to these questions and in so doing would build one of the largest and most successful broadcasting systems in the world.

Yet the industry itself was not a unified and monolithic enterprise. Though NBC and CBS quickly became the two major players, exerting strong oligopolistic control over radio broadcasting in the United States, they also competed with each other and with the ever-more-powerful forces of the advertising industry. In chapter 2, "'Always in Friendly Competition': NBC and CBS in the First Decade of National Broadcasting," Michael J. Socolow traces the productive rivalry between the two major U.S. broadcasting networks. Advertising agencies began to dominate radio program production and often struggled with the networks for control over content. Combined, the radio networks, the advertising agencies, and the taken-for-granted American public created what some have called the golden age of U.S. radio broadcasting. However, forces arguing for radio to be constructed as a public service medium also ensured that the Communications Act of 1934, which created the Federal Communications Commission, would oversee the nascent medium with an eye toward the public interest. "Sustaining" programs, produced by the networks without sponsorship, provided education, religious programming, cultural events, and public affairs discussions. David Goodman discusses the evolution of this particular program form in chapter 3, "Programming in the Public Interest: *America's Town Meeting of the Air.*" Yet as his chapter demonstrates, race and ethnicity remained trouble spots for American radio. Many groups remained outside radio's emergent public sphere, including the voice of America's rising labor movement, described by Elizabeth Fones-Wolf and Nathan Godfried in chapter 4, "Regulating Class Conflict on the Air: NBC's Relationship with Business and Organized Labor."

From a collection of individual stations offering an eccentric mix of local entertainments, radio had grown by 1938 into an enormously profitable industry and a central focus of American life. Advertising agencies, networks, and stations, with a heavy dose of Hollywood, created unique new forms of entertainment, information, and expression. Though primarily intended to sell consumer goods, the avenues of innovation opened up by this amazingly successful medium allowed a variety of programs, genres, stars, and audiences to emerge that spoke to the hopes, fears, and desires of the American public. New organizations like the National Association of Broadcasters sprang up to lobby and speak for the new industry, and trade journals such as *Broadcasting* and *Sponsor* were initiated to serve them (and serve historians of the medium today). Ratings systems were devised so that advertisers could begin to understand this new creature, the radio public, and fan magazines rose up to cater to the audience's insatiable interest in their new radio friends. By 1937, 74 percent of America's households owned at least one radio set, and radio listening occupied on average more than 4.5 hours per day. The American broadcasting network had emerged as an institutional and cultural form central to national identity and American life.

1

NBC and the Network Idea

Defining the "American System"

MICHELE HILMES

NBC: the National Broadcasting Company. The name itself, so familiar by now we scarcely give it any thought, lays out the three factors crucial to understanding not only how NBC came to be but also how broadcasting emerged as one of our primary engines of cultural production around the globe.[1] First, *national:* when RCA announced the formation of its new radio "chain" in 1926, it introduced the first medium that could, through its local stations, connect the scattered and disparate communities of a vast nation *simultaneously* and address the nation as a whole. Thus radio could become a powerful means of creating and defining a national public, sorely needed in those nation-building years between the two world wars.

Second, *broadcasting:* this word was coined to denote a new form of communication that emerged in the early 1920s, one that emanated invisibly from a central source and passed with ease through not only physical but social and cultural barriers to reach listeners as private individuals in their homes. More accessible, more exotic (where did that distant station come from?), yet more intimate than any former medium, it created new forms of community and new modes of creative expression.

Third, *company:* In the United States, unlike most of the rest of the world, broadcasting would develop as a primarily privately owned enterprise, a business responding to market conditions rather than an organ of the state or a public service institution. Yet its power and centrality to national interests meant that it would also come under closer scrutiny and accept the basic compromise of government regulatory oversight to a far greater extent than other media, even in the United States with its First Amendment protections. These three factors—the accessibility and simultaneity of broadcasting, its unique capacity to link a nation and construct a feeling of national identity, and the private ownership that led quickly to advertising as an economic base—defined American broadcasting as a system sometimes imitated, sometimes reviled, around the world.

NBC was the first to put the three together. It positioned itself as "America's network," just as the British Broadcasting Company (BBC) was Britain's network and as other nations would soon form national networks, even though by contrast NBC would remain a private, not a public, corporation. Soon, in the national spirit of commercial competition, it would be joined by its closest rival, CBS. This chapter will trace the origins of the commercial network system of broadcasting as worked out by NBC and its parent company RCA in the 1920s and 1930s, looking at the essential tensions that drove its growth and the cultural results of its pioneering efforts. American radio negotiated a space for itself between principles of social diversity and cultural standardization, between forces of national integration and local independence, and between First Amendment–protected freedoms and the need for regulatory control. These tensions, often reductively articulated as a conflict between radio's public service responsibilities and its commercial economic base, resulted in the affiliate/network structure and the system of sustaining and sponsored programs pioneered by NBC in the 1920s and 1930s. This particular compromise was unique to the United States and represents the central innovation of the American system.

Chaos and Control

The story begins in the United States in the early decades of the twentieth century. By 1917, the year that the United States entered World War I, amateur experimentation with the wireless transmission of Morse-coded messages had already reached a fairly sophisticated level of organization. Groups like the American Radio Relay League had formed, organizing networks, holding yearly meetings, and devising a philosophy of what they called "citizens' radio": a vision of wireless broadcasting open to all, each person both a sender and a receiver of messages, untrammeled by either government restrictions or business considerations. Unlike the countries of Europe, at war since 1914 and still settling tense political conditions in the early 1920s, the United States allowed and even encouraged active amateur experimentation and growth, shutting amateur stations down only from 1917 to 1919. The war motivated rapid development of wireless technology, as well as training of thousands of young men and women as wireless operators, many of whom would pioneer radio broadcasting after the war as coded signals gave way to speech and music over the air (S. Douglas 1987, 1999; Hilmes 1997).

Among these amateurs was a young Russian Jewish immigrant named David Sarnoff, who by 1916 was already employed by the leading radio company operating in the United States, American Marconi, owned by its British parent corporation. Much has been made of Sarnoff's famous "radio music box" memo, which may have been written that year, in which he suggested that radio might become a popular means of listening to music carried invisibly over the airwaves into the home. In fact he was only one of many amateurs and experimenters already put-

FIG. 1 David Sarnoff at his desk at NBC headquarters, September 1941. (Library of American Broadcasting)

ting such ideas into effect nightly in garages and attics across the nation.[2] He was uniquely placed to implement the notion, however, and it seems likely that his enthusiastic participation in the amateur free-for-all of the postwar years influenced his understanding of the medium in many profound ways.

Sarnoff's immigrant origins point to another important factor in radio's developing role in U.S. society. Immigration to the United States had increased steadily through the turn of the century, reaching a peak in 1920, when nearly 35 percent of the U.S. population either had been born in a foreign country or had at least one foreign-born parent. In many large industrialized U.S. cities, that proportion exceeded 50 percent (Dinnerstein and Reimers 1975, 40). The wave of immigration of the 1860s through the 1920s brought, not the Anglo Saxon and Northern European Protestant settlers of the early period, who had tended to settle in rural areas on independent farms in the best Jeffersonian tradition, but shiploads of economic and political refugees from the "less civilized," poorer, mostly eastern and southern parts of Europe—Ireland, Italy, Poland, and the Balkans. The majority of these immigrants were Roman Catholics and Jews, crowding into tenements in the nation's exploding and expanding cities. Fears of cultural disintegration and lack of national cohesion began to circulate. How could the United States assimilate these swarming, disparate hordes? How could an American national identity be maintained in the face of this overwhelming diversity?

Most social theorists of the day agreed that communication was essential and that the expanding arena of popular media and entertainment, if properly supervised, could draw diverse populations into the social order; without such supervision, cultural chaos could spin out of control. In addition, experience with propaganda during the First World War had left the nation wary of the power that media offered the state and powerful groups and even more suspicious of the dangerous political currents swirling around on the street level during this tumultuous postwar period. Radio both promised a solution to these problems and threatened to exacerbate them. From the beginning, however, it was clear that issues of national identity and social control, in tension with traditional American values of diversity and freedom of expression, were too important to be left to chance, or the market, alone.

The Local and the National

Many Americans believed that the government, most likely the Department of the Navy, would need to take charge of the new medium; others deplored the amount of government intervention into private life that had occurred during the war and were determined that radio should remain in private hands. One important compromise was reached in March 1919, when the General Electric Corporation (GE), a leader in radio technology, negotiated to sell all rights to the important Alexanderson alternator to the British Marconi Company. This would have given Marconi a virtual world monopoly on state-of-the-art radio equipment. A young Franklin Delano Roosevelt, then assistant secretary of the navy, stepped in to propose that instead the government use its leverage to force the American Marconi company to sell its assets to GE and withdraw from the U.S. market in exchange for key patent rights abroad. Government and corporate interests cooperated to define and defend radio as a crucial national medium, an arrangement that would be replicated around the world.

In October 1919, GE, with the guidance of the federal government, formed a wholly owned subsidiary, grandly titled the Radio Corporation of America (RCA). Westinghouse, the American Telephone and Telegraph Corporation (AT&T), and the United Fruit Company became partners in RCA in 1920. This national organization brought together the major companies involved in radio research to pool their patents and coordinate the development of radio in the United States. RCA's charter stipulated that its ownership must be 80 percent American, that its board of directors must consist entirely of U.S. citizens, and that one member must be a representative of the government (Sterling and Kittross 2001, 58). David Sarnoff, formerly of American Marconi, became general manager. In 1930 he would be named president of RCA, from which position he would direct the continuing development of NBC.

This early attempt to exert some kind of national control over broadcasting would have a great impact on the equipment-manufacturing and station-building business; however, radio broadcasting itself—actually providing some form of content over the airwaves—was still a remote enough concept in 1919 that no provisions were made for a national broadcasting service (unlike the situation in 1922, when the BBC debuted). U.S. amateurs' early and extensive involvement in wireless telephony meant that over the next three years not only the members of RCA but thousands of individuals, nonprofit organizations, religious groups, small companies, and related commercial concerns such as newspapers, department stores, and movie theaters (also chicken farms, hardware stores, laundries, and a myriad of others) applied for and received licenses to broadcast with very little thought of interference or overlap.

By 1922 the unchecked diversity and populism of the airwaves provoked the first major move to rein it in: the creation by the U.S. Department of Commerce of the Class B license, which was distinguished from the more general Class A license in that it allowed approved broadcasters to shift their operations to a less crowded frequency in exchange for certain promises of quality in performance (Bensman 1976, 550–51). Most notably, these stipulations included a ban on the playing of recorded music (at least in part a reaction to the social panic over African American–rooted jazz that had recently swept the country) and a mandated preference for more expensive live performance that would persist into radio's heyday. This also brought into the picture the American Society of Composers, Authors, and Publishers (ASCAP), a powerful music rights organization interested in ensuring that royalties would be paid for live radio performances, and that development in turn inspired the foundation of the National Association of Broadcasters (NAB) in 1923 to negotiate on behalf of the emergent industry.

RCA itself, along with its constituent partners GE, Westinghouse, and AT&T, was among the first to obtain the new Class B licenses; meanwhile, amateurs faced increasing restrictions on the content of their broadcasts and would soon be banished to another part of the spectrum completely. Setting an important precedent for the field of radio, government and big business, working together, had come up with a way to "improve" broadcasting and restrict its access to "responsible" parties without making any actual First Amendment–infringing rules as to what content radio broadcasting should provide, and also without restricting the field to a single, state-licensed broadcaster, as was about to happen in England (M. Goodman and Gring 2000). However, the concept of radio as a truly open medium, accessible to all, had clearly been compromised in favor of more powerful, socially central groups: citizens' radio no more. Class B licenses became available by the end of 1922. Though their frequency and name changed in the aftermath of later regulatory decisions, many of the Class B licensees remain on the air today and would form the backbone of network operations.

Despite its socially and politically exclusionary intentions, the Class A and B distinction also worked to confirm the principle of locally licensed stations, establishing for American radio a firm basis in *localism* rarely found in other nations.[3] Even at the height of network radio, a mid- to large-size U.S. city typically offered anywhere from five to ten or more locally operated radio stations, most of them unaffiliated with a network[4] and thus open to a plethora of community-originated, syndicated, ethnic, foreign-language, and marginal programming. Network affiliates preserved a high level of local identity and content; they were responsible for programming much of the broadcast day—not least in the area of local news—and could reject network programs in favor of their own, though the networks' steady undermining of this right of preemption would provoke the "chain broadcasting" investigation of 1938–41, as Christopher H. Sterling discusses in chapter 5.

Radio in the United States would thus develop in a productive tension between the local and the national, in strong contrast to the highly centralized national systems established in many other countries. Localism's central position in the U.S. system of radio—as indeterminate and contradictory a concept as it has proven to be in application—not only reflected the facts of U.S. radio's early history but also functioned as the guarantor of decentralization, both cultural and political, so vital in American political thought and so deeply rooted in the diversity of American cultural origins and influences. To further this policy, U.S. regulators regarded allocation of "the maximum technically feasible number of stations around the country" as a vital part of their task (Newton 2003, 870). One of the first actions of the Radio Act of 1927 was to divide the nation into five zones for frequency allocation purposes; the Davis Amendment in 1928 required equality of allocation across the zones.

In most other nations, such as France and Britain, both localism and cultural diversity took a back seat to a centralized, state-mandated monopoly and a carefully constructed homogeneity of culture and address. Some, like the Netherlands, allocated broadcasting outlets to established pillars of social and political power, such as religious and political groups. Switzerland and Belgium focused on linguistic regions. Localism was America's bottom-up answer to such top-down determinations, and one factor that troubled many observers about the formation of networks linking such local stations into New York–based chains was the subversion of localism that they seemed to imply. The relationship of NBC and CBS to their affiliates would thus not only form the backbone of commercial broadcasting's economic system but also become the primary source of contention between broadcasters and their critics and regulators.

The Birth of Networks

The first steps toward the formation of NBC were taken both by RCA and by AT&T. In 1922, RCA established WJZ, later to become the flagship station of its Blue network. At first based in Newark, New Jersey, it would move into New York City the following year, building state-of-the-art studios in the Aeolian Building on 42nd Street just off Times Square. AT&T opened its pioneering station WEAF that same year a little further uptown, where it would undertake some of the first experiments in chain broadcasting—tying two or more stations together via telephone wires to create the first network. Later, it would be sold to RCA and become the key station of NBC's Red network. Over the next five years, both of these early Class B stations came up with many of the programs and practices that served as prototypes for American radio. Bertha Brainard, WJZ's first program manager, who later served as station manager and then NBC's first director of commercial programming, originated one such show in 1922 that took advantage of WJZ's enviable location: the alliteratively titled *Bertha Brainard Broadcasting Broadway*. Bringing Broadway stars to the microphone for interviews and skits, and eventually airing entire stage productions, this program represented radio's ability to translate and enhance existing cultural forms in a broadcast format, a concept that would soon be extended to symphonies, jazz bands performing in hotels and ballrooms, sports events, and political conventions.

During this early period, WJZ's economic function within RCA was to provide incentive for the purchase of radio receiver sets and not to make a profit itself. Thus much of WJZ's schedule consisted of programs provided free of charge—and broadcast without charge by the station itself—by those with services to promote or goods to sell. Prominent among such early program providers were magazines and newspapers, music publishers and talent agencies, hotels, department stores, and theaters.

Nearby, AT&T's station WEAF took a different approach. Since AT&T, by agreement with its RCA partners, was not in the business of selling radio receivers, it came up with an economic model based on that of the telephone: toll broadcasting. WEAF invited would-be sponsors to purchase time, in fifteen-minute or half-hour installments, to deliver their sales message along with entertainment for a fee, just as a telephone caller paid a fee to make use of telephone lines. One of its earliest successes was *The Eveready Hour*, sponsored by the National Carbon Company (maker of Eveready batteries) and produced by their advertising agency, N. W. Ayer. This early hit show was based on a vaudeville variety format that starred ukulele-strumming Wendell Hall, "the red-headed music maker," and a group of recurring performers. AT&T also used WEAF to experiment with one usage of radio that centrally featured AT&T's unique control over telephone landlines that stretched across the United States. Starting with just two or three stations linked together by wires, by early 1924 AT&T had connected stations in twelve cities for a special broadcast of the Republican National Convention. By October 1924, a regular three-hour block of programs was offered daily, and by the spring of 1925 thirteen stations in twelve cities had joined the chain. *The Eveready Hour*, airing on Tuesdays from 9:00 to 10:00 p.m., formed a cornerstone of the schedule. RCA also experimented with linking stations, but without access to AT&T's telephone network they were restricted to leasing lower-quality telegraph lines from Western Union.

Growing disputes over the division of the burgeoning radio business among

RCA's sometimes restless partners led to a series of lawsuits and a decision reached by arbitration in November 1925 that ended AT&T's foray into radio station ownership and programming. Its continuing monopoly over telephone landlines, however, would keep the company in a profitable position at the heart of network broadcasting. In July 1926, AT&T sold WEAF to RCA and retreated to its primary business, the manufacture of telephone equipment and the provision of landlines and service. Just two months later, on September 9, 1926, RCA announced the launch of its new business in momentous terms:

> ANNOUNCING THE NATIONAL BROADCASTING COMPANY, INC. *National radio broadcasting with better programs permanently assured by this important action of the Radio Corporation of America in the interests of the listening public.* . . . The purpose of that company will be to provide the best programs available for broadcasting in the United States. . . . The Radio Corporation of America is not in any sense seeking a monopoly of the air. . . . It is seeking, however, to provide machinery which will insure a national distribution of national programs, and a wider distribution of programs of the highest quality. [emphasis in original][5]

RCA's linking of "national" with "quality," along with its disclaimer of intention toward monopoly, would provide the nascent network's keynotes throughout its early years. The monopoly issue, however, would not soon go away.

NBC expanded its programs over two networks, the Red, anchored by WEAF, and the Blue, captained by WJZ. Over the next two decades they would both grow exponentially but unevenly, as the Red remained the more popular and commercial, and thus the more profitable, while the Blue linked lower-power stations into a less commercial network but one that showcased NBC's primary nonsponsored public service (sustaining) cultural and educational programs.

This much radio power in the hands of one company began to cause concern among political leaders, social reformers, and smaller radio operators alike. American radio companies followed the developments in Britain closely. They were aware of the BBC's state-chartered monopoly of national network broadcasting that had begun to emerge as early as 1924, as the early BBC (a private organization of manufacturers, much like RCA, until its nationalization in 1926) began to centralize broadcasting and close down local stations. Fears of a similar monopoly were circulating in the U.S. press (along with a considerable amount of admiration for the British system and a desire for the U.S. to emulate it), and the monopoly status of AT&T in the telephone field and RCA in the radio manufacturing arena added to these concerns (Hilmes 2003).

Meanwhile, American radio still operated under the rather loose system of licenses administered by the Department of Commerce. A series of radio conferences had been called by Commerce Secretary Herbert Hoover from 1922 to 1925 in an attempt to amend the by now out-of-date Radio Act of 1912 and address the relative scarcity of available frequencies compared to the number of would-be users. Here, fears of monopoly, both state and commercial, competed with the threat of perceived chaos in the air, both technical and cultural. In 1926 a lawsuit filed by the Zenith Corporation against Secretary Hoover, questioning the legal basis of any of his regulatory decisions, was decided in favor of Zenith, and "in a period of seven months, more than 200 new stations went on the air, creating intolerable interference in major urban areas" (Sterling and Kittross 2001, 98). Commercial stations—which had invested significantly in their radio operations—found themselves drowned out by wayward enthusiasts and pressed for a solution, not least among them the newly launched NBC network and its powerful parent, RCA. In February 1927, Congress finally passed a new Radio Act that created the Federal Radio Commission (FRC) in an effort to bring order to the airwaves. Not just technical issues were at stake; reimposition of social order would be one of the tasks of the new commission as well.

During this early period, regulators paid limited attention to the experimentation with networking going on at AT&T and RCA; with a plethora of ideas swirling around about how radio might be organized, the FRC initially concentrated primarily on the pressing issue of local station licensing. Given the preexistence of hundreds of local stations, already well established and broadcasting a variety of entertaining, informative, and promotional messages in their separate localities, U.S. radio regulators focused on the contentious process of balancing regional allocation of licenses—no congressman wanted to see his district lose any service—and on the difficult task of reconciling free-speech protections with the development of some kind of criteria as to which applicant might receive such local preference.

Networks and Affiliates

Passage of the Radio Act of 1927 ushered in the era of network dominance, despite its framers' ambivalence about NBC's emergent chain and its parent RCA's monopoly in the radio market. Though cautions against monopoly were sounded throughout the act, with so many voices in the airwaves dispersed unevenly about the country, chaos seemed to be a more pressing problem than monopoly. The FRC's first task was to restructure the system for assigning station licenses. After coming up with a plan for dividing radio stations into three categories based on service requirements and signal strength—clear channel, regional, and local—across the five regions, the FRC next devised criteria on which to base licensing assignments. In 1928, General Order 40 developed a framework that created a preferred category of "general public interest" stations—commercial stations selling time to any and all—and gave such stations higher power and more favorable frequency allocations. Those owned and operated by nonprofits, schools, religious and social organizations, and political groups—including labor unions—were classified as "propaganda" stations: stations committed to representing only one point of view or set of interests and thus not open to the general public. These stations were to be discouraged, and many of them soon found themselves assigned to shared frequencies operating on the lowest power.[6] General public interest stations—a category that included all the powerful clear-channel and most of the regional licensees—were constrained to operate only in the "public interest, convenience, and necessity," a phrase borrowed from public utility law and never clearly defined.

This distinctly American conception of the public interest, privileging commercial business operations over nonprofit public service, was the exact reverse of the BBC's definition, which considered commercial broadcasters inherently private and thus not able to operate in the service of the public. It demonstrates the "Progressive compromise" between government and business so influential in the shaping of American broadcasting (Hilmes 2006). Rather than making licensing decisions that might violate First Amendment freedoms by giving preference to one group's point of view over another, the FRC deflected the issue by turning control of broadcasting speech over to the marketplace. Commercial stations would sell time freely to all on the basis of their ability to pay, not the content of their speech, and with many small, local stations available in every market, every voice could find an audience; this was the concept. National broadcasting, however, would be dominated from the beginning by large commercial corporations, and decisions made on the basis of their corporate interests would influence the scope of radio's free speech.

Within three years of the act's passage and the extensive reassignment of frequencies that followed, hundreds of small, nonprofit stations had lost their licenses or gone out of business due to unfavorable time and frequency assignments, while the more powerful stations owned by larger commercial interests thrived. Many of them received the clear-channel assignments that enabled them to be heard across large sections of the country. Starting out with 28 affiliates by the end of 1927, NBC claimed 71 by 1930, 88 by 1934, and 182 (53 Red, 60 Blue, 69 that alternated) by the end of 1940. CBS's growth was equally impressive; debuting a year after NBC in 1927 and purchased by William Paley in 1928, it went from 17 affiliates that year to 112 in 1940 (Sterling and Kittross 2001, 830–31). Though networks owned and operated some of their stations, all affiliates were local stations licensed to serve a specific geographical area, most of them owned by local businesses or other organizations in the community.[7] They elected to air NBC or CBS programs for part of their broadcast day or in many cases, during the first decade, switched from NBC to CBS depending on the program and local audience tastes. The rest of the time they provided either locally produced or, increasingly, syndicated recorded programs. In 1929, the three networks (NBC-Red, NBC-Blue, and CBS) combined put out approximately 351 hours of national programs per week; by 1935 that figure had risen to 809, and by 1941 it was 1,078—distributed over four networks by then, since the new Mutual Broadcasting System had joined the competition in 1934 (Sterling and Kittross 2001, 848). This meant that most affiliate stations broadcast local, or at least locally selected, programming for much of their day, with network programs aired largely at night and at certain key parts of the daytime. In 1939, NBC provided approximately sixteen hours of programs to its affiliates each day, stating as its philosophy, "To help create a true democracy of the air, NBC has sought to preserve the individuality which characterizes every station's approach to its own audience" (NBC 1939, 14–15). Of course, affiliates had to agree to clear the best parts of their schedules for network transmissions, leaving only late night, early morning, and weekend daytime hours for expressing such individuality.

The economic system worked out by NBC and its affiliates in the early years proved cumbersome as network broadcasting expanded. Networks provided two classes of programs to their affiliates: commercial (sponsored by advertisers) and sustaining (nonsponsored, produced by the networks themselves or by nonprofits). NBC paid its affiliates a flat fee to take the commercial programs, since the network was compensated by sponsors on the basis of the number of stations, and hence listeners, they could provide, but it required its affiliates to pay the network for sustaining programs. Stations might do this to fulfill their own public service obligations or to attract an audience to higher-quality programs than could be produced locally; they could then sell advertising spots adjacent to these broadcasts to local sponsors.

However, as Michael J. Socolow discusses in the next chapter, as CBS grew into a full-size network William Paley recognized that a simpler and more beneficial system would be to eliminate the revenue stream from the affiliates and replace it with tighter guarantees that a station would accept and air the *entire* network schedule of programs, both commercial and sustaining. NBC adopted his system in 1935, and it became an increasingly controversial aspect of network operations during later regulatory investigations, which Christopher H. Sterling analyzes in chapter 5.

Sponsored and Sustaining Programs

During this early period, the networks briefly enjoyed more creative control over broadcast production than they would again until the 1960s. Part of the task of the nascent NBC was to step up its own production of programs; rather than relying solely on other self-promoting businesses to fill up the broadcast hours, NBC itself, as its announcement promised, would take responsibility for the production of network programs in the name of quality (as the BBC had been doing in Britain since the early 1920s). In November 1926, Bertha Brainard, newly named director of commercial programming, wrote to a potential client: "This department secures suitable talent of known reputation and popularity, creates your program and surrounds it with announcements and atmosphere closely allied with your selling thought."[8] One function of sustaining programs was to attract advertisers; these programs might be unsponsored for a period of time, but it was the networks' hope that a sponsor would quickly pick them up.[9]

By 1932, however, sponsors came to perceive that they—or more likely, their advertising agencies—might more successfully produce programs "allied with their selling thought" than could a network whose loyalties were divided. By the mid-1930s, almost all evening programs, and a large proportion of daytime programs, were originated and produced by sponsors and advertising agencies. During the

FIG. **2** Bertha Brainard, early program innovator, WJZ station manager, and NBC's first director of commercial programming. (Library of American Broadcasting)

daytime, in fact, networks frequently sold time in hour-length blocks to big advertisers like Procter & Gamble, who might produce four fifteen-minute serials, each promoting a different P&G product. Sponsors effectively took out long-term leases on a particular day and time slot, filling it with the program of their choice, and since networks had very little stake in programs, sponsors frequently moved them to a rival network if a better deal, or a better time, was offered.[10]

Thus, although NBC and CBS can take credit for originating early forms of many radio broadcast genres that still exist today on television — the variety show, the serial drama, the quiz show, the news commentary, the homemaker talk, the public affairs program, and many more — it was in the creative meetings and planning sessions of advertising agencies and their sponsors that these genres developed and grew into staples of modern popular culture. NBC had promised quality national programs; sponsors took that promise and ran with it, all the way to the bank. On the way they innovated cultural forms today known around the world.

In 1931 NBC President Merlin Aylesworth wooed John F. Royal, station manager of the powerful independent station WTAM-Cleveland, to the post of NBC vice president of programming, a new position supervising both commercial and sustaining program production. His background in vaudeville and his firm belief in the value of established entertainment forms on radio helped usher in the years now often thought of as radio's "golden age" (Hilmes 1997). If sponsors were willing to take on the responsibility of providing programs to the network, programs that would attract large audiences and bring big-name stars to the air, Royal was willing to work with them and allow them creative independence—along the lines of a vaudeville house manager, inviting in different acts. Sponsors could provide larger budgets than NBC could afford to expend across its schedule, hastening the transformation of the network to a time broker and, increasingly, censor of programs created outside Royal's immediate direction. RCA's acquisition of the film studio RKO in 1929, in response to the coming of sound to American cinema, only accelerated the creation of big-name, big-budget productions that inspired the shift to sponsor control.

Many of NBC's first commercial successes came in the variety format, inspired by vaudeville and often named after their sponsors: *The Fleischmann's Yeast Hour*, starring Rudy Vallee; the *RKO Theater*, sponsored by RKO; *The Camel Pleasure Hour* (Camel cigarettes); *Jones and Hare*, the "Interwoven Pair," sponsored by Interwoven Socks; and so on. *The Jack Benny Program*, which debuted in 1932, sponsored by Canada Dry, settled down in 1934 with Jello and became the jewel in NBC's entertainment crown. As the 1930s progressed, serial drama and comedy programs rose in popularity, from *The Goldbergs* and *Amos 'n' Family* (Standard Brands), and *First Nighter*, an early dramatic anthology program (sponsored by Campana Balm).

The comedy serials would survive and reach their peak of popularity in the 1940s with *The Great Gildersleeve* (Kraft), *The Life of Riley* (Procter & Gamble), *The Aldrich Family* (Procter & Gamble), *A Date with Judy* (Tums), and many more, some of which would carry over into early television. And the thriller drama would go from relative obscurity to enormous popularity in the late 1930s and early 1940s, though here NBC's roster took a back seat to those of its rivals CBS and Mutual. However, NBC's *Mr. District Attorney* (Bristol Myers) achieved some of the highest ratings in that category, as did *Mr. and Mrs. North* (Jergens Lotion). Other serials, mostly with domestic settings and attracting a primarily female audience, would be transferred to daytime schedules in the mid-1930s as the networks increasingly defined daytime as the province of women, both as audiences and as producers. By 1940 more than fifty different serials filled the daytime hours on the four networks, often gaining ratings higher than their comedy and thriller equivalents; they included *Ma Perkins* (Oxydol), *The Story of Mary Marlin* (Ivory Soap), *The O'Neils* (also Ivory), *Pepper Young's Family* (Camay Soap), *Stella Dallas* (Phillips), *Vic and Sade* (Crisco), and *The Guiding Light* (White Naptha). It's easy to see why these were dubbed soap operas.

By 1936, sponsors' appetite for name-brand stars had moved the center of radio production from New York to Hollywood. NBC built a state-of-the-art production studio at the corner of Hollywood and Vine to complement its stunning new headquarters at Rockefeller Center in the heart of Manhattan. In addition, both NBC and CBS started their own talent bureaus in the 1930s, finding another income stream in providing the acting and musical talent that the agencies and sponsors required. NBC remained committed to the idea of the network as primarily a facilitator (and profit taker) of programs produced outside its immediate purview. CBS, however, would begin in the late 1930s to take a more active role in creating or commissioning programs, for which it would then seek out sponsors. Douglas Gomery in chapter 9 explores the difference this would make to NBC's and CBS's fortunes in the early years of television.

Another significant change in network operations would occur in the mid-1930s as the broadcasting industry responded to pressures for reform. The debates that preceded and shaped the Communications Act of 1934 both solidified corporate control of radio and placed new public service requirements on broadcasters. Both NBC and CBS expanded and changed their definition of sustaining program production. Now sustaining programs became the primary venue for a version of "quality" that competed with that of the commercial programs. This definition had been heavily influenced by the example of the BBC, often invoked during the regulatory debates by educators and broadcast reformers, and was based on notions of education, information, and cultural uplift (Sterling 2003, 1354–56).

Sustaining public service programs produced by the networks during this period included public affairs discussions such as *America's Town Meeting of the Air* (NBC-Blue, 1935), which David Goodman analyzes in depth in chapter 3, and *The University of Chicago Round Table* (NBC-Red, 1932) initiated by Judith Waller, NBC's head of the central division of public service programming. Sustaining "quality" music programs included not only broadcasts by the NBC Symphony Orchestra, directed by Arturo Toscanini (NBC-Red, 1936), but also regular performances by the Cincinnati Conservatory Symphony, the Metropolitan Opera, the Westminster Choir, the New York Philharmonic, the Salt Lake Tabernacle Choir, the Cleveland Symphony Orchestra, and many more. The daytime, early evening, and late evening hours were filled by much sustaining "light" music by such artists as Art Tatum, the Ink Spots, and a warbling host of lesser-known sopranos, tenors, quartets, and duos.

Sustaining dramatic anthology and "informative drama" shows included *Radio Guild Dramas* (NBC-Blue, 1930), *The American School of the Air* (CBS, 1933), the *Columbia Workshop* (CBS, 1936), *The World Is Yours* (NBC-Red, 1935), produced by the Smithsonian Institution, and many others. Free airtime and production support for informational "talk" programs were provided to groups such as the Academy of Medicine, the Federation of Women's Clubs, the U.S. Department of Agriculture, the National Parent-Teachers Association, and the American Medical Association. Provision of religious programs had been taken into network hands in the wake of Father Coughlin's controversial career, and by 1937 NBC's roster included *The Catholic Hour*, *Message of Israel*, *National Radio Pulpit*, the *Devotional Program*, and *Religion in the News*. Regular news programs tended to be sponsored, although the controversy-provoking character of news commentary often meant the departure of sponsors, so that the networks sustained these programs for at least part of the time. During

World War II, the networks would work closely with the Office of War Information and other government and military agencies to provide a much-expanded schedule of public service and informative programming.

As can be seen from the examples above, the networks approached sustaining programs much as they did sponsored shows: they provided airtime (in this case, for free) to selected organizations and interest groups who themselves created and (with NBC's assistance) produced their programs. With a few significant (and much-trumpeted) exceptions, NBC played not so much a creative as a gatekeeper role, just as with commercial programs; in both arenas the networks developed policies that permitted some groups easy access to the airwaves and barred or discouraged others. They worked most comfortably with mainstream groups and those with government and big business credentials; many groups deemed controversial, such as labor unions (discussed by Elizabeth Fones-Wolf and Nathan Godfried in chapter 4) and smaller, less well-established religious groups, could neither purchase time on the air nor obtain free time from the networks under sustaining-program policies. They were effectively banned from the public airwaves. Though local stations chose separately whether to permit those whom the networks rejected to be heard over their wavelengths—Father Coughlin, for example, cobbled together his own ad hoc network of local stations for his radio addresses in the 1930s—in 1939 the National Association of Broadcasters amended its code to follow network policies.

For evangelical and nonmainstream religious groups, the Mutual network provided a home (Hangen 2002); for labor unions, it would take federal intervention in the 1940s to redress their exclusion. And many issues remained too hot to handle during much of network radio's history, especially anything having to do with America's continuing and central problem of racial exclusion and discrimination, as David Goodman discusses in chapter 3 and as David Weinstein takes into the war years in chapter 6. Not until World War II, when the need for national unity brought a redefinition of inclusion, would African Americans gain more access to the airwaves. This led to an increased awareness of the discrimination faced by minority and subordinated groups, in society and on the radio (Savage 1999).

Conclusion: The American System

By the late 1930s, broadcasting in the United States, led by NBC, had evolved into a system that significantly differed from the vision of broadcasting of the 1920s. The commercial success of radio as an advertising medium, and the pre–New Deal decision to make public service broadcasting an adjunct to commercial radio, led to the dominance of the commercial sponsor and its advertising agency in the creative process of producing popular radio programs. American radio became a cultural form that incorporated advertising into its very substance more thoroughly and intrinsically than any other medium of expression. The networks had been transformed, in the space of just a few years, into middlemen that supplied airtime, talent, and studio assistance to a wide variety of program providers: commercial, governmental, and civic. They would slowly begin to regain control over program production in the 1940s, but not until the 1960s in television would networks come again to dominate program selection, scheduling, and production as they had in radio in the 1920s.

Local stations continued to produce local programming, but those that affiliated with a network became far more profitable by turning more and more hours of their broadcast days over to network programs. Tighter contracts mandated fewer opportunities for opting out in favor of local tastes and interests, and this would be one of the primary concerns of the Roosevelt administration's investigation into chain broadcasting completed in 1941. Its findings led to the antiduopoly rule, requiring NBC to divest itself of one of its networks. The Blue chain was spun off in 1943 to become the American Broadcasting Company (ABC) in 1945.

However, the debates leading up to the Communications Act of 1934 introduced some important reformist concepts into American broadcasting that had not factored into earlier decisions. Most significant was the example of the BBC, which in the 1930s grew into the leading public service broadcasting system in the world. Many of radio's most avid reformers, and a good many of the terms of the debate, had been influenced by concepts and practices developed in Britain. NBC, in particular, maintained close ties to the BBC. NBC's president, Merlin Aylesworth, had become quite friendly with John Reith, the BBC's longtime head, and Reith himself saw NBC as the most responsible and respectable of the broadcasting networks in the United States. Though Reith's and others' hopes for a less commercialized service in the United States would be disappointed, the way sustaining programs and quality broadcasting were defined and understood after the passage of the act owed much to the example set by the BBC, particularly in the areas of music and drama.

Outside these areas, the United States' definition of quality and public service in broadcasting differed sharply from that of other nations. First, in the United States, neither commercialism nor popular entertainment was seen as incompatible with public service. Networks, sponsors, and regulators all believed that reaching the broad consuming public with entertaining programs was a public service in itself and could be used to promote not only goods and services but also cultural, social, and political ends. This comfortable definition placed some groups, particularly those that challenged the commercial system itself—such as labor unions— at a distinct disadvantage. But it did create a populist address that reached out to the middle- and working-class public, including women, far more effectively and inclusively than its state-chartered public service counterparts (Hilmes 2007). Second, decentralization of culture and the importance of the local played a primary role in U.S. ideas of public service; both the network/affiliate structure and the displacement of production, even of sustaining programs, onto outside groups and organizations demonstrated this principle in action. Not until the World War II years would NBC and CBS take on significant public service program production themselves, including regular network news reporting.

In 1937, NBC produced a glossy pamphlet celebrating the commencement of its second decade of broadcasting. Noting that "fully 70% of the 19,842 hours of network broadcasts in 1937 consisted of sustaining programs," the booklet promised to describe "NBC's march along the airways to greater service in the national benefit during 1937." News, international broadcasts, and the access that NBC had given federal government officials and departments led the presentation of proud moments, followed by separate chapters on educational, religious, and "serious" music and drama programs, with sports bringing up the rear. "And popular entertainment too!" was the title of the last section; the book ended with a two-page list, in very small print, of NBC's sponsors, titled "The Sponsor's Part in NBC's Service to the Public." Clearly a picture was being painted here of the sustaining tail wagging the commercial dog, ignoring the actual preponderance of commercial programming in terms of both audience popularity and the bottom line. Yet to dismiss this activity and its system of compromises and tensions as purely commercial is to misunderstand the American context that produced it. NBC became America's network because it negotiated the complexities and contradictions of its unique time and place. Its survival—despite profound changes to the network over the years, which this volume documents—and the spread of many of its innovations around the world testify to its central creative position in twentieth-century culture, and beyond.

Notes

Abbreviations

NBC/WHS National Broadcasting Company Archives, Wisconsin Historical Society

1. David Sarnoff himself suggested some alternative names in a letter he wrote to General Electric in 1922, proposing a company that would acquire and operate the broadcasting of RCA partners (except for AT&T): "the Public Service Broadcasting Company" or the "American Radio Broadcasting Company." Letter reprinted in Lichty and Topping (1976, 163–64).

2. NBC emphasizes Sarnoff's famous memo in *Brought to You in Living Color* (2002). It is reprinted in full in the pamphlet *Broadcasting in the Public Interest*, published by NBC in 1939.

3. This was affected, of course, by the United States' geographic size and access to spectrum space: a vast continent to cover, and only Canada and Mexico to contend with in frequency allocations, very different from the situation in Europe.

4. Though by 1947, network radio's apogee, 97 percent of stations were affiliated with a network, 46 percent were affiliates of Mutual, which had a much looser arrangement with its affiliated stations and provided fewer hours of national programming. See Sterling and Kittross (2001, 830–31).

5. The full announcement is reproduced in NBC (1939, 10–12).

6. Federal Radio Commission, *Third Annual Report of the Federal Radio Commission to the Congress of the United States Covering the Period from October 1, 1928 to November 1, 1929* (Washington, DC: U.S. Government Printing Office, 1929), 32–36; see also McChesney (1993, 23–29).

7. NBC reported owning ten stations in 1939 and managing—providing both network

and local programs for—five more, though these stations were owned by others. See NBC (1939, 15–16).

8. Bertha Brainard to C. B. Donovan, Acme Apparatus Company, November 26, 1926, Box 2, Folder 3, NBC/WHS.

9. John F. Royal, "The Network Program Department," Box 13, Folder 27, NBC/WHS.

10. Llewellyn White (1947) provides an extensive and highly critical analysis of the economics of network operations in his study done for the Commission on Freedom of the Press in 1947.

2

"Always in Friendly Competition"

NBC and CBS in the First Decade of National Broadcasting

MICHAEL J. SOCOLOW

On the night of November 11, 1933, the National Broadcasting Company celebrated the opening of its new Radio City facilities in the heart of New York City. Radio City's shining lights and soaring architecture sharply contrasted network radio's bright promise with the economic despair gripping the nation. NBC's stars celebrated the world's most technologically sophisticated broadcasting facilities in a program beamed around the globe. Invited to the festivities, but not asked to participate, was William Paley, the thirty-two-year-old president of NBC's rival, the Columbia Broadcasting System (CBS). Merlin Aylesworth, NBC's president, sent Paley a personal note shortly before the event. "In the spirit of battle both your Sales and Program Departments and mine will try to show how much better they are," Aylesworth wrote. "This is natural, but when all is said and done we should boost each other and radio. I never make a speech . . . dealing with radio broadcasting that I do not refer to you and Columbia always in kindly terms and as though we stood for the same cause always in friendly competition."[1]

Aylesworth's phrasing nicely encapsulates the relationship between America's two original commercial broadcast networks. The rivalry between NBC and CBS in the first decade of national broadcasting has never been adequately detailed. Between 1926 and 1936, NBC and CBS competed for listeners, advertising dollars, prestige, the services of popular entertainers, and, perhaps most importantly, the loyalty of affiliated stations around America. This rivalry could be fierce at times; the chains closely monitored, and tried to counter, each other's moves. Yet the competition would always be tempered by a mutual understanding among CBS and NBC executives that the economic development, political goals, and regulatory stability of the nascent industry required cooperation. The chains never attacked each other in public, nor did they engage in competitive price discounting for advertisers. They refrained from starting bidding wars for affiliates for most of the decade. These actions would have threatened the fragile political and economic stability of chain broadcasting. Executives of both chains understood that a publicly subtle and understated rivalry best served the interests of national commercial broadcasting.

NBC: America's Monopoly Chain

From the inception of NBC, the Radio Corporation of America (RCA) demonstrated an intense concern over the public perception that it maintained a monopoly in national network broadcasting. "No Monopoly in Radio," declared the September 13, 1926, public announcement of the National Broadcasting Company: "The Radio Corporation of America is not in any sense seeking a monopoly of the air. That would be a liability rather than an asset. . . . *If others will engage in this business the Radio Corporation of America will welcome their action, whether it be cooperative or competitive*" (118).[2] RCA executives raised the specter of monopoly to deflect criticism they considered inevitable. In its seven years of existence, critics regularly targeted RCA, accusing the company of employing unfair and illegal practices to control American radio manufacturing and marketing. Although RCA owned only 50 percent of NBC, the corporation's executives knew its establishment would appear to be another example of "radio's octopus" further extending its tentacles. RCA and its partners established an NBC Advisory Board to defuse criticism, and statements made by top executives were designed to cultivate the public perception that NBC would always place public service before corporate profit (Benjamin 1989).[3] Graciously inviting competitors to the field of national broadcasting offered evidence of RCA's good intentions.

Despite this public endorsement of competition, NBC had been established precisely to limit competition in network radio. Before 1926, two independent radio chains offered programming schedules to affiliated stations via dedicated wire lines. RCA, Westinghouse, and General Electric operated the WJZ network from WJZ-Newark, New Jersey. That chain utilized modified Western Union telegraph lines to deliver programming to affiliated stations. The WEAF network, owned by the American Telegraph & Telephone Company, connected stations via the landlines of the AT&T network. In addition to these technical differences, the chains maintained one significant policy difference: while WEAF introduced toll broadcasting—in which interested parties paid for the use of the network—the WJZ network offered its broadcasting facilities for free. The WJZ network existed solely to stimulate consumer demand for its founders' products: radio receivers and equipment. Because the WEAF chain siphoned revenue from AT&T, the telephone company commercialized the airwaves to help recoup its investment (G. H. Douglas 1987; Smulyan 1994).

This situation—in which one chain attempted to sell something (time on the air across several stations) that the other chain offered for free—created economic difficulties for both chain operators. "It used to disturb us greatly," remembered one AT&T executive, "to have WJZ . . . go out to the same advertiser that we were

trying to sell . . . and say, 'we'll give you time for nothing if you will put your program on WJZ.'"[4] Running competitive networks exacted a toll from their corporate owners. Between December 1924 and July 1926, RCA's market capitalization
fell from almost $91 million to $59 million; operating the unprofitable and increasingly costly WJZ network played an important role in the decline.[5] Although
WEAF's revenues would exceed its expenses by the close of 1925, chain broadcasting
cost AT&T more than $100,000 a year in 1923 and 1924 (Banning 1946, 268).

The creation of NBC in 1926 ended this fiscal uncertainty. Following a contentious series of negotiations, the two chains were brought together under one ownership group (Rosen 1980, 85–91). RCA, General Electric, and Westinghouse purchased WEAF and its network from AT&T in exchange for $1 million and a
generous contract guarantee for leased telephone lines. The new ownership announced the formation of NBC and opened the schedule of both networks for sale.
The creation of NBC legitimized the market for time on the nation's airwaves and
ensured fiscal stability in the field of network radio. Although network broadcasting would henceforth develop as a monopolistic commercial enterprise, the nascent industry's economic certainty heartened many. "Anyone who wishes to rival
this chain, having sufficient capital and brains, will find it possible," an editorial in
Radio Broadcast stated. "Broadcasting stations can be combined and wire lines hired
to link them. Commercial broadcasting has not yet developed to the point where
two competing chains can be profitably maintained. When that day comes the rival chain will come into being promptly."[6]

Despite this confident assertion, the unsettled state of radio regulation in 1926
proved far more critical in dissuading competition than commercial development
or the lack of "sufficient capital and brains." A court decision in April 1926 inval-
idated the existing framework for broadcast regulation. Consequently, between April
1926 and November 1928 hundreds of stations sprang forth on the American airwaves. Enthusiastic broadcasters created radio chaos by purchasing and operating
transmitters without considering issues of interference. Many of these enthusiasts
jumped long-established wavelength assignments and created severe difficulties for
both listeners and broadcasters (Slotten 2000, 37–42). The broadcasting industry,
and the public to a large extent, demanded that the government respond with a
new radio law. "The establishment of rival chains is a prospect impossible of con-
summation as long as the ether remains overcrowded," the editors of *Radio Broadcast* concluded in early 1927.[7]

Congress responded by passing the Radio Act of 1927. The act established the
Federal Radio Commission (FRC) and inaugurated a new regulatory process in
American broadcasting. From now on, every station would have to apply, and then
reapply, for wavelength assignments. Although the act empowered the FRC to immediately begin limiting access to the airwaves, the reestablishment of an ordered
radio spectrum would not be completed until late 1928. Yet it was within this chaotic
atmosphere that NBC's chief rival would emerge.

CBS: The Origins of Competition

Shortly after receiving word of the formation of NBC, Arthur Judson, a well-known New York City musician's agent, arranged a meeting with RCA's David Sarnoff. Judson later claimed that Sarnoff encouraged him to assemble an artists' bureau for NBC, and in September 1926 Judson incorporated the Judson Radio Program Corporation. When Sarnoff failed to follow up on that (disputed) conversation, Judson arranged a second meeting to solidify the arrangement. At that appointment Sarnoff brusquely rejected Judson's offer to work with NBC. As he left Sarnoff's office, a frustrated and angry Judson informed the RCA chief of his intention to create a rival to NBC (Barnouw 1966, 193–95).

Judson knew nothing of the broadcasting business. His principal aim was to find employment for his musicians. Shortly after the second meeting with Sarnoff, he discussed his radio chain idea with George Coats, a stock promoter he knew through friends at the New York Philharmonic. "Neither of us was interested in broadcasting," Judson remembered. "I was interested in music and Coats was interested in making money, with a quick [stock] turn-over, if possible."[8] Coats and Judson recruited Major J. Andrew White, an important figure in early radio, to front the enterprise. In a direct rebuke to NBC's monopoly, the men named the company they incorporated on January 27, 1927, the United Independent Broadcasters, Inc. (UIB). Throughout early 1927 Judson, Coats, and White pursued the requisite capital to break into national broadcasting. The first news of their endeavor appeared in the *New York Times*, which reported that the Paramount-Famous-Lasky movie corporation and the Columbia Phonograph Company would join together to back the chain. The idea behind the new chain "was said to hinge around the dramatizing of first run motion pictures and the exploitation of phonograph records on the radio."[9]

In fact, Paramount would not invest in the chain until after it had been broadcasting for over a year. Columbia Phonograph's commitment, while not substantial, came at a steep price: the phonograph company insisted that United Independent's chain be named the Columbia Phonograph Broadcasting System. Judson, Coats, White, and the other UIB shareholders agreed. Political connections were employed to secure the AT&T lines, and the new chain was publicly announced. "Nothing will help the broadcasting situation so much as real competition to the N.B.C. chains," wrote the editors of *Radio Broadcast*, arguing that a "nip and tuck battle for program supremacy" would benefit radio listeners, vendors of radios, advertisers, and even the competing chains.[10] On the evening of September 18, 1927, the Columbia Phonograph Broadcasting System inaugurated its chain radio service by airing a performance of the opera *The King's Henchman.*[11]

NBC's one-year head start proved a significant handicap to Columbia. During that initial year, NBC's promoters and salesmen traveled the country, impressing advertisers, their agencies, civic groups, and local station operators with their expertise. In April 1927, NBC established its Pacific Coast network. From key station

KPO-San Francisco, where it housed new offices and studios, NBC-affiliated stations up and down the Pacific Coast broadcast national-quality programs supplied by the chain.[12] Only weeks after Columbia's debut, NBC moved into its modern fifteen-story NBC Building on Fifth Avenue in New York City. Throughout 1927, AT&T and NBC engineers worked diligently to install the dedicated transcontinental radio circuit that would permanently link NBC's Pacific Coast chain with its east-of-the-Rockies "basic" chain (the permanent connection between Denver and San Francisco was completed on December 24, 1928) (Goldsmith and Lescarboura 1930, 170). With almost no evidence to prove the sales effectiveness of radio, NBC's sales force was still able to secure eighty-two different advertising accounts before the end of 1927.[13] Despite these auspicious moves, Merlin Aylesworth told the Federal Trade Commission in December of that year that NBC had not yet "broken even" in terms of profitability. In fact, NBC had an operating deficit of $464,585 in its first fourteen months of existence.[14]

Profitability also eluded the founders of the Columbia chain. Before Columbia aired its first program, George Coats signed sixteen stations to remarkably generous—and completely impractical—affiliation contracts. Coats promised to purchase from each station a minimum of ten hours a week at $50 an hour (this was NBC's standard station compensation rate). With sixteen stations, this committed Columbia to $8,000 per week in station compensation alone. These promises were made before the chain hired its first performers, paid for its AT&T lines, or secured a single advertiser. Columbia Phonograph agreed to operate the network under these conditions, but after just a few months, with a reputed loss of over $100,000 per month, the record company sold the operating rights back to the shareholders of United Independent and abandoned the business. A desperate Judson contacted Leon and Isaac Levy, the brothers who owned Columbia's key affiliate, WCAU-Philadelphia, for assistance. Ike Levy arranged a meeting with Jerome Louchheim, the owner of the Keystone State Construction Corp. Louchheim envisioned using the chain for his political interests (his business relied on public contracts), and in November 1927 he committed $150,000 toward the now renamed Columbia Broadcasting System. Louchheim's investment, combined with additional capital provided by the Levy brothers, kept the chain alive.[15]

Major White immediately contacted each affiliate to renegotiate the relationships. CBS would no longer guarantee a minimum income. If a station wanted to remain with the network, CBS would remit to the station $50 per hour sold to an advertiser. The affiliated station could then purchase nonsponsored (sustaining) programs for the same price. The chain would cover all expenses for the programming. By removing the minimum compensation guarantee and directly tying affiliation costs to advertising sales, the new terms provided enough financial relief to ensure CBS's survival.[16]

Though the new contract eased the immediate financial burden for United Independent, CBS's parent company continued to hemorrhage money. *Fortune* would later call United Independent a "mere shoestring" operation and a "miserable ra-

dio adventure." [17] Yet the chain's troubles were not entirely the result of misman-
agement. The FRC's reorganization of the radio spectrum was not completed until
November 1928; in the interim the overcrowded airwaves continued to hinder the
business of radio broadcasting. To ensure adequate coverage in Chicago in 1927–28,
CBS needed to sign affiliation agreements with three different stations; NBC, operating two networks, required five Chicago affiliates.[18] By mid-1928 Louchheim
wanted out, and he and the Levy brothers discussed shutting down the chain. By
that time the partners had invested almost $1 million with little success. Scouting
around for a new investor, Louchheim and Leon Levy focused on the sponsor of
CBS's most successful program. The Congress Cigar Company of Philadelphia paid
for *The La Palina Smoker*—a popular musical variety show. Leon Levy's brother-in-
law, William (Bill) Paley, the twenty-seven-year-old son of the owner of Congress
Cigar, supervised the program. Louchheim and Levy persuaded Paley to purchase
Louchheim's investment in UIB in September 1928, and once more the chain was
rescued (S. Smith 1990, 62–63).

Paley's ascension brightened the troubled atmosphere at CBS. His enthusiastic
salesmanship and expansive vision for the chain paid immediate dividends. In a little over three months (between September 1928 and January 1929), CBS increased
its affiliate roster from twenty-two stations to forty-seven. In December 1928, Paley purchased WABC-New York; no longer would the chain be forced to work
around an unreliable affiliate situation in the city housing America's foremost advertising agencies. One month later, after Paley merged United Independent into
CBS and relaunched the network amid much fanfare, he would triumphantly announce that Columbia constituted "the largest regular network of stations in radio
history."[19]

Paley also proved shrewd in his personnel choices. One of his first new hires was
Sam Pickard, one of the original FRC commissioners. Together, Pickard and Paley came up with a brilliant new business model for network radio. Because CBS
was not selling much of its sustaining programming, and the chain still ran into
clearance problems on key local stations, the network proposed a new arrangement.
Henceforth, it would offer its affiliates free national quality sustaining programming in exchange for a guaranteed option on any of that station's time. The precise amount of compensation for sponsored broadcasts returned to each affiliate
would be negotiated between the chain and each station on the basis of several
variables (Barnouw 1966, 251). This new CBS contract highlighted the different
business models of NBC and CBS. Until 1935, NBC would charge its affiliates for
sustaining programming; these costs, as well as network clearance issues (NBC's
standard contract lacked CBS's option-time clause), regularly created tension between the older chain and its local broadcast partners. In 1935, after the standard
CBS contract had proven significantly advantageous to the junior chain, NBC
adopted identical terms for all its affiliates.

The biggest coup in Paley's first year of ownership occurred in June 1929, when
he convinced Paramount's Adolph Zukor to invest $3.8 million in a 50 percent own-

ership stake in CBS (S. Smith 1990, 84–85). "The network, inside of a year and a half, had risen in value from one hundred thousand dollars to seven million, six hundred thousand dollars," Arthur Judson recalled, noting that "in back of this were few physical assets: just ideas, the station WABC, and the agreements with the stations comprising the chain. Really, it had all been built up on ideas and hustling ability."[20] Less than a month after securing the Paramount investment, CBS moved its offices into a new skyscraper on the corner of Madison Avenue and Fifty-second Street in New York City. Between August 1928 and August 1929, CBS's billings increased sixfold. By the end of that year (1929), CBS reported a net income of $474,203; its time sales increased from $1,409,975 in 1928 to $4,453,181 in 1929.[21]

During this period of rapid expansion, CBS rarely explicitly acknowledged its older rival. Executives of both chains, in this formative period, understood that for the habitual listener American radio remained a primarily local or regional phenomenon. NBC and CBS executives were far more interested in promoting national commercial broadcasting than with establishing a rivalry between their brands. Promotional materials reflected this concern about competing with popular local stations; thus a 1929 CBS sales pamphlet noted that "the great majority of listeners who can receive network programs . . . will naturally tune to them because of their marked superiority over the average local program," without once mentioning NBC.[22]

Competition and Cooperation, 1930–33

Despite CBS's impressive gains, NBC dominated network radio in its earliest period. In every aspect of the business, from programming to advertising revenue, total number of affiliates to public recognition, NBC's performance surpassed that of CBS. Beginning in late 1928, NBC operated two truly national networks, while CBS was forced to rely on affiliation with Don Lee's Pacific Coast chain in order to cover the nation. NBC sold $15.7 million of airtime in 1930, while CBS did $6.9 million worth of business. In 1931 those numbers reached $20.4 million for NBC and $10.4 million for CBS.[23] NBC promotional materials emphasized the disparity between the chains; a booklet for advertisers published in the mid-1930s proudly noted that 74 percent of the total "money spent for advertising time on national networks" in the first six months of 1930 was earned by NBC.[24] "The National Broadcasting Company in the early 1930s had practically no competition," remembered NBC executive Mark Woods.[25]

NBC's early economic dominance was closely linked to its programming success. Early network radio relied heavily on musical programs—in a typical month (September 1932), 66.3 percent of all network programs were music.[26] It was a new program format, introduced by NBC in 1929, that sparked a revolution in American listening habits. The *Amos 'n' Andy* program, a minstrel comedy, began airing on the NBC-Blue network for Pepsodent toothpaste that fall. *Amos 'n' Andy* earned the highest ratings ever recorded in the history of American broadcasting; it was truly a national phenomenon. Its primary legacy, according to Francis Chase (1942), lay in the fact that it "did the preliminary work of conditioning listeners across the nation to following a continued radio program" (181). For two fifteen-minute blocks a night, six days a week, America halted to hear Freeman Gosden and Charles Correll perform. *Amos 'n' Andy* created an intense audience loyalty to NBC that the chain extended with other spectacularly popular programs. Only a few months after the debut of *Amos 'n' Andy*, NBC packaged a program for Fleischmann's Yeast starring Rudy Vallee (originally titled *The Rudy Vallee Orchestra*). Vallee "offered his audiences a singing lover, one who was sophisticated, romantic, vulnerable . . . and accessible to them in their home." His enormously popular program ushered in the craze for crooners on American radio (McCracken 1999, 365). NBC introduced the first regularly scheduled evening radio drama, *First-Nighter*, in 1930; that program also secured a wide and loyal following. In the 1931–32 season, NBC aired all sixteen programs with a Crossley, Inc. Cooperative Analysis of Broadcasting (CAB) rating over 20.0. CBS's most popular program, still *The La Palina Smoker*, earned a 12.0: a respectable rating, but one dwarfed by the 53.4 scored by *Amos 'n' Andy* and the 36.5 earned by Vallee's musical variety program (Summers 1958/1971, 19–23).

CBS packaged its own *Amos 'n' Andy* knockoff *(Two Black Crows)*, but the show failed to find an audience. Paley and his small staff realized that CBS needed to challenge NBC in two key areas: program popularity and audience metrics. Though the two were clearly linked, CBS launched dual initiatives. Shortly after Paramount partnered with CBS, Paley established the Columbia Concerts Corporation and then Columbia Artists, Inc. Tasked with finding and promoting new talent, these artists' bureaus had a significant advantage over NBC's equivalent: CBS could offer prospective radio talent a Paramount screen test. This Paramount connection allowed CBS to better NBC in the competition to sign a promising young singer named Bing Crosby in 1931.[27] In terms of decision making in general, and talent cultivation in particular, CBS's smaller size made it more nimble and quick to capitalize on new opportunities. One early CBS executive remembered that Paley "never had to go ask anybody else, board of directors or anybody else, for a decision on anything."[28] Paley and his CBS executives discovered, promoted, and sold such talents as the Mills Brothers, Tony Wons, Kate Smith, and Morton Downey. The junior chain could not match NBC's dramatic and comedy programming success in these years, but by cultivating new voices for appreciative advertisers and listeners CBS continued its vigorous growth.

Throughout 1931–32, NBC programming head John Royal became more concerned with CBS's programming. He demanded to know why CBS's ratings were improving more than NBC's. The primary reason, according to one key NBC executive, was that many NBC musical programs "are a little over the heads of the average audience." "NBC is undoubtedly raising audience appreciation of good music to a higher plane by its courage in presenting the better things in musical composition, even though they are less popular with the masses," Frank Arnold ex-

FIG. **3** John Royal, former station manager of WTAM Cleveland, appointed NBC's first vice president for programming in 1930. Under him Bertha Brainard managed commercial programs and Phillips Carlin handled sustaining production. (Library of American Broadcasting)

plained.[29] A second reason offered was that NBC was willing to attempt innovative programming strategies, whereas CBS either followed popular musical formulas or copied NBC. "While we are 'pioneering,' Columbia is selling its shows to the people," Royal angrily responded. CBS's promotional materials were also beginning to upset him. "They are not always the greatest in the world, but they certainly make the public believe they are."[30]

While CBS's talent development and promotional moves proved effective, remedying the disparity in Crossley ratings presented a more difficult task. Paley hired Paul Kesten in 1930 to direct CBS's sales promotion, and he immediately implemented significant new research efforts. Kesten commissioned Price, Waterhouse & Co. to complete annual studies of "radio network popularity based on a nationwide audit." When an industry newsletter published the results of one early CBS survey proving that "Columbia listener interest in cities where the survey was made was now in excess of the N.B.C. blue and red networks," David Sarnoff asked Aylesworth to investigate the claim because "it seemed . . . so much at variance with any impression I hold on the subject."[31]

Importantly, CBS's surveys did not ask audience members to identify a favorite chain or program. Instead, listeners were asked what stations they listened to on what days and times, and CBS then correlated responses with chain affiliation. CBS argued that this was the proper methodology to employ because surveys regularly showed that "the name of the station tends to impress itself especially strongly on the mind of the listener," whereas listeners were less able to identify chains.[32] Listeners in this period were often confused as to chain identification; some believed CBS was actually one of NBC's networks (Razlogova 2003, 90). To counter NBC's advantage in the Crossley ratings, which focused on program preferences, CBS claimed that their research provided "the only direct measurement of network popularity and size of network audience."[33]

Although CBS's successes enlivened the rivalry between 1930 and 1933, the crushing economic conditions, combined with a rising popular critique of commercial radio, forced the two networks to cooperate. The largest commercial threat to the industry emerged with the widespread production of transcribed, or electrically recorded, programs. Advertisers aired these recordings on key local affiliates. They usually paid the station's full advertising card rate, an amount that always exceeded the amount the networks remitted to their affiliates. "Spot" broadcasting, so-called because the advertiser could pick the spots, or selected markets, to air a program without purchasing a chain, frightened both CBS and NBC executives. When *Broadcast Advertising* reported in October 1930 that "spot broadcasting is increasing much more rapidly than chain broadcasting," their fears were proven.[34] Between late 1929 and 1932, several NBC affiliates began to reject chain offerings in favor of these recorded programs. One Detroit station, after cutting off NBC's popular *Chase & Sanborn Hour* at midpoint, claimed it earned eight times more money airing a thirty-minute transcription program than it would have earned by airing the entirety of the NBC show.[35] Although CBS, with its option-clause contract, was far more protected than NBC, it also recognized the threat. To counter transcriptions, executives of both chains defined and aggressively promoted live, wire-distributed programming as the only authentic system for national broadcasting. The chains cultivated a powerful ally in this fight: the FRC. All recorded programming, by FRC General Orders 16 and 52, had to be announced as such. When the transcription companies lobbied the FRC to do away with the stigmatizing announcement, the chains argued that this was an attempt to deceive the listener. The FRC commissioners agreed; they consistently refused to alter their strict rules regarding the required announcement of recorded programming (Russo 2004a, 4–17).

The chains also cooperated in less public ways. During this period CBS and NBC executives monitored each other's station relations very closely, but neither exploited the other's problems. In 1929 NBC was hit by the "Ohio rebellion" when executives with WLW-Cincinnati and WTAM-Cleveland threatened to end affiliation unless NBC offered them amounts closer to their standard advertising rates. WLW ("the nation's station") eventually carried out the threat and abandoned NBC; NBC fixed its WTAM problem by purchasing the station and bringing its feisty manager,

John Royal, to New York to work for the chain.[36] CBS executives were undoubtedly aware of NBC's problems in Ohio, but they did not intervene. To meet the WLW and WTAM demands would have thrown the entire compensation structure of chain broadcasting into chaos. Executives of both networks understood that a bidding war for affiliates anywhere would destroy the system everywhere.[37] Occasionally stations would end affiliation with one network with the intention of joining its rival (as did WHAS-Louisville, which left NBC in 1932 for CBS), but the chains did not actively solicit these moves or offer additional compensation for them.

A severe drop-off in advertising revenue between early 1932 and the summer of 1933 forced executives of the two chains to discuss their mutual problems. In an effort to control fees paid to musicians and other radio artists, CBS and NBC explored the possibility of merging their artists' bureaus.[38] Employees of both chains shared confidential information about steps being taken to economize at their respective companies.[39] Thus the summer of 1932 saw the networks simultaneously announcing severe employee layoffs and pay cuts. In June, more than a hundred employees were let go from CBS and the rest had to absorb a 15 percent pay cut; that same month NBC fired 195 employees.[40] In July, when CBS announced a reduction in its advertising rates, NBC declared a 10 percent pay cut across the board for all employees.[41] When the fiscally strapped organizers of the Los Angeles Olympics asked a $100,000 fee for the exclusive rights to broadcast the games, both networks flatly rejected the offer. The American public missed live reports of athletic competition; only digests of highlights were heard each evening, by Grantland Rice for NBC and Ted Husing for CBS.[42]

In the fall of 1932 both networks announced a new policy of accepting advertising that quoted prices (direct advertising) to stimulate ad sales.[43] The decision paid immediate dividends, as did the influx of revenue generated by the political contests of the fall of 1932.[44] Yet the chains were not quite out of the woods. In December NBC further cut its already meager spending on sustaining programs. John Royal vehemently protested the move, noting that NBC's "sustaining programs now are not of high quality" and that it would surely create more tension between NBC and its affiliates.[45] The new year dawned with few signs of economic renewal, and the national broadcasters continued to expect the worst. Although CBS's savings from the previous year allowed it to produce a tiny profit in the first quarter of 1933, Paley warned Aylesworth that CBS anticipated a "tremendous decrease in billing" in the second quarter of 1933. "We are . . . scrutinizing our overhead very carefully," Paley noted.[46] The belt tightening at both chains continued throughout most of the year. In March, NBC shocked the industry when it announced that service on its second West Coast network extension—the so-called Gold network—would be discontinued.[47] Until January 1936, when NBC reconstituted a second transcontinental chain in order to strengthen the NBC-Blue network, NBC would not sell time to sponsors on two truly national networks. The decision to limit the reach of NBC-Blue had important ramifications for the network as a whole. The most successful advertisers began to favor NBC-Red for their programs, and NBC executives encouraged the trend. By concentrating the most popular programs on the Red network, NBC bolstered its advertising rates by creating an artificial scarcity of premium time for sale. The Blue was left to wither, primarily as a public interest network or a chain designed to serve underserved audiences (K. Miller 2002, 64). Even after the decision to end the Gold network, David Sarnoff questioned whether it was "essential that NBC maintain a Pacific coast organization" of any substance. Noting that CBS lacked a Pacific Coast operation, Sarnoff wanted to know "whether or not there is any opportunity for NBC to save money" by entirely eliminating its Pacific Coast operations.[48] Despite these discouraging signs, 1933 also brought a few glimmers of hope. By that fall, revenue showed signs of a rebound, and NBC moved into its lavish new Radio City headquarters.

The Rivalry Intensifies: 1934–36

In the fall of 1934, four well-established broadcasters with national reputations announced the formation of a new chain. All four had once been affiliated with either CBS or NBC but had left the chains over unfair compensation. Thus the licensees of WOR-Newark, WLW-Cincinnati, WXYZ-Detroit, and WGN-Chicago incorporated the Mutual Broadcasting System in Illinois in October 1934.[49] Mutual, however, was designed to be a different type of network. It would be primarily a program exchange and syndication service for the four stations (and, later, others who joined). Mutual paid its stations their full rate card for broadcast time minus a 5 percent commission and expenses. All programming would be produced by the local stations; Mutual itself would have no studios and employ no radio artists. It would essentially take America's best local programming and nationalize it, while fairly compensating everyone involved. The establishment of Mutual was greeted enthusiastically by stations around America; the frustrated affiliates of NBC-Blue proved especially appreciative.

The emergence of Mutual occurred at a particularly difficult time for NBC. While NBC still dominated the airwaves with America's most popular programs— nineteen of the twenty-five top-rated programs in 1933–34 aired on NBC—the disparity between it and CBS was rapidly closing.[50] CBS developed—and retained— several hit programs in 1933–34. Joe Penner's program for Fleischmann's Yeast and the Burns and Allen show for White Owl cigars both surpassed CAB ratings of 30 that year, and CBS even stole two popular NBC programs. It lured Will Rogers's Gulf Oil program and the *Court of Human Relations* from NBC (Summers 1958/1971, 37–49). By 1935, CBS was demonstrating a new aggressiveness in programming that greatly disturbed NBC officials. In September of that year CBS executives let John Royal know that CBS intended to end the three-year understanding between the networks that they "would not buy sporting events of any kind for sustaining purposes." The issue was simple: CBS had never aired a heavyweight championship fight, and NBC's success in obtaining and selling exclusive rights to the most popular programs on the American airwaves hurt CBS financially. To Royal, the timing of the meeting was particularly suspicious; he was convinced that CBS intended to purchase the World Series from Major League Baseball before lining up a sponsor—something neither chain had ever done. "We must meet this challenge," Royal told his superior. "They have thrown down the gauntlet and I think we should give them a darn good licking. My suggestion is that we go out and buy all the important events now. Most of them we can sell. We might have to take a loss on one or two, but in the long run we will keep NBC out in front where it belongs."[51]

Sports programming was not the only locus of CBS's belligerence. Paley's chain began maneuvers to capture several of NBC-Blue's most prestigious outlets in this period. CBS executive William Ackenberg traveled throughout the states, tasked with holding confidential discussions with disaffected NBC stations.[52] Word quickly got back to NBC, and rumors spread that CBS intended to start its own second network. This plan, an NBC executive concluded, "would seem to be a logical move for CBS. . . . The broadcasting business is good and there is pressure for satisfactory network time."[53] Several NBC executives pressed their superiors to strengthen the Blue network in order to counter CBS. Niles Trammell suggested changing the name of the Blue network "to the Victor Broadcasting Company, or something of that nature" in order to build a new brand identity for the chain.[54] These ideas were motivated by the regular complaints of the Blue affiliates, who were angered that their chain—which only a few years earlier had aired *Amos 'n' Andy*, *The Jack Benny Program*, and other popular shows—was being neglected.[55] Noticing those changes at NBC, CBS salesmen had begun to sell advertisers on "the idea that the Blue Network is the third network."[56]

The tensions produced by NBC's affiliate difficulties and CBS's aggressive moves came to a head in April 1935. In a series of angry phone calls and meetings, NBC's Richard Patterson and CBS's Bill Paley argued over who, in fact, had first abrogated the agreement not to pursue each other's stations. Paley admitted that though the two networks "did have an agreement that we wouldn't raid each other's stations" it was "NBC [that] came along and broke it" by enticing CBS's Norfolk affiliate to join NBC. When Patterson replied that the Norfolk station solicited NBC affiliation after leaving CBS on its own, Paley called this "just a case of technicalities." After the phone call, Patterson felt that Paley "would not be satisfied until he was even." In an earlier conversation Patterson "tried to get Paley to calm down." Paley claimed that "all bets were called off by you a long time ago" and that CBS would increase its hostility toward its older rival. "I can't tell you how many of your stations we turned down," Paley couldn't resist adding.[57]

CBS did convince KSL-Salt Lake City and WRVA-Richmond to defect, but its big prize was the capture of WJR-Detroit (S. Smith 1990, 89–90). CBS capitalized immediately on the WJR deal. The chain boosted the station's power from ten thousand to fifty thousand watts, and it published a special promotional brochure to notify advertisers.[58] Although most of CBS's attempts to lure NBC stations failed, the older chain was forced to pay additional compensation to retain the services of its affiliates.

These affiliate raids came at the worst possible time for NBC. Beginning in January 1935, NBC intended to finally establish a uniform policy for all its affiliates.[59] NBC's most pressing problem, before CBS began its actions, concerned its relationship with its affiliates. For years, NBC had been surreptitiously paying key strategic stations additional compensation in a series of special deals to ensure program clearance. This led "to the inevitable result of increasing the demands of other station managers," thus "precipitating the crisis" facing NBC in 1934. "Unless the network can be established on a sound and mutually advantageous basis," Richard Patterson warned the board of directors, "the future of NBC is anything but bright." A new relationship between NBC and its affiliates needed to be forged. The new plan, developed with the assistance of consultants from Trade-Ways, Inc., called for "an absolutely uniform treatment of all associated stations and the complete elimination of special deals."[60] Because the elimination of special deals was sure to provoke rancor among key NBC affiliates, NBC needed to feel secure about CBS's intentions. "It was the understanding throughout the management of our company at the time we began negotiations of the new station plan that both networks were convinced of the desirability of maintaining stability in regard to stations in the public interest as well as in the interests of the stations and the networks," NBC's Frank Mason wrote in 1935 after watching CBS's moves. "This confidence turned out to be badly founded."[61]

CBS's unwillingness to maintain the agreement concerning raiding each other's affiliates and its new aggression in programming were matched by an unprecedented public relations effort. That campaign culminated in a fawning *Fortune* magazine profile that left NBC executives fuming. Richard Patterson angrily stated that "there was a feeling that CBS was trimming NBC on all fronts."[62] Bill Paley began to cast himself as the leader of the chain broadcasting industry. He answered the vociferous criticism from the public and Congress over the commercialism on the airwaves with a widely publicized new set of policies (S. Smith 1990, 142–44). These included limits on the amount of advertising in any particular program, strict vetting of children's entertainment by a psychologist, and the discontinuance of "discussion of bodily functions or disturbances in terms not generally acceptable in social groups." The move was widely praised; the chair of the Federal Communications Commission (FCC) hailed Columbia's "wise leadership."[63]

A shrewd analysis in *The Washington Post* noted that "N.B.C.'s policies have been just about the same as Columbia's recently announced ones, except that N.B.C. has said little about them."[64] In mid-1934 NBC began to seriously address complaints about crude and suggestive humor and obnoxious advertising on its airwaves. By November, its Department of Continuity Acceptance, under the supervision of Janet MacRorie, had started its supervisory work.[65] In the discussions leading to the founding of the department, NBC executives considered notifying CBS of their plans. By raising standards alone, NBC executives worried that they might "drive certain advertisers off NBC networks and force them to go on CBS."[66] Thus NBC had already begun to quietly police its scripts when CBS made its public announcement and garnered terrific publicity. This stung NBC's senior managers particularly hard; when one asked NBC executive Edgar Kobak to explain what the CBS announcement meant to NBC, Kobak answered that the junior chain was actually "following our lead."[67]

Yet nothing disturbed NBC's senior executives more than CBS's financial success in these years. When the *New York Times* published CBS's consolidated net profit for the year 1934 in March 1935, David Sarnoff was stunned. The figure appeared inordinately high. NBC executives had never publicly segregated NBC's performance from its parent company, RCA. Sarnoff spent the rest of 1935–36 obsessing over the comparative financial performance of both networks.[68] He would forward each new CBS claim or publicity pamphlet to his executives, demanding explanations and more vigilance.[69] The reports grew consistently worse; one June 1936 memo from NBC treasurer Mark Woods stated that "for the first year in the history of the company, CBS is consistently topping the NBC revenue on its Red network. . . . Their total rate for all stations of $18,395 is $2,355 higher than our rate of $16,040."[70] CBS, Woods explained, was enjoying more success in having advertisers purchase every station on its chain. By the end of the year Sarnoff demanded another detailed comparison of the two networks.[71]

CBS, throughout 1936, continued to grow. In August the FCC approved its purchase of KNX-Los Angeles, for $1,250,000. Shortly after completing the purchase, CBS built two huge thousand-seat studios to accommodate new productions.[72] The network then began the process of setting up a Pacific Coast organization. CBS's Don Thornburgh asked Don Gilman of NBC's Los Angeles office for advice. When Gilman reported on the meeting to his superiors, his generosity annoyed Roy Witmer, NBC's sales chief. Witmer instructed Gilman to limit any assistance to CBS, noting that "we have been good Samaritans to Columbia long enough."[73] Morale at NBC bottomed out by the end of 1936. "It is a problem to sell the public on the National Broadcasting Company," John Royal reported, "but I think our greatest problem, right now, is to sell it to our own organization."[74]

The increased tension between the chains in these years did not come at the expense of continued cooperation in various areas. The chains still worked closely together on educational programming.[75] They relied on each other in the face of external criticism from independent radio educators who sought to use the Hatfield-Wagner Amendment to reserve broadcast space for nonprofits. They continued to support the same policies and legislation in Washington. Both chains cooperated extensively with the Roosevelt administration, and both vigorously defended the American system of commercialized broadcasting (Craig 2000, 78–83).

The intensification of the rivalry between CBS and NBC appears to be a natural evolution. As more advertising revenue flowed into national broadcasting and the political and regulatory stability of the American system became assured, the concerns over the stability of the industry that had forced the chains to cooperate eased substantially. Additionally, the successful entrance of Mutual into the field of national broadcasting catalyzed a new competitive environment for broadcast outlets. The genteel environment of the early cooperative competitors gave way to a more pronounced rivalry. CBS and NBC cooperated when necessary, but the necessity lessened considerably by the end of this first decade.

The rivalry between CBS and NBC created America's enduring love affair with the broadcast media. CBS and NBC fought for talent, prestige, and audience interest. This competition created new radio stars, developed new program formats, and cultivated new audiences. John Royal would later remember these early years as key to establishing the powerful dynamic relationship between Americans and their mass media. "Competition in our business," Royal remembered three decades later, was "the biggest thing that went towards the success for radio in this country."[76]

Notes

Abbreviations

LAB   Library of American Broadcasting, University of Maryland

NBC/LC   National Broadcasting Company Collection, Motion Picture, Broadcasting, and Recorded Sound Division, Library of Congress

NBC/WHS National Broadcasting Company Archives, Wisconsin Historical Society

RPP   Radio Pioneers Project, Oral History Research Office, Columbia University

1. "Radio City Studio Dedicated by NBC," *New York Times*, November 12, 1933; M. H. Aylesworth to William S. Paley, November 2, 1933, Box 16, Folder 65, NBC/WHS.

2. See "Announcing the National Broadcasting Company, Inc.," September 13, 1926, reprinted in Sterling and Kittross (2001).

3. Dane Yorke, "The Radio's Octopus," *American Mercury*, August 1931.

4. "The Reminiscences of Mark Woods," 1950, 18, RPP.

5. "One Share of Stock = One Radio Set," *Radio Broadcast*, July 1926, 214; Radio Corporation of America, *Annual Report, 1924* (1925), 7–8, and *Annual Report, 1925* (1926), 9, both in Folder 500, NBC/LC.

6. "Changes in Radio 'Big Business,'" *Radio Broadcast*, October 1926, 476.

7. "Danger of Monopoly in Broadcasting," *Radio Broadcast*, March 1927, 464–65.

8. "The Reminiscences of Arthur Judson," 1950, 11, RPP. The precise origins of the company that would become CBS were disputed by Coats. He claimed that while staying at the Astor Hotel in New York City he had come across a meeting of broadcasters negotiating musical rights with representatives of songwriters. After meeting a few radio executives he promptly decided to enter the business. He claimed to have contacted Arthur Judson when he realized that broadcasting's chief revenue would derive from supplying musicians to broadcasters—and not from operating stations. For this version of the story, see Chase (1942, 40–43) and White (1947, 33).

9. "And All Because They're Smart," *Fortune*, June 1935, 80; "New Chain of Stations Will Exploit Movies," *New York Times*, June 23, 1927, 22.

10. "The Columbia Broadcasting Chain," *Radio Broadcast*, October 1927, 347.

11. H. C. Cox, "Columbia Chain in Debut Today," *New York Times*, September 18, 1927, 14; "'King's Henchman' Led by Taylor over Radio," *New York Times*, September 19, 1927, 32.

12. "New Radio Chain to Open April 5," *New York Times*, March 26, 1927, 12; "New Radio Chain Will Open Tonight," *New York Times*, April 5, 1927, 32.

13. Erwin, Wasey & Company, *A Study of Radio as an Advertising Medium*, January 1928, Pamphlet File 129, NBC/LC.

14. "Says Radio Chain Is Losing Money," *New York Times*, December 2, 1927, 18; Federal Communications Commission (FCC), *Report on Chain Broadcasting* (1941; reprint, New York: Arno Press, 1974), 17.

15. Ike and Leon Levy Oral History, 8–10, Transcript AT–12/17, LAB.

16. "And All Because They're Smart," 148–51.

17. Ibid., 80.

18. John W. Spalding, "1928: Radio Becomes a Mass Advertising Medium," *Journal of Broadcasting* I (Winter 1963–64), 31–44, reprinted in Lichty and Topping (1975, 220–21).

19. Columbia Broadcasting System, *Broadcast Advertising—The Sales Voice of America*, 1929, 13, Pamphlet File, LAB; "Columbia System to Extend Chain," *New York Times*, December 12, 1928, 41; "New Columbia Chain Starts on Air Jan. 8," *New York Times*, December 14, 1928, 33.

20. "Reminiscences of Arthur Judson," 23–24.

21. FCC, *Report on Chain Broadcasting*, 24.

22. CBS, *Broadcast Advertising—The Sales Voice of America*, 1929, 15, Pamphlet File, LAB. NBC officials also refrained from mentioning CBS. NBC President Merlyn Aylesworth noted that "the Columbia Broadcasting Company . . . also occupies a field in sponsored broadcasting" (de Haas 1928/1974, 243). Importantly, Aylesworth only mentions Columbia in a short passage designed to deflect criticism of commercial broadcasting.

23. FCC, *Report on Chain Broadcasting*, 27, 24.

24. *NBC Networks: Facts and Figures* (New York: NBC, 1930), 5, LAB.

25. "Reminiscences of Mark Woods," 58.

26. *Forward into 1933: The Record of NBC in 1932* (New York: NBC, 1933), 8, LAB.

27. John F. Royal, interview by William S. Hedges, 1954, 6–7, Transcript AT–29, LAB.

28. Earl Gammons Oral History, 13, Transcript AT–56/92, LAB.

29. F. A. Arnold to John F. Royal, May 10, 1932, Folder 433, NBC/LC.

30. John F. Royal to G. F. McClelland, May 12, 1932, Folder 433, NBC/LC.

31. CBS, *A Study of Radio Network Popularity*, 1930, LAB; David Sarnoff to M. H. Aylesworth, August 6, 1931, Box 45, Folder 21, NBC/WHS.

32. CBS, *Study of Radio Network Popularity*, 15, Pamphlet File, LAB.

33. CBS, *The 4th Study of Radio Network Popularity Based on a Nation-Wide Audit Conducted by Price, Waterhouse & Co., Public Accountant* (New York: CBS, 1934), 14, LAB.

34. "Are the Chains Losing Their Grip?" *Broadcast Advertising*, October 1930, 8.

35. "Recordings: Their Place in Broadcasting," *Broadcast Advertising*, July 1931, 5–6.

36. "NBC Assumes Control of WTAM," *Broadcast Advertising*, November 1930, 28.

37. It is difficult to prove the existence of this "gentleman's agreement" because it was only referred to once NBC executives accused CBS of breaking it. One finds mention of "problems of common interest to CBS and NBC about which we had understandings with CBS" in a memo from Alfred H. Morton to Mark J. Woods, December 8, 1936, Box 45, Folder 20, NBC/WHS. See also Frank E. Mason to Richard C. Patterson, June 6, 1935, and note titled "Telephone Conversation—Mr. Paley and Mr. Patterson 4–15 1935 4:50 p.m. re: Raiding Each Other's Stations," both in Box 35, Folder 39, NBC/WHS.

38. Edward Klauber to M. H. Aylesworth, December 8, 1931, Box 7, Folder 108, NBC/WHS.

39. A. L. Ashby to G. F. McClelland, June 30, 1932, Box 45, Folder 21, or Box 7, Folder 108, and R. C. Patterson Jr., to M. H. Aylesworth, August 30, 1933, Box 16, Folder 65, both in NBC/WHS.

40. "CBS Retrenches," *Broadcasting*, May 15, 1932, 8; "NBC Cuts Staff," *Broadcasting*, June 1, 1932, 10.

41. "CBS Station Rate Cuts Begin Sept. 1," *Broadcasting*, July 15, 1932, 15; "NBC Orders Pay Cut," *Broadcasting*, July 15, 1932, 14.

42. "Won't Pay Olympics," *Broadcasting*, July 15, 1932, 19; "$100,000 Demand Bars Broadcast of Olympics," *Broadcasting*, August 15, 1932, 6.

43. "Ban on Price-Quoting Is Lifted by Nets as Incentive to Sales," *Broadcasting*, September 15, 1932, 29.

44. Martin Codel, "Price Quoting Held an Advertising Stimulus," *Broadcasting*, October 1, 1932, 5.

45. Richard C. Patterson Jr. to John F. Royal, December 20, 1932, and John F. Royal to Richard C. Patterson Jr., December 22, 1932, both in Folder 31, NBC/LC.

46. William S. Paley to Merlyn Aylesworth, February 27, 1933, Edward Klauber to M. H. Aylesworth, February 14, 1933, and "Analysis of Comparative Statements CBS and NBC," March 1, 1933, all in Box 16, Folder 65, NBC/WHS.

47. Richard C. Patterson Jr. to all departments, March 18, 1933, File 305, NBC/LC.

48. David Sarnoff to Richard C. Patterson Jr., October 7, 1933, File 284, NBC/LC.

49. FCC, *Report on Chain Broadcasting*, 26–27.

50. Trade-Ways, Inc., *Selling Broadcast Advertising: A Handbook for Network Salesmen* (1933), IV-14.

51. John F. Royal to Richard C. Patterson Jr., October 1, 1935, Box 35, Folder 39, NBC/WHS. An earlier discussion of cooperation in not purchasing sporting events can be found in the minutes of the "Operating Committee Meeting—Chicago, September 17, 1934," 2, Folder No. 831, NBC/LC.

52. Frank E. Mason to Richard C. Patterson Jr., June 16, 1935, Box 35, Folder 39, NBC/WHS.

53. David Rosenblum to Frank Mason, June 7, 1935, Box 35, Folder 39, NBC/WHS.

54. Niles Trammell to R. C. Patterson Jr., October 26, 1935, Folder 299, NBC/LC. On the need to strengthen the Blue, see Frank E. Mason to Richard C. Patterson Jr., June 16, 1935, Folder 293, NBC/LC.

55. Frank E. Mason to Richard C. Patterson Jr., June 16, 1935, Box 35, Folder 39, NBC/WHS.

56. Frank E. Mason to R. C. Patterson Jr., October 24, 1935, Folder 299, NBC/LC.

57. "Telephone Conversation—Mr. Paley and Mr. Patterson, 4–15, 1935 4:50 p.m.," R. C. Patterson to Mark Woods, April 19, 1935, and R. C. Patterson Jr. to David Sarnoff, April 23, 1935, all in Box 35, Folder 39, NBC/WHS.

58. CBS, *The World's Largest Radio Chain Adds Another Link*, 1935, Box 35, Folder 39, NBC/WHS.

59. "A Report of the Operations of the National Broadcasting Company, Inc.," 1934, 14–15, Folder 265, NBC/LC.

60. All of these quotations are from "Report of the Executive Vice President to the Board of Directors, First Six Months, 1934," 1934, 6, Folder 1040, NBC/LC.

61. Frank E. Mason to Richard C. Patterson Jr., June 6, 1935, 4–5, Box 35, Folder 39, NBC/WHS.

62. "Control Board Meeting," July 30, 1935, Folder 782, NBC/LC.

63. "The Broadcasters Wake Up," *Washington Post,* May 17, 1935, 8. The FCC replaced the FRC in 1934.

64. Katherine Smith, "Probable Effect of Columbia's New Program Policy Analyzed; Action Praised," *Washington Post,* May 19, 1935, 15.

65. Janet MacRorie, "Report of NBC's Department of Continuity Acceptance for the Year 1935," 2, Folder 63, NBC/LC.

66. David Rosenblum to File, November 8, 1934, Folder 63, NBC/LC.

67. Edgar Kobak to Richard C. Patterson Jr., 17 May 1935, Box 35, Folder 39, NBC/WHS.

68. See, for instance, David Sarnoff to L. R. Lohr, February 27, 1936, Box 45, Folder 2, NBC/WHS.

69. Handwritten note signed "DS" on the report "Measuring Radio Audiences: A Critical Analysis of Current Techniques," Box 45, Folder 20, NBC/WHS.

70. Mark Woods to L. R. Lohr, June 13, 1936, Box 45, Folder 21, NBC/WHS.

71. David Sarnoff to Lenox R. Lohr, December 14, 1936, Box 45, Folder 21, NBC/WHS. See handwritten note "Mr. Lohr—are their claims correct?" signed "DS" on Victor M. Ratner to Mr. David Sarnoff, November 11, 1936, E. P. H. James to L. R. Lohr, November 14, 1936, and William C. Gittinger to David Sarnoff, June 8, 1936, all in Box 45, Folder 20, NBC/WHS.

72. "Artists See Air Productions Centered in Hollywood Soon," *Washington Post,* May 24, 1936, 8.

73. Don Gilman to Lenox Lohr, July 10, 1936, and Roy Witmer to Lenox Lohr, July 22, 1936, both in Box 45, Folder 20, NBC/WHS.

74. John F. Royal to Lenox R. Lohr, October 7, 1936, Box 45, Folder 20, NBC/WHS.

75. R. C. Patterson Jr. to John F. Royal, February 8, 1935, Box 35, Folder 39, NBC/WHS; Alfred H. Morton to Mark J. Woods, December 8, 1936, Box 45, Folder 20, NBC/WHS.

76. John F. Royal, interview by William S. Hedges, 1954. Transcript AT-29, LAB.

3

Programming in the Public Interest

America's Town Meeting of the Air

DAVID GOODMAN

America's Town Meeting of the Air (ATMA) was broadcast on the NBC Blue network from 1935 until 1943, and then on ABC radio from 1943 to 1956. *ATMA* was the jewel in the crown of NBC's public service programming, an oft-cited piece of evidence that the network was responsible and civic minded and already effectively carrying out the public service work of a national broadcaster. Radio had provoked fears that democracy might be compromised in a society in which public opinion could be manipulated by broadcast propaganda. Less well remembered is the way it also stimulated new hopes for American democracy, the prospect of historically novel levels of democratic awareness and activism in citizens. The history of *ATMA* reminds us of the civic ambition of golden age network radio and allows interpretive study of a relatively neglected topic—the by turns productive and disabling tensions always, I argue, evident between the commercial and public service roles of the American radio networks, and at NBC perhaps most of all.

A National Radio Forum

ATMA was an initiative of the League for Political Education, founded in 1894 after the defeat of a women's suffrage amendment in New York. The league sought to continue the struggle for women's rights by general political education. George V. Denny Jr., a former drama teacher and professional actor, was appointed the league's associate director in 1930 and became director in 1937, his career already boosted immeasurably by his national prominence as on-air host of *ATMA*. He soon changed the league's name to Town Hall Inc., thus cementing its association with the successful radio show.

In the wake of the compromise brokered over the 1934 Communications Act, the networks in the mid-1930s recognized their urgent need for public service programming—in part to counter well-publicized accusations that they were not serious about it (Committee on Civic Education 1936). NBC adopted programming such as *ATMA* because it was convinced that—politically—the survival of the "American system" of commercial broadcasting depended upon it. But the networks were also concerned to keep their audience. They sought public service programs that combined undeniable educational and civic value with entertainment. This was the distinctively American settlement of the struggle over radio: not the complete bifurcation between public service programming and commercial entertainment that appeared in many nations but rather the invention of a hybrid of the two. John Royal, vice president for programs at NBC, who championed *ATMA* as his pet project, had worked as a promoter of circus, vaudeville, and opera. He understood show business and no doubt appreciated the theatrical air that Denny— who described himself as part educator and part entertainer—gave *ATMA* from the start.

ATMA was a radio forum, begun at a time of national interest in forums of all kinds. As superintendent of Des Moines schools, John W. Studebaker had organized a demonstration program of public forums that met after hours in school buildings. Appointed U.S. Commissioner of Education in 1934, he began a Federal Forum project (1936–41) that saw two and a half million citizens attend its "modern American town-meetings" (D. Goodman 2004). Studebaker was convinced that radio could play an important role in forum development. The radio industry watched Studebaker's activities at the Office of Education anxiously, ready to counter any suggestion that radio's civic role could be handled effectively only by a government broadcaster. Studebaker could be "dangerous," John Royal warned other NBC executives in 1935.[1] But the network also saw opportunity in the government interest in forums. After the announcement of the Federal Forum project NBC was, Royal recalled, "besieged from various sides with Town Hall suggestions." NBC decided in 1935 to move quickly to get a forum program to air and selected as its partner the League for Political Education.[2]

The Idea of *ATMA*

The moving force behind *ATMA* was George V. Denny Jr. Born in 1899 in Washington, North Carolina, he spent six years in military school, then studied commerce at the University of North Carolina, where he acted with, and from 1924 to 1926 managed, the famous Carolina Playmakers. He briefly acted on the New York stage and then directed the extension program at Columbia University. Like John Studebaker, he came to the metropolis from the provinces bringing a self-consciously optimistic message about restoring democracy: "It may seem rather presumptuous at first," he remarked at Harvard University in 1937, "for a Southerner to come to the birthplace of the American town meeting to urge its revival" (Denny 1937, 101). While the Iowan Studebaker was drawn to the public school as a natural site for public discussion, for Denny as a southerner the disembodied medium of radio seemed to hold the greatest democratic potential. Broadcasting could bring the

FIG. 4 On the stage of *America's Town Meeting of the Air*. From left to right: Jonathan W. Daniels, George Denny Jr., Senator Homer Ferguson, G. O. Shepherd, Mrs. George Denny Jr., James H. Glen, and Chet Welchel. (Library of American Broadcasting)

same discussion to all, even in places where racial segregation prevented genuinely open public conversation and where the public school was hardly a symbol of a shared and democratic space.

Denny began each show with "Good evening, neighbors." The suggestion was that radio could make neighbors of the entire nation. Critics have pointed to the ways in which the ideal and rational public sphere celebrated by the early Habermas was a masculine space: "[T]he exclusion of women," Habermas himself acknowledged in 1992, "has been constitutive for the public sphere" (428). Denny's public sphere, in these terms, had some feminine as well as masculine qualities. He wanted it to be both a site for rational discussion and a place of empathy and connection where all would be neighbors as well as citizens and where the process of discussion would be as important as its conclusions. Nevertheless, in the first eight years, men outnumbered women as speakers on *ATMA* by ratios of between five to one and fourteen to one per season.

Denny was an entrepreneur of a single idea: "If Democrats go only to hear Democrats and Republicans go out only to hear Republicans and Isolationists to hear

Isolationists, can we possibly call this an honest or intelligent system of political education? The morons could do as much if they were properly labelled."[3] The story Denny always told about the origins of *ATMA* was that the idea came to him while walking home one evening, when one of his neighbors said of another that he "would rather be shot than caught listening to Roosevelt on the radio." Denny told of his response: "Here's a man who just won't listen. Even with the radio right there in his room and a chance to hear what the other side has to say for itself, he deliberately closes his mind. . . . Talk about dangers to democracy—*There's* the real danger!" "I determined then," he recalled, "to try to develop a radio program where he would have to listen to the other side in order to hear his own side presented."[4] Attentive listening was a precondition for empathy. "If we are even to approach an understanding of each other's problems," he wrote, "we must surely be willing to hear each other's point of view stated" (Denny 1937, 117). Town Hall assisted the formation of listening groups that would hear the program together and hold their own postbroadcast discussions. By 1940 there were more than three thousand *ATMA* listening groups around the country.

Denny repeated tirelessly that the aim of *ATMA* was to revive the spirit of the old New England town meeting, and the show was presented with some self-consciously revivalist elements. The audience at Town Hall was ushered into its seats by "pleasant-looking women, wearing attractive colonial dresses" (M. L. Ely 1937, 42–43). Each show began with the announcement that the broadcast came from "historic Town Hall in New York City"—though the building had opened as recently as 1921. The Town Hall idea was based upon a theory of modernity. In modern society, a sympathetic book on *ATMA* argued, "radicals group with radicals, conservatives with conservatives, rich with rich, poor with poor, educated with educated, uneducated with uneducated, native with native, foreign with foreign." In such a world, tolerance becomes merely "a willingness to let those who hold strange points of view go off somewhere else and talk about them" (Overstreet and Overstreet 1938, 111–12). Denny understood his project as one of restitution, reinstating an old form of engaged community discussion. The challenge to democracy, he thought, was whether it was possible "for a highly complicated, industrialised, citified civilization to conduct its affairs by those modes of common discussion and mutual understanding that were successful in a village society" (Overstreet and Overstreet 1938, 6). The question remained for Denny an open one. He simultaneously participated in and rejected the trope that democracy belonged to the past.

ATMA as Radio

ATMA was broadcast live in front of an audience. That audience gave the show much of its interest as radio, and an air of danger that studio discussion programs, such as NBC's *University of Chicago Round Table*, with their comfortable suavity, quite lacked. Most of the *ATMA* broadcasts came from Town Hall, on Forty-third Street, though in later years the program also regularly went on the road. Denny as moderator allowed the audience to be heard, and publicity made much of the rowdiness this produced—"spectator-hecklers" is how *Movie-Radio Guide* described the audience.[5] Denny, observed another magazine, "didn't invent heckling, but he is the first man to organize it and sell it as headline entertainment."[6] The live audience—in Town Hall usually about 1,500 people—contributed a great deal to the atmosphere and sound of the show. Listeners at home were aware of the reactions of the live audience and would comment in letters on what they heard and surmised about it.

Each *ATMA* broadcast began with the ringing of a bell and a town crier calling "Town meeting tonight!" and announcing the topic of the evening's discussion. There were two, three, or four speakers of contrasting views, and they spoke from prepared scripts—they met on the morning of the broadcast and could spend the afternoon revising their scripts.[7] Audience questions had to be written and had to consist of less than twenty-five words; then they had to be approved by a committee, which was vigilant in weeding out "personal" questions. The question period, live on national radio, was a significant innovation in American broadcasting. It created an unprecedented sense of a national public sphere of live debate. The *New York Times* critic applauded the "freedom and informality" of *ATMA*—almost a parallel, he thought, "to the amateur hour, another of 1935's popular radio events."[8] It was partly this live question time that made *ATMA* successful as radio in the 1930s context, in which there was, as Jason Loviglio (2002) has observed, a fascination with the possibility of broadcasting the "voice of the people." NBC's *ATMA* thus seemed to many a timely program, fulfilling some of the cultural and civic promise of radio while also providing an edge-of-the-seat tension in its concluding minutes as it flirted with the danger of national broadcast of live comment from ordinary people.

Denny was by training an actor, and his instincts were theatrical. The three things that went to make up *ATMA*, he once wrote, were "educational integrity, showmanship, and fair play."[9] He always defended the necessity of "showmanship" in communicating ideas to the public. Jesus of Nazareth, he asserted, "used methods to get his message to the masses that would be characterised by today's academicians as pure showmanship."[10] There was considerable theatricality to the *ATMA* broadcasts—from the opening town crier to Denny's quick repartee as he managed the question time. Denny's initial pitch to NBC had even suggested that the questioners and hecklers on the show might be professional actors.[11] He also had a clear sense of the proper drama of a town meeting. In a 1941 letter about a live town meeting he was to chair, he wrote: "I trust you will suggest to the speakers that they emphasise their differences in their opening presentations, as there will be ample time to stress their points of agreement during the discussion period."[12] Part of the theater of town meetings was to dramatize the power of discussion to bring opponents closer together.

Many *ATMA* listeners in the early years readily understood the need for the program and praised it warmly.[13] "Public response to this program has been little short of astonishing," Robert Ely and George Denny reported.[14] *ATMA* received an average of 1,103 letters a week in its first year and 1,542 the next season. From the 1937–38 to the 1940–41 season, it was averaging more than 2,000 letters a week and the most popular broadcasts were generating over 4,000.[15]

Many letters offered thanks for a radio program suitable for the intelligent listener: "There are many whole evenings when I do not care to turn on the radio," wrote one listener, "because there is nothing which would engage the interest of an intelligent person."[16] Another listener observed, "[T]here has never been a time when it was more important for intelligent people to use every means at hand to strengthen democracy."[17] *ATMA*'s most enthusiastic listeners understood and adopted its rhetoric about the urgency of its civic work and warmed to its interpellation of them as intelligent listeners.

One of the things these self-identified "intelligent listeners" prided themselves on was their openness. They understood themselves as receptive to new information and open to reasoned persuasion. Research on *ATMA* listeners in 1936 by psychologist Hadley Cantril of Princeton University found that 50 percent "usually" continued discussion after the program finished and that 34 percent reported having changed their opinions as a result of listening.[18] "There are some mighty important revelations here," Denny responded, "particularly the 34% changed opinions."[19] In the climate of 1930s liberalism, changing the opinions of listeners was the agreed measure of success of a radio forum. Prejudice—immovable, fixed belief—was understood to weaken democracy. Only when citizens were open to reason and new knowledge could democracy thrive. It was notorious that propaganda changed minds, and there was a great desire to demonstrate that reasoned debate could do so as well.

ATMA in Practice

ATMA in its early years gave time to advocates of alternative social, political, and economic systems and did not allow listeners to think of existing social, political, and economic arrangements as natural or inevitable. The opening program featured a communist, a socialist, a fascist, and a democrat. *ATMA* in the 1930s placed the free-market capitalist system under scrutiny. It was allowed to ask fundamental social and political questions and to present a range of genuinely differing views. Topics covered in the early years included social security, economic cooperatives, the Townsend plan, unions, world peace, unemployment, propaganda, and foreign policy in a democracy.

Under the initial 1935 agreement, NBC was to pay all expenses, while the league was to have final authority in the choice of speakers and topics. But when Denny first sent NBC a list of possible speakers, it objected to the inclusion of communist leader Earl Browder.[20] The first *ATMA* broadcast asked, "Which Way America? Fascism, Communism, Socialism, Democracy?" but the communist speaker was A. J. Muste, chair of the Workers Party of the United States, not Browder. Town

Hall nonetheless continued to proclaim *ATMA*'s openness to all views. In a 1938 interview, Denny reported proudly that "Communists frequently are in our audience on Thursday evenings airing their views and asking questions."[21] Clarence Hathaway, editor of the *Daily Worker*, spoke on *ATMA* in 1938, and Earl Browder did so in January 1939. Hathaway received applause for his statement that he wanted the kind of democracy "that will give to all of us an equal economic opportunity."[22]

After the Nazi-Soviet pact of August 1939, and in the context of Martin Dies's House Un-American Activities Committee's investigations, Denny's views on the selection of speakers began hardening. Town Hall agreed in December 1939 that neither Earl Browder nor German-American Bund leader Fritz Kuhn would be invited on the program in future.[23] A Town Hall press release under Denny's name and sent to the Dies Committee stated that because of the external loyalties they served, neither Browder nor Kuhn was "entitled to the privileges of fair competition in debate."[24] By 1940, Denny's ideal for *ATMA* had to this extent been significantly modified.

A recurring issue was whether NBC would sell *ATMA* as a commercial program. The network kept the question alive by dwelling on the cost of the program. During negotiations for the 1936–37 season, Denny reported: "[T]he only change asked for by the National Broadcasting Company in view of their financial situation, was that we provide a clause in the contract permitting them to change the night of the broadcasts and the place if necessary in case they had a commercial contract offered for that time." But NBC was hardly in financial trouble in 1936 — it had made $3.6 million profit in 1935.[25] For their part, NBC executives professed a suspicion of Denny. Walter Preston at NBC warned: "Denny, as you know, is quite famous for his razzle-dazzle type of approach. . . . [W]e have too frequently in the past awakened to the realization that Denny slipped something over on us."[26]

When NBC cried poor, Denny reminded it of the responsibilities of a national broadcaster and mobilized support for retaining *ATMA*'s sustaining, noncommercial status. He told NBC in 1939 that "the interests of NBC and Town Hall and American democracy will best be served by continuing on the present basis. . . . [W]e have a tremendous responsibility to the nation."[27] In 1940, NBC executives were again querying the expense of the program. RCA president David Sarnoff asked for figures. "It is now costing us $1100 per week, or $28,600 per season," reported John Royal, "Do we wish to renew it?" When Royal sought the advice of NBC educational counselor James Angell, the strongest argument he could put in favor of retaining the show was that he would not like to see CBS pick it up.[28]

ATMA survived for twenty-one years. The NBC hierarchy had a clear sense among themselves of the worth of the program in political capital, even as they wished to produce it as cheaply and uncontroversially as they decently could. NBC did, moreover, keep *ATMA* as a sustaining program. It was ABC, which inherited the program after NBC divested its second network, that commercialized it, gaining the sponsorship of *Reader's Digest* for the 1944–45 season. From 1947, ABC sold the program as a "cooperative," with the cost shared among several local sponsors.

"Prestige—at a price you can afford," read the sales brochure. "This stimulating forum is your opportunity to acquire a background of prestige for your sales messages—prestige that pays off in profits." *ATMA*'s stature and influence diminished a little in the postwar years, and commercial sponsorship was one of the changes that wore away at the distinction of the show.

Cosmopolitans, Nationalists, and War

The outbreak of war in Europe, and the divisive question of American involvement in that war, dramatically changed the environment in which *ATMA* operated. One observer noted an alteration in the Town Hall audience—their manner was now "inflammable," their questions "bitterly phrased." Denny feared for the first time that "the audience would get completely out of control."[29] Serious commentators wondered whether forum programs, and particularly *ATMA* with its live question period, ought to continue if the United States did enter the war.

ATMA's preoccupation with international relations and war grew dramatically in the later 1930s. In 1935–36 three out of twenty-nine programs dealt with the international situation; in 1936–37, three out of twenty-four; in 1937–38, as the crisis in Europe deepened, seven out of twenty-six; in 1938–39, fourteen out of twenty-six, including such topics as "How Should the Democracies Deal with the Dictatorships?" and "Should Our Neutrality Act Be Repealed?" In 1939–40, eight out of twenty-seven shows dealt with the international situation. But in 1940–41, *ATMA* was turned over to the war debate for twenty-seven of the twenty-nine shows. Week after week, listeners were confronted with questions such as "Is This Our War?" "How Should We Meet Totalitarian Aggression in the Americas?" "Is a Hitler Defeat Essential to the United States?" "Should Our Ships Convoy Materials to Britain?" "Must America and Japan Clash?" and "Must We Fight Japan?"

It is not surprising that the relentlessness of this attention to the war question struck many isolationist listeners as excessive. For them the question was settled, and *ATMA*'s repeated posing of it was proof of its war-mongering and un-American character. Such listeners concluded that the whole claim of *ATMA* to be open and democratic was a sham. "As a listener I think some of these debates are trumped up to present the views of those who have the money and power," wrote a woman from the Bronx, "regardless of democratic procedures that you constantly chatter."[30]

A perception was clearly growing among a section of *ATMA*'s audience that the program represented the views of eastern elites rather than those of ordinary Americans. During the 1939–40 season it became "more difficult than ever to keep the objective viewpoint which the Town Meeting has so faithfully maintained in the past."[31] On the war issue more than any other the *ATMA* audience seemed to diverge from the ideals of the program makers. There was a stream of virulent correspondence from a troubling racist minority among isolationists, who alleged that the program had become a forum for internationalist elites, Jews, and foreigners who held un-American views.

There had been charges that the speakers and/or audience of the program presented foreign views since the inception of *ATMA*. In 1935 a man from New Jersey reported that he had heard in the "background of noise" during one program "continuously broken English of Italian, English, German or Jewish flavours." He proposed that "at least three generations of American citizenship" be required of people who spoke on the radio.[32] Early in the history of *ATMA*, questioners were required to give their name before asking a question. This requirement was dropped after many listeners wrote in claiming that most of the names sounded foreign and advocated alien or communist views.[33] A Californian listener detected a "consistently sympathetic attitude of your NY audience to anything foreign particularly Russian or Communistic—and almost as consistently antagonistic to anything American."[34] *ATMA*'s claim to being a neutral space, a genuine public sphere, was already being contested. The war debate would very significantly increase the intensity of that contestation.

Any discussion of possible U.S. involvement in foreign war provoked passion. But there was a deeper sense in which *ATMA* began to alienate some listeners, even as it continued to appeal to those self-identified "intelligent" listeners who had always warmed to its questioning of orthodoxies, its commitment to the process of discussion and openness to change. Isolationist listeners were likely to object to New York cosmopolitanism, but they also often astutely discerned and rejected *ATMA*'s belief in the redemptive power of open discussion. *ATMA* sought to persuade Americans that the truth was complex and might not be grasped immediately. Fifty percent of those in Cantril's survey preferred that no definite solution to problems be arrived at on the show. In a handbook for those directing discussion groups, Denny (1940) warned that "it is rarely possible and often undesirable to attempt to arrive immediately at conclusions about the subjects discussed on the Town Meeting program. . . . [J]udgement should be reserved on a great many proposals" (23–24). Some Americans viewed this open-mindedness with suspicion, as a sign of dissembling rather than intelligence. *ATMA*'s commitment to fostering democracy had a relativist and cosmopolitan edge to it that divided listeners.

Isolationist listeners had a very different conception of the working of the radio forum than did *ATMA*'s producers. They saw their task as restoring the full identity—racial, religious, political, personal—of the disembodied voices they heard on their radio. The common accusation of their letters was that Town Hall's espousal of internationalism was but further evidence of Jewish and radical domination of New York City and its institutions. "Look beyond the Hudson," one listener advised, "for real patriots."[35] A man wrote from St. Louis to accuse *ATMA* of an attempt at "Manhattanizing the nation."[36] "Those noisy Jews, who packed the Town Hall Meeting of the Air tonight, spoiled the program for the listening audience," wrote "Twelve Listeners" from Brooklyn in 1941. "[T]he Jews, by their actions, convince the radio listeners that, as far as they are concerned, Hitler is 100% right."[37] These listeners identified *ATMA* as being partisan and interventionist at home as well as abroad.

Denny struggled in this environment to maintain the separation, so important to him, between personal and public considerations. In April 1941, *ATMA* asked, "Should Our Ships Convoy Arms to Britain?" The speakers were the Republican former senator from Vermont, Ernest W. Gibson, now national chairman of the Committee to Defend America by Aiding the Allies, and Senator C. Wayland Brooks, Republican of Illinois and a decorated World War I veteran, who opposed convoys. The speakers presented their cases passionately. They seemed to understand that, for the radio audience, their identity was important. Brooks was introduced as "one of America's most decorated war veterans," and he used this authority to argue that "if those who vote for war, had to fight the wars, there would be much less war in the world." When Gibson countered that he was an officer in the Cavalry Reserve, Brooks scoffed that "a Reserve Officer in the Cavalry is a long way from the convoy 3000 miles away across the sea. (Applause)."[38] In question time, Denny endeavored to keep such "personal" issues out of the discussion. A man in the audience tried to ask Brooks whether he had voted for Wendell Willkie in the 1940 presidential election. "That is a personal question," remonstrated Denny. "[I]t is out. Please don't ask personal questions. You take up too much time."[39]

This broadcast unsettled Chester S. Williams, director of the U.S. Office of Education's Federal Forum project. He wrote to Denny afterwards to say he thought this *ATMA* "got no where, was highly irrational and destructive of that public attitude of respect for the deliberative process." The live audience encouraged participants to speak "according to crowd psychology rather than according to living room conversation." Forums of this kind served the cause of totalitarianism rather than democracy, creating "that disgusted state of mind which is ready to embrace a dictator rather than carry on with a confusion of tongues." The "crucial question" of war and peace held the most danger—"This thing can wreck American democracy."[40]

Denny replied saying *ATMA* had for a time tried programs less structured around conflict, but they "were accused on all sides of being dull." It was only with the heat of the Lend Lease debates that the audience came back: "[W]e must remember that the human being is still an emotional animal primarily, and thinks only when he is absolutely forced to do so."[41] Both Denny and Williams were privately admitting to some despair by mid-1941 about the capacity of the ideal radio forum to cut through the emotion of the moment. The project of maintaining a space for civilized "living room conversation" about war and peace seemed increasingly unrealistic.

This despondency was no doubt enhanced by the fact that Denny's own sentiments were internationalist and cosmopolitan, in a nation where there had been a clear isolationist majority. He was arguing in 1936 that "the development of science and international trade has made us citizens of the world in which we all have common interests and common problems."[42] He developed early a revulsion for the race-based terror of Nazi Germany, for the way it "ruthlessly murders and persecutes helpless minorities," and he believed that such regimes ultimately posed a threat to American democracy.[43] By 1940, he held clearly interventionist views, arguing that "we should at once throw all the resources of this nation behind the Allies" to preserve the democratic way of life throughout the world.

So it was in confronting evidence of the immovable isolationism of many *ATMA* listeners that Denny began to grow more pessimistic about establishing the discursive and participatory democracy he had hoped for. In 1939 he told a luncheon at Town Hall that his four years of experience with *ATMA* had led him to conclude that "human nature is innately decent and instinctively prefers fair play to foul, good to bad, and truth to deception."[44] But in the following years, his thinking became gloomier. The view that discussion was an end in itself came to seem less and less plausible to him. What if, after all the reasoned discussion, a significant section of the American population still came only to the conclusion that democracy was broken because a Jewish and/or Communist conspiracy controlled their world? What if they stubbornly retained their conviction that identities were fixed and interests were unassailable by reason?

Through the war years, though, Denny continued to struggle to retain his liberal conviction that there a public sphere of discussion could be kept separate from issues of identity. In one 1944 *ATMA* broadcast, Denny ruled an isolationist question to radio commentator H. V. Kaltenborn out of order:

> Lady: Mr Kaltenborn. Do you believe in freedom of speech on the air for internationally minded news commentators while Americans who believe in the preservation of our national sovereignty, such as Wheeler, Lindbergh, and Father Coughlin, are denied this privilege?
>
> Mr Denny: I am sorry. That is obviously a question that any judge or any person of fair play would rule out. . . . It is of a personal character and has no place in this discussion tonight. I am very sorry the lady asked it.[45]

After this broadcast, Denny received many angry letters. Some of them insinuated that Denny himself must be Jewish and/or communist: "The red Christ-killers have not been ruled out of order when they packed the Town Hall for 'all out for War.'"[46] "You lousy Jews had better stay in New York where you are surrounded by all the Yiddish," read one postcard, sent from a Veterans Hospital in Kansas and addressed to "Abe Shitsky alias George Denny."[47] In a crisis, Americans seemed to Denny less and less likely to be able to discuss important issues without resorting to emotional and personal vituperation. As *ATMA* speakers insisted on elaborating who they were, it became more and more difficult for Denny to police the line that no "personal questions" were to be allowed. The war was a personal question in a way that Denny's liberalism found difficult to recognize.

Once the United States was in the war, Denny reluctantly began to argue that "Tolerance, Reason and Justice," the cornerstones of the Town Hall faith, were no longer enough. Unity was now an important desideratum, and *ATMA*'s methods might not produce it. In a 1943 speech, Denny expressed new reservations about freedom and rationality. Freedom, he said, "desirable as it is, is just about the most

dangerous thing in the world," for "implicit in freedom is the right to be and advocate evil as well as good, injustice as well as justice, and to practice foul rather
than fair play." Reason was a "dangerous and docile instrument. It may be used as
readily by a Machiavelli or a Goebbels as by a Washington, a Jefferson or a Lincoln." For years one of Denny's favorite methods of explaining the Town Hall idea
had been to produce a ball that was black on one side and white on the other. Things
appear differently to us from our different vantage points, he would say, but discussion can help us understand and overcome our differences. By 1943 Denny had
a profoundly more pessimistic conclusion to draw from the black and white ball:
"[T]he tragedy is that we cannot turn our problems around so simply. Each of us
is bound by all of his yesterdays."[48] He had lost much of his earlier confidence that
discussion could trump history.

In June 1943 Denny was invited by Elmer Davis, director of the Office of War
Information, to visit Britain "as a speaker to interpret American life and war effort"
and to lead forum discussions. The trip to England was clearly a transformative experience for Denny. He reflected in a letter in 1945 that "[n]o one thing in my past
experience has been quite as rich in deepening my understanding than the trip to
England in the fall of 1943."[49] This was personally too a difficult time. He had married Mary Yellott, a fellow Carolina Playmaker, in 1924, and they had had three
children. She was granted a divorce in Reno on September 1, 1943, citing cruelty.[50]
In April 1944 George married again, to Jeanne Sarasy, a younger woman who had
appeared on a 1941 *ATMA* discussion entitled "What Is American Youth's Moral
Code?" and who was then hired as an assistant on the show. There is also some
suggestion that Denny was wrestling with depression. In a 1943 letter to an English
friend, he said he had been busy on the tour and so "haven't had much time with
The Shadows."[51]

In a diary kept on the British trip, Denny was more revealing of his underlying
anxieties about his project than he was anywhere in his public speeches or writings.
On September 19 in London: "Got into a hot argument with C about Intellect,
Reason, Emotions, where our moral sense comes from, heredity, etc. . . . I do have
some difficulty explaining the genesis and perpetuation of our moral sense on
grounds other than environmental influences, present and as far back as you wish
to go. Yet it must be there. I'll keep looking for it." Why was it so important to Denny
to believe that there was an innate moral sense? He was beginning to retreat from
the relativism of the Town Hall philosophy; openness and tolerance, letting the
other speak, were no longer enough in a world of evil. If discussion was not anchored by some innate moral sense, what grounds were there for optimism about
the outcome? All the training in the world might still have no effect. Even democracy itself began to seem no longer a self-evident good. "The more I see of democracy in action," he wrote in his diary, "the more I want to write my book on Dangerous Democracy": "If you want proof of how abysmally our education has failed,
just talk to some of the officers in the army who have been watching the young
men and women come in from all walks of life. How can you have self-gov't based

on so little knowledge or understanding by ignorant and selfish selves?"[52] His travels in England and across the United States had left him, he told an audience in 1943, "extremely pessimistic": "I do not think that any man can look at the affairs of the world today, and think ahead five, ten, fifteen years, in the light of what he sees, without being terribly pessimistic. It all adds up to chaos, debt, competition of the most ruthless kind, nationalisms gone wild, and another great war, followed by a civil war, followed by race wars."[53]

Denny was thus preoccupied in 1943 with, among other things, the dangers that race and racial prejudice posed to democracy. He, like other democratic reformers of his generation, had thought of discussion as a cure for the class-related tensions of the Depression era. He espoused a developed form of civic nationalism, which had come by the end of the 1930s into collision with what Gary Gerstle (2001) has referred to as the "enduring potency of the racialized tradition of American nationalism" (161). On his return from Britain, in a 1943 letter to Elmer Davis, Denny reflected revealingly on the continuing motivation for his work: "Coming from the South as I do I have also seen men move about in gangs and mobs. I have seen a skillful organizer for the Ku Klux Klan meet in a public school building and, appealing to the prejudices of his hearers, organize a Klan. I witnessed mass meetings before the war and saw thousands of our own citizens have their prejudices cultivated and their hatreds against their fellow citizens intensified. . . . I hope not to see this again."[54] This southern experience of racial hatred, never recalled publicly, was, I suspect, an important source of Denny's lifelong commitment to a more rational and discursive public sphere and part of the reason for his despair at finding his national radio forum assailed by prejudice.[55]

Late in the war Denny did steer *ATMA* toward some direct and surprisingly frank discussion of American racial issues. At its inception, *ATMA* had been almost exclusively preoccupied with New Deal–era questions of class and state intervention rather than race. The growing international focus brought it to grips with race issues elsewhere in the world, but late in the war it turned at last to some African American speakers and open debate about American racial issues: in 1944 Langston Hughes spoke on "Let's Face the Race Question," and in 1945 Richard Wright participated in "Are We Solving America's Race Problem?"

In 1939 Denny had made a rare overt political judgment in telling a reporter that he considered the outrages committed by the Nazis in Germany "not comparable to the Russian purges." "At least in Russia, they were punishing what they considered political crimes," he said, whereas in Germany the regime was "torturing a minority whose only crime was their race."[56] Race prejudice was quite apparently for Denny the most destructive and irrational element in political life and first among the threats he perceived to modern civilization. In a 1940 address, he said it was a moot question whether humanity had progressed or retrogressed. When he listed the "unsolved economic, social and political problems of the past four thousand years," race was first among them, then religion, nationalism, population, distribution of natural resources, government, money, labor, capital, and human greed.[57]

Despite the New York overlay, Denny was still in many ways a southern liberal, with a deep and abiding sense of the destructiveness of the ideas and practices of racial supremacy.

After the War

After the war, *ATMA* struggled to find a role and a market for itself at home but moved onto the international stage. George Denny was sent to advise General MacArthur on the democratization of Japan.[58] He became an articulate cold warrior, very hostile to the Soviet Union, in favor of outlawing communist parties all over the noncommunist world. In 1948, on the five hundredth edition of *ATMA*, the program returned to the question posed on the first broadcast, "Which Way America—Fascism, Communism, Socialism, or Democracy?" But this time there was no possibility of having communists or fascists speak for themselves. Denny made it clear in his introduction that communism and fascism were forms of totalitarianism and that "we are not impressed by the propaganda demands of the advocates of totalitarianism to use the principles of democracy to advance the cause of a form of government which would destroy those principles." The speakers chosen to talk about communism and fascism were vigorous opponents of those doctrines.[59] Denny became an advocate of a world government that could police the world against the "gangster" states of the communist bloc and a vocal opponent of the United Nations, which purported to represent communist as well as noncommunist nations. This, he argued, was as if the city of Chicago had decided to have Al Capone's control over the city recognized by giving him a seat on the council.[60]

Denny and Chester Williams took *ATMA* on a world tour in 1949—to London, Paris, Berlin, Vienna, Rome, Ankara, Tel Aviv, Cairo, Karachi, New Delhi, Manila, Tokyo, Honolulu, Washington. The touring party included Walter White of the National Association for the Advancement of Colored People (NAACP) and Edith Sampson of the National Council of Negro Women to counter the impression, held by many, that America's troubled race relations undermined its arguments for democracy. The group, "greatly aided by the Negro members, effectively set forth the steps being taken and progress being made against lynching, disfranchisement, segregation and discrimination in America."[61] By 1950, *ATMA* was being broadcast internationally on the Voice of America. Denny wrote: "People in any country who hear the program know they are listening to democracy in action."[62]

ATMA survived until 1956 on ABC radio. In February 1952, *ATMA* premiered on ABC television on Sunday night, but by April—after internal disputes at Town Hall—Denny had been replaced as host of both radio and television shows. He went on the lecture circuit. "A New Idea in 'Debates'! Now hear BOTH sides of important issues facing all Americans interpreted by ONE speaker qualified to discuss them with objective impartiality." George Denny debating with himself was marketed as "unusual and provocative" entertainment: "Mr Denny's original form of platform discussion might well be termed 'one-man debates.' They implement his lifelong belief in the necessity for the free and unfettered exchange of opposing views. . . . Mr Denny is introduced by the chairman, first in his capacity as speaker for the affirmative side, then in his role as speaker for the negative side."[63] By the 1950s, Denny's form of democratic showmanship had become all show. Detached from a movement that saw in organized discussion a new and enlivened democratic future, his stage performance had become merely a novelty act.

The hopes for radio as a democratic and transforming medium faded. Political discussion between people of opposing views became routinized, clearly not something that was going to change the world. The range of divergent views that could be represented in the media narrowed. And in the Cold War context, the urgent need for democratizing American society became a less acceptable theme than the need to bring American democracy—understood now as an existing achievement rather than a work in progress—to the rest of the world.

Genuinely innovative and influential from its inception, *ATMA* was buffeted by the crisis over American intervention in World War II. The agonized debates about American participation in the war, and the continuing strength of racial nationalism in the United States, put unbearable strains on the belief that rational public discussion would produce a better and more tolerant society. The voices speaking back from the active but stubbornly unempathetic and tenaciously prejudiced radio audience dented faith in radio's capacity to create a new national yet neighborly democracy. As Denny adapted to the Cold War context, he came to see his show's mission as more international than national, and the program thus served as a mirror of American national preoccupations.

ATMA was one of NBC's most significant public service programs. It was for NBC in its heyday a great success story—a program that both presented and provoked national debate. It provided a practical demonstration of a new kind of radio public sphere, one that was both constrained and enabled by the network's commercial basis. It is timely to remind ourselves of the hopes that were once held for it.

Notes

Abbreviations

GDP   George V. Denny Jr. Papers, Manuscript Division, Library of Congress

THI   Town Hall Inc. Papers, Manuscripts and Archives Division, New York Public Library

NBC/WHS   National Broadcasting Company Archives, Wisconsin Historical Society

RF   Rockefeller Foundation Archives, Rockefeller Archives Center

1. John Royal to Richard Patterson, May 3, 1935, Box 108, NBC/WHS.

2. John Royal to David Lawrence, April 27, 1935, and John Royal to David Rosenblum, April 23, 1935, both in Box 34, Folder 8, NBC/WHS.

3. Speech by Denny, April 3, 1936, League for Political Education Spring Luncheon, Series 1, Box 24, GDP.

4. Frederick L. Collins, "He Makes Democracy Think!" *Liberty*, December 9, 1939, 41–45.

5. "America's Town Meeting of the Air," *Movie-Radio Guide*, December 13–19, 1941, 38.

6. Collins, "He Makes Democracy Think!" 44.

7. The transcripts of each broadcast were published by Columbia University Press as *Town Meeting: Bulletin of America's Town Meeting of the Air*, and listeners could purchase copies at ten cents each.

8. *New York Times*, June 30, 1935.

9. "Freedom of Discussion," *United Business Men's Review*, December 1943, 4.

10. George V. Denny Jr., "Education and Leadership in Democracy," address to Town Hall luncheon, April 12, 1939, 3, GDP.

11. Margaret Cuthbert to Richard Patterson, April 8, 1935, Box 34, Folder 8, NBC/WHS.

12. Series 1, Box 1, Folder 2, GDP.

13. For a study of the fan mail received by *ATMA* for the 1937–38 season, see Sayre (1939).

14. Report of the Officers to the Trustees of the League for Political Education, July 2, 1935, THI.

15. Minutes of Meetings of Executive Committee, May 1939–April 1941, and President's Report, May 1939, both in Box 13, THI.

16. C. Healy, Oak Park, IL, to Town Hall, November 1, 1935, Box 16, THI.

17. "Report of Advisory Service," Chester D. Snell, Director, in *Annual Report of the Town Hall Inc. Season, 1939–40*, THI.

18. Reported in *New York Sun*, December 5, 1936.

19. George Denny to John Marshall, October 30, 1936, Box 271, Folder 3233, RF.

20. Franklin Dunham to Alfred Morton, September 23, 1935, Box 34, Folder 6, NBC/WHS.

21. *Town Meeting*, January 24, 1938, 32.

22. *Town Meeting*, February 7, 1938, 17.

23. Minutes of Town Hall Executive Committee Meeting, December 18, 1939, THI.

24. "Statement by George V. Denny Jr., President, The Town Hall, Inc." n.d., Series 1, Box 20, GDP.

25. Minutes of the Meeting of the Executive Committee, May 11, 1936, THI.

26. W. G. Preston to S. Strotz, November 25, 1940, Box 80, Folder 101, NBC/WHS.

27. George V. Denny to John Royal, October 18, 1939, Box 66, Folder 12, NBC/WHS.

28. David Sarnoff to Niles Trammell, January 11, 1940, John Royal to Niles Trammell, February 23, 1940, and James Angell to John Royal, Feb. 26, 1940, all in Box 74, Folder 28, NBC/WHS.

29. Herbert Lyons Jr., "Free Speech in Action," *New York Times*, May 25, 1941, X8.

30. Stella Westhof to Town Hall, February 28, 1941, Box 18, THI.

31. Report of Radio Forum Division, prepared by Marian S. Carter, Director, in *Annual Report of the Town Hall Inc. Season, 1939–40*.

32. Franklin Church to Town Hall, November 23, 1935, Box 77, THI.

33. *New York Sun*, April 24, 1937.

34. R. H. Goodell (Glendale, CA) to Town Hall, April 22, 1937, Box 76, THI.

35. John Brown to Town Hall, January 9, 1941, Box 18, THI.

36. Joseph Donovan to Town Hall, January 14, 1940, Box 18, THI.

37. "Twelve Listeners" to Town Hall, January 9, 1941, Box 18, THI.

38. "Should Our Ships Convoy Arms to Britain?" *Town Meeting*, April 7, 1941, 12–14.

39. Ibid., 20.

40. Chester S. Williams to George Denny, April 4, 1941, Box 8, THI.

41. George Denny to Chester S. Williams, April 16, 1941, Box 8, THI.

42. Speech by Denny, April 3, 1936, League Spring Luncheon, Series 1, Box 24, GDP.

43. George Denny, "Democracy and Leadership—An Address Delivered at the Commencement Exercises at Temple University 13 June 1940," Series 2, Box 3, GDP.

44. Denny, "Education and Leadership," 1.

45. *Town Meeting*, April 6, 1944, 20.

46. Unsigned letter to George Denny, April 7, 1944, Box 19, THI.

47. Ed Hall to Town Hall, n.d., Box 19, THI.

48. Series 1, Box 26, GDP. Denny recycled his stories and speeches often; some of the same sentences appear in an interview with Denny in the *New York Times*. S. J. Woolf, "The Umpire of the Town Meeting," *New York Times*, June 6, 1943, VI:16.

49. George Denny to Major Stanley Dyment, January 16, 1945, Series 1, Box 23, GDP.

50. *New York Times*, September 2, 1943, 13.

51. George Denny to Lady Judith Listowel, October 8, 1943, Series 1, Box 23, GDP.

52. Series 1, Box 23, Folder 1, GDP.

53. "Freedom of Discussion," *United Business Men's Review*, December 1943, 5.

54. George Denny to Elmer Davis, November 20, 1943, Series 1, Box 23, GDP.

55. This feeling would have been reinforced in 1945 when, in response to an appearance on *ATMA* by African American novelist Richard Wright, Town Hall received many "long passionate" angry letters from white listeners. See Savage (1999, 218).

56. *Boston Sunday Post*, January 22, 1939, 5.

57. Denny, "Democracy and Leadership," Series 2, Box 3, GDP.

58. *Variety*, March 12, 1947.

59. *Town Meeting*, March 16, 1948, 4.

60. George Denny, "US Must Organize Real United Nations or Face Destruction," *Wichita Beacon*, November 26, 1950.

61. World Town Hall Seminar, *Report to the President of the United States*, Washington, DC, October 18, 1949, 3, 6.

62. Town Hall, Inc., publicity brochure, 1950.

63. Flyer, GDP.

4

Regulating Class Conflict on the Air

NBC's Relationship with Business
and Organized Labor

ELIZABETH FONES-WOLF AND NATHAN GODFRIED

For millions of Americans, the Great Depression represented the failure of the nation's economic and political systems to provide for the general welfare. As a result, working-class Americans participated in a massive wave of militant actions that challenged American capitalism and democracy. In the midst of the rising class conflict, both business and organized labor sought greater access to broadcasting. Radio offered to these competing forces a new means for winning the allegiance of workers and the public. Programming that overtly promoted business or labor ideology, however, posed special problems for the networks, which generally shied away from controversy. Like religion and politics, strikes and class conflict were "dynamite" that might alienate listeners and attract the wrath of regulators.

This essay explores the National Broadcasting Company's relationship with business and organized labor during the 1930s and World War II, an era of volatile class relations. In particular, it examines how the network viewed the demands of both unions and corporations for airtime with caution but tended to treat business more favorably than labor. NBC's programming policies reflected its corporate status and its dependence on business advertising. Not surprisingly, network executives eagerly sought corporate institutional programming, which carried relatively subtle messages designed both to improve the corporate image and to promote business values, and welcomed business-backed news commentators who regularly attacked labor. Fearful of antagonizing New Deal regulators, however, the network refused to allow corporations and business organizations carte blanche access to the airwaves. In this era, it was necessary to provide at least the facade of fairness.

While NBC executives put the welcome mat out for their business colleagues, they placed severe limitations on unions' use of their network. Like CBS and many local stations, NBC refused to sell time to unions. During the 1930s, the network sought to meet its public service responsibilities and to placate organized labor by providing union leaders with limited amounts of free time for speeches and by currying favor with conservative labor leaders like William Green, president of the American Federation of Labor (AFL). While the AFL seemed satisfied with NBC's crumbs, the newly formed and much more militant Congress of Industrial Organizations (CIO) criticized organized labor's limited access to broadcasting. During World War II, both labor groups stepped up pressure on the network for more equitable treatment. Wartime exigencies and regulatory pressures eventually forced NBC to provide unions with wider access to the airwaves. But such changes did not fundamentally alter the network's primary allegiance to its corporate sponsors.

Labor, Business, and NBC before World War II

"Political censorship, both flagrant and subtle," observes historian Daniel Czitrom (1982), "characterized commercial radio from the beginning" (81). During the late 1920s and early 1930s, civic, educational, religious, farm, and labor groups, concerned that increasingly powerful private broadcasters had little interest in protecting a diversity of opinion on the air, fought for public control of radio. They contended that radio should serve the public interest and that "commercial broadcasting was inimical to the communications needs of a democratic society" (McChesney 1993, 94). As reformers saw it, radio was too powerful a medium to be controlled by companies driven solely by the profit motive.

The struggle for a diversified radio system ended unsuccessfully with the passage of the Communications Act of 1934, which established the Federal Communications Commission (FCC). While the American system of broadcasting remained predominantly privately owned and profit driven, the government required stations to operate under a mandate to serve "in the public interest, convenience, and necessity." The FCC issued licenses to stations for short terms and could deny renewal if there was evidence of violation of federal regulations. It required stations to present a balanced, well-rounded schedule of programming, representing a variety of political viewpoints (McChesney 1993; Smulyan 1994).

Through much of the 1930s, the FCC applied its authority cautiously and maintained friendly relations with the broadcasters. Still, the "threat of government mischief haunted the industry," especially the networks, NBC and CBS (Steele 1985, 18). Although not under the immediate jurisdiction of the FCC, they owned some of the most powerful local stations. In some ways, the networks were more politically vulnerable than local stations. Broadcast reformers' charges that the networks had gained monopoly control of the industry raised the specter of potential antitrust litigation and other kinds of regulation. There was some basis for industry fears of greater government supervision. In the late 1930s, the FCC chided NBC for several broadcasts that some listeners found offensive. Responding to congressional pressure at about the same time, the FCC began an investigation into chain broadcasting, which resulted in the requirement that NBC divest itself of one of its two networks (see Sterling, chapter 5 of this book). In 1941, the FCC launched an inquiry into newspaper ownership of broadcast stations. Given this pressure, broadcasters sought "to foster a spirit of accommodation with the administration" (Ewen 1996, 251; Steele 1985,17–25, 127–36).

Beyond fear of government interference, radio stations were also concerned about maintaining public goodwill. Desiring to maximize their audiences and their advertising revenues, broadcasters were leery of airing programs that might alienate potential listeners or advertisers. Thus stations and the networks censored scripts to eliminate not only controversial issues but also anything that might be considered in poor taste or offensive. At NBC, John Royal, the network's vice president for programming, established the network policy of "giving offense to no one."[1]

To reduce the possibility of further federal regulation, the networks generally discouraged criticism of government policy and shied away from selling time for programs on subjects that they deemed controversial. The National Association of Broadcasters (NAB) officially endorsed this policy in 1939 when it adopted a new voluntary code of ethics. As part of this policy, the networks attempted to maintain an attitude of political neutrality. In July 1936, NBC reminded station managers that "none of our news broadcasts, commercial or sustaining, must in any way reflect political opinions or take partisan views on any issue" (Craig 2000, 124). Broadcasters met the mandate that they operate in the public interest and that they offer a balanced schedule by sponsoring public service programs. These included talks on current political, economic, and social questions by government officials, representatives of organized social groups, and other public figures. It was the broadcasters themselves who determined which subjects were of public interest and which groups were legitimate representatives of particular issues. The discussion of controversial issues theoretically required that each side of a question receive equal time. In the early part of 1935, however, only 5 percent of NBC network time went to this kind of programming, and only a small proportion of these shows addressed issues of a controversial character.[2] To varying degrees, local stations followed the network policies on controversial issues. As a result, unable to buy time and with little free time available, advocates of dissident political or social views, such as socialists, pacifists, communists, or promoters of birth control or racial equality, were often denied access to the airwaves (Craig 2000, 72–75, 100–101, 114).

Labor was one of the victims of the broadcasters' restriction on freedom of speech. In the 1930s and 1940s only two small radio stations, WCFL in Chicago and WEVD in New York, were committed to broadcasting labor issues. Most unions relied for airtime on stations that generally hesitated even to appear to serve as a platform for organized labor. NBC and CBS refused to sell time to unions for national broadcasts, asserting that they sold time only for the advertising of goods and services and never for propaganda or controversial public issues. In 1937, CBS president William S. Paley defined propaganda as "any attempt to influence legislation, regulation, taxation and the like." The networks viewed unions as agents of propaganda and thus classified them as inherently controversial.[3]

NBC adhered so strictly to this rule that it initially banned a broadcast of *Pins and Needles*, the acclaimed Broadway musical by the International Ladies Garment

Workers Union (ILGWU), arguing that the show's songs were full of controversial subjects. The network agreed to air the show only after the producers cut numbers like "Doing the Reactionary" and "Sing Me a Song of Social Significance." In addition, the show's songwriter, Harold J. Rome, had to revise the lyrics of "One Big Union for Two," deleting references to court injunctions, closed shops, scabs, and lockouts (Denning 1997, 202–3). Executive John Royal allowed the song "Sunday" to remain in the broadcast only after he was convinced that it was strictly a romantic tune and was not critical of the economic system.[4] To justify their refusal to sell time to labor unions and other groups, the networks claimed that they fulfilled their public service mission by providing ample free time for groups to discuss controversial issues, including labor. Each year NBC and CBS broadcast parts of the AFL and later CIO conventions and Labor Day speeches by prominent union leaders. They also opened the airways to unions for speeches at several other times during the year (Godfried 1997, 145). In 1936, for instance, in addition to his Labor Day address, labor leader John L. Lewis spoke over the networks on July 6 and again on December 31.[5] During the 1930s, NBC demonstrated its commitment to providing representation to all political and economic viewpoints by giving time for speeches by Socialist Party leader Norman Thomas and occasionally even by the Communist Party leader Earl Browder. Thomas, who often spoke about labor issues, admitted that he served as NBC's "pet radical." As he put it, he was valuable to NBC "as proof of [its] liberalism" (Brindze 1937, 174–75; Godfried 1997, 150).

As a result of network policies, relatively little airtime went to labor. Unable to buy time, labor essentially depended on the networks' largesse. Free airtime was available only for issues that the networks deemed of sufficient public interest. NBC denied Norman Thomas's request to discuss Mayor Frank Hague's attack on workers seeking to organize Jersey City, arguing that it was not a public issue. Executive John Royal contended that the meaning of " 'public issue' . . . is a matter of opinion" and asserted that NBC did not "permit free *speech* on the air. We *do* permit free discussion, under radio's editorial judgment." In December 1939, in another internal memo, Royal admitted that the network had "never given much time to labor as labor—there have been occasional talks by the A F of L and the CIO."[6]

On the few occasions when the networks scheduled a labor speaker, only rarely did all affiliated stations carry the broadcast. Networks required affiliates to carry sponsored programs, such as *Fibber McGee and Molly*, *The Jack Benny Program*, or the *Ford Sunday Evening Hour*, which offered classical music with short intermission talks by William J. Cameron, Ford's director of public relations, who often spoke about political issues from a conservative perspective. But the networks allowed local stations to accept or reject unsponsored or sustaining programs. Thus, as American Civil Liberties Union secretary Hazel L. Rice observed, "[E]very station on a network must have the Ford hour, with Mr. Cameron's little talk in the middle of the hour, [but] should Mr. [John L.] Lewis follow him (and the only way he could do it would be to have the time given to him) all the affiliated stations could cut him off if they chose to." Local affiliates did indeed often refuse to carry network labor speeches. ILGWU president David Dubinsky, for instance, spoke over NBC at 6:15 p.m. on April 14, 1938. Workers in Los Angeles, Montreal, and Fall River, Massachusetts, many of whom had gathered at their union headquarters, were disappointed when their local stations failed to pick up NBC's coast-to-coast broadcast.[7]

Until World War II, there was little consensus within the labor movement about its treatment by broadcasters. Most federation leaders were satisfied with the operation of the existing broadcasting system. Indeed, with little interest in using radio for organizing, few AFL unions clashed with broadcasters over access. NBC in particular had long curried favor with the AFL, which it considered the most responsible element of the labor movement. The network appointed AFL president William Green to its National Advisory Council and happily gave the AFL leadership airtime for speeches. A man of limited imagination, Green had little understanding of radio's potential power, regarding it primarily as an educational and public relations tool to provide evidence of organized labor's responsible behavior. In 1936 NBC President Merlin Aylesworth sent Green a "gilt-edged pass" to the NBC Studios with the message that he hoped Green would "use it often." Green responded by praising the networks for their generosity to organized labor.[8]

Within the AFL, however, there were those who had a more ambitious vision for the future of labor and radio. Even before the advent of radio networks, local labor groups feared the political and economic power of business-owned and commercially oriented radio stations. In 1926, the Chicago Federation of Labor (CFL) founded WCFL as a "non-profit, listener-supported station, dedicated to serving the interests of workers and their communities," and in 1927 the socialists founded WEVD in New York City. During the 1930s and 1940s, both stations provided labor with airtime in their cities. Moreover, under the leadership of CFL secretary Edward Nockels, WCFL helped lead the battle to save broadcasting from monopolistic control, arguing that the networks and commercial stations failed to serve the public interest (Godfried 1993; Godfried 1997, 149–57, 203–4).

Nockels's attacks on NBC's role in the "radio trust" did not stop WCFL from purchasing selected programming from the network during the 1930s. In 1934, NBC and WCFL negotiated a tentative agreement that would have given the labor station free network programming, offered the AFL a weekly show on the network, and provided NBC with additional access to markets in selected areas of the nation. While NBC president Aylesworth did not object to complying with William Green's occasional requests for airtime, he feared the possibility of "a series of Labor programs offered to our Associated stations under the immediate direction of Nockels . . . and in the form of attacks on employers, etc." The proposed deal fell through when the network legal counsel warned that the provision calling on WCFL to build stations in other parts of the country and then to lease those stations to NBC for a nominal fee clearly violated the Communications Act's prohibition on trafficking in licenses. Nockels, never entirely comfortable with the agreement, quickly returned to condemning the networks' monopolization of the airwaves and promotion of private property rights over the public domain (God-fried 1997, 149–56).[9]

In the late 1930s, the CIO also began challenging the broadcasting status quo. CIO leaders like John L. Lewis, Homer Martin, and James Carey were impressed by radio's ability to shape public attitudes and influence political and economic power. At one point United Automobile Workers (UAW) president Homer Martin boasted that, "by use of radio alone, we could whip any auto company." Occasionally NBC did allow speeches by CIO leaders, but industrial unionists were still frustrated and angered by their limited access to the air.[10]

Broadcasters proved much more accommodating to the use of radio to sell the political and economic agenda of business. This is not surprising given that the networks were corporations themselves and dependent on business sponsorship of their programming. NBC executives, however, understood that the regulatory structure made it imperative that the network avoid overtly promoting business interests. Still, in the 1930s, as the Depression deepened and public hostility toward business intensified, networks encouraged companies to use radio as a public relations tool. Exploiting fears about the future of the free enterprise system, NBC urged industry to "campaign for public favor as never before." It advised, "Get your story across through the greatest force the world has ever known for influencing lives and thoughts—Radio."[11] Broadcasters like NBC could argue that radio was even more effective than the printed word in selling ideas as well as products, pointing to a *Fortune* magazine survey that found radio had higher credibility among Americans than the press (Stott 1973, 80).

Beginning in the 1930s, a number of major firms began sponsoring nationally broadcast programs with institutional messages aimed at creating a positive corporate image. NBC eagerly sold airtime to General Motors, Westinghouse, DuPont, Texaco, and Firestone for classical music programs and serious dramas. In the belief that public hostility toward industry was the result of a lack of knowledge, companies used these programs to present information about their labor policies, safety record, and support for charities. In an "informative and confidential fashion," General Motors spokesmen mixed discussion of the technical problems of automobile construction and driving safety with occasional remarks on wage levels and the benefits of the American economic system (Sethi 1977, 7–10).[12]

NBC executives worked hard to recruit the DuPont institutional program, *Cavalcade of America*. The 1930s had been a public relations nightmare for the chemical manufacturer, which had been tagged with a "merchant of death image" by the Senate committee investigating World War I munitions profits. The DuPont family also worried about the popularity of the New Deal and the increasingly militant labor movement, which they believed would destroy the freedoms associated with American capitalism. Through its historical drama series, the DuPont company sought to refurbish its image while taking subtle shots at the Democrats. The radio program reminded the public of the "origins of our unique freedom through dramatic stories of the men and women who won it, of those who fought to hold it."[13] Designed to be inspirational, it focused on the lives of such prominent Americans as Thomas Jefferson, Daniel Boone, Robert E. Lee, Tom Paine, and Roger Williams. The show's commercials emphasized the contributions of the company's products to American society. Each episode concluded with the slogan "Better Things for Better Living through Chemistry." Despite the efforts of NBC to woo DuPont, the program premiered in 1935 on CBS. Through the late 1930s, NBC continued to lobby DuPont for its institutional business. To win DuPont's confidence, among other goals, NBC sought to demonstrate its sympathy for conservatism by hiring James Rowland Angell, a prominent conservative and critic of the New Deal, as the network's director of radio education. By January 1940, NBC executives had succeeded in convincing DuPont to shift its program to NBC (Marchand 1998, 218–23; Bird 1999, 66–82, 101–4).

While DuPont may have contended that they were simply seeking goodwill for their firms, other business programming was overtly political. In the mid-1930s, the Crusaders, an organization of conservative business leaders opposed to "all forces destructive to sound government," sought airtime for a weekly program that dismissed the problem of unemployment and defended American industry while attacking the New Deal and its regulatory agencies (Barnouw 1968, 14–15, 34). The National Association of Manufacturers (NAM) also developed a radio series, *American Family Robinson*, that fought the New Deal and organized labor. This program, which NAM offered to NBC in 1934, taught economic lessons and argued that Roosevelt's social policies were utopian and disruptive (Ewen 1996, 317–18; Tedlow 1979, 60–73). NBC, however, rejected both programs. Fearful of government intervention, the network refused to allow business carte blanche to the airwaves. Network vice president of programming John Royal worried about associating NBC too closely with antiadministration business organizations, and he refused to sell time to the Crusaders.[14] The network also rejected NAM's program, *American Family Robinson*, characterizing it as "decided propaganda" and thereby forcing the employers' association to rely on small non-network stations for airtime. According to Royal, some members of NAM believed that NBC was going to "give them unlimited time." But, he argued, although "they are our biggest clients, there is a much bigger question facing [us]. That is the very question of our existence for 'public interest,' convenience and necessity."[15] The network nevertheless wanted NAM's business and encouraged the employers' association to develop a more acceptable institutional program (Bird 1999, 28–29, 53–56).

Network principles on controversial programming placed impediments to business self-promotion but certainly not insurmountable barriers. NBC's policies were often inconsistent. During the 1936 election, for instance, the network sold time to the American Liberty League, another anti–New Deal business organization (Barnouw 1968, 14–15).[16] Similarly, it normally refused to allow discussion of controversial issues, like strikes, on commercial programs. Indeed, at the April 1938 meeting of the NBC's National Advisory Council, network president Lenox Lohr asserted that, "if a motor company were having a strike and should attempt to use their time to influence public opinion on the subject, we would stop them from presenting such a case in time sold for advertising a product." But in early 1937, NBC permitted General Motors to use the intermission of its *General Motors Concert Hour* to make a subtle attack against the Flint sit-down strikers, who had forced the closing of several of the corporation's plants. The GM announcer never specifically mentioned the strike but instead defended the "age-old principle of the right to work." He contended that "whether one shall work—how one shall work—when one shall work—has from the earliest days of our national existence been the acknowledged right of each one of us to decide for himself, with no man's interference." The appeal was "so cleverly done" that NBC's John Royal felt confident in taking "a chance on it."[17]

Despite its pretensions of nonpartisanship, NBC was also much more likely to give time to business than to organized labor. During April 1935, for instance, NBC broadcast speeches by fifteen business leaders representing some of the most powerful corporations in the nation, including Lammot DuPont, American *Cynanamid* Company president William B. Ball, GM president Alfred P. Sloan, and General Electric vice president T. K. Quinn. The only labor speaker to grace NBC's microphone during that period was ILGWU president David Dubinsky, reporting for fifteen minutes on an international labor conference in Geneva, Switzerland. While NBC ultimately decided against selling the Crusaders airtime, during the spring and summer of 1935 it allowed the Crusaders to organize a series of probusiness speeches. The Crusaders, however, were not identified as the sponsors, and the series was carried as an unsponsored, network-supported sustaining program.[18]

Wartime Changes

Corporations, civic and social groups, and the federal government all increased their use of radio during World War II. NBC and other networks demonstrated their patriotism by providing time and resources for such programming. Noncommercial government propaganda shows from the Treasury Department, the War Department, the Office of War Information, and other agencies constituted the bulk of public service programming offered over radio during the war (Horten 2002, 41–65; Savage 1999). The Red Cross and other private social service organs also used radio to promote their activities and needs to the public (Blue 2002, 154–55).

Businesses' use of radio to promote corporate ideology expanded during World War II, much to the delight of NBC and other broadcasters. Individual corporations eagerly exploited the war to improve their image. Corporate publicists trumpeted the business contribution to the war effort and promoted the "fifth freedom," the freedom of enterprise. They also fed the deluge of antilabor propaganda that permeated the American media during much of the war. The high wartime excess profits tax, combined with the Treasury Department decision allowing corporations to deduct advertising costs from taxable income, encouraged companies to engage in this kind of advertising. Radio played an important role in the campaign to sell American business and its ideology during World War II. Because of paper shortages, advertising in the print media decreased slightly during the war, while radio's advertising volume almost doubled. Networks and individual stations found sponsors for even the most unpopular time slots, which in the past had been filled by sustaining programming. Historian Gerd Horten suggests that radio was more effective in promoting the business message than the print media. By fusing advertising and entertainment, radio "provided the most powerful and persuasive medium for advertising before and during the war years" (Barnouw 1968, 166; Horten 2002, 101).

As part of its effort to win public goodwill, businesses dramatically enlarged their institutional programming. Corporate sponsorship of high culture featured prominently in their strategy. With no consumer products to sell, more American companies began to underwrite prestigious arts organizations, which in the past had struggled for sponsorship (Marchand 1998, 332–33; Barnouw 1968, 166). NBC convinced General Motors to assume sponsorship of the newly created NBC Symphony Orchestra under Arturo Toscanini. GM used the show to "tell the facts of its wartime production" to the public "in accompaniment of this great music." The program enabled General Motors executive Charles Kettering to speak directly to the American people on a weekly basis. His stories of how the corporation's "technical and managerial genius" contributed to the war effort reinforced the auto company's extensive newspaper and magazine advertising campaign (Horten 2002, 105; Marchand 1998, 338).

The war finally enabled NAM to obtain a regular program on network radio. In the spring of 1941, NBC agreed to provide time to the manufacturers' association. That decision enabled NBC to solidify its position with NAM, which, network executive Phillips Carlin observed, "after all, is our bread and butter — their advertisers."[19] During that year NBC broadcast *Defense for America* on Saturday nights. Later during the war, NBC carried NAM's *This Nation at War*. All these programs featured the story of industry's contribution to the war effort. NAM reporters visited important centers of defense production, describing the production process and interviewing workers at their factory benches, plant superintendents, government officials, and business leaders. Visiting Weirton Steel Company in June 1941, NAM found evidence of the "American spirit of free enterprise" in a "great American symphony of men, machines and management, working in perfect harmony" to prepare "our nation for any emergency." *Defense for America* regularly reminded listeners that managers and workers were "girding to defend the American way of life, a way of life that rests on a base of three inter-dependent freedoms . . . representative democracy, civil and religious liberties and free enterprise." The general manager of station WKPT of Kingsport, Tennessee, lauded the program as "without a doubt the most inspiring [program] on the air."[20]

Business Sponsorship of News Commentators

Business also helped shape Americans' understanding of the world through the sponsorship of radio commentators. Radio news commentary became popular during the 1930s but expanded dramatically during World War II. The U.S. entrance into the war further heightened interest in the news, and the percentage of network and local radio time devoted to news and commentator programs increased significantly. By 1944, about 18 percent of commercial network time was devoted to news, and news shows were second only to dramatic production in attracting advertising (Craig 2000, 217–21; Horten 2002, 25–33).[21] Commentators were hired by either the networks, local stations, or commercial sponsors. While many firms shied away from controversial commentators for fear of offending potential customers, businesses sponsored some of the most conservative commentators of the era.[22]

NBC hosted two such business-backed commentators, Upton Close and H. V. Kaltenborn. In September 1942, Shaeffer Pen Company hired Upton Close to provide a Sunday afternoon political commentary over the network. Close had appeared sporadically on NBC news programs from 1934 to 1941, but with corporate sponsorship he felt freer to express his opinions. He attracted a large audience during the first years of the war, when his bitter denunciations of the Roosevelt administration, American labor, the Soviet Union, and Great Britain "seemed to express the pent-up feelings of a sizable group of listeners."[23]

For much of the 1930s, H. V. Kaltenborn was an obscure CBS news analyst whose unsponsored newscast was carried by the network at a variety of unpopular times. In September 1938, however, Kaltenborn gained national attention as he provided an anxious American public with almost continuous coverage of the Czechoslovakian crisis. After this exposure, General Mills briefly became Kaltenborn's sponsor. General Mills promised Kaltenborn complete "freedom of selection and expression." But after just thirteen weeks, the firm backed out of the relationship when Catholic groups, angry at Kaltenborn's views in support of the besieged Republic in the Spanish Civil War, threatened to boycott the company's products. Kaltenborn found a more supportive sponsor in Pure Oil, which picked up his program in the spring of 1939 and shifted it to NBC. Broadcast five times a week during prime evening hours, Kaltenborn's show became one of the top-ranked news programs (Clark 1968, 309–10). Kaltenborn was highly critical of the Roosevelt administration's management of the wartime economy, contending that government policies hindered war production. Moreover, he carried on a virtual crusade against the labor movement, asserting that "labor union practices are injuring and destroying America's war effort" (Clark 1965, 502). Kaltenborn opposed wage increases for workers and lashed out bitterly against wartime strikes. In covering strikes, he frequently aired partisan statements from company officials and ignored the union response. For instance, in October 1942, he reported only on the company side of a dispute at a Chrysler plant, quoting a management spokesman who described a walkout as "definite sabotage against the nation's war effort." Kaltenborn blamed

FIG. **5** Hans V. Kaltenborn, news commentator. His popular *H. V. Kaltenborn Edits the News* program on NBC, sponsored by Pure Oil, criticized wartime policies and angered many with its probusiness, antilabor politics. (Wisconsin Center for Film and Television Research)

the wartime strikes on "a pro-labor Administration," complaining that "for ten years, we have pampered the labor unions to the point that they act like spoiled children whenever they don't get what they want." Business groups were so pleased with Kaltenborn's broadcasts that they asked NBC if they could buy recordings (Clark 1965, 499–502; Chester 1947, 389–427, esp. 404, 423).[24]

Labor Countermoves

Both the AFL and the CIO were angered by the business-sponsored programming, which they viewed as part of a "huge and sinister" antilabor propaganda campaign designed to deprive workers of hard-fought social and economic gains. They argued that the press and radio gave a very lopsided picture of the relative contributions of labor and industry to the war effort. According to the CIO, corporate goodwill programs and institutional advertising constantly emphasized the war achievements of business without giving credit to unions or the workers who made the production records possible. Union leaders blamed radio commentators as well as the daily press for the growing public hostility toward labor during the war, pointing in particular to stories exaggerating the numbers of strikes and the extent of absenteeism. They attributed the quick passage of the Smith-Connally antistrike bill to "the barrage of misinformation thrust into the air by radio commentators."[25]

Labor combated the business radio campaign with protests aimed at the networks, local stations, sponsors, and the FCC. Kaltenborn's crusade against organized labor in particular generated widespread opposition. Unionists across the country demanded that NBC bar Kaltenborn from the air. The Duluth local of the Textile Workers Union advised NBC in March 1942 that "labor is fed-up with Mr. Kaltenborn's false charges," which were "hindering war production."[26] The AFL complained to NBC after Kaltenborn asserted in a March 1942 broadcast that "no man can produce war material in any of the major war plants of the United States without first paying tribute to a labor union." AFL publicity director Philip Pearl condemned the statement as "vicious labor-baiting" and asked the network, "[W]here does Kaltenborn get the gall to spread over the radio" such "malicious anti-labor propaganda?" Such assertions, he continued, "have been, for many years, the last refuge of chiseling, labor-hating employers, the scum of industry." Eighteen months later, a disgusted federation turned to the FCC after Kaltenborn declared that nonunion aircraft plants had a better production record than unionized plants. When Kaltenborn refused either to produce evidence for his assertion or to broadcast a retraction, AFL president William Green demanded from NBC and the FCC "summary and remedial action" against this "flagrant abuse of the right of free speech."[27]

Unions representing hundreds of thousands of workers launched boycotts against Kaltenborn's sponsor, Pure Oil (Clark 1968, 316–19). By late spring 1942, Pure Oil dealers were already feeling the impact of the boycott. The local Pure Oil agent in Duluth asked the company to discontinue the program immediately, and in 1943 the West Virginia agent complained that "business is too damn hard to get at this time to pay somebody to drive business away from you." F. H. Marling, the company's advertising director, advised Kaltenborn that, "if this sentiment from our field sales organizations spreads, we will be up against serious trouble."[28]

Despite this economic pressure, Pure Oil president Henry May Dawes continued to support Kaltenborn. The company contended publicly that it had no control over Kaltenborn's broadcasts; privately Dawes urged Kaltenborn to moderate his commentary. To reduce tension, Kaltenborn met with AFL officials in December 1943 and promised to "do his utmost" to emphasize more frequently "labor's constructive achievements." But Dawes never asked Kaltenborn to make significant changes. He confided to Marling that Kaltenborn's broadcasts "appealed powerfully to all of my personal feelings and instincts." He continued that "our stockholders would certainly be willing to take any losses" as a result of the controversy. Appreciative that Pure Oil Company was "sufficiently courageous" in the face of the labor movement's "very vigorous and widespread criticism," Kaltenborn continued throughout the war to speak the "unpleasant truths" about unions (Chester 1947, 410–27).[29]

Although Kaltenborn caused discomfort within the network, NBC regularly renewed his contract. In June 1940, after he "gave labor hell for striking" at a New Jersey shipyard, NBC news director A. A. Schechter complained to network president Niles Trammell that the commentator had violated "one of the fundamentals of the news business" by getting "into strikes of labor." As Schechter saw it, strikes, "along with religion or politics" were "dynamite!" Schechter worried that "we are now treading on dangerous ground" and suggested putting "this fellow in a corner" and talking "sense to him." Kaltenborn was clearly violating both NBC network policies and the NAB code. But news commentary was a lucrative business, and ultimately NBC's primary concern was avoiding offending sponsors. Thus the network never cracked down on Kaltenborn, for "as long as Pure was happy, so was NBC" (Clark 1968, 319).[30]

In the case of union-sponsored programming, however, most broadcasters adhered rigidly to the NAB code that forbade selling airtime to labor. Subjects deemed appropriate when proposed by business were judged controversial when presented by labor. Business, for instance, had no difficulty obtaining airtime to boast about its wartime achievements, but similar labor programs were routinely rejected.[31] While NBC welcomed corporate sponsorship of commentators, when the CIO considered sponsoring a commentator the network made it clear that it would frown on any such program.[32]

Labor for Victory

But the war and the necessity to promote capital-labor unity did strengthen labor's demand for more equitable treatment from broadcasters. In 1941, after Mutual and NBC had given time to NAM and the Chamber of Commerce for business defense programs, both the AFL and the CIO began lobbying the networks for their own regularly scheduled defense shows. Initially all the networks resisted. Finally, in the spring of 1942, as a "public service," NBC granted labor a fifteen-minute weekly sustaining program, *Labor for Victory,* with the AFL and CIO broadcasting on alternate weeks.[33]

Ostensibly, the program's primary purpose was to acknowledge labor's participation in the war effort. By giving labor a regular forum, NBC also sought to mute the flood of unionists' complaints over H. V. Kaltenborn's attacks on organized labor. Having established a labor program, the network advised Kaltenborn's critics that unions now had their own show, albeit one that was supposed to be noncontroversial and to focus only on labor's contribution to the war effort. *Labor for Victory* also served as a justification for NBC to deny unions any additional airtime over the network. In a December 1942 program, American Small Business Organizations, Inc. denounced unions on the air for striking during wartime and urged that strikers be shot. An NBC assistant manager responded to labor's demands for time to answer the attack with a statement that he saw "no reason why labor should have time on the air" because unions already had a weekly program. If anything, he argued, NAM should get "free time every week because of the 'Labor for Victory' program" (Godfried 1997, 209).[34]

Labor for Victory was a milestone because it technically provided organized labor with a national platform. But the show was broadcast at an unpopular time, and only 44 of the 150 NBC affiliates, less than a third of the network, agreed to carry it (Barnouw 1968, 230). Both the AFL and CIO appreciated NBC's providing regular access to network radio, but the CIO recognized that a single weekly fifteen-minute period on one network, at a time when the audience was small, did not "in any way compare in frequency, regularity or good timing with the time afforded to business and employer interests."[35]

NBC envisioned that *Labor for Victory* would be nonpartisan and noncontroversial. Network executive William Burke Miller made clear that the network never intended that the program serve as an "open forum for labor."[36] The AFL, led by William Green, who continued to have a close relationship with NBC, was grateful to the network for the airtime and had little problem with these restrictions. It used its segments to inform the American people what labor was doing to win the war, showcasing the role of individual unions in boosting production and stressing labor's good relationship with management (Barnouw 1945, 80–81).[37] The CIO emphasized some of the same themes as the AFL, but many of its programs focused on more politically sensitive issues, such as taxation, rationing, absenteeism, inflation, economic reconversion, and racial discrimination (Barnouw 1945, 80–81).[38] NBC repeatedly censored the CIO's segment of *Labor for Victory*, contending that it was too controversial. In the spring before the 1944 elections, tensions between NBC and the CIO escalated as the two sides clashed over a drama encouraging listeners to register and vote. The network finally canceled the show, citing a concern about political partisanship. Skeptics questioned the network's justification, suggesting that NBC considered any CIO program, even on a nonpartisan theme, controversial since it might help win Roosevelt's reelection.[39]

In January 1945, NBC finally bowed to pressure from the CIO and the AFL as well as from the ACLU and the FCC to allot labor a more permanent presence on the network. Throughout the war, the CIO had been conducting a vigorous campaign for greater access, and after the cancellation of *Labor for Victory* the federation joined its rival in demanding the same rights as business. For years the ACLU had also been wrestling with the problem of achieving fair and equitable treatment of labor on the air. It pushed both the NAB and the networks to ameliorate the antilabor and probusiness bias in broadcasting. Similarly, under the leadership of FCC chairman James Lawrence Fly, the commission fought for democracy within the media. Fly was highly critical of the broadcasters' refusal to sell time to labor and in 1943 made the sale of NBC's Blue network contingent upon the new owners' promise to sell time to organized labor (Barnouw 1968, 188–90). Under the weight of this pressure, NBC joined CBS and the newly minted American Broadcasting Company (ABC) in allotting the AFL and the CIO free time for weekly public service programs. By the summer of 1945, as a result of the CIO's campaign, the NAB code prohibiting the selling of time to labor had been repudiated. That fall Mutual and ABC began selling time to labor (Fones-Wolf 2000, 290–94, 300). NBC, however, steadfastly refused to sell time to unions.

Conclusion

NBC's relationship with business and organized labor changed, but only slightly, during the Great Depression and World War II. The network nurtured the interests of the business community, aiding in both the sale of capitalist products and the promotion of capitalist ideology. NBC remained reluctant, if not actively hostile, about providing an avenue for the dissemination of opposing viewpoints or challenges to the status quo. This applied equally to perspectives offered by organized labor and by proponents of racial equality. As Barbara Savage (1999) points out, NBC "was routinely more cautious about programming on race relations" than CBS (177). When pressured by outside forces, such as CIO militants in the late 1930s and 1940s, and threatened with greater government oversight, as occurred during the war, NBC acquiesced to provide a modicum of fairness in addressing controversial social and political issues, including the class conflict on the air.

Notes

Abbreviations

ACLU   American Civil Liberties Union

ALUA   Archives of Labor and Union Affairs, Walter P. Reuther Library, Wayne State University

FCC   Federal Communications Commission

ILGWU   International Ladies Garment Workers Union

KC   Kheel Center for Labor-Management Documentation and Archives, Martin P. Catherwood Library, Cornell University

NBC/LC National Broadcasting Company Collection, Motion Picture, Broadcasting, and Recorded Sound Division, Library of Congress

NBC/WHS National Broadcasting Company Archives, Wisconsin Historical Society

1. John F. Royal to Niles Trammell, March 2, 1933, Box 361, Policy-Program Policies, 1926–34 Folder, NBC/LC.

2. Report of the President of the National Broadcasting Company to the National Advisory Council, May 1935, David Rosenblum to R. C. Patterson Jr., April 16, 1935, and "Policy on Public Service Programs," enclosed in R. C. Patterson Jr. to David Sarnoff, April 30, 1935, all in Box 359, Policy-Program Policies, 1934–37 Folder, NBC/LC.

3. William S. Paley to John R. Royal, June 2, 1938, Box 357, Policy-Program Policies, 1938 Folder, NBC/ LC; William S. Paley, *The American System of Broadcasting*, 1938, University of Oregon Library.

4. *Variety*, February 9, 1937.

5. Harry Boyer to John L. Lewis, July 6, 1936, Reel 6, Pt. 1, and Kathryn Lewis to Philip Murray, December 24, 1936, Reel 12, Pt. 1, both in the microfilm collection "CIO Files of John L. Lewis," published in book form as *CIO Files of John L. Lewis*, ed. Martin Paul Schipper, John Llewellyn Lewis, and Randolph Boehm (Frederick, MD: University Publications of America, 1988).

6. John F. Royal to Janet MacRorie, August 21, 1939, Box 77, Folder 70, and John F. Royal to Niles Trammell, December 14, 1939, Box 108, Folder 40, both in NBC/WHS.

7. Hazel L. Rice to John W. Love, December 28, 1937, Vol. 1011, ACLU; Hannah Haskell to I. Lutsky, April 18, 1938, and Montreal Dressmakers Union Local 262 to Hannah Haskell, April 14, 1938, both in Box 80, David Dubinsky Papers, ILGWU Records, KC.

8. M. H. Aylesworth to William Green, January 3, 1936, Box 46, Folder 47, NBC/WHS.

9. M. H. Aylesworth to R. C. Patterson Jr., December 18, 1934, and A. L. Ashby to R. C. Patterson, December 27, 1934, both in Box 99, Folder 77, NBC/WHS.

10. CIO Executive Board Minutes, July 2, 1936, Box 14, Katherine P. Ellickson Papers, ALUA.

11. S. H. Walker and Paul Sklar, "Business Finds Its Voice," *Harper's Magazine*, January 1938, 122.

12. Harvey Pinney, "The Radio Pastor of Dearborn," *Nation*, October 1937, 374–76.

13. *Original Radio Script of Abraham Lincoln from the Cavalcade of America*, February 13, 1940 (New York: Harcourt Brace, 1940), back cover.

14. Frank M. Russell to R. C. Patterson, October 26, 1934, and John F. Royal to Frank Mason, June 7, 1934, both in Box 25, Folder 29, NBC/WHS.

15. John F. Royal to William Hedges, November 1, 1934, and John F. Royal to Richard C. Patterson, February 20, 1935, both in Box 39, Folder 40, NBC/WHS.

16. Lenox R. Lohr to Jouett Shouse, June 18, 1936, Box 43, Folder 34, NBC/WHS.

17. Memorandum of Minutes of the Eleventh Meeting of the Advisory Council of NBC, April 12, 1938, Reel 21, NBC/WHS; L. H. Titterton to William Burke Miller, January 11, 1937, Policy-Program Policies, Box 358, 1929–50 Folder, NBC/LC; John F. Royal to David Sarnoff, January 25, 1937, Box 53, Folder 45, NBC/WHS.

18. Report of the President of the National Broadcasting Company to the Advisory Council of the National Broadcasting Company, Ninth Annual Meeting, May 27, 1935, Vol. 769, ACLU; Frank E. Mason to John F. Royal, May 29, August 17, 1934, Box 25, Folder 29, NBC/WHS.

19. Minutes, Red Network Planning and Advisory Committee, NBC, October 30, 1941, Box 3, William Hedges Papers, WHS.

20. *Variety*, February 26, March 26, 1941; "Highlights of the 1943 Public Information Activities," n.d., Acc. 1411, NAM 3/842; *Defense for America*, script, June 21, 1941, Box 418, Box 419, NBC/WHS.

21. "Interest in Newscasts Soared in 1943," *Broadcasting* 24 (January 1944): 13.

22. Norbert Muhlen, "The Canned Opinion Industry," *Common Sense*, October 1946, 9–11; "Radio: Political Threat or Promise? The Network's Influence on the Public Mind," *Commentary*, March 1947, 201–09.

23. Muhlen, "Canned Opinion Industry," 204; Dixon Wecter, "Hearing Is Believing," *Atlantic Monthly*, August 1945, 54–61.

24. H. V. Kaltenborn, "Address of H. V. Kaltenborn, 3 Sept. 1942," Box 164, H. V. Kaltenborn Papers, WHS; A. A. Schechter to C. L. Menser, March 23, 1942, Box 88, Folder 3, NBC/WHS.

25. AFL, *Proceedings*, 1942, 138; CIO, *Proceedings*, 1943, 57; *Variety*, June 30, 1943.

26. Charles Morrison and Anne Gerlovich to NBC, March 31, 1942. Also see, among many others, Glenn Chinander to NBC, March 17, 1942, and Leonard Lageman to NBC, March 16, 1942, in Box 88, Folder 3, NBC/WHS.

27. Philip Pearl to Kenneth H. Berkeley, March 25, 1942, Box 429, NBC/LC; *Radio Daily*, October 21, 1943; *Labor Review*, October 8, 1943.

28. *Variety*, June 30, 1943; G. F. Kielhack to F. H. Marling, April 28, 1942, J. E. Jones to F. H. Marling, March 26, 1943, and F. H. Marling to H. V. Kaltenborn, April 29, 1943, all in Box 150, H. V. Kaltenborn Papers, WHS.

29. Henry M. Dawes to F. H. Marling, March 24, April 3, 1942, H. V. Kaltenborn to Frank Ferrin, March 22, 1943, and H. V. Kaltenborn to F. H. Marling, April 9, 1943, all in Box 150, Kaltenborn Papers, WHS; *Labor Review*, December 3, 1941.

30. A. A. Schechter to Niles Trammell, June 3, 1940, Box 78, Folder 8, NBC/WHS.

31. James Fly to Charles Webber, May 8, 1943, Box 310, FCC.

32. *Variety*, June 9, 1943; Testimony of Len De Caux, in U.S. Senate, Committee on Interstate Commerce, *Hearings on S. 814, a Bill to Amend the Communications Act of 1934*, 78th Cong., 1st sess., 1943, 577.

33. CIO Executive Board Minutes, March 24, 1942, ALUA; "Labor Goes on the Air," *Time*, April 20, 1942, 69.

34. A. L. Ashby to William Burke Miller, April 6, 1942, Box 88, Folder 2, NBC/WHS.

35. Testimony of Len De Caux before FCC, September 20, 1943, Box 2, De Caux Papers, ALUA.

36. "Report for the Board of Directors' Meeting 10 April 1943," Box 943, NBC/LC; William Burke Miller to Al Kiefner, April 8, 1942, Box 88, Folder 2, NBC/WHS.

37. Transcript of interview with Peter Lyon, November 27, 1944, File B0232, Bureau of Applied Research Papers, Electronic Data Services Offices, Lehman Library, Columbia University; *Federation News*, November 21, 1942; Script, "Labor for Victory," July 4, 1943, Box 443, NBC/WHS.

38. *CIO News*, June 29, December 12, 1942, January 10, 1944; Minutes, CIO Executive Board, February 5–7, 1943, ALUA.

39. *Variety*, May 24, June 4, 1944; Philip Murray to Niles Trammell, n.d., Box 2, De Caux Papers, ALUA.

Transitional Decades
1938–60

Introduction to Part Two

Transitional Decades, 1938–60

MICHELE HILMES

During the war years of the 1940s, radio broadcasting gained more importance in American life than ever before. Yet its very centrality made it a controversial medium in which many conflicts of American society played themselves out. Demagogues like Father Coughlin, the "Radio Priest," inflamed the debate in the late 1930s, leading to a series of decisions that restricted the scope and depth of political discussion on the airwaves. Franklin Delano Roosevelt's administration, far more activist than that of his predecessor Herbert Hoover, instituted a New Deal for radio, investigating its practices and mandating a series of reforms, including the ban on dual network ownership that forced NBC to sell off its Blue network in 1943. The network would return as the American Broadcasting Company (ABC) and would provide serious competition to its parent in later decades. In chapter 5, "Breaking Chains: NBC and the FCC Network Inquiry, 1938–43," Christopher H. Sterling examines the FCC hearings and subsequent reforms.

At the same time, as the war heightened the need to define "who we are and why we fight," radio offered increased opportunities for less powerful social groups to demand the ability to speak for themselves, to address the inequities and anti-democratic aspects of American life. For the first time, programs that explicitly addressed the history of racism and prejudice in the United States reached a broad public on the airwaves. Programs and news about the Holocaust going on in Europe, though slow to emerge, showed how radio could serve as America's conscience. David Weinstein considers the factors that both inspired and inhibited such programming on NBC in chapter 6, "Why Sarnoff Slept: NBC and the Holocaust." Though these first efforts were cautious and hampered by oppositional views, they contributed to the momentum that would lead to civil rights reforms and greater ethnic and religious tolerance after the war. Other programs recruited American women into a newly defined sphere of paid work and public service.

Advertisers, stations, networks, and government agencies worked hand in hand, though not without friction, to build public morale and spread important wartime information and encouragement. Programs produced for American troops abroad boosted morale overseas. News coverage developed enormously but still struggled with the conflicts between commercial and informative agendas, between self-interest and objectivity. And meanwhile, television hovered in the wings. Though it would not be allowed on the public stage until the postwar years, important decisions affecting American television for the next fifty years were made during this period in a close collusion between government and industry, as the American public looked the other way.

Broadcasting as an industry emerged from the war years in a much strengthened position, despite the controversies surrounding it. Television would fulfill the promises that radio had made, and so often broken, decades before. It would be the shining light in the center of the home, delivering the same utopian promises that radio had offered a few decades previously. By 1961, 89 percent of U.S. households owned at least one television set, and the five hours a day previously devoted to radio had shifted to the new medium—as radio listenership fell to its lowest ever, less than two hours per day. Yet the war years had set the terms of an argument that would focus attention on television's darker side, notably its established position in the pockets of commercial networks and sponsors. Television's amateurs, far from the inventive individuals in garages and attics who had built up early radio as a practice and a set of ideals, were engineers and scientists in the laboratories of RCA, CBS, and General Electric. Cold War tensions only heightened the close relationship between government and industry. And despite considerable social unrest brewing among America's minorities, labor unions, and redomesticated former wartime workers, television promised a normalizing nation the good life and sought to represent it in no uncertain terms.

Regulatory decisions consolidated the big networks' hold over the developing medium and put them in a strong position once the FCC freeze on TV station licenses ended in 1952. Television programs drew directly on radio. NBC and its two competitors, CBS and ABC, encouraged the transition to TV by siphoning off radio profits to support the new medium, and they encouraged sponsors, advertising agencies, and stars to jump onto the TV bandwagon. This left radio to fend for itself, and an era of black radio entrepreneurs blossomed. The all-music DJ format emerged from black radio practices, and a new kind of music filled the airwaves. Rock 'n' roll debuted as a musical form arising out of the collision of black and white audiences and crossover DJs in the newly available sphere of radio. Yet television's capacity to make racial representation newly visible, along with pressure for greater social equality after the war, made NBC and the other networks more mindful of the role they played in holding America's unequal racial hierarchies in place. Murray Forman traces the efforts NBC made to address issues of race and inclusion in chapter 7, "Employment and Blue Pencils: NBC, Race, and Representation, 1926–55."

A brief period of live drama influenced by the New York theatrical scene brought bold fare to the small screen and launched dozens of careers. Many consider this TV's golden age. The sponsor continued to hold the upper hand in television production, and major advertising agencies like J. Walter Thompson provided some of the earliest experimentation in the new medium, even as the networks struggled to regain the control over production programming that they had lost in the early 1930s. Michael Mashon brings this innovative period to light in chapter 8, "NBC, J. Walter Thompson, and the Struggle for Control of Television Programming, 1946–58."

Variety shows, westerns, and situation comedies also thrived and prospered. The situation comedy, in particular, would bring a feminine voice to prime time and soon dominated television schedules. News experimented and adapted to the visual demands of television, as did sports. The daytime remained a relatively undeveloped part of the schedule until the late 1950s. And although NBC made its shift to television with a technological and economic head start over all the others, its adherence to older practices of sponsor dominance caused an abrupt ratings slide in the mid-1950s, a drop from which it would not recover for over a decade. Hollywood forces moved eagerly into production for the new medium, and the "package show," shot on film by independent star-centered production companies but distributed by major studios, gradually became the norm. NBC lost ground by failing to respond to these new factors quickly enough, as Douglas Gomery argues in chapter 9, "Talent Raids and Package Deals: NBC Loses Its Leadership in the 1950s." Yet NBC's color standard prevailed, and soon color television would become the norm in the United States. By 1960, the network would boast 214 affiliates, 42 percent of the nation's total, and network advertising revenues (for all three networks) exceeded $800 million.

All was not entirely rosy. Fears about television's effects on children emerged and would spread like wildfire in the next two decades. Broadcasters already showed disturbing signs of putting commercial ends above public interest responsibilities, despite the high-flown rhetoric surrounding television's debut. Such rhetoric could be deployed very effectively to squash competition—as with the rival technologies of theater television and subscription TV. The classic network system, with its tight, centralized control and limited program offerings, was about to take center stage. This crucial postwar period introduced most of the major factors that would position television as America's primary medium in the next decade. But it had also sowed the seeds of weakness and dispute that would trouble the next turbulent era.

5

Breaking Chains

NBC and the FCC Network Inquiry, 1938–43

CHRISTOPHER H. STERLING

The potential impact of federal regulation of broadcasting has been hotly debated virtually from the beginning of the radio business. As regularly scheduled commercial networking began in 1926–27, the degree to which network operations might come under government oversight was added to the policy pot. A decade later, the thriving National Broadcasting Company, which operated parallel (but by no means equal) Red and Blue networks, became the chief target of a government inquiry that would dramatically change the radio industry. The 1941 chain broadcasting rules of the Federal Communications Commission (FCC) (and their affirmation in a landmark decision by the Supreme Court in 1943) are still widely cited decades later.

As a result of those legal decisions, NBC was forced to divest its weaker Blue network, a move that marked a watershed in the network's affairs. As long as it operated both Red and Blue networks (into the early 1940s), NBC dominated radio. After the chain broadcasting proceedings and the war, NBC became merely another, albeit important, part of a rapidly expanding industry. The changing position of the network and its affiliates offers a useful example of a company operating under and changing because of government pressure.

A Growing Concern

A central precedent for the government's future action appeared even as NBC was forming. The Radio Act of 1927 included a provision allowing the new Federal Radio Commission (FRC) to "make special regulations applicable to radio stations engaged in chain broadcasting" (sec. 4[b]). *Chain* was the regulatory term for what later became known as networking, the linking of two or more stations in order to simultaneously share identical programming, a process that had been experimented with in the years before the law passed but that was just beginning to occur on a regular basis in 1926–27. The provision was carried over without change in the Communications Act of 1934 as section 303(i).

That precedent in place, two things eventually triggered growing government concern about radio networks in the 1930s. The first was the increasing control of the Columbia Broadcasting System (CBS) and NBC networks over many aspects of their affiliate stations' operations. In 1933, NBC inaugurated an "option time" policy that gave it the right to demand use of an affiliate's most valuable broadcast hours with just twenty-eight days' notice. The policy covered all time for Pacific Coast stations because of the time zone difference (Warner 1948, 474). A year later, NBC entered the program transcription (recording) business, soon developing its "Thesaurus" music service for station use. This formed part of a $5 million business by 1938 (easily $50 million in 2005 dollars) that tripled in value just three years later (519). The networks also developed artists' bureaus to represent their own on-air talent, a rather obvious conflict of interest. In 1936 NBC changed its affiliation contracts to bind stations for five years (rather than the former one year), even though the network itself continued to be bound only for a year. The new contracts also tightened territorial exclusivity of programming so that affiliates could not carry offerings from other networks (470–71). CBS policy closely paralleled NBC in each of these moves except that it operated only one, albeit highly successful, network.

The second factor that would eventually prompt the government to act was the arrival of the Mutual Broadcasting System in 1934, and its subsequent difficulty breaking into the network business. Mutual found it hard to affiliate with stations (especially those with high power or located in large markets), as nearly all were already tied to either CBS or NBC. Mutual had an even harder time attracting advertisers because of the discount structure NBC offered to buyers of time on both of its Red and Blue network affiliates. Mutual was soon making it clear to the FCC, among other government agencies, that the evolving structure of the industry made it almost impossible for a new player (and competitor) to establish itself in commercial radio. Internal NBC accounting confirmed Mutual's concern: of total broadcast advertising volume from 1935 to 1937, NBC's two networks took 29 percent, CBS 20 percent, and Mutual less than 2 percent—the remainder was local or regional advertising.[1]

NBC's surviving records make clear that starting in the mid-1930s the network was considering selling Blue, both to reduce the various monopoly concerns already cropping up in Washington and to increase its profit margin.[2] But NBC officials were sharply divided: some suggested other options, such as combining Red and Blue into a single supernetwork or developing two separate but still RCA-owned subsidiaries.[3] Memos flew back and forth and meetings were held to assess "what to do about the Blue." This flow of internal memos made clear that the basic Blue Network was "admittedly inferior to the basic Red" because it did not offer as strong a national service in terms of either programming or affiliate stations and that "efforts to build up the Blue Network during the past two years have been unsuccessful."[4] Blue's operations were said to total 45 percent of NBC expenditure, while yielding only a quarter of its revenue. More than one recommendation went to NBC president Lenox Lohr and board chair David Sarnoff citing the many potential advantages of selling Blue and making as much as $10 million ($6 million would have come from the three Blue owned-and-operated stations in New York, Chicago, and San Francisco), somewhat more than $100 million in 2005 value.[5]

By the time the FCC began its network inquiry in 1938, network officials had finally all agreed *not* to sell Blue (partially due to fears of what might happen to the network in the hands of a competitor) but instead to work harder to overcome the "inferiority complex" Blue employees faced in selling advertising time.[6] By early 1940 a plan was forming to make Blue more fully independent *within* RCA, with separate management and personnel. The network's very name was seen as part of its "second-class" image problem; among new names considered were the Victor Broadcasting System, the American Broadcasting Company (or System), and even the Public Broadcasting Service.[7] The decision to build up Blue relied in part on a misreading of the regulatory situation. As NBC's vice president in Washington told the network president, "I cannot conclude . . . that we will be forced to or asked to dispose of the Blue Network."[8]

The FCC Inquiry

The FCC network inquiry got its immediate impetus from Congress. Early in 1937, three resolutions in the House and one in the Senate called on the FCC to investigate monopoly in radio, especially the growing dominance of the networks, though they were then just a decade old. To some extent, the move paralleled the probe that the FCC had just initiated into newspaper ownership of radio stations, an investigation prompted by White House concern about conservative newspaper editorial positions. The proposed network inquiry, in contrast, would focus on potential economic constraints rather than political point of view.

Reading the clear congressional signals, on March 18, 1938, the FCC adopted General Order 37 (under provisions of sec. 303[i]) to undertake an investigation "to determine what special regulations applicable to radio stations engaged in chain or other broadcasting are required in the public interest, convenience or necessity."[9] Three weeks later, a special committee of four commissioners (Sykes, Brown, Walker, and chairman McNinch) was appointed to conduct the network study as commission Docket 5060.

Chain broadcasting hearings got underway at the FCC on November 14, 1938. First to be heard from was RCA president (and NBC board chairman) David Sarnoff. After stating that he welcomed the investigation, and after providing background on the development of NBC (Sarnoff 1939, 5), Sarnoff responded to questions from the FCC's general counsel and commissioners, most of which focused on program control and censorship, not on network structure. NBC president Lenox Lohr and other network officials were also heard and questioned. By the final day of the hearings on May 19, 1939, the sessions had met some seventy-three days spread over six months, ninety-six witnesses had been heard, 707 exhibits had been entered, and 8,713 pages of transcripts had been produced. The committee then began to draw up a report with conclusions and recommendations.

As the FCC investigation began, NBC's two networks held contracts with 161 affiliates (many could be switched to either Red or Blue), CBS had contracts with 113, and the struggling Mutual network had 107 smaller, often rural and less powerful outlets. Between them, NBC and CBS controlled 92 percent of total nighttime station transmitting power. They also earned half of total industry revenues, retaining 73 percent and paying out the remainder to their affiliates. NBC gave a 25 percent volume discount based on purchases of advertising time on both of its networks and offered easily twice as many program (and thus advertising) hours as CBS or Mutual did. NBC affiliation contracts did not specify whether a station was part of the Red or Blue networks, giving the New York–based company even more control (Warner 1948, 516).

As the investigation continued, the October 1939 World Series would provide further proof to the FCC of the excessive power CBS and NBC had over their affiliates. Despite being under government scrutiny, CBS and NBC both refused to allow their affiliates to carry World Series baseball games because Mutual had been designated the only network carrier, and neither of the older networks wanted to assist their newer competitor. Thus "thousands of potential listeners failed to hear the World Series of 1939."[10]

Unexpectedly, the FCC's authority to act on the business arrangements of its licensees was thrown into question in an unrelated case. In its March 25, 1940, decision *Sanders Brothers Radio Station* (309 U.S. 470), the Supreme Court noted that the Communications Act "does not essay to regulate the business of the licensee. The Commission is given no supervisory control of the programs, of business management, or of policy" (Warner 1948, 524). The networks quickly used this decision to argue that the FCC held no jurisdiction where they were concerned and that the act left matters of industry structure and operation to the courts or the Federal Trade Commission. As will be seen, the Supreme Court would hold otherwise.

On June 12, 1940, the FCC network study committee (by then made up of commissioners Brown, Walker, and Thompson) issued a draft report, recommendations, and a five-volume digest of the evidence it had heard. On its first page the committee concluded that "these materials form an adequate basis upon which the Commission may proceed to a consideration of the need for a revision of its licensing policy in the radiobroadcast [sic] field in order to correct the serious inequities and arbitrary practices which have developed in connection with chain broadcasting."[11]

The committee focused specifically on the "grossly inequitable relation between the networks and their outlet stations to the advantage of the networks" based upon "contractual arrangements forced upon stations seeking affiliation with a network," which made the stations the "servant of the network rather than an instrument for serving the public interest." The report felt it might well be necessary for "networks to be licensed by the commission." More specifically, the committee concluded that, "by means of its two separate and distinct networks, N[BC] is able to prevent competition from other networks and stations in many areas. It is able, too, by its right to determine whether a station is to be on the 'Red' network or the 'Blue,' to determine the earnings of the station and the availability of program service to thousands of listeners [even in] areas served by only one of its two networks."[12] At the same time, the committee recognized the many positive benefits of networking, noting that it sought to balance the playing field between stations and networks to allow the former (the commission's licensees) to better serve the public interest.

Not surprisingly, these tentative conclusions raised a storm of protest in the broadcast business—in many cases from the very affiliates the FCC professed to be trying to help. CBS and NBC understandably led the charge. Claims that the FCC was trying to wreck the industry, worries about the impact on First Amendment freedoms, and arguments that the commission lacked authority to undertake such changes filled the press and various filings for reconsideration with the regulatory authority. At the same time, and perhaps more closely gauging the regulatory climate, both CBS and NBC (by midyear headed by Niles Trammell) sold their artists' bureaus in 1940, removing one relatively minor bone of contention with the FCC (Warner 1948, 518).

Wrapping up their research efforts, the FCC held two days of oral arguments about its research and preliminary report in early December 1940. In the meantime, the networks had all acquired more affiliates—NBC's two chains now had 214 (many of them shared), CBS 121, and Mutual about 160 (Warner 1948, 516). As before, however, the Mutual outlets were smaller and used less power than was the case for the other networks. Presaging the future, longtime NBC treasurer Mark Woods noted that, "by the end of 1940, National Broadcasting Company was in certain departments [already] a dual organization—one for the red and the other for the blue Network. There were two sales departments, two program departments, two promotion departments. During 1941 this separation process was greatly accelerated."[13]

More quietly, Woods admitted in a confidential memo that "*the fact is* that the Blue Network is operating at a loss," which would be greater in 1941 than in 1940. Further, NBC was seeing things more clearly now: the expected final FCC report would almost certainly "contain divorcement demands that the Blue Network be separated from RCA and NBC."[14] Just six weeks later, Woods was proved correct.

Decision

The commission's final *Report on Chain Broadcasting*, issued May 2, 1941, was based on a 5–2 vote, with commissioners Case and Craven dissenting and arguing that their colleagues were overreaching the agency's powers. The 139-page report included eight regulations that were to become effective in ninety days. All were indirect in that they were to be enforced at the licensee level (where the FCC held the power of authorization) rather than at the level of the networks themselves (where the law was less clear). Most sought to strengthen the affiliates' ability to negotiate about programs, option time, or advertising rates with networks. The seventh rule (sec. 3.107) called for the prime structural change: "No license shall be granted a standard broadcast station affiliated with a network organization which maintains more than one network: *Provided,* That this regulation shall not be applicable if such networks are not operated simultaneously, or if there is no substantial overlap in the territory served by the group of stations comprising each such network."[15]

The rule clearly implied that NBC, as the only national broadcaster operating two networks—now a violation under FCC rules—would have to divest itself of one of its networks in order to comply. Given the financial success of the powerful Red network, there was little doubt that Blue would get the boot. The many regional radio networks (such as Yankee in New England and Don Lee in California) were unaffected by the decision.

Though surely no surprise given widespread reporting on the inquiry starting in 1938, the FCC's final network rules still hit the industry hard. Trade and network publications rapidly speculated on what the new commission rules would require. Meeting in St. Louis at the National Association of Broadcasters (NAB) convention, "all broadcasters, with the exception of the Mutual affiliates, expressed general disapproval of these [new FCC] regulations."[16] A CBS booklet titled *What the New Radio Rules Mean* claimed that "these orders strike at the heart of American radio broadcasting. . . . [They are] the first paralyzing blow at freedom of the air . . . [and] will establish radio monopolies in many sections of the country which are now served by competing stations. . . . [They] may, in the end, encourage the government to take over broadcasting altogether. Meanwhile it opens the door to the complete domination of radio by whatever government happens to be in power" (CBS 1941, 2–4).

These were strong, indeed overwrought words in an era when people were well aware of Nazi radio propaganda. And they were ironic given that the rules were an attempt to *reduce* monopoly control of radio. Nor was there anything in the FCC decision to suggest even remote thoughts of a government takeover. But such sweeping public comments were common—and sometimes persuasive—in the attacks on the FCC's network rules.

Hearings and Appeals

The FCC action quickly provoked strong counterpunches. Broadcasters turned first to Congress, hoping for legislation that might overturn the FCC decision. Just three days after the report appeared, Senator Wallace White (R-ME)—who had been instrumental in the passage of the 1927 and 1934 laws—introduced a bill calling for an investigation of the commission and its suggested rules. White received strong support from CBS and NBC, as well as the NAB, then meeting in Washington.

Thus the first arena for public debate became the Senate's Commerce Committee hearings on the White bill during several days in June 1941. The FCC and the Mutual network countered that no congressional study was needed, as the FCC evidence was plain (T. Robinson 1943/1989, 70–71).

NBC president Trammell was chief among industry figures encouraging congressional action to restrain the FCC initiative. By this point his networks served 233 affiliates (130 Red and 103 Blue) (Warner 1948, 512). The ongoing Senate hearings were risky because they effectively delayed network legal appeals (given that appeals might conflict with possibly helpful congressional action).[17] In his testimony, Trammell expressed fear that "the confusion and chaos that must follow the sudden removal of the business and contractual props upon which chain broadcasting now rests will signal the assumption of more and more control by the Commission. Neither the industry nor the F.C.C. has any illusions about that."[18] Naturally, he said not a word about NBC's earlier internal studies proposing some kind of Red-Blue split.

Under sometimes fierce questioning from committee chairman Burton K. Wheeler (R-MT), Trammell tried to defend his network's policy of binding affiliates for five years while the network was tied to only one and at the same time underscored NBC's commitment to extensive public service programming (so long as it was supported at least indirectly by revenue from popular commercial programs). Trammell kept emphasizing how difficult untangling Red and Blue would be (though network internal documents dating back to 1935 make clear that most details had already been thoroughly gone over). Further, he suggested that any attempt at a sale would probably break up the network, given that CBS and Mutual were likely to poach affiliates. While conceding that Red was stronger in both affiliates and popular programs, he would not admit what he knew privately—that Red made money while Blue was by then costing more than it earned given that many programs were offered on a sustaining basis.[19]

Trammell did warn that any divestiture of Blue would probably cause a drop in public service programming. In an internal report to his superiors, a Pacific Coast NBC official underlined the problems Blue faced, no matter who owned it: "Our Blue Network is still overloaded with educational, agricultural and public service features. . . . They are not audience building shows nor do they compel the attention and interest of prospective sponsors or agencies."[20] Meanwhile, both CBS and NBC argued with the commission over rule details, and during the summer of 1941 their implementation date was postponed several times. On September 12, the commission issued a supplemental report (by the same 5–2 vote) that amended three of the rules to a minor degree but made no major changes.

Having exhausted their procedural options, and foreseeing no bill from Congress, CBS and NBC brought suit against the commission to stay the rules while substantive appeals continued. An injunction was finally granted (Warner 1948, 525). But late in 1941, building on the FCC's findings, the Justice Department filed antitrust suits against the two networks in the U.S. District Court in Chicago. Early in January 1942, Mutual joined the fray with its own private antitrust suit against RCA and NBC, seeking $10 million (about ten times that in 2005 values) in damages. Thus began the court proceedings that would eventually lead to the landmark Supreme Court case.

In the meantime, RCA chief David Sarnoff announced in early January 1942 that Blue had become a separate subsidiary of RCA.[21] As Mark Woods later put it, "This move was made in response to changing conditions and the general attitude of the government."[22] FCC chairman James Lawrence Fly tried to calm the fears of Blue's affiliate stations meeting in Chicago by assuring them that "the destiny of the Blue Network is to become a full-fledged, independent and competitive network in its own right."[23] On June 1, 1942, the Supreme Court accepted the network case for argument. At the end of the month, FCC chairman Fly said that if the FCC lost this final appeal the commission would seek more specific legislative authority to regulate the networks.

Nearly a year later, the final knell for NBC's dual network operations sounded when, on May 10, 1943 (two years and a week after the FCC rules had been issued), the Supreme Court announced its decision in *NBC v. United States*, finding for the FCC and against the networks. In a twenty-seven-page opinion authored by Justice Felix Frankfurter and joined in by five other Justices, the Court concluded that "the Communications Act of 1934 authorized the Commission to promulgate regulations designed to correct the abuses disclosed by its investigation of chain broadcasting. . . . [and] we find that the action of the Commission was based upon findings supported by evidence and was made pursuant to authority granted by Congress (319 US 190 at 216)." Throughout the opinion (still widely cited decades later), the majority made clear their feeling that the FCC's powers were expansive and flexible rather than narrowly defined. Justices Murphy and Roberts strongly dissented (two other Justices did not participate in the case), the latter having authored the *Sanders* decision of 1940, which implied a narrower view of FCC authority. They argued again here that Congress granted more limited authority to the FCC than the commission's network rules implied. Trade press reports emphasized many of their points as central to network appeals to Congress to pass new legislation overriding the Court.

NBC president Trammell sent a telegram to all affiliates announcing the decision.[24] The network trade weekly *Broadcasting* reported that the industry, "stunned by the severity of the Supreme Court opinion," was "girded for a last-ditch effort" before Congress.[25] Senate hearings began on a new White-Wheeler bill to roll back the new rules, reorganize the FCC, and make its duties more specific—and limited.[26] Nothing, however, came of this final attempt to override the commission's network rules.

The failure to pass legislation was caused by several things, chiefly timing—the country was now in the midst of World War II and more fundamental concerns dominated Congress—but also continuing New Deal suspicions of big business on

FIG. **6** FCC chair James Lawrence Fly addressing the NBC Blue affiliates meeting in Chicago on January 15, 1942. (Library of American Broadcasting)

the part of the Democrats (who controlled both houses). Network chiefs were unable to garner much sympathy when congressmen heard complaints about network monopoly practices from stations in their local districts.

Blue Departs

Facing reality, NBC prepared to sell Blue. As the certainty of selling became more evident, some forty firms expressed interest in buying Blue—depending, of course on the price. Many steps to separate Blue had already been taken. As far back as January 1942, telegrams from New York had instructed Chicago and Hollywood production centers to identify the network as "The Blue Network" rather than "NBC-Blue," as had long been the practice.[27] The Blue Network Inc. was set up as a separate RCA subsidiary under the laws of Delaware.[28] All through that year, internal memos spelled out the complex details of dividing people, facilities, real estate, and programs between Red and Blue services.[29] RCA provided $1 million in cash (about $10 million in 2005 values) to help tide Blue over during the transition, this largely in lieu of formerly shared facilities and services.[30] But at the same time, and more behind the scenes, Blue was stripped of some assets NBC wished to retain: several important Blue affiliates switched to NBC-Red (KDKA among them), though eighteen new stations (some former Mutual affiliates) joined Blue and forty more outlets sought to. Even so, Blue still lacked any stations in at least seven states. Mark Woods was named to head the increasingly independent network and its 550 employees (Trammell would serve as board chair until Blue was sold). Rental agreements were drawn up for Blue's continued use of RCA Building spaces until new headquarters could be found.

After considerable negotiating, in late July 1943, NBC sold the Blue network to Edward J. Noble, owner of station WMCA in New York. The agreed price was $8 million (equivalent to about $88 million in 2005 values). As the sale included station WJZ in New York (Blue's flagship), Noble agreed to sell WMCA to an outside buyer. (Noble had made his initial money selling Life Savers candy and later had served in the federal government as the first head of the Civil Aeronautics Authority and then as undersecretary of commerce in the Roosevelt administration, stepping down in 1940.)[31] The FCC approved the sale on October 12, 1943 (it was required to make a decision because of the three owned-and-operated station licenses involved), and two days later the sale took place.

In late December, Time Inc. purchased 12.5 percent of Blue's common stock from Noble, and Chester J. LaRoche, former chairman of the Young & Rubicam advertising agency, bought an equal amount. Network president Mark Woods bought 3 percent.[32] It was now widely recognized in the radio business that since Blue could no longer rely on the revenues of the more successful Red network it would have to become far more commercial. Blue announced plans to sell $44 million in advertising time in its first year as an independent operation. As Niles Trammell had warned the Senate back in 1941, Blue would in the future carry fewer of the public service programs that held little interest for most listeners or advertisers.

Aftermath

The economic or structural meltdown of broadcasting, so often predicted by many radio industry leaders in the face of the FCC rules, failed to materialize. Instead, driven by an expanding postwar economy, a rapid increase in the number of AM broadcasting stations—from about 900 after the war to some 2,500 by the early 1950s—helped to weaken the networks' strong hold on the business. There was plenty of revenue for all these radio stations—at least until television's competition began to bite. Radio continued with four national networks (now owned by different firms) and a dwindling number of regional services. There were a few attempts to start up additional national radio chains—one of them centered on FM stations (which were not an important factor in radio until the late 1960s and reached dominance only by 1980). But these failed as audience and advertisers began the shift to television. By the mid-1950s, the radio networks had dwindled to mere shadows of their former glory.

Blue increasingly separated itself from its former colleagues at Red and RCA. For a time, Blue rented its old space in the RCA Building, but it soon moved to new facilities. Though it had been proposed years earlier that Blue be renamed the American Broadcasting Company (ABC), only at the beginning of January 1945 did the renaming finally occur.[33] In the immediate postwar years, ABC broke the longtime network ban on recorded programs and attracted the hugely popular Bing Crosby, among others, to its network. ABC also expanded quickly to purchase owned-and-operated television stations in five major markets. Lacking sufficient capital to create and operate an effective television network, however, Noble sold out to United Paramount Theaters, headed by Leonard H. Goldenson, for $25 million in early 1951, a deal finally approved by the FCC two years later.

With the legal battle and sale behind it, NBC also quickly moved on. Within a year, internal publications for employees made no reference to the former dual-network operation (NBC 1944a, 1944b). The company's public *Annual Review 1944–45* also made no mention of Blue or all the legal activity of the previous several years, detailing only the work of the Red network, now simply called NBC (NBC 1945). Famous New York anchor station WEAF became WNBC in 1946 (and four decades later would be sold). CBS would pull ahead of NBC with its famous late 1940s "talent raids" (see Gomery, chapter 9), and the resulting radio ratings success would translate to television's first decades as well.

The FCC's 1941 network rules that had formed the basis for the long legal battle were extended to television in 1946, two years before any video network had begun operation. In the mid-1950s, the FCC again considered network control of programming and advertising, focusing this time on television, but no major structural changes in network operations resulted. An FCC office of network study continued to make policy recommendations into the 1960s. Only years later (in 1977), at the start of the FCC's effort to deregulate broadcasting, were the network rules eliminated for radio. Early in the new century, they were finally removed for television as well,[34] for by then broadcast networks were rapidly losing audience share to newer services. In one sense, however, the chain broadcasting conflict of more than sixty years ago continues to have an effect. The Supreme Court's 1943 *NBC* decision is still widely cited in both FCC and court decisions as a landmark statement supporting the principles of both the 1934 Communications Act and FCC discretion in regulatory initiatives.

Notes

Abbreviations

NBC/LC   Motion Picture, Broadcasting, and Recorded Sound Division, Library of Congress

NBC/WHS National Broadcasting Company Archives, Wisconsin Historical Society

1. G. W. Payne to Mark Woods, March 4, 1937, NBC/LC File 510.
2. Frank Russell to Lenox Lohr, September 26, 1936, NBC/LC File 300.
3. Harry Wilder to Richard Patterson Jr., June 28, 1934, NBC/LC File 998; R. Witmer to Lenox Lohr, October 12, 1937, NBC/LC File 300.
4. David Rosenblum to David Sarnoff, October 2, 1936, NBC/LC File 300.
5. Ibid.
6. See NBC/LC File 301.
7. Niles Trammell to Lenox Lohr, April 1, 1940, NBC/LC File 302. In the end, no name change was forthcoming while Blue remained part of RCA.
8. Frank Russell to Lenox Lohr, January 9, 1940, NBC/LC File 302.
9. FCC, *Report on Chain Broadcasting* (1941; reprint, New York: Arno Press, 1974), 95.
10. Ibid., 52.
11. FCC, "Report of the Committee Appointed by the Commission to Supervise the Investigation of Chain Broadcasting," mimeo, June 12, 1940, i, author's files.
12. Ibid., ii, v, 78.
13. Statement of Mark Woods on Behalf of Blue Network Co., Inc., in U.S. House, Committee on Interstate and Foreign Commerce, *Proposed Changes in the Communications Act of 1934: Hearings on H.R. 5497*, 77th Cong., 2nd sess., April–July 1942, pt. 3, p. 1052.
14. Mark Woods to Niles Trammell, March 22, 1941, NBC/LC File 302.
15. FCC, *Report on Chain Broadcasting*, 92.
16. Niles Trammell to the NBC Board, June 6, 1941, NBC/LC File 945.
17. Trammell to the NBC Board, June 6, 1941, NBC/LC, File 945.
18. Statement by Niles Trammell, President, National Broadcasting Company, in U.S. Senate, Committee on Interstate Commerce, *To Authorize a Study of the Radio Rules and Regulations of Federal Communications Commission: Hearings on S. 113*, 77th Cong., 1st sess., June 2–20, 1941, 461.
19. Ibid., 484–95.
20. "Let's *DO* Something about the *Blue*," June 19, 1941, NBC/LC File 998.
21. Press release of January 9, 1942, NBC/LC File 128.

22. Statement of Mark Woods, 1052.

23. James Lawrence Fly, speech of January 15, 1942, NBC/LC File 128.

24. NBC/WHS Box 114, folder 20.

25. "Nets Prepare to Operate under New Rules," *Broadcasting* 17 (May 1943): 7.

26. U.S. Senate, Committee on Interstate Commerce, *To Amend the Communications Act of 1934: Hearings on S. 814.* 78th Cong., 1st sess., November–December 1943.

27. NBC/LC File 303.

28. Press release of January 9, 1942, NBC/LC File 128.

29. NBC/LC File 303.

30. Statement of Mark Woods, 1052.

31. Press release of July 30, 1943, NBC/LC File 128.

32. Box 114c, Folder 34, NBC/WHS.

33. Press release of January 1, 1945, NBC/LC File 128.

34. FCC, "FCC Eliminates the Major Network/Emerging Network Merger Prohibition from Dual Network Rule," press release, April 19, 2001.

6

Why Sarnoff Slept

NBC and the Holocaust

DAVID WEINSTEIN

World War II had a profound impact on all American broadcast genres, including drama. NBC produced hundreds of dramatic programs about war, freedom, fascism, and democracy between 1938 and 1945. Before Pearl Harbor, the networks discouraged radio dramatists from broadcasting overt political messages, but writers used thinly veiled metaphors calling attention to the fascist threat at home and abroad. After the United States entered the war, dramatic productions became a primary vehicle for addressing the question of why America was fighting. Many radio dramas emphasized the strength of the American army, the skill of its soldiers, and the value of military service. Other programs focused on the nature of the enemy, highlighting Japanese and German duplicity, cruelty, and antipathy to core American values of democracy and freedom. In extolling the American way of life, dramas portrayed the United States as a melting pot of economic opportunity and tolerance. Optimistic radio plays attempted to counter racism and prejudice and to build unity by recognizing the contributions of racial, ethnic, and religious minorities to the broader American culture (Hilmes 1997; Blue 2002; Savage 1999). Programs that took a more nuanced or pessimistic look at the politics of racism or anti-Semitism were far less common.

In fact, of the thousands of dramas produced during the war, few depicted anti-Semitism at home or the plight of Europe's Jews abroad with the depth and complexity afforded other wartime subjects. Two programs—*The Second Battle of Warsaw* (NBC-Blue, 1943), by Irving Ravetch, and *The Battle of the Warsaw Ghetto* (NBC-Red, 1943), by Morton Wishengrad—focused on Jewish armed resistance to the German army in the Warsaw Ghetto.[1] Starting in 1944, NBC also aired a series, *The Eternal Light*, that explored several topics, including anti-Semitism, of particular interest to Jews. Although starting in the late 1930s institutional constraints worked against the production of programming on politically divisive issues such as anti-Semitism, prominent programs such as the Warsaw Ghetto dramas and wartime episodes of *The Eternal Light* managed to break through these constraints. In doing so they illustrated the political and aesthetic possibilities of dramatizing these topics and suggested that radio had the potential to present strong dramatic stories and make powerful statements in response to the great political and moral challenges facing the nation. The paucity of additional, similar dramas on either NBC or the other networks invites a look at the politics and practices of network radio drama during the war years. One of the central questions of this chapter, and indeed for historians generally, is, Why was network radio drama almost completely silent regarding the plight of Europe's Jews?

Dramatic Omissions

Radio network producers certainly could not have been ignorant of conditions in Europe. The country's major newspapers and news magazines provided numerous articles and reports on Jewish refugees, anti-Jewish laws, deportations to concentration camps, massacres, and, by the end of 1942, the systematic murder of Jews in Nazi-occupied territories.[2] Influential political journals such as the *New Republic* and the *Nation* ran several essays calling attention to Nazi persecution of Jews starting in 1933 (Lipstadt 1986; Abzug 1999). Popular magazines also drew attention to the problem. *Reader's Digest,* for example, published a passionate article by Ben Hecht in February 1943, warning that of the six million Jews in Europe "almost a third have already been massacred . . . and the most conservative of the shopkeepers estimate that before the war ends at least another third will have been done to death."[3] The *New York Times* and several other newspapers carried detailed information on the horrors of Auschwitz and Birkenau in the summer of 1944.[4]

These articles were seldom on the front pages of America's leading newspapers. At a time of war, when there was a great amount of international news, battle reports tended to dominate the daily headlines, and editors did not make the Jewish crisis in Europe a priority. In addition, many reporters and editors were overly cautious and required very high standards of proof for reports on Nazi violence against civilians. In some cases, journalists could not confirm the accounts of witnesses, including individuals who escaped the villages and ghettos of Nazi-controlled Europe. Reporters did not want to compromise their credibility by spreading stories of atrocities that could be seen as anti-Nazi propaganda. Nevertheless, as historian Deborah Lipstadt (1986) demonstrated in her study of the American press's reporting of the Holocaust, "There was practically no aspect of the Nazi horrors which was not publicly known in some detail long before the camps were opened in 1945" (235).

Like the newspapers, the radio networks did not offer detailed, comprehensive news coverage of the genocide. But starting in the late 1930s, as part of their European reporting, both CBS and NBC aired numerous stories on anti-Semitic laws, deportations, and massacres (Fine 1988). In November 1938, radio broadcasts covered the German attack on Jewish homes, businesses, and synagogues known as *Kristallnacht.* The networks aired speeches by prominent religious, political, and educational leaders—including Thomas Dewey, Herbert Hoover, and Alf Landon—expressing outrage at Germany's brutality (Lipstadt 1986, 99; Diamond 1969). On the evening of November 15, 1938, the NBC-Blue network interrupted its scheduled "light opera hits" for a special report by White House correspondent George R. Holmes. Listeners learned that at a press conference of "special significance" earlier in the day President Roosevelt had condemned Nazi Germany and announced the recall of American ambassador Hugh Wilson. Roosevelt's statement at the press conference conveyed the "disgust of the American people over the atrocious happenings in Germany over the past week," Holmes explained.[5]

Over the next several years, correspondents continued to report on Nazi violence toward Jews. In December 1942, for example, Edward R. Murrow authoritatively told listeners that "millions of human beings, most of them Jews, are being gathered up with ruthless efficiency and murdered. . . . The phrase 'concentration camps' is obsolete, as out of date as 'economic sanctions' or 'non-recognition.' It is now possible to speak only of extermination camps" (Murrow 1967; Fine 1988, 10).[6] However, even Murrow, a premier journalist who was well aware of Nazi cruelty, was not prepared for what he saw in Buchenwald shortly after it was liberated by the Allies in April 1945. In what remains one of the most well-known and powerful news reports in radio history, Murrow walked through the camp, speaking with survivors and describing the conditions under which Buchenwald operated. In a sign of how skeptical the public was of such reports of German cruelty and how difficult it was for Americans to fully comprehend the extent of Hitler's Final Solution, Murrow beseeched his listeners, "I pray you to believe what I have said about Buchenwald. I have reported what I saw and heard, but only part of it. For most of it I have no words."[7]

Starting in 1937 and continuing through the end of the war, Jewish organizations regularly aired fund-raising appeals that supplemented the mainstream media coverage with specific, up-to-date reports on the dire situation in Europe. Between 1937 and 1943, at least eighteen programs produced by Jewish organizations highlighted such issues as anti-Semitism in Europe, the refugee problem, and resettlement in Palestine. Ten of these broadcasts aired on NBC (Zahavy 1959,168–93; Fine 1988, 5–6, 12).[8] The appeals featured speeches by religious figures, politicians, scientists, writers, and actors. For example, over the years, Albert Einstein, Eddie Cantor, Sam Jaffe, Paul Muni, and other luminaries appeared alongside Jewish political and religious leaders. Several broadcasts attempted to attract listeners by supplementing the speeches with a mixture of comedy, music, and short drama. The broadcasts kept the Jewish crisis in the public eye, even though the audience for these appeals was small.

Jewish Identities on the Air

Radio dramas could have played an important political and aesthetic role by presenting powerful personal stories based on information available from news reports and Jewish organizations. However, with a few exceptions to be discussed below, the networks and their sponsors were reluctant to present dramas that were too critical of the Nazis and, more generally, anti-Semitism. Several institutional barriers militated against such programming, as did the viewpoints of various Jewish writers and performers. Arthur Miller, for example, wrote several plays for CBS starting in 1941. At the time, Miller viewed Judaism as "dead history." In his autobiography, *Timebends* (1995), Miller remembered that he and his new wife, Mary Grace Slattery, had seen their renunciation of religion as a political act. "Both of us thought we were leaving behind parochial narrowness of mind, prejudices, racism, and the irrational, which were having their ultimate triumph, it seemed to us, in the fascist and Nazi movements" (70). Miller and other progressive radio writers, Jewish and non-Jewish, were most interested in addressing issues of social class, economic inequality, rising fascism at home and abroad, and racism. Conditions in America were far worse for blacks than they were for Jews. Dramatists believed that they had a better chance of influencing American public opinion and political policy regarding race and other domestic issues. As director and writer William N. Robson told an audience at the annual Institute for Education by Radio meeting in 1943, "We have a little back-yard cleaning to do right here: we cannot fight to protect the Jew in the ghetto of Warsaw and allow the Negro to do only spade work in the armed forces. . . . If we are going to make the world safe for all peoples—a phrase I just coined—we had better make sure that we mean it at home" (Mac-Latchy 1943, 58; Blue 2002, 28).[9]

Jewish performers on the air, including several of radio's biggest names, similarly stifled any talk of Jewish identity. However, these actors, mostly comedians, were motivated less by progressive politics than a desire for national popularity beyond the country's urban, ethnic areas. Jewish comedians like George Burns, Jack Benny, and Eddie Cantor played characters based on themselves in programs that mixed elements of the situation comedy and the variety show. But Jewish identities had little place in their on-air personas. Occasionally, Benny and others introduced Jewish supporting characters who provided comic relief with their funny accents and stereotypical behavior. For historian David Marc, Burns and Benny are prime examples of influential broadcast comedians who "created not only public masks, but fictional domestic sitcom milieus that in no way indicated Jewish background, culture, or religion." The "middle-American" settings of their programs enabled Benny and Burns to reconstruct their personas from "culturally marginal" Jewish Americans into "unhyphenated" Americans (Marc 2003, 199–200; Howe 1976, 565–69; Jenkins 1992, 175–83). These performers normally did not talk about Jewish culture and identity in their prewar shows, and during the war they may have been daunted by the aesthetic challenge of seamlessly inserting material on anti-Semitism into plotlines. In addition, jokes about prejudice and Nazi brutality didn't accord with the breezy tone of radio comedy. Instead, Benny and others supported the war effort by offering sketches and gags about lighter topics: conservation, rationing, and life in the Army (Horten 2002).[10] Even *The Goldbergs*, a more serious comedy-drama that pivoted on the central family's Jewish identity, rarely referred to the Jewish dimensions of the events in Europe (Weber 2003, 118).[11]

The experience of Eddie Cantor illustrates some of the dangers of identifying too closely with Jewish culture and politics. For more than thirty years, starting in the 1910s, Cantor was consistently one of America's most popular stage, film, and radio performers. In his study of early 1930s film comedy, media historian Henry Jenkins presents Cantor as the prime example of the star who purged overt markers of his Jewish identity so that he could appeal to national audiences outside the northeastern cities. After several films featuring Jewish stars of the Broadway stage—like Cantor and Fanny Brice—bombed at the box office, studios determined that "jokes that were vitally connected with the experiences of urban viewers were either too obscure or too painful to be accepted by regional spectators" (Jenkins 1992, 183). In his film and radio work of the 1930s, Cantor sharply curtailed his use of Yiddish phrases or unfamiliar references to New York cultural landmarks. Discussion of Jewish rituals and identity was out of the question. So, for example, Cantor celebrated Christmas each year on the air but talked of no Jewish holidays.

At the same time, like several other Jewish stars of film and broadcasting, Cantor offered coded references to his background that Jewish and some non-Jewish audiences would appreciate (Jenkins 1992, 182). Magazine and newspaper articles also provided markers of Cantor's heritage. In 1935, for example, *Time* labeled Cantor a "good Jew" because of his Jewish charity work and his political activity. The article noted that Cantor was born "Izzy Iskowitch" on Manhattan's East Side.[12] On his weekly CBS program, Cantor sometimes reminisced about growing up in New York's rough Lower East Side neighborhood, a center of Jewish (and non-Jewish) immigration during the early twentieth century.[13] He also made jokes based on the assumption that listeners would know that he was Jewish. In an episode with Broadway singer-actress Ella Logan, for example, Cantor requests an Irish song. He tells Logan, "You know, an Irish song gets me right here. Most people don't know it, but my real name isn't Cantor."

Logan replies, "Oh, I think most people know that."

Cantor pauses for a second while the audience laughs, then delivers the punch line, "You mean the world knows my secret? That my name is really Shaughnessy O'Cantor, as fine a boy as ever did live in the County Cork?"[14]

Away from his prime-time program, Cantor spoke more freely and directly about his Jewish identity and the problems facing Jews. Cantor was the most vocal radio star in America regarding the dangers of anti-Semitism. Both before and after America's entry in World War II, he was the featured attraction at numerous charity luncheons and benefits that were covered in daily newspapers and sometimes broadcast live on network radio.[15] Cantor spoke powerfully about the bleak prospects of Europe's Jews while also drawing attention to the threat of domestic anti-Semitism. In 1935, for example, he addressed a Los Angeles B'nai Brith convention about the "precarious times" in which Jews were living. "You know the situation in Europe as far as Jews are concerned, but I doubt if many of you know how close to the same situation we are in America." Cantor then turned his attention to the anti-Semitic Father Charles Coughlin, who was at the height of his influence. "Father Coughlin is a great orator but I doubt he has a sincere atom in his entire system. We Jews have nothing to fear from good Christians. We are their brothers and sisters. But I am afraid of people who pretend to be good Christians."[16]

Throughout the late 1930s, Cantor continued to denounce anti-Semites in the United States and the Nazis in Europe, while working to raise money for the evacuation of Jewish children. In April 1938, the press reported on Cantor's remark to a conference of Hadassah, a Jewish women's organization, that he and his wife had received Nazi death threats. In addition, Cantor's sponsor, RJ Reynolds (Camel cigarettes) was threatened with a boycott by pro-German groups if Cantor remained on the air.[17] However, these threats did not deter Cantor. In August 1938, he publicly criticized Henry Ford, who had a history of anti-Semitism, for accepting a medal from Hitler. Cantor called Ford "a damned fool for permitting the world's greatest gangster to present him with this citation. I question Mr. Ford's Americanism and I question his Christianity."[18] As Cantor biographer Herbert G. Goldman noted (1997), such outspokenness on a controversial subject was unprecedented for a radio actor of Cantor's stature. "For Cantor, representative of major sponsors' products, it meant risking major income and, quite possibly, his entire career" (187–88).

The following year, Cantor paid for his anti-Nazi activism. On the afternoon of June 13, 1939, he addressed the New York chapter of Hadassah. The meeting took place at the World's Fair Temple of Religion. In the speech, which was not broadcast, Cantor implied that leading industrialists were bankrolling prominent anti-Semites such as Coughlin and Senator Robert Rice Reynolds of North Carolina. "These men," said Cantor, referring to the influential figures behind Coughlin and Reynolds, "are not only the enemies of Jews, but of all Americans." Coughlin had an active and vigilant following at the time. In addition, Cantor probably did not endear himself to the powers at the North Carolina–based tobacco company that sponsored his program by singling out the state's junior senator.[19] Within days, Cantor's *Camel Caravan* was taken off the air by RJ Reynolds and the William Esty Agency, even though Cantor was one of radio's most popular performers.[20] Looking back on the event, Cantor (2000) said that the speech "not only cost me $585,000, but threatened my radio career for good" (224–25).

Cantor missed the entire 1939–40 radio season. He returned to the air only after Jack Benny intervened on his behalf by calling a different agency, Young & Rubicam. Starting with the 1940–41 season, Cantor had a new sponsor, Bristol-Meyers, and a new network: NBC. As it was preparing to promote the Cantor show, Young & Rubicam expressed concerns over the performer's declining popularity and his recent political activity, lamenting Cantor's "unfortunate attack on Father Coughlin." Working with Cantor's personal publicist and representatives from NBC, Young & Rubicam decided to "present Cantor to the public strictly as a funny man, and [to] try to avoid any publicity that would indicate that Cantor ever has a serious thought or is guilty of a serious deed." The agency insisted that "if Cantor does some kind deed for the poor, or for the war refugees, etc., it should be in private and without publicity."[21] Cantor steered clear of controversial politics on his comedy-variety show during its thirteen-year run on NBC. However, away from the program, Cantor continued to appear at Jewish charity events and appeals to help war refugees. He used these occasions to speak against the Nazis both on and off the air.

The most powerful figure at NBC during the war years was David Sarnoff, a Russian-born Jew who came to America at the age of nine in 1900 and, like Cantor, grew up on the Lower East Side of New York during the first decade of the twentieth century. In many ways, Sarnoff's story was typical of the many Jews who ascended to influential, public positions in business and government during the 1920s and 1930s. Sarnoff did not deny his Jewish heritage, but for him Jewish identity was tied more to culture than to politics and religion. For example, at a 1945 luncheon held at the Waldorf-Astoria celebrating the first anniversary of *The Eternal Light*, Sarnoff joked about Jewish dietary laws, speaking "not as a theological Jew, but as an expert gastronomical Jew." Sarnoff continued nostalgically about how he missed eating authentic Jewish dishes, such as gefilte fish, and how he wanted to "go downtown and really live life all over again."[22]

Despite this affection for Jewish foods and neighborhoods, Sarnoff did not speak out for Jewish causes above other social, political, or economic issues. Biographies of Sarnoff, written by relatives and former colleagues, chronicle the anti-Semitic slights and barriers that Sarnoff encountered as he rose through the executive ranks of RCA (Dreher 1977, 25; Bilby 1986, 54–55, 188–89). But Sarnoff focused on other issues in his public statements and speeches, rarely drawing attention to his Jewish identity by talking about his experiences with prejudice or speaking against the problem of anti-Semitism in America and abroad. Such a public stance on a sensitive political issue, especially in the late 1930s, could have damaged NBC's standing in the eyes of sponsors and provided fodder for the many anti-Semitic groups and organizations looking for evidence that influential Jews were pushing the country toward war. According to Sarnoff's friend and biographer Kenneth Bilby, a longtime RCA executive, Sarnoff "had been appalled by the menacing anti-Semitism of the Nazis. Reports of the notorious 'Kristallnacht' . . . left him with mingled feelings of apprehension and rage." Yet Sarnoff did not respond to the pogrom by speaking out publicly against the Nazis or recommending American diplomatic or military action. Instead, he decided he could best fight Nazi practices by lobbying the government to purchase RCA electronic equipment to be used in defense (Bilby 1986, 138; Lyons 1966, 235–36).

After December 7, 1941, as radio began producing anti-Nazi propaganda, Sarnoff still did not encourage NBC executives or advertising agencies to create network programming that would draw attention to the plight of Europe's Jews. In fact, sensitive to the anti-Semitic charges that Jews controlled the media and that

World War II was a "Jewish war," Sarnoff spread the word that he did not want specifically Jewish programming to receive undue prominence on the network. In one instance, Erik Barnouw, who was the supervisor of an NBC wartime series called *Words at War*, planned to produce a drama that was critical of anti-Semitism. The program was rejected by NBC, according to Barnouw, for two reasons: the network was concerned that it would have to give equal time to the opposite point of view, and, "because Sarnoff was Jewish, it would be embarrassing to him because it would be said that NBC was 'Jew-dominated'" (Culbert 2002, 487). In other instances, Sarnoff spoke of NBC's most prominent Jewish program, *The Eternal Light*, not as a uniquely important Jewish program but as one of many religious shows that demonstrated America's lack of prejudice and openness to religious freedom (Wyler 1986–87, 18).[23]

More broadly, radio executives consistently trumpeted the industry's neutral stand on American involvement in the war, including assistance to England. Assurances that radio would not be used to "influence action or opinion of others" started in 1939 and continued even after the United States declared war on Germany. Between 1939 and 1942, the networks, the National Association of Broadcasters, and the Federal Communication Commission each issued formal policies prohibiting radio time from being used for advocacy (Dryer 1942, 160; Barnouw 1968, 134–36; Culbert 1976, 7). While much of the regulation and examination of political bias focused on news and commentary, dramas also were vetted. As the *New York Times* reported in 1940, "The dark headlines of war, which so often offer excellent plot structures, are being very carefully handled, and in ninety-nine out of 100 cases are taboo. In years to come they may be taken out of the morgue for dramatization, but when as fresh as they are today they are likely to pluck at the nerves—to fan war hysteria." Janet MacRorie, NBC's head of Community Acceptance, explained, "What we aim to avoid is propaganda in the guise of drama."[24]

Public statements by industry figures could be deceptive. As several historians have noted, despite a superficial "neutrality" and "balance," the networks aired a disproportionate amount of programming that supported intervention against Germany before Pearl Harbor (Culbert 1976, 5–7; Steele 1985, 135–46; S. Douglas 1999, 161–85; Hilmes 1997, 235). Dramatists like Archibald MacLeish, Orson Welles, and Arch Oboler used thinly veiled allegories to warn of the dangers of fascism, although, before December 7, 1941, network bans on "propaganda" precluded them from opposing Nazism more explicitly (Blue 2002, 79–89; J. Smith 214–15; Barnouw 1968, 64–73; Oboler and Longstreet 1944, 78). In 1942, Oboler looked back at the frustrating prewar situation, suggesting that there was a special place in the afterlife reserved for "radio network executives, advertising agency department heads, manufacturers of assorted objects advertised over the airwaves, and—radio writers. . . . [T]he devil in Hell alone knows what measure of responsibility is theirs for the national indifference with which pre-war America" contemplated the rise of fascism in Europe (Dryer 1942, 239).

Dramatic Exceptions

After Pearl Harbor, the industry was more welcoming of antifascist programs, but few dramas examined anti-Semitism. The political and institutional constraints described above still mandated that the dramas conform to certain rules: programs were not to emphasize Nazi atrocities, focus on the victimization of Jews, or explicitly advocate U.S. political or military action to fight anti-Semitism. Nevertheless, working within these constraints, writers who wanted to examine the problems facing Europe's Jews found an appropriate vehicle in the story of a small and courageous group of Jews in the Warsaw Ghetto who battled the vastly more powerful German army in 1943.

The Second Battle of Warsaw, by Irving Ravetch, was part of *Free World Theatre*, a four-month series that aired over the NBC-Blue network on Sunday evenings starting in February 1943 (Blue 2002, 149–51, 314–15; Ravetch 1944). *Free World Theatre* was conceived, produced, and directed by Arch Oboler. The series' Hooper ratings hovered at around 2.0, a figure that was average for sustaining programming but low compared to most commercial offerings. However, its ratings were not of paramount concern to NBC. Every week, NBC aired several war-related series and additional special broadcasts to satisfy the patriotic listeners, public service requirements, and wartime government agencies.[25] In fact, the network was rewarded for its commitment to *Free World Theatre* with a formal letter from the Office of War Information (OWI) shortly after the show's debut. The OWI predicted that *Free World Theatre* would "contribute greatly to a better understanding of many of the basic issues of this war."[26]

Oboler wanted to craft a series for the "upper ten-percent intelligent quotient of the radio audience [who] were not listening to the ordinary bludgeoning war messages" (Oboler and Longstreet 1944, xiii). He advertised that the wartime stories would originate from ideas or statements by poets, philosophers, and politicians ranging from Walt Whitman to Franklin Roosevelt.[27] The producer-director hired big-name Hollywood talent for his series: *The Second Battle of Warsaw*, for example, starred John Garfield and Ann Baxter. Oboler also enlisted the help of the Hollywood Writers Mobilization, a quasi-government organization that worked with the OWI to recruit some of Hollywood's best writers, including Samuel Raphelson and Budd Schulberg. Novelist Pearl Buck, who started writing for radio during the war, also contributed to *Free World Theatre*.[28] Irving Ravetch, twenty-two years old at the time and a recent graduate of UCLA, was not yet in this class when he wrote *The Second Battle of Warsaw*. However, Oboler had a good eye for talent. Ravetch is best known today for the work he did after leaving radio: he and his wife, Harriet Frank Jr., wrote *Hud* (1963), *Norma Rae* (1979), and several other films. As the son of a rabbi, Ravetch may have had a particular passion for the subject of European Jewry and knowledge of Jewish history and contemporary life. Ravetch told one interviewer that he learned to write at a young age "because a poor rabbi mobilizes his entire family to help. My job was to write bar mitzvah speeches for the young men when they reached thirteen" (McGilligan 1990, 187).

The Second Battle of Warsaw aired on June 14, 1943, less than a month after the Germans declared final victory over the surprisingly resilient Jewish resistance in Warsaw. For American listeners, the story of brave anti-Nazi fighters had obvious resonance. The radio program opens solemnly: "This we bring you now is the truth. Remember that, you who listen—this is the truth! It happened in your time! It happened—and is happening." In the program, Ravetch depicts the brutal killing of the Warsaw Ghetto's Herzog family: two children, their father, and their grandfather. However, Ravetch does not allow the Herzog family and others in the ghetto to serve as mere symbols of resistance to the Nazis. The Herzogs are Jews in Poland; as such, they have unique problems. Early in the story, a member of the underground visits the family and gives them the choice of being smuggled across the border or of fighting. In a pointed criticism of Allied refugee policy, the grandfather, Dovid, recognizes that flight is not an option because of immigration quotas. He observes bitterly that even if the family made it out of Poland they would face "the freedom of starvation and hopelessness on a ship that never stops. . . . I am too old and tired for such a journey" (Ravetch 1944, 227). Instead, the grandfather argues that it is more noble to stay and fight. Here, Ravetch depicts the Warsaw Jews as martyrs for the Allied cause in the sort of lofty proclamation typical of wartime drama: "There is only one way for free men to die. And that is in defense of freedom. Children, what is freedom? Only a word? No! If we want it, we must struggle every day of our lives to win it anew, only so we can be worthy of it" (1944, 228). In doing their part for freedom, the Herzogs hope that others will join the fight against the Nazis. "Awake, Herzogs throughout the world! To arms," cries grandfather Dovid (1944, 229). During the battle, the family members fight bravely, but they die one by one. At the end, only the boy, Zelbel, survives. As the program ends, Zelbel issues a stark challenge to the Allies, asking, "Will the world know. . . ? Or are we alone here?" (235).

Morton Wishengrad uses the story of the Warsaw Ghetto to advance similar themes in his *Battle of the Warsaw Ghetto*, which received far more contemporary attention and remains a favorite of old-time radio fans.[29] The American Jewish Committee (AJC), the most established American Jewish charity organization, produced the program for NBC.[30] The program was circulated by the Writers' War Board as the featured script for October 1943 and selected by Erik Barnouw the next year for his anthology *Radio Drama in Action: Twenty-Five Plays of a Changing World*. *The Battle of the Warsaw Ghetto* was presented on NBC three times during the war years. It premiered over the Red network on October 3, 1943, during the ten days between Rosh Hashanah and Yom Kippur. Wishengrad's play addresses questions of guilt, moral responsibility, and atonement that are central to Jewish thought and practice during this time of the year. The program aired again in December 1943 during Chanukah and in January 1945 to celebrate the liberation of Warsaw. Together, the three broadcasts drew more than twelve thousand letters from listeners

(Barnouw 1945, 33). The response is all the more extraordinary considering the air-time: all three programs aired on Sunday afternoons when there were relatively few listeners.

During the early 1940s, the word *Jew* was rarely spoken in network radio drama, and the Hebrew language was not used at all. However, Wishengrad signals his intention to violate taboos before any dialogue is spoken: *The Battle of the Warsaw Ghetto* starts with a cantor singing "El Moleh Rachamim," a Jewish song of mourning, in biblical Hebrew. An anonymous narrator then introduces the story of the thirty-five thousand Jews who stood their ground against the Third Reich. "Twenty-five thousand fell. They sleep in their common graves but they have vindicated their birthright."[31] The narrator is then replaced by a new voice: a character, Issac Davidson, who was killed in Warsaw and tells his horrible story in an understated tone from the grave. Davidson serves as the narrator for the remainder of the program, though the anonymous narrator returns in a brief coda. Wishengrad's elegy for Warsaw's dead is bleaker than Ravetch's in that escape from Poland is never presented as an option. The Jews of the ghetto must fight. They are moved by a combination of honor and desperation. Wishengrad eulogizes the "ten thousand brave, hopeless, tragic men who seized sticks and stones and knives and fists and charged the tanks and tried to halt the trucks."[32] The alternative to armed resistance is clear. Men, women, and children are packed into "black trucks," and sent to concentration camps (which Wishengrad identifies by name) and certain death in "a lethal gas chamber, an electric cell, a poison pit, an execution field."[33]

Wishengrad is even more pointed than Ravetch in his criticism of the Allies. "When we were starving, we beseeched the civilized world for food, when the plague struck us, we appealed for simple things, soaps, medicines, tools for our physicians, but when the black trucks came we no longer asked for rescue and for mercy, we asked for weapons," narrator Davidson explains. "Through the Polish underground, which carried our appeals, we asked England, Russia and the United States for weapons. There came your answer: resolutions of sympathy."[34] In a final scene, as the resistance is defeated, a man dying alongside Davidson provides a dignified epitaph, directed at the Allies, for the Jews of the Warsaw Ghetto. "It is not for thee to complete the work [of the resistance], but neither art thou free to desist from it."[35] The play ends by evoking a long Jewish history of fighting, despite enormous odds, to win freedom and survive oppression. The anonymous narrator returns with a poetic prayer from Warsaw as the cantor chants "El Moleh Rachamim" again in the background. "Give me grace and give me dignity and teach me to die; and let my prison be a fortress and my wailing wall a stockade, for I have been to Egypt and I am not departed."[36]

In both of the Warsaw Ghetto radio plays, Jews are presented as self-reliant. They need assistance but are capable of fighting alongside the Americans as allies, not victims. While each drama points out moral and political failings of American policy regarding European Jews, the programs do not focus on the most important and controversial political question of the day: immigration quotas for European refugees. Instead, they emphasize Jewish courage and dignity. Using the conventions of wartime drama, the programs invite viewers to conflate the Jewish fighters with the more commonly portrayed Allied soldiers in battle and to understand that the values and interests of Jews are not different from those of other Americans or the country as a whole. This argument was a central component of the strategies by mainstream Jewish organizations to fight anti-Semitism. Jewish groups drew attention to conditions in Europe and quietly lobbied the government to admit more refugees, but they were careful not to push too hard lest the war against the Nazis become a "Jewish war." Rather than portraying anti-Semitism as a specifically "Jewish problem," advocacy organizations worked more broadly to stress that all prejudice and bigotry was undemocractic and un-American. They also fought anti-Semitism by emphasizing positive images of Jews rather than offering legitimacy to the accusations of anti-Semites by answering these charges directly (Dinnerstein 1994, 147). More frank and nuanced discourse about anti-Semitism in America and Europe was reserved for the Jewish press, Yiddish radio, and other forums in which the audience was almost exclusively Jewish (Kelman forthcoming; Grobman 1978).

The most successful network radio program about Jewish life, NBC's *The Eternal Light* (1944–82), emphasized Jewish contributions to American and world history. Resistance to anti-Semitism was a more subtle, secondary theme. In fact, the weekly series gave the two primary creative people behind *The Battle of the Warsaw Ghetto*—writer Wishengrad and producer Milton Krents—an opportunity to continue their collaboration and expand upon the Jewish history themes that first surfaced in *The Battle of the Warsaw Ghetto*. The landmark public service series was produced by the Jewish Theological Seminary (JTS), "the rabbinical academy and intellectual center of the conservative movement, which was then the fastest-growing branch of organized Judaism in the United States" (Shandler 1999, 61). According to Krents, in 1944 NBC was looking to fill a gap in its religious public service offerings. *Message of Israel*, which debuted on NBC in 1934, was moving to the newly formed ABC network, and NBC wanted another Jewish program to take its place. Krents had ambitious plans for *The Eternal Light*, as did the head of the JTS, Louis Finkelstein. Krents and Finkelstein wanted to present an original drama each Sunday morning on the new program.[37] *The Eternal Light* occasionally dramatized stories from the Bible, but its episodes moved beyond this popular source of religious drama to cover the gamut of Jewish history, theology, and culture.

At the time, radio drama on religion was aesthetically risky. While most religious figures in broadcasting were comfortable delivering sermons, there was no model for a weekly drama series. Furthermore, drama production was an expensive endeavor requiring researchers, writers, actors, music, and an office staff to coordinate each production. One early *Eternal Light* budget, for example, estimated production costs at $27,200 per week, not including music.[38] Nevertheless, Krents and Finkelstein believed that they needed to move beyond the standard religious fare on the air. As Finkelstein wrote in a March 1944 letter, soliciting support for the new program, "Religious programs are extremely unpopular. Broadcasting com-

FIG. 7 David Sarnoff in discussion with Louis Finkelstein, head of the Jewish Theological Seminary and producer of *The Eternal Light* series, in an NBC studio in the early 1950s. (Courtesy of the Ratner Center for the Study of Conservative Judaism, The Jewish Theological Seminary)

panies give time to churches as the newspapers give space to reports of sermons— unwillingly. This is because no group has learned to express the ideas of religion simply enough."[39] Ultimately, Krents and Finkelstein believed that drama had tremendous potential to reach a broad audience of Jewish and non-Jewish listeners who might not tune in to a more conventional program. They also were savvy enough to recruit Wishengrad, one of radio's top dramatists, as the staff writer.

The Eternal Light was hailed as a new kind of religious program soon after its October 8, 1944, debut. As Jack Gould wrote in a *New York Times* review, "Technically [*The Eternal Light*] is listed as a 'religious program,' but that is to do it a gross disservice. More accurately, and perhaps primarily, it should be described as a series of fine and sensitive dramas which stand very much on their own merit as radio plays."[40] Moreover, the distribution numbers vindicated the JTS's choice of drama. *The Eternal Light* started on a respectable forty-five NBC affiliates across the country, including markets where there were no large Jewish populations, and grew to one hundred stations by 1954. NBC and the JTS claimed that *The Eternal Light* had a devoted audience of six million listeners (Shandler and Katz 1997).[41] *The Eternal Light* also helped NBC and its affiliates satisfy FCC rules, which required stations to air religious programming, and the wartime OWI. In fact, NBC listed *The Eternal Light* in its monthly log of war-related programming because the series provided "rich stimulation of the spirit of brotherhood among all men" and exposed the dangers of "intolerance."[42]

During the war years, *The Eternal Light* usually did not present contemporary stories about anti-Semitism or conditions in Europe. The first set of thirteen dramas explored historic synagogues and Jewish communities from around the world; the next series introduced biographies of Jewish heroes: rabbis, scientists, politicians, community leaders, and biblical characters. The only contemporary European story was "Monsieur Levy Passes Over," a moving 1945 Passover program set in a recently liberated French village. As a Jewish American soldier wanders through an abandoned synagogue, he discovers a Frenchman, Monsieur Levy. Initially the soldier mistakes Levy for a sniper. However, he soon learns that Levy has been "hiding like an animal from the Nazis" for the past four years and has emerged as one of only two Jews in the village to have survived Nazi occupation. The American soldier and his fellow GIs pass the helmet to raise funds for the synagogue's restoration. They then pitch in to create a Passover service.[43]

Several wartime *Eternal Light* dramas included metaphoric references to the conditions in Europe, presenting inspirational stories of Jewish physical and moral strength in times of great crisis. The stories served as reminders to listeners that Jews had endured and triumphed over persecution. Short sermons by Jewish leaders at the end of each episode made the connections between history and present-day conditions explicit. "The Black Death," for example, takes place in the German city of Mayence, where Jews are blamed for spreading bubonic plague during the fourteenth century. The program has strong formal and thematic similarities to *The Battle of the Warsaw Ghetto*, including a narrator who tells the story from the grave. The narrator, Judah, is one of many Jews, confined to a ghetto, who contemplate armed resistance in the face of an enemy that wants to destroy them. In this version, however, the narrator is killed when he tries to leave the ghetto and "appeal to the humanity" of his oppressors. His fellow Jews stay behind and fight bravely, but are all killed. In a talk after the play, Rabbi Mordecai M. Kaplan of the JTS places Wishengrad's story in the broader context of the history of anti-Semitism, linking "the martyrdom of the Jews during the pestilence of fourteenth-century Europe" and the "wholesale slaughter of three million Jews of twentieth-century Europe."[44] Another wartime episode of *The Eternal Light* profiles Henrietta Szold, the founder of Hadassah. The program highlights Szold's humanitarian work with Jewish refugees in Palestine during the 1930s, when "a storm broke over Europe, and darkness fell, and Zion prepared to receive the fugitives."[45]

Conclusion

Given what we have learned about Nazi Germany since the end of the war, it seems clear that the radio industry should have done more to oppose the Nazis before

Pearl Harbor and to alert Americans to the horrors to which Jews were subjected under Nazi rule. However, in the context of the times, the question of why the industry acted as it did becomes more complicated. The political, economic, and social conditions in America during the late 1930s and early 1940s militated against a large-scale rescue of European Jews. The questions of whether America could improve the status of Jews in Germany or admit more Jewish refugees from Europe were related to broader domestic political issues regarding immigration, unemployment, anti-Semitism, and, before Pearl Harbor, isolationism. America's response to Nazi persecution of Jews divided the Roosevelt administration and pitted powerful political figures, interest groups, private agencies, and federal government institutions against each other.[46] In this environment, American Jewish organizations and prominent individuals struggled to find ways to help Europe's Jews while affirming loyalty to American cultural values and military goals.

Historically, the broadcast networks have tried to avoid taking sides in such heated and vexing matters, rather than providing moral or political leadership by advocating unpopular causes or publicizing controversial issues. During the late 1930s and early 1940s, radio writers, who were most active in the fight against fascism, did not place a priority on exploring the problem of anti-Semitism in America and Europe. Many others at NBC, from Eddie Cantor to David Sarnoff, were governed even more strongly by sponsors, government regulators, and public opinion. The business culture of radio demanded that programming not offend advertisers, politicians, federal workers at the FCC and OWI, and large segments of the public. NBC aired several powerful dramas as unsponsored public service programs on Sundays, when listenership was low and the programs may not have been scrutinized as closely by regulators. Although the audience for these Sunday dramas was relatively small, NBC's wartime public service provided an important venue for serious programming that boldly presented the concerns of a religious minority at a time of great crisis. What's more, radio programs like *The Battle of the Warsaw Ghetto* and *The Eternal Light* served as early attempts to find a dramatic language that could articulate the suffering of Europe's Jews and find inspiration in Jewish heroism from ancient times through the war years. In the postwar years, radio and television writers continued to grapple with the political, aesthetic, and moral challenges of representing the Holocaust.

The author thanks Charlotte Bonelli, Tom Doherty, Eric Frazier, Michael Henry, Michele Hilmes, Chuck Howell, Ellen Kastel, Ari Kelman, Rebecca Sandler, Michael Socolow, and Rachel Weinstein for their assistance.

Notes

Abbreviations

AJC   American Jewish Committee Oral History Library, Jewish Division, New York Public Library

FAC   Fred Allen Collection, Rare Books and Manuscripts, Boston Public Library

JTS Records of the Jewish Theological Seminary, Joseph and Miriam Ratner Center for the Study of Conservative Judaism, New York

LAB Library of American Broadcasting, University of Maryland

NBC/LC Motion Picture, Broadcasting, and Recorded Sound Division, Library of Congress

OWI Records of the War Office of Information, National Archives

UWC Motion Picture, Sound, and Video Records, University of Washington Collection, National Archives

1. The Warsaw Ghetto dramas were apparently among the earliest and most prominent programs to focus on Nazi violence and Jewish resistance to this violence, but they were not the only such dramas. A catalog and analysis of all programs that included references to anti-Jewish violence in Europe during the war years is beyond the scope of this essay. In addition, there are no extant records and descriptions of all wartime radio dramas, so it is impossible to determine how many dramas dealt with the subject.

2. Why the American press reported the Holocaust as it did and how press coverage influenced the American public's knowledge of the Holocaust are beyond the scope of this essay. For more on these questions, see Lipstadt (1986), Leff (2005), and Hollander (2003).

3. Ben Hecht, "Remember Us," *Reader's Digest*, February 1943, reprinted in Abzug (1999, 147). This *Reader's Digest* article was a condensed version of a longer essay that first appeared in the February 1943 *American Mercury*. Also see Lipstadt (1986, 187).

4. Daniel T. Brigham, "Inquiry Confirms Nazi Death Camps," *New York Times*, July 3, 1944, 3.

5. "George R. Holmes," November 15, 1938, NBC-Blue, reel-to-reel tape from transcription disc, RWA-3146-A4, NBC/LC. Fine (1988, 4) gives the date of the broadcast as November 18, 1938, but all other sources indicate that it was November 15, 1938.

6. Murrow's report aired four days before the Allies issued a joint statement condemning the Nazis' "bestial policy of cold-blooded extermination."

7. Edward R. Murrow, "Buchenwald, 04/15/1945," 200-MR-3964, Audio Recordings Forming the Milo Ryan Phonoarchive of Radio Newscasts Relating to World War Two and Special Coverage of Other Historical Events, circa 1931–circa 1977, Record Group 200-MR, UWC; transcript in Murrow (1967, 90–95).

8. NBC, "War Effort Report, May 1–31, 1944," unpublished report, Box 649, Entry 103, Record Group 208, OWI; "Jewish Charities Program," November 28, 1940, NBC-Blue, reel-to-reel tape of transcription disc, RWA-4862-A3–4, NBC/LC; "United Jewish Appeal of 1943 for Refugees, Overseas Needs and Palestine," April 11, 1943, NBC-Red, reel-to-reel tape of transcription disc, RWA-5776-A3–4, NBC/LC.

9. The date of the Institute for Education by Radio meeting at which Robson delivered this speech is not provided. Thus it is not clear whether Robson could have been alluding to the Warsaw Ghetto radio programs discussed later in this essay. However, it is likely, based on references at other sessions, that the conference took place between April and August of 1943. For more on the politics of writers, see Blue (2002, 17–46), Hilmes (1997, 236–64), and J. Smith (2002, 209–30). For some of the most significant dramas, see Barnouw (1945).

10. A discussion of the aesthetic challenges of presenting Nazi cruelty in popular art during the war is beyond the scope of this essay. However, it should be noted that both Charlie Chaplin (*The Great Dictator*, 1940) and Ernst Lubitsch (*To Be or Not to Be*, 1942) demonstrated

satirical possibilities for narrative film. Jack Benny starred in Lubitsch's great satire of War-saw under German rule.

11. Weber also identifies a few exceptional episodes of *The Goldbergs*, including an April 1939 Passover program in which a rock "crashes through the window of the Goldbergs' home," an allusion to *Kristallnacht*.

12. "Cantor on Coughlin," *Time*, July 15, 1935, 43. Cantor was actually born Edward Is-rael Iskowitz. Newspapers provided extensive coverage of Cantor's activities supporting Jewish causes. Features in radio fan magazines, which were more subject to the influence of network and agency publicists, generally did not refer to Cantor's Jewish background or po-litical activities.

13. See, for example, *Time to Smile*, with Al Jolson and Dinah Shore, NBC-Red, June 4, 1941, MP3 file, author's collection. Hasia Diner (2000) notes that it was only after World War II that the Lower East Side emerged as "American Jewish sacred space." During the 1930s, the Lower East Side was seen more broadly as a "broad urban borderland, a sprawl-ing zone where pockets of Jewish life functioned alongside areas shaped by other peoples, many of whom were also newcomers to America" (44, 165).

14. *Time to Smile*, with Ella Logan, NBC, February 21, 1945, MP3 file, author's collection.

15. James Fisher (1997) identifies six different radio appearances by Cantor on broad-casts for Jewish charities between 1936 and 1943. He also provides citations to numerous newspaper articles about these events (130–35, 213–67). Also see Kramer (1992).

16. "Cantor on Coughlin," 43; Kramer (1992, 223).

17. "Cantor Assails Hitler," *New York Times*, April 1, 1938, sec. 1, p. 9; "Cantor Says Nazis Threaten His Life," *Hollywood Reporter*, April 1, 1938, 3; Goldman (1997, 198). Cantor had just broadcast his first program with a new sponsor, Camel Cigarettes, at the time of the re-marks. It is not clear whether Cantor's previous sponsor, Texaco, released Cantor in response to his anti-Nazi activity.

18. "Ford Denounced by Eddie Cantor over Nazi Medal," *Washington Post*, August 4, 1938, 2.

19. "Cantor Warns Jews at Fair's Hadassah Day," *New York Herald Tribune*, June 14, 1939, 17; Goldman (1997, 210–11). For more on Reynolds, including his anti-Semitism, see Pleas-ants (2000).

20. "Camels Stall on Ed Cantor," *Variety*, June 21, 1939, 31; "Camel Gives Cantor Go-By," *Variety*, June 28, 1939, 23; Koseluk (1995, 366–74). It is difficult to corroborate Cantor's story regarding the agency's motivations for dropping him. By 1939, Cantor had slipped from the height of his popularity, but he still was relatively popular with listeners. His pro-gram averaged a 20.1 rating, the twelfth highest ranked program on radio, during the 1938–39 season. A June 1939 *Radio Guide* poll of more than seven hundred thousand listeners ranked Cantor as the fourth most popular comedian on the air. Moreover, Cantor remained pop-ular with listeners after he returned to radio, starting with the 1940–41 season.

21. Thomas to Harrington, August 15, 1940, unpublished memo, scrapbook, pf Ms. 2003.G3.1, FAC.

22. "Luncheon Meeting: Jewish Theological Seminary," typescript, October 1, 1945, 11, Box 46, Record Group 1-C, General Files, JTS.

23. Ibid., 12.

24. "Impacts of War on the Air," *New York Times*, August 18, 1940.

25. NBC also occasionally broadcast war-related series on the Blue network and coop-erated with the OWI to insert war messages into popular series that were not otherwise fo-

cused on the war. See C. E. Hooper, Inc., "National Evening Programs: War Effort Programs," May 30, June 15, and June 30, 1943, unpublished reports, Box 705, Entry 117, OWI. For more on the relationship between the networks and the OWI, see Horten (2002). Several reports on NBC's wartime programming are available in Boxes 644–49, Entry 103, OWI.

26. Douglas Meservey to Charles Barry, February 24, 1943, Box 600, Entry 93, OWI. Within two months, the OWI decided to withdraw its name from the credits of *Free World Theatre*, citing concerns with the quality of the program. The government agency also believed that *Free World Theatre* "often came dangerously close to being political propaganda." The OWI internal letter does not provide details regarding Oboler's political transgressions. Cornwell Jackson to Don Stauffer, April 10, 1943, Box 625, Entry 95, OWI; Philip Cohen to Cornwell Jackson, April 12, 1943, Box 625, Entry 95, OWI. See also Blue (2002, 151).

27. The connections between these ideas and the radio stories was not always clear. *The Second Battle of Warsaw*, for example, was based on a statement by Lillian Hellman, but the published version of the play does not reprint the statement or refer to it in the script. See Ravetch (1944). The OWI noted that "there is rarely any relationship between the as-broadcast scripts and the statements that allegedly inspire them." See Jackson to Stauffer, April 10, 1943.

28. Blue (2002, 145–51) discusses the Writers' War Board and the Hollywood Writers Mobilization. For a list of *Free World Theatre* writers, see Oboler and Longstreet (1944, vii–viii). Also see Erik Barnouw's introduction to "Will This Earth Hold?" in Barnouw (1945, 18).

29. As recently as 2004, the Gotham Radio Players performed *The Battle of the Warsaw Ghetto* at the annual Friends of Old-Time-Radio convention in Newark, NJ.

30. Milton E. Krents, interview by Jill Levine, November 12, 1979, transcription of audiotape, tape 1, 56–57, AJC.

31. Morton Wishengrad, *The Battle of the Warsaw Ghetto*, typescript, October 1943, pamphlet 2803, LAB. Subsequent citations are to this version of the drama, unless noted. The play was published with slight revisions in two books: Barnouw (1945, 31–45) and Wishengrad (1947, 32–45).

32. Wishengrad, *The Battle of the Warsaw Ghetto*, 6.

33. Ibid. In subsequent published versions and radio productions of the play, the phrase "electric pit" was changed to "electric furnace."

34. Ibid., 6–7.

35. Ibid., 9. The line is taken from the *Pirke Avot*, one of the central books of Jewish teachings. See Erik Barnouw's introduction to *The Battle of the Warsaw Ghetto* in Barnouw (1945, 33).

36. Wishengrad, *The Battle of the Warsaw Ghetto*, 10.

37. Krents, interview by Levine, tape 1, p. 69. It is difficult to determine which man, Krents or Finkelstein, first had the idea to build a series around dramas rather than sermons. Krents remembers approaching NBC with the idea for drama, then pitching the idea to Finkelstein. In a February 22, 1944, letter to a donor, Finkelstein outlines a series that would rotate between four different formats each month. One week would feature a lecture; the second, a roundtable discussion; the third, a reading from Jewish Scripture; and the fourth, a drama. It is not clear whether Finkelstein was working with Krents at this time. See Louis Finkelstein to Mrs. Felix Warburg [Frieda Schiff Warburg], February 22, 1944, Box 41, Record Group 1-B, General Files, JTS. See also Wyler (1986–87, 19); Shandler and Katz (1997).

38. Milton Krents to Louis Finkelstein, August 8, 1944, Box 36, Record Group 1-B, General Files, JTS. According to Marjorie Wyler, longtime director of public relations at the

Jewish Theological Seminary, the cost of each weekly episode at this time was $22,000. See Wyler (1986–87, 19).

39. Louis Finkelstein to Mrs. Felix Warburg [Frieda Schiff Warburg], March 2, 1944, Box 41, Record Group 1-B, General Files, JTS.

40. Jack Gould, "The Eternal Light," *New York Times*, December 17, 1944, sec. 2, p. 9.

41. See also, for example, Jewish Theological Seminary of America, *6,000,000 Listen. . .*, ca. 1947, Box 1, Morton Wishengrad Papers, JTS; "Report to Board of Overseers," typescript, December 1948, Box 26, Record Group 11C, Communications Department, JTS; *The Eternal Light*, "Fact Sheet," typescript, October 22, 1953, Box 26, Record Group 11C, Communications Department, JTS; Milton Krents to Rabbi Moshe Davis, March 11, 1957, Box 26, Record Group 11C, Communications Department, JTS.

42. See, for example, NBC, "War Effort Report, October 1–31, 1944," unpublished report, Box 648, Entry 103, OWI.

43. "Monsieur Levy Passes Over," *The Eternal Light*, April 1, 1945, NBC, reel-to-reel tape from transcription disc, RWA-67490-B3–4, NBC/LC.

44. "The Black Death," *The Eternal Light*, November 5, 1944, NBC, audiotape, author's collection. Morton Wishengrad, "The Black Death," in Wishengrad (1947, 140). Wishengrad's script uses the spelling "Mayence" rather than the more common "Mainz."

45. "Henrietta Szold," *The Eternal Light*, April 22, 1945, NBC, audiotape, author's collection.

46. Breitman and Kraut (1987, 2). The question of what, if anything, these powerful American individuals and institutions could have done to save more European Jews is still a matter of debate among historians. There is a large amount of historical literature on American reaction to the Holocaust. Medoff (1996) provides a useful review of several works and positions.

7

Employment and Blue Pencils

NBC, Race, and Representation, 1926–55

MURRAY FORMAN

Throughout its first quarter-century, NBC regularly encountered the complexities of representing race in its program development and broadcasting. After its start in 1926, the network struggled to appease audiences who were offended by the portrayal of black characters or by the language and terms employed in relation to citizens of the African American community. The network's explicit attempts to address racial issues and to conform to standards of propriety and "good taste" also reflect the ways that American cultural values were understood at various historical junctures.

In what follows, I will illuminate NBC's responses to what was widely described as the nation's "Negro problem" and the ways the network reacted to complaints about its representation of blacks in broadcast drama and the use of derogatory terms, especially in song lyrics. Crucial to NBC's evolving racial policy in the postwar era was the network's program to reach out to the nation's black community, devising a coherent response to racial discrimination and initiating what network executives eventually termed the "Integration without Identification Policy," developed in collaboration with the Joseph V. Baker and Associates public relations firm between 1950 and 1954.

NBC Radio and Content Monitoring

In a letter addressed to "R.C. of America" in 1926, NBC's first year of operation, Mrs. Charles F. Reid, a self-described "ardent radio fan" from Baltimore, Maryland, wrote about her experience while tuned in to a featured performance by a popular singer of the day, Wendell Hall:

> Tonight, having a number here to hear the Victor Concert which we enjoyed, we were very much humiliated by having Mr. Hall refer to our race (Colored) as Darkey, after

I had just told them of his exceptional ability as a broadcasting artist. . . . This word Darkey is considered a slander to us, which I do not think is sanctioned by you. An explanation will be much appreciated to show those present that such is not to be expected in the future from station W.J.L.[1]

The letter offers evidence of listeners' critical reception skills and willingness to act on their own behalf to challenge or admonish the broadcast networks for perceived breaches in good taste and propriety. The writer's respectful tone notwithstanding, the letter indicates a serious issue that would hound NBC for the next several decades as network executives struggled to formulate a consistent policy on racial representation in radio and, later, television broadcasting.

Despite David Sarnoff's lofty claims about the educational, artistic, and cultural virtues of radio broadcasting, NBC and the other network broadcasters were inured by years of social conditioning, producing the context for racial insensitivity and at times outright bigotry in radio programming and content. Underscoring the problem was the blackface tradition exploited by minstrel and vaudeville acts. According to Michele Hilmes (1997), "Vaudeville blackface teams made a smooth transition onto radio in the mid-1920s. . . . Many network programs featured either 'exotic natives' or minstrel teams in their overall continuity" (80). Early radio minstrel routines extended the reach of conventional blackface performances that depicted woeful or blissfully ignorant southern blacks and a host of other stereotypical identities. Freeman Gosden and Charles Correll first broadcast their successful creation *Amos 'n' Andy* on Chicago radio station WMAQ in 1926; the station was subsequently acquired by NBC, and the program premiered on the national network in 1929. Although the program appealed to white and black audiences alike, it was not uniformly accepted, causing heated debate about the dilemmas of racial representation and listening pleasures in American radio broadcasting (MacDonald 1992; M. P. Ely 1991; Hilmes 1997; Bogle 2001; Doherty 2003; Pondillo 2005).

The burgeoning network was at this stage still defining itself as a corporate broadcasting entity, and NBC executives wrestled with programming issues in their effort to balance engaging content with what was socially acceptable. As network radio gradually penetrated the American heartland, broadcasters began to recognize vast regional differences in the parameters of social acceptability relating to race. NBC's early intent to sanitize its broadcast content is evident in numerous internal corporate memoranda from the early and mid-1930s, suggesting that the network executives were conscious of the potential negative impact of airing offensive or objectionable material. For instance, in a 1932 memo sent by NBC vice president of programming John F. Royal to Bertha Brainard, director of commercial programming, Royal explains, "[I]t is imperative that from this date on no remarks of questionable nature be permitted in our continuities. . . . [R]adio got its great start by giving clean, wholesome entertainment . . . and we must stop material in bad taste."[2]

Royal was undoubtedly referring to the radio trend toward performances fashioned in the burlesque, music hall, and vaudeville traditions; prior to his career at

NBC, Royal had himself been a manager in the Keith-Albee vaudeville theater chain (Gilbert 1940; Bergreen 1980), so he had a keen insider's perspective on the aesthetics and conventions of vaudeville routines, including minstrel skits and black-face performances. A radio man with NBC since 1929 (when he became manager of Cleveland station WTAM), Royal was appointed vice resident of programming in 1931, whereupon it fell to him to monitor scripts and broadcasts in order to appraise content and ensure that general standards of propriety were maintained. In his role as program monitor, however, Royal articulated the still-evolving distinctions between public and private reception that radio broadcasting enabled; further, he was instrumental in delineating NBC's early broadcast profile for millions of home listeners. NBC's interpretation of good taste and what was acceptable radio fare for domestic reception in the 1930s, it seemed, was to be defined for the public by John F. Royal and employees in the network's Program Department.

Although there was ample concern about bawdy, ill-conceived sexual humor, NBC's Program Department was also cautious about the language and discourses of race, ethnicity, and religion, recognizing that offhanded comments or distasteful song selection could raise the ire of a large audience bloc. While vaudevillian humor was frequently distasteful, it was minstrel skits or racially tinged song lyrics that most regularly provoked angry responses from black listeners. The often insensitive lyrical traditions of Tin Pan Alley and the "coon song" genre, popular since the late nineteenth century, had survived well into the 1930s, emerging as common fare on NBC's early radio broadcasts. Most perplexing were the southern songs (such as "Darktown Strutters Ball," "Mississippi Mud," "My Old Kentucky Home," "Kentucky Baby," "My Curly Headed Baby," or "Way Down upon the Swanee River") and much of the Stephen Foster songbook, all of which regularly articulated the basic tenets of racial discrimination and contained derogatory references to blacks.

In 1934, the network published the *NBC Program Policies and Working Manual* inscribing the basic guidelines for scripts and broadcast content, including the network's stance on lyrical transgressions and racial insensitivity. The manual was intended to standardize the approach to continuity issues in the Program Department and throughout the network, yet there was a notable element of insensitivity in the way the Program Department conducted its own business. Commenting on the network's content and continuity acceptance in 1935, John Royal revealed his own tendencies toward racial bigotry even as he attempted to assert the network's new formal policy: "We should eliminate the word 'nigger' wherever possible. Of course, these darkies put a lot of pressure on us and they are sometimes too exacting, and there are certain songs where the word 'nigger' must be used. However, it is wise to cut it out as much as possible."[3]

In 1938, the network reiterated its internal guidelines, distributing a general memorandum to its employees concerning racial language and bigoted discourse, particularly in popular songs: "Please let this serve as a reminder that songs containing the words 'nigger,' 'darky,' and 'coon,' etc. in the title and lyrics should not be programmed. These always bring complaining letters from negro listeners and if this can be explained to sponsors or program builders they surely will see the wisdom of not including anything on programs which may be offensive to any peoples."[4] As the rationale for content monitoring indicates, however, it was not the commitment to respectful representation of blacks that motivated the network's policy but the desire to protect sponsors' interests by avoiding inappropriate content that might taint their corporate or product image. This perspective dominated at NBC through the 1940s and into the 1950s.

Context for Change: A Nation in Transition

As the nation recovered from World War II, there was an intense focus on domestic issues, with efforts across multiple sectors to readjust to new social and cultural realities. Under the government administrations of Democratic presidents Franklin D. Roosevelt and Harry S. Truman, American blacks had won unprecedented rights, including the right to fair employment after Roosevelt's 1941 decree giving black laborers access to jobs in the nation's defense and munitions factories. By the time he became president in 1945, Truman had come to realize that Negro conciliation was essential to the Democrats and also to his own political future. Between 1945 and 1948, Truman went on record as a staunch advocate of civil rights, amplifying the discourses of liberty, justice, and equality that were already emanating, with rising urgency, from black rights organizations.

As Barbara Savage (2002) explains, "Harry Truman's open rhetorical embrace of the central claims of African-American activists carried enormous symbolic power in the national discourse of the politics of race, in which radio played an important role" (249). She notes that Truman's unprecedented June 1947 radio address to the National Association for the Advancement of Colored People (NAACP), broadcast live from the steps of the Lincoln Memorial on the mall in Washington, D.C., was significant not only because it announced an important administrative policy initiative in a speech to the NAACP but also because Truman boldly employed the airwaves to introduce his civil rights agenda to the American people and to the world.

With the federal government positioned to "show the way," as Truman declared in his speech, major corporations slowly responded to the new labor environment, revising their hiring and employment practices either proactively or under criticism from black community leaders. NBC had confronted its own crisis in 1945 when it had been the defendant in a case heard before the newly formed New York State Commission against Discrimination (the first such office in the nation) after a formal complaint had been filed by the NAACP. The NAACP and other organizations remained watchful of the broadcast networks in the areas of representation and employment, gaining credibility among their constituencies for their unbending dedication to the black cause.

Media historian J. Fred MacDonald (1992) positions television's emergence, and with it NBC's corporate retooling, within this vital transitional phase in American society: "The politics of postwar America also encouraged many to envision a bright, bias-free future in television. The new medium emerged in the midst of a liberal, reform-minded period in history" (5). As the Truman administration's race initiatives resonated powerfully throughout the country, national policy began to make inroads into the corporate arena as well. NBC director of personnel Ernest de la Ossa illustrated the extent to which the network had adopted the Truman government's discourse when he outlined NBC's employment policy to a group of network executives and members of the national Negro press in 1950: "Applicants are considered for positions on the basis of their education, experience, and ability. Selection is made in terms of their qualifications without regard to race, color, or creed."[5]

Through the 1940s and into the early 1950s, however, NBC's record of employing blacks was abysmal, and although critics from black civil rights organizations assailed NBC for lagging behind its competitor CBS in its racial policies, it was probably not much worse than many other corporations of similar scale. In 1950, of an estimated two thousand NBC employees at the network's New York headquarters, only thirty-five were black, and of these only one (a recording technician named Ray Hall) was a trained professional; the rest were primarily clerical or custodial hires. When De la Ossa announced that the network had a pressing need for trained technicians, black leaders challenged the network to reserve positions for qualified black applicants.

The personnel director expressed the network's commitment to hiring black employees, adding that in any newly integrated labor environment there was also often a period of what he termed adjustment, during which blacks and whites had to learn to work side by side.[6] By the late 1940s and early 1950s a convergence of forces—encompassing black rights policies, an energized black community, empowered civil rights organizations, the emergence of television, and the desire among NBC and its sponsors to reach an estimated fifteen million black consumers—compelled the network to look outside its ranks for assistance in managing community relations with the nation's black constituency.

Race and NBC's "Blue Pencil" Specialists

With increasing frequency influential organizations such as the NAACP, the National Urban League, and a growing number of locally active groups representing black labor interests (such as the New York–based Negro Actors Guild or, after 1951, the Coordinating Council for Negro Performers) raised methodical and vocal opposition to demeaning portrayals of blacks on radio and television. The Negro press campaigned publicly for fair and equal treatment of blacks in broadcasting; Harlem's newspaper of record, the *New York Amsterdam News*, reported concerns among blacks in June 1948 that the NBC radio program *National Minstrels* might reproduce the racially degrading content associated with traditional minstrel performances.[7] The show's producers (the Gale advertising agency) defended the production and its potential audience appeal, stressing that with an all-black cast and careful script oversight "National Minstrels will be a radio show that they will be proud to associate themselves with." The reporter suggests, however, with no apparent irony, "The network has no fear that Southern stations will refuse to air the show. The minstrel is 'a natural' to please whites." However, Lucky Millinder, the African American host and musical director of *National Minstrels*, was granted special oversight of the program's content as "the person who will check the script or throw out anything he believes to be offensive to Negroes."[8] Millinder's role, referred to unofficially as script policeman, and officially as continuity acceptance, was a designation that acquired considerable importance as NBC honed its policies of racial representation in the early 1950s.[9]

NBC's Continuity Acceptance Radio/Television Department was guided by basic standards of "common sense" and "good taste" that were defined in various network manuals and internal memos.[10] The department's stated mission was "based on the belief that, by maintaining high program standards, we are in a better position to fulfill our responsibility to serve the public, and at the same time— to build a better advertising medium for ethical advertisers."[11] Continuity acceptance executives and employees were charged with the responsibility "to negotiate all changes in script material with either the agency for the sponsor of the program in cases of sponsored programs, or pertinent NBC personnel responsible in cases of sustaining material."[12] The work involved evaluating radio and television scripts prior to production, monitoring broadcasts for general appropriateness, ensuring consistency in the application of content standards, and responding to audience complaints about questionable or offensive performances.

NBC further defined continuity acceptance as "a form of public relations. Its purpose—to create harmony between the advertiser and the radio listener and good will for NBC."[13] Despite this idealistic description, however, continuity acceptance was also a means of protecting the network and its sponsors from audience complaints, organized protests, or lawsuits; advancing the causes of civil rights and improved race relations was secondary. With the black press (including the *New York Amsterdam News*, the *Chicago Defender*, and the *Pittsburgh Courier*) closely scrutinizing the developments in television programming, the networks sought to avoid public reprimands for repeating the worst errors of the radio years.

Referring to himself at one point as a "blue pencil specialist," continuity acceptance manager Stockton Helffrich described his work as simple editing, a process that entailed evaluating programs and, when necessary, removing questionable material—blue penciling—before airtime in order to improve programming for broadcasting "to a family or a home audience."[14] In a basic sense, the blue-pencil duties of the continuity acceptance manager involved censorship, and as Helffrich's reference to family listeners implies, the editing was informed by a set of assumptions about middlebrow sensibilities and an ideological alignment with liberal middle-class values.

There are numerous examples of the scope of the blue-pencil work at NBC with the rise of television. In early 1950, a series of memos circulated between Helffrich and longtime programming employee Edna Turner pertaining to the January 31 broadcast of *The Original Amateur Hour*, hosted by Ted Mack. At issue in this instance was the broadcast performance by a white contestant, a farmer from upstate New York, whose rendition of "Without a Song" included a reference to "darkies."

In his message, Helffrich explained that NBC was taking a hard-line approach to derogatory language and racial epithets and expressed dismay that the song had aired at all, since the production notes for *The Original Amateur Hour* explicitly indicated that the phrase "darky's born" should have been substituted with the more neutral phrase "man's born." The show's production notes (dated January 31, 1950) further give instructions that another song, "Shine," be similarly amended, removing the term *colored boy*. Apprising fellow NBC executive Jack Hein of the situation and reminding him of the network's "policy on racial considerations," Helffrich states, "[Y]ou probably don't know that around epithets descriptive of various races and creeds we have had considerable to-do. We carefully delete words like 'mick' or 'kike' or 'coon.'"[15]

In another example of the responsibilities of NBC's continuity acceptance manager, Helffrich received several letters and memos following Lena Horne's February 25, 1951, appearance on the network's broadcast of the *Colgate Comedy Hour* with host Eddie Cantor. Horne was famous for her energetic performances and for her beauty, making her an ideal candidate for television's unique visual demands. Attesting to this, the *New York Amsterdam News* had reported roughly a month earlier that Horne was scheduled to make her "teevee debut as guest hostess" alongside Sid Caesar and Imogene Coca on NBC's broadcast of *Your Show of Shows*.[16]

Despite a persistent "willingness to sing and dance in blackface" (Pondillo 2005, 107), Eddie Cantor was a staunch supporter of civil rights and was among a handful of early television hosts (including Steve Allen, Arthur Godfrey, Dennis James, Ted Mack, and Ed Sullivan) with national network contracts who vocally defended the inclusion of black artists on their shows. The entertainment trade journal *Variety* noted that Horne's guest turn on *Colgate Comedy Hour* would coincide with Brotherhood Week and that, "besides singing, Miss Horne will join Cantor in a pitch on racial and religious understanding."[17] Despite this socially progressive element to the broadcast, Horne's act was criticized, not only for the bold "U-shaped" plunge of her gown's décolletage (said to surpass even that of talk show host Faye Emerson, whose attire generated a moral panic and a public relations crisis at CBS in this same period), but also for the character of the performance itself.

According to the assistant general manager at Philadelphia station WPTZ-TV, "[H]er action and her style of delivery made her performance border dangerously on the obscene."[18] This perspective strays perilously close to a racialized interpretation of Horne's performance, raising stereotypes of the oversexualized body of the black female. A further letter, from a North Carolina attorney, lightly chided the network for broadcasting Horne's "immodest display" (which he described as an "outrageous affrontery [sic]," unsuitable for his home) while directing his real indignation to a distinctly racial issue: "[T]his Horne woman may be a good singer but if I am not misinformed she is a woman that married a white man and we still have a large number of states that make such a marriage a crime."[19]

Assessing the broadcast after receiving 183 letters of complaint (most associated with a Pennsylvania-based correspondence "crusade") and letters from several more regional station managers who had been forced to contend with viewer outrage, Helffrich referred NBC staff once again to the network's continuity acceptance criteria and the need to apply standards consistently. He explained that the responsibility was ultimately the show director's, noting that in this case aesthetic precautions should have been more carefully observed: "I understand now that the daring of the gown, and the excessive cleavage, were noted at the dress [rehearsal]. Some of the shadows accenting Miss Horne's interesting bosom were eliminated by increased lighting, but on the actual show said higher lighting wasn't used *and* Miss Horne added a bit more oomph to her rendition than used at the dress."[20]

As this example of a relatively minor continuity crisis indicates, television created an entirely new set of aesthetic and performance issues to contend with. Yet in maintaining professional standards the entire broadcasting industry was also obligated to alter or redesign content and programming to accommodate the political and cultural transitions in postwar America, including those pertaining to race. In this sense, NBC sought to maintain its solid standing as a well-intentioned and socially responsible institution even as it strove to engage new audiences, expand its profits, and reinforce its overall financial status.

Joseph V. Baker: NBC's Eyes and Ears in the Black Community

Stockton Helffrich conceded in 1950 that in its racial policy and content control NBC was not the industry leader, trailing rival network CBS in the area of race relations: "As the public criticism mounted, including some poor publicity for NBC in articles blasting at us, our Management finally decided that NBC would follow CBS precedent by deleting objectionable terminology from classical lyrics and generally recognize constructively the resentment felt against us."[21] As was its practice in the technical and programming realms, NBC sought to outperform its industry competitors by revising its race policies and embarking on a fresh initiative with several key objectives: to ameliorate the negative effects of racial discrimination by opening the radio and TV airwaves to black entertainers; to ensure that potential black consumers and audiences were not alienated from the network; to garner goodwill and win concessions from the national black leadership; and to establish closer working relations with the nation's black communities. To achieve its goals, NBC hired Joseph V. Baker, an African American public relations expert from Philadelphia, for his assistance in navigating the potential pitfalls of representing blacks in radio and television and ensuring greater interaction between NBC's executives and America's increasingly influential black leaders.

Baker was crucial to the network's development of a racial policy in the years immediately preceding the civil rights movement. Regarded among NBC's executives as an effective and savvy professional with an apparent capacity to navigate elite executive boardrooms and local political backrooms with equal ease, Baker rapidly emerged as a gatekeeper at NBC, facilitating access to the network among the black press while functioning as NBC's eyes and ears within the black community. According to Barbara C. Harris (whom Baker hired for an entry-level position in 1949, and whom I interviewed in 2005),[22] in the early to mid-1950s the Joseph V. Baker and Associates agency consisted of about four account executives and another five or six support staff. Despite the agency's small size, however, Baker had signed contracts with some of the titans of U.S. industry, including the DuPont Corporation, U.S. Steel, American Tobacco, the Association of American Railroads, and the Hamilton Watch Company. Several of the agency's corporate clients were also early sponsors of television programs, an interesting overlap of interests and a good example of the dynamic interplay between public relations firms, advertising agencies, corporate sponsors, and the broadcast networks that had intensified in the immediate postwar period. When Baker was first contacted to work with NBC in 1950, the agency was already under contract with NBC's parent company, RCA.

As Harris explains, "[W]e counseled corporations at the point of their approach to the black community. That was our key assignment; that's what we did." But another reason NBC hired Baker was the network's urgent desire to tap into black America's consumer clout. In 1949 the advertising trade paper *Sponsor* featured a much-cited study on "the forgotten 15,000,000," touting the consumer power of African American radio listeners who collectively wielded an estimated annual spending capacity of ten billion dollars. As *Sponsor* reported, "[T]hough there are social segregation, economic and political barriers, civic and fraternal restrictions, there are nevertheless no such things as 'segregated ears'."[23] Suggesting ways to appeal to black consumers, *Sponsor* warned that black radio audiences were often critical of blacks' being cast in subservient domestic roles and stated that "Negroes, more perhaps than most minority groups, are considerably touchy about the elements relating to the Negro race in advertising copy directed to them particularly."[24]

The first explicit evidence of Baker's arrangement with NBC is found in a June 5, 1950, letter addressed to network executive Sidney Eiges, vice president of continuity acceptance. Here, Baker defines his new role with NBC as "Special Counsel for National Broadcasting," a designation that he implies is somewhat of a misnomer since the agency will be working with various media, especially the "Negro press." Baker itemizes his main responsibilities with NBC within four main categories:

1. To be totally responsible for NBC Press Relations as they affect approximately 100 Negro newspapers and magazines;

2. Engineer and execute projects designed to close the gap between NBC and the Negro Community;

3. Counsel Program as regards what might be done and what should be avoided in order to constructively handle the sensitive nerve-ends of 14,000,000 potential listeners whose prior conditioning makes them unresponsive to ordinary approaches;

4. Be "on call" to Personnel for counsel relative to emergency situations which will inevitably arise and also as regards the possible addition of Negro employees when and if their hiring looms.[25]

Douglas Battema (2002) interprets Baker's reference to "prior conditioning" of the black population as an allusion to their latent "distrust of white institutions and technology that did not operate in their own interest" and suggests that Baker's real challenge was to help NBC "make its presence felt, to ensure that its ideological message prevailed over the concerns, reservations, and hesitations of African-Americans" (18).

In November 1950, Baker requested that in his new role he be granted access to several of the network's vice presidents, including monthly meetings with programming and continuity acceptance heads Charles Barry, Sidney Eiges, Stockton Helffrich, and Ernest de la Ossa of the Personnel Department.[26] This proximate interaction with the network's executive tier reinforced Baker's influence at NBC and concentrated his power among the black press. In Baker's view, strengthening ties with the "Negro community" was essential if NBC truly wanted to correct past wrongs and proactively chart the future course concerning hiring practices and programming. It was his further belief that by doing so NBC might gain considerable capital among blacks, dispelling the lingering impression that CBS was both more sensitive to black interests and more assertive in hiring blacks in a variety of roles. With NBC's public relations staff, Baker strategically placed himself in the middle, devising a strategy to forge and maintain "cordial relations with the national Negro community."[27] Correspondence among NBC executives reveals Baker's central role in helping NBC to convey network policies and various promotional or public relations information to the African American community, improving NBC's race relations through more frequent and intimate communication with black-owned newspapers across the country. In one corporate initiative, Baker was enlisted as the publisher of the *RCA Baton,* a monthly newsletter on TV and radio entertainment. Introduced in 1950, the *Baton* was published in Philadelphia by the Baker agency "on behalf of artists, products, and services of the Radio Corporation of America." The newsletter served as a public relations organ for the RCA/NBC corporate family, emphasizing profiles of and achievements among black technicians, performers, and other employees, including disk jockeys, camera operators, and stenographers.

The *Baton* also published articles and programming updates of interest to network listeners and viewers, including descriptions of radio and television broadcasts that either included black performers or in some way encompassed thematic content of perceived relevance to blacks. In addition, the publication promoted new RCA technologies and consumer items, providing potential black consumers with product information and pricing. Baker regarded the *Baton* as a dual-purpose medium, engaging RCA and NBC employees while also functioning as a means to communicate the corporate stance on race issues—what he referred to as "the 'big policy' in the RCA Family"[28]—to leaders of the nation's black community and the press.

Baker embarked on his new duties with NBC on a grand scale by organizing a series of "roundtables" bringing NBC executives together with representatives of America's black press in New York, Chicago, and Los Angeles. At these sessions, Baker played a prominent and multifaceted role as a facilitator, gatekeeper, and liaison between the executives and the journalists, whose lines of professional access to broadcast executives were often severely restricted by systemic and systematic racial discrimination.

The first of the National Broadcasting Company and the Negro National Community roundtable sessions met in New York on October 25, 1950, and set the tone for future gatherings. The proceedings featured a Who's Who of the northeastern Negro press as well as several leaders of progressive black organizations, including the National Urban League. Sidney Eiges outlined NBC's mission:

> We feel a keen lack of contact with you very people in the room here and with the Negro press or the colored press. It seems to us and it does not seem to us—it is true— that we hear from you only in cases of crisis . . . and it seems that today has been the only time when we have contact with you. And we feel very remiss on our part. . . . That is one of the purposes that we have engaged Joe Baker to help us, and this is one of the first steps we have taken to sort of break the ice and get to know you better.[29]

The roundtable sessions were designed to address two central concerns: hiring practices at NBC and the network's portrayals of black characters. NBC executives candidly admitted that they could do more to ensure that blacks were hired in technical and production departments, noting that with sufficient access to educational programs blacks would eventually acquire the necessary credentials and experience to rise in the industry. As Barbara Harris recounts, the Baker agency's work "resulted in a number of black people being hired by corporations in professional capacities. A number of companies hired black professionals as a result of our counseling their personnel and industrial relations officers." RCA and NBC recruited prospective engineers among graduating students at black colleges, fulfilling Sidney Eiges's promise to increase the number of blacks working at the network while also ensuring that blacks already employed with NBC were identified for internal promotion whenever suitable.

Members of the black press were also eager to learn how the network vetted program scripts and the company's logic in responding to perceived slights against black characters, raising the issue of "blue pencil" editing. In this regard, Stockton Helffrich explained how Joe Baker's participation was a considerable boon to the Continuity Acceptance Department: "We tried to do what we think is right, but we don't always know how, and it has been quite a help to us to have someone to refer the so-called borderline problems to."[30] Indeed, extant NBC documents reveal that Baker frequently assessed program scripts and song lyrics for "sensitivity," basing his decisions on what he thought black audiences would find permissible.

In one case Baker was asked to review a script that included a performance of "Song of the South" with racially insensitive lyrics, and another time he evaluated a proposal to revive the Eugene O'Neill play *The Emperor Jones*.[31] Baker did not rely merely on his own subjective assumptions about suitability but consulted with what he described as "a representative segment of the Negro Press." As he wrote in his verdict on the O'Neill play that he forwarded to the network executives: "I should like you to know that I am not opposing these presentations because I think it is the thing to do. Rather, I am trying to set in focus the actual situation as it is likely to be reviewed by the great majority of Negroes. . . . [T]here was, in the judgment of the persons to whom I talked, the ready concession that, artistically, 'The Emperor Jones' has value. However, that could also be true of 'The Birth of a Nation,' which Negroes still despise and oppose."[32]

According to Harris, the Baker agency "had no direct impact on programming *per se* but . . . [w]e were able to influence the thinking of the people who were responsible for programming and to get them to make the kinds of changes that would get black people to realize that the network was sensitive to their interests." Baker alleviated the stress among NBC's white continuity acceptance managers who had little experience with or insight into black cultural sensibilities. As William Brooks, vice president in charge of public relations, commented in 1951: "Joe Baker and his organization have been a great help in this continuity acceptance field because a lot of times in the past we haven't known where to go to get the information to guide us. And by referring it to Joe and getting the proper organizations, we have been put in the groove so that we have avoided a lot of things that might have happened prior to having this organization."[33] Brooks elaborated on Baker's involvement, at one point half-jokingly distancing himself and NBC's executives from the decision-making process and effectively placing responsibility firmly in Baker's corner: "We are working on these lyrics, and we have had borderline cases—and I am very glad that we have Joe Baker because we can put a lot of these things in his lap now and he has to find out. And if anybody questions us, then we say that Mr. Baker advised us along this line. . . . But we are trying to find out for ourselves."[34]

Baker also proved helpful in another capacity, assisting NBC executives in their formulation of responses to letters of complaint about programming issues, often from black viewers who felt slighted or offended by NBC's programming decisions. On one occasion, however, the request for Baker's help followed a searing letter from a white Memphis, Tennessee, television viewer who voiced his support for

Georgia Governor Herman Talmadge's infamous 1952 pronouncement against "broadcast miscegenation," or the mixing of races on television shows.[35] The correspondence excoriated NBC for portraying blacks and whites together in its various broadcasts:

> Down here in Memphis, Tenn., we are limited to your outlet. We can't turn to Columbia or American for a change of programme and have to take what you offer. Can't we have one program without a bunch of niggers? I like negroes and have employed as many of them as most people but I do not care to have them in my home, as guest and to be a participant with *white* people. I really think it is insulting to try and stuff the negroes down our throat in order to commerciaise [*sic*] your soap or some other product. . . . We sure will be glad when we can get Columbia or any other programme that isn't of a *nigger* origin![36]

Helffrich turned to Joe Baker for help in crafting the network's response to the rant, admitting his incapacity to properly address the issues raised by the irate viewer: "Will Joe Baker . . . let us know of phrasing he thinks might be good. Joe has after all lived with and dealt with the problem for many more years than I have and I defer to his seniority."[37]

Among Baker's most important and lasting contributions at NBC was his collaboration with NBC executives in the formation of the network's Integration without Identification policy. Harris explains, "This was developed for integrating black people into regular television shows in roles [in] which they might be found in everyday life," including mailman, teacher, parole officer, and other occupations. The intent was "to move beyond the roles of domestic service and to quietly integrate people into the cast without calling undue attention to it." This policy was followed up by Baker's proposals to introduce black directors and playwrights to the network and to consider programming possibilities for all-black casts (an option that tended to privilege song-and-dance variety shows and that typically did not rile audiences who subscribed to the Talmadge doctrine).

Referring explicitly to the Integration without Identification policy in a memo sent to Charles Barry, Stockton Helffrich describes his skepticism about a proposal to produce an all-Negro broadcast called *The Hominy House* that was, in his estimation, not "right for NBC at all" due to stereotypical "jive terms" and "lines written in consciously bad English." In a testament to Baker's influence, Helffrich states, "[T]he rule of thumb NBC is following under the aegis of Joseph Baker favors Negro 'integration without identification.' That doesn't exist here in my opinion."[38] By 1953, the entertainment trade magazine *Variety* trumpeted NBC's successes with its racial policy, reporting that the "'talent has no color' projects had boosted the number of black performances to 1,540 on radio and 913 television appearances."[39] A production of *Philco TV Playhouse* was also positively cited for its casting of a young Sidney Poitier "in a role of a parole officer which in no way identified the role as being played by a Negro."[40] NBC's racial policy successes stood in sharp contrast to the public relations fiasco experienced between 1951 and 1953 at rival network CBS, where the airing of the televised version of *Amos 'n' Andy* created "two years of bad press and harmful boycotts" (Doherty 2003, 80).

In another NBC coup, baseball star and civil rights icon Jackie Robinson was hired to lead the WNBC-WNBT Music Foundation as the director of community activities at the new nonprofit agency. With funds administered by NBC, the foundation's stated goals were to "provide record players and record libraries to all organizations that require them," concentrating on facilities serving "the poor, the elderly, or the infirm."[41] NBC, it seemed, was turning the corner, having redefined its commitments to race relations and improving black representation over the air and in the workplace.

In mid-1953, however, *New York Amsterdam News* columnist Alvin Webb reported that tense "personal issues" had developed between Baker, whom he referred to indirectly as "the Philadelphia p.r. man," and members of the black press, who increasingly believed that Baker had "sold them out to NBC." As Webb explained, Baker's critics were alleging that he had "set up a segregation press conference, and, at the same time, muffled the voices of Negro writers, a vicious and hypocritical situation." Webb also targeted NBC executives, implying that they had abandoned Baker as his opponents had rallied against him, leaving him to deal with the black press on his own and distancing themselves from the growing controversy.[42] Baker was also under attack from black arts groups and civil rights organizations that demanded "plums with the crumbs," declaring that NBC could do still more for black actors seeking access to radio and television.[43] Baker's effectiveness as a gatekeeper to the network was waning as his influence and goodwill with the black community eroded, leading some organizations to attempt to circumvent him and deal directly with the network brass.

Webb continued his critique of Baker and NBC in August 1953, reporting that the Council of Negro Performers had been taken to task by others in the black community for appointing "an NBC representative" to its board of governors, hinting at Baker's identity, and noting that "it is a well-known fact that the new board member has frequently been delegated by his employers to carry out the duties of an appeaser." Webb clearly held Baker in disdain, dismissing his tactics at NBC as insufficient in the struggle for racial equality in broadcasting. Adopting a contrary agenda, Webb promoted "aggressiveness and militancy rather than the passive resistance method" in order to win "full integration of the Negro performer and artist."[44]

Wearied by the personal attacks and by the lack of network support, Baker officially severed his professional relations with the network in the summer of 1954, explaining to NBC president Sylvester "Pat" Weaver that the public relations firm had no "desire on our part to have our relationship renewed." Though Baker was clearly adamant in his decision not to return to NBC, he expressed satisfaction with his accomplishments over the previous several years, specifically mentioning NBC's Integration without Identification policy as a point of pride.[45]

FIG. **8** Nat King Cole on stage with Betty Hutton on the *Nat King Cole Show*, December 3, 1957. (Library of American Broadcasting)

Conclusion

Joseph Baker's departure from NBC coincided almost precisely with the birth of the civil rights movement, overlapping as well with the monumental U.S. Supreme Court decision *Brown v. Board of Education* in May 1954. During this period, columnist Alvin Webb's appeal for more aggressive methods of resistance was realized as black civil rights activism emerged in multiple forms and more direct protest tactics evolved. Baker's system of "appeasement," it seems, was out of tune with the groundswell of rebellion sweeping the nation. Yet through its relationship with Joseph V. Baker and Associates NBC was undoubtedly better prepared to address the legitimate concerns and criticisms of the nation's black community as the country continued to struggle through its racial crisis. In his tenure as consultant to the network, Baker helped to transform NBC's corporate culture, ushering in a new era of awareness and social responsibility at the network.

As this narrative illustrates, from its inception NBC was conscious of the importance of racial representation, and it sought to mitigate the negative effects of objectionable and racially insensitive programming or content. The work did not end in 1954, however, and the network continued its attempts to advance black entertainers and other professionals within its ranks. In November 1956, Nat King Cole's program premiered with much initial hype but without a sponsor. The show was continually in a financial crisis, but NBC provided extensive support (underwriting it through most of its duration) and labored to establish sustaining sponsorship. The efforts proved fruitless, however, and the show was dropped in December 1957. Though frustrated and fatigued by the ordeal, Cole expressed his gratitude to NBC: "The network supported this show from the beginning. . . . From Mr. Sarnoff on down, they tried to sell it to agencies. They could have dropped it after thirteen weeks. . . . Madison Avenue is afraid of the dark" (Watson 1998, 33). This, too, might be read as an outcome of a thirty-year process and a turning point, not only in America's race relations, but also in the evolution of NBC's content and programming.

I offer very special thanks to Bishop Barbara C. Harris for sharing her experiences of working at the Joseph V. Baker and Associates agency. I am also indebted to Douglas Battema and Elena Razlogova for sharing material based on their excellent research and to Michele Hilmes for her astute suggestions. This chapter benefited from the funding support of the National Endowment for the Humanities.

Notes

Abbreviations

NBC/WHS   National Broadcasting Company Archives, Wisconsin Historical Society

1. Mrs. Charles F. Reid to Radio Corporation of America, March 26, 1926, NBC/WHS.
2. John F. Royal to Bertha Brainard, December 12, 1932, NBC/WHS.
3. John F. Royal to Janet MacRorie, May 1935, NBC/WHS.

4. NBC to employees, December 8, 1938, NBC/WHS.

5. Ernest de la Ossa, comments in "The National Broadcasting Company and the Negro National Community: A Roundtable, Oct. 25, New York," 1950, transcript, NBC/WHS.

6. Ibid.

7. *National Minstrels* featured host Lucky Millinder leading his fifteen-piece orchestra as well as Annisteen Allep, the "blues singer and comedian" Bull Moose Jackson, and the "balladeer" Paul Brecker.

8. S. W. Garlington, "Radio Row: Producers Assure Public 'Minstrels' Will Be Okay," *New York Amsterdam News*, June 5, 1948, 14.

9. The minstrel show format was also relatively common on early television, with network broadcasts occasionally featuring minstrel vignettes (such as the October 8, 1950, and October 28, 1951, CBS broadcasts of the *Fred Waring Show*) and regional programs in the South and West also maintaining the tradition. Among these were the 1948 broadcast of *Mississippi Minstrels* on KTSL-TV in Hollywood, California, and *McMahon's Minstrels* in 1950 and *Tiny Stowe's All Star Minstrels* in 1951, both on Los Angeles station KTTV.

10. For a detailed account of NBC's Continuity Acceptance Radio/Television Department and its manager, Stockton Helffrich, see Pondillo (2005).

11. NBC, *NBC and You: Operations and Employee Relations Policies Manual* (New York: NBC, 1948), 31, NBC/WHS.

12. Ibid.

13. Ibid.

14. Stockton Helffrich, comments in "The National Broadcasting Company and the Negro National Community: A Roundtable."

15. Stockton Helffrich to Jack Hein, February 3, 1950, NBC/WHS.

16. S. W. Garlington, "The Amusement Row," *New York Amsterdam News*, January 20, 1951, 20.

17. "Lena on Cantor's TV," *Variety*, February 21, 1951, 29.

18. Rolland V. Tooke to Sheldon B. Hickox Jr., February 26, 1951, NBC/WHS.

19. Harry Brown to NBC, February 26, 1951, NBC/WHS.

20. Stockton Helffrich to William F. Brooks, March 2, 1951, NBC/WHS.

21. Stockton Helffrich to Jack Hein, February 3, 1950, NBC/WHS.

22. Barbara C. Harris was hired by Joseph Baker in 1949, at the age of nineteen. She became president of Joseph V. Baker and Associates in 1958, a position she held until 1968.

23. "The Forgotten 15,000,000," *Sponsor*, October 10, 1949, 25.

24. Ibid., 54. A second installment of the story appeared in *Sponsor* two weeks afterward, providing case studies of effective advertising and programming considerations in black consumer markets. Then, three years later, when television had expanded substantially as a major broadcast medium, *Sponsor* revisited the topic, describing steady increases in black household income and an overall rise in national economic buying power in the intervening period. The later *Sponsor* article provides figures indicating that, despite generally lower income levels than the white average, television sales among black consumers were robust, and the new medium was emerging rapidly as a viable advertising outlet for reaching black audiences. "The Forgotten 15,000,000 . . . Three Years Later," *Sponsor*, October 10, 1952.

25. Joseph Baker to Sidney Eiges, June 5, 1950, NBC/WHS.

26. Joseph Baker, "Agenda for Discussion (NBC Conference)," n.d., ca. 1950, NBC/WHS.

27. Sidney Eiges to Samuel Chotzinoff, June 14, 1951.

28. Baker, "Agenda for Discussion."

29. Sidney Eiges, comments in "The National Broadcasting Company and the Negro National Community: A Roundtable."

30. Stockton Helffrich to Jack Hein, February 3, 1950.

31. The script by playwright Eugene O'Neill is written in stereotyped black vernacular, replete with multiple references to "niggers."

32. Joseph Baker to William F. Brooks, November 24, 1950, NBC/WHS.

33. William Brooks, "Interracial Relations," NBC internal document, January 16, 1951, NBC/WHS.

34. Ibid.

35. "Webs Brush off Talmadge Beef on Negro Talent," *Variety*, January 9, 1952.

36. Ben Warfield to NBC, January 1952.

37. Stockton Helffrich to Anita Barnard, January 30, 1952, NBC/WHS.

38. Stockton Helffrich to Charles Barry, November 12, 1951, NBC/WHS.

39. "NBC's 'Talent Has No Color' Projects," *Variety*, March 18, 1953, 1. NBC's curious evaluating system for black performances counted the number of blacks on air at any given moment. Thus, if the Duke Ellington Orchestra, with twenty-six members, appeared on radio seventeen times, as they did in 1952, the network claimed 442 blacks on the air. The cynical view invites speculation that if the network booked more frequent choir or orchestra appearances they could therefore quickly improve their figures.

40. Ibid., 3.

41. "Jackie Robinson to Direct New Community Project," *NBC Chimes*, January 1953, 10.

42. Alvin Webb, "Footlights and Sidelights," New York Amsterdam News, July 18, 1953, 24.

43. "Negro Acts Appeal to Webs for 'Plums for Crumbs,'" *Variety*, January 28, 1953, 1.

44. Alvin Webb, "Militant Action Urged in TV Fight," New York Amsterdam News, August 8, 1953.

45. Joseph Baker to Sylvester Weaver, July 13, 1954, and Joseph Baker to Sidney Eiges, July 13, 1954, both in NBC/WHS.

8

NBC, J. Walter Thompson, and the Struggle for Control of Television Programming, 1946–58

MIKE MASHON

Television is a profit-maximizing set of entities, an industry whose success is largely measured by its ability to deliver viewers to advertisers. This puts the sponsor at the center of program strategies. Thus we must acknowledge the complex relationship between networks and advertisers, two industries whose differing responsibilities and sometimes conflicting needs produce the programming. Never was that set of determinants more in flux than in the period between 1946 and 1958. Among the many changes within the television industry during this time, none was more dramatic, or had more lasting consequences, than the transition in sponsorship trends. In 1946 television inherited an industrial structure from radio that relied on advertiser-produced programming; by 1958 sponsors were buying commercial spots on shows owned or licensed by the networks.

At the center of this evolution were two businesses — the National Broadcasting Company and the J. Walter Thompson advertising agency — whose histories are inextricably entwined. Their corporate behavior, within the broadcasting industry as well as toward each other, reflects the enormous changes that took place in television during the period. In particular, their early collaboration on two programs, *Hour Glass* and the *Kraft Television Theatre (KTT)*, illustrates the problems inherent in the shifting relationship between sponsors and networks that would eventually lead to the end of the sponsor-dominated system of broadcast production that had prevailed in radio since the 1930s.

Early Developments in Television

Both NBC and CBS devoted much effort and expense to their experiments with television during the 1930s, especially NBC, since it served as a laboratory for parent company RCA's manufacturing work. Several advertising agencies also began preparing for the new era, especially Thompson, where the Radio Department assumed responsibility for the company's ventures in television. The plans for NBC-TV proceeded along two tracks: creation of the network, including five owned-and-operated (O&O) stations in New York, Washington, D.C., Chicago, Cleveland, and Los Angeles, and improvements in the amount and quality of network programming.

NBC executives initially envisioned that network production would be locally based: that is, programs would originate from the affiliate station and be sent to other stations in the chain, but they would be sponsored by a different local advertiser in each city. The fear was that no one sponsor would be willing to pay for the entire network, at least until television production techniques and costs had stabilized. However, by early 1946 several internal studies indicated that local advertisers were unwilling to support high-cost programming, so landing national advertisers was made a top priority. Further, concentration of production in New York, Chicago, and Los Angeles—the three principal entertainment centers in the United States, and also, not coincidentally, the locus of advertising agency power—made network, not local, production more economically feasible.[1]

The point of producing programs was, of course, to make the network an attractive buy for national advertisers. However, most large companies were apprehensive about television. The unknown costs of the new medium constituted the greatest element of uncertainty. Television was considered a risky and potentially unprofitable investment until its saturation level increased. With the bare bones of a network on the East Coast and individual stations operating in Chicago and Los Angeles, the medium was available only to a fraction of the nation, with the number of actual viewers being an even smaller percentage.[2]

NBC was compelled to use loss leader tactics as a way of overcoming advertiser reluctance to enter unfamiliar territory. The network hoped to offer complete in-house packages (programs put together by the network itself and sold to advertisers) priced at 15 percent below cost and, for those sponsors who furnished their own shows, deep reductions in both time and facilities charges. Despite the blandishments of discounts and time franchises (a classic "get in on the ground floor" appeal), in 1947—the year that WNBT in New York went to seven-days-a-week programming—there were only fourteen advertisers on the network, sponsoring less than half of NBC's total television broadcast hours. Still, the network was obliged to provide a substantial program service in order to promote the buying of TV sets and, in turn, to attract paying customers, even if that meant the majority of the schedule would initially be unsponsored.[3]

Placing a show on the schedule was a cumbersome process, whether the show was an in-house or outside package. No single individual was responsible for overseeing shows brought to the network by potential sponsors, advertising agencies, or independent producers. The result was chaos. NBC's Sales Department (whose bailiwick was ostensibly the sale of network time) occasionally mediated negotiations between advertisers looking for a program and producers or agencies seeking sponsors for their shows. If the groups reached agreement, the department considered its participation a success, and a segment of the schedule was filled. The Sales Department was not, however, concerned with the quality of programming provided by NBC, only with fitting together package, sponsor, and time slot. NBC executives feared there was no mechanism by which the network could keep truly awful shows off the schedule. To rectify this situation, program manager Ted Mills suggested appointing a program liaison "whose job is that of supplying NBC audiences with quality, the one person to whom program quality—and not the easiest, most available program—is the total emphasis. . . . We 'pioneers' should do everything we can to start television off at the highest level possible, and for my dough, the biggest threat to high standards is from the agencies in its early years."[4]

While it would take several months for NBC to act on Mills's recommendations for program quality control, his denigration of advertisers reflected a deep corporate skepticism about the ability of agencies to deliver distinctive programming. Few executives had ever seriously suggested that television would develop as anything other than a commercial medium, but there was considerable sentiment at NBC that program creation and execution would best be left to the network. However, the personnel demands and expense of television production made it impossible for any network to produce all its programming in house. Thus, as in radio, agencies assumed a major role in the initial evolution of the television schedule.

Hour Glass

J. Walter Thompson, however, never vacillated over the new medium. Thompson's first postwar moves into television were modest: purchasing "time signals" (ten-second spots giving the current time) for Elgin and placing travelogues for Pan Am on WNBT in 1945. Their first serious programming attempt came in May 1946 with *Hour Glass*, a variety show sponsored by Standard Brands for their Chase & Sanborn and Tenderleaf Tea lines.

Hour Glass is a seminal, almost completely forgotten program in early television, yet one whose production history exemplifies the issues faced by networks, sponsors, and agencies. It was Standard Brands advertising director Donovan B. Stetler who approached the agency about getting the company into television, mainly with the intent of establishing a time franchise. Sponsor and agency took several months to decide on the show's format, eventually choosing variety for two reasons: it allowed for the network and agency to experiment with other forms (comedy sketches, musical numbers, playlets, and the like); and Thompson and Standard Brands had previously collaborated on the successful radio variety show *Chase & Sanborn Hour*.[5]

The show represented a steep learning curve for Thompson, Standard Brands, and NBC. The lines of responsibility were not completely defined in these early years, and the nine-month run of *Hour Glass* was punctuated by frequent squabbling among the principals. Each show was assembled by seven Thompson employees, led by radio producers Edmund Rice and Harry Hermann. They worked as a tag team, each one putting together a show over two weeks in a frenzy of production. The first week would be spent writing the script and booking acts through Thompson's Talent Department. The script was finalized by week's end, when NBC would be informed of scenery needs. Monday was the first cast rehearsal at the agency offices, and the first camera run-through at WNBT's studios came on Wednesday. There would be one more rehearsal on Thursday afternoon before airtime at 8:00 p.m.[6]

The format of the show was familiar to *Chase & Sanborn Hour* listeners, which was precisely the way John Reber, the powerful head of all broadcast programming at Thompson, wanted it. In carrying over Thompson's radio strategy into television, Reber accentuated star power as the means of drawing the largest audience (Hilmes 1997). Various guests such as Bert Lahr and Jerry Colonna hosted the first several shows, but later the emcee spot was filled by actress Helen Parrish, who predates Milton Berle as television's first home-grown star. *Hour Glass* featured different performers every week, including Peggy Lee and—in one of the first examples of a top radio star appearing on network television—Edgar Bergen and Charlie McCarthy in November 1946. The program also showcased filmed segments produced by Thompson's Motion Picture Department; these ranged from ads to short travelogues. Every episode also included a ten-minute drama (usually adapted by Ed Rice), which proved to be one of the more popular portions of the show.[7]

Rice and Hermann made several alterations to the show (after receiving Reber's blessing): establishing Helen Parrish as the permanent hostess in order to maintain a sense of continuity, restricting the amount of time per act to keep the show moving at a brisk clip, and integrating pitches for Standard Brands products throughout the hour. The actual length of spots varied dramatically during the show's run. Initially the live commercials were more than three minutes long, while filmed spots were as long as five. After a few months viewer response (tabulated by the agency's Research Department) indicated that ads should be held to no more than two minutes.[8]

It must have been the curiosity factor that prompted some stars to appear on the show because they certainly were not paid much money. *Hour Glass* had a talent budget of only $350 a week, hardly more than scale for a handful of performers. Still, Standard Brands put an estimated $200,000 into the program's nine-month run, by far the largest amount ever devoted to a sponsored show at that time. Thompson paid all production staff salaries plus $150 an hour (about $1,200 a week) for rehearsal time at WNBT.[9]

Although Thompson and Standard Brands representatives occasionally disagreed on the quality of individual episodes, their association was placid compared to the constant sniping that was the hallmark of the agency's relationship with NBC. It started with Thompson objecting to the small studio space and escalated when the network insisted that an NBC director manage the show from live rehearsals through actual broadcast. From NBC's perspective it was a reasonable request; they were providing airtime and studio space at such a deep discount that they lost money on the show (the usual time charge for Studio 3-H was $750 an hour, $600 more than Thompson was billed), and they considered all agency personnel to be untutored in the expensive ways of television. The network was similarly displeased that Thompson refused to clear its commercials with NBC before airtime.[10]

Reber, characteristically, saw this as an unjustifiable encroachment on Thompson's responsibility to the client. He was especially incensed that neither Rice nor Hermann was allowed to transmit instructions directly to NBC personnel but rather had to ask the network director to relay information. Although much of NBC policy regarding studio work was based on regulations prohibiting nonunion personnel from supervising union members, Reber interpreted NBC's actions as a preemptive move for creative control of the show.[11]

In February 1947, Standard Brands canceled *Hour Glass*. They were pleased with the show's performance in terms of beverage sales and overall quality, but they were leery about continuing to pour money into a program that did not reach a large number of households (it is unclear if the show was broadcast anywhere other than NBC's interconnected stations in New York and Philadelphia). The strain between NBC and Thompson played a role as well. This struggle for control was apparently not an isolated example in the industry. Referring to the *Hour Glass* cancellation, an editorial in *Televiser* noted that "stations who have set sights on retaining studio control of programs are forcing a 'war of control' by the attitudes of working staff who reflect management, according to these same agency men. Many agency men have complained that they were told to go 'sit in the client's booth' while the station aired the sponsor's show." Still, *Hour Glass* did provide Thompson with a blueprint for the agency's most celebrated production, *Kraft Television Theatre*.[12]

Kraft Television Theatre

The hour-long *Kraft Television Theatre* drama on NBC proved to be one of the most durable and honored programs of the golden age, staying on the air until 1958. When Kraft executives approached their Thompson representatives in late 1946 about putting together a plan for television, John Reber and his colleagues, having achieved some measure of satisfaction with the playlet segment of *Hour Glass*, suggested a longer dramatic format. This dovetailed nicely with Kraft's overall marketing strategy in the late 1940s, which stressed the concept of "gracious living," an appeal to middle-class, suburban, family values. *KTT* was to feature quietly paced, intimate dramas; as one Kraft representative put it, the show would be a "respectful guest in America's living rooms."[13]

Kraft Television Theatre premiered on May 7, 1947, with a drama called "Double Door," starring John Baragrey and directed by NBC staff director Fred Coe. As had been standard practice in the radio era and would continue to be in television, Thompson rented studio space from NBC at the network's Rockefeller Center headquarters. Costwise, it was a modest production; the "time and talent" costs were only $3,000, of which $1,200 went for talent.[14]

The time charge involved not only the use of NBC's facilities but also the transmission charges for use of the coaxial lines that connected the six cities along the network. Although *KTT* quickly established itself as a critical favorite, in Kraft's estimation the show was only as useful as its ability to move product. In this it succeeded beyond everyone's greatest expectations. Sales of advertised products rose dramatically in television cities and, even more importantly, a poll conducted by *Television* magazine in November 1947 showed that *KTT* had the highest sponsor identification of any show on television.

Kraft and Thompson prided themselves on keeping costs at a minimum in the early years of *KTT*. The dramatic emphasis was on warm and engaging family fare ("realism with a modest moral," as one executive put it) solicited from young playwrights in New York; all performers were selected by Thompson's Casting Department. Although the show was almost entirely an agency product (Thompson employees Stanley Quinn and Maury Holland were the producer/directors, Ed Rice was the Kraft liaison), NBC took a great interest in the program's operation—too much, in fact, for John Reber's liking.[15] In the fall of 1947 NBC Television producer Fred Coe argued that the network should have more input into the editorial content of *KTT*. This proved to be a real sticking point for Reber, who strongly believed that the agency should control every aspect of a program in order to harmonize the entertainment and advertising segments. In Reber's mind, Thompson's allegiance was to Kraft's wishes, not those of NBC. Reber also insisted that agency employees be denied on-screen credit for their efforts, making exceptions only for stars, writers, and in some cases directors. In short, nothing was allowed that might detract from audience identification with the sponsor.

Coe and several NBC executives were unwilling to allow the agencies such latitude in programming decisions. NBC policy in early 1947 stated that the network would exercise exclusive control over all its televised productions; agency personnel could serve as creative liaisons, but whatever happened in the studio was the responsibility of the network. For Reber, this dictum was intolerable, for it essentially removed Thompson from the loop once the script was written. He had swallowed his reservations on *Hour Glass* by granting NBC control of physical production, but since *Kraft Television Theatre* represented a considerable investment for both the agency and sponsor, and since television was gaining national prominence, more was at stake for Thompson, and the agency's disagreement with NBC intensified. Coe was adamant, however, that all creative decisions made in the studio would rest with him, and he asked NBC president Niles Trammell to intercede with Thompson on his behalf.[16]

The stalemate turned out to be short-lived. In November 1947 NBC announced that it would allow agency directors and producers to directly supervise productions at network facilities and simultaneously increased the rates agencies paid for use of those facilities. It was a victory for Reber and other like-minded agency personnel, but NBC's capitulation was based less on pressure from Madison Avenue than on economic and creative concerns. Several NBC executives argued strongly that it was

FIG. **9** Behind the scenes on the set of the *Kraft Television Theatre*'s production "Of Famous Memory," March 21, 1951. Nancy Marchand played Queen Elizabeth I, a role that required her to age from twenty-five to seventy-five in the course of an hour. Often makeup technicians had less than three minutes to effect the changes between scenes, given the hectic pace of live television drama. (Wisconsin Center for Film and Television Research)

manifestly impossible for the network to hire enough people to support an operation providing live programming from 6:00 to 11:00 p.m. seven days a week because the medium's demands were just too great. They reasoned that it took months to produce motion pictures and Broadway plays, yet television's insatiable appetite for programming demanded fresh material every day. Investing such responsibility with one or two people was a recipe for formulaic productions, they contended, and if Thompson and Kraft wanted to take that risk, then they were welcome to it.[17]

The Philosophy of Scheduling

For many Madison Avenue agencies, however, the mysteries of television threatened to disrupt previously efficient media departments. The larger shops such as Thompson, Young & Rubicam, and BBDO had already developed television expertise by 1948, but the vast majority of agencies found themselves at the bottom of a very steep learning curve. As a result, the 1948 and 1949 seasons served as a rough shakedown for the entire industry. Although it was by no means clear in 1948 just who would dominate television programming, for the most part agencies seemed to expect that the medium would be a version of the radio model with a variety of program sources, while the networks—in their private deliberations at least—made it clear they intended to concede as little power as possible. Nonetheless, all participants agreed that extensive television broadcasting could not be initiated without the production input of advertisers; thus an uneasy truce settled over the industry.

One question that lingered—and received an inordinate amount of attention in trade journals—was the issue of sponsor identification, a bedrock fundamental of broadcast advertising. The idea was simple: if a consumer made the connection between a show and its sponsor, then inevitably an intangible called the "gratitude factor" would emerge; the grateful viewer would buy, for example, Texaco gasoline to thank the company for sponsoring *Texaco Star Theater.* Early research indicated that sponsor identification was indeed more powerful on television than radio; one survey by Young & Rubicam in 1948 concluded that over 80 percent of all viewers could correctly match a television show with its sponsor, twice the rate of radio (and there was an almost 100 percent recognition of Milton Berle and Texaco). Of course, identification depended almost entirely on the practice of single sponsorship, which at this stage of television development was still the norm. A perusal of the programs offered in the fall 1948 schedule is testimony to efforts to link show and sponsor: *Camel Newsreel, Chevrolet Tele-Theater, Philco Television Playhouse, The Swift Show,* and so on.

The promise of a financial bonanza in television invested practically every aspect of the new medium, including scheduling, with a sense of urgency. A network that could attract the largest audience share would be sure to reap the greatest profits. One important aspect of this enticement was the concept of "audience flow," the idea of capturing viewer attention and holding it through a seamless continuity between programs. When he arrived at NBC as vice president for television programming in 1949, Sylvester L. "Pat" Weaver found a schedule that was without direction; as he described it, "Programs landed next to each other by mere chance, with each agency building its show in a way that was aimed at nothing more than keeping the client happy."[18]

In a sense, Weaver was slightly off the mark. Agencies were, of course, deeply concerned with their own shows, devoting considerable research to determine the proper time slot. For example, Thompson purchased 9:00–10:00 p.m. Wednesday on NBC for Kraft in 1947 (this at a time when they literally could have gotten an option on any period they desired) because their research showed that Wednesday was the night people were most likely to be at home. Further, the agency did not want *Kraft Television Theatre* to interfere with Thursday night's *Kraft Music Hall* on radio (Hawes 1986, 138–39).

At the same time, agencies were anxious about programs either adjacent to or competing against their shows. Sponsors recognized the time franchise as a double-edged sword—once a time period was purchased, the buyer was powerless to move if challenged by a popular show on another network—so they spent a great deal of time worrying about adjacent programs. A long-standing scheduling theory in radio held that shows of similar format or genre should not be broadcast consecutively for fear that the audience would grow bored and change stations. This attitude changed in late 1940s on radio with the advent of block programming on independent stations, but the concept did not immediately transfer to television. Many believed that the medium's perceptual demands made it difficult for the viewer to endure more than an hour or so of the same type of program.[19]

A sponsor's biggest fear was that their show would suffer by being placed next to a weak program providing an insufficient lead-in audience. This led to enormous headaches for the networks, and in many instances they could not satisfy the demands of one advertiser without antagonizing another. Thompson, for example, was particularly insistent that NBC protect *Kraft Television Theatre* by strengthening the program lineup before 9:00 p.m. The agency was horrified to discover in April 1948 that *KTT* was being clobbered in the Hooper Teleratings (which at this point measured New York audiences only) by boxing on WABD, the DuMont station.[20]

It is indicative of how important *KTT* was to NBC that the network promptly reshuffled the Wednesday night schedule, replacing a quiz and a cooking show with two musical variety programs. Because *Americana Quiz* was sponsored by the Encyclopedia Britannica and *In the Kelvinator Kitchen* was paid for by Kelvinator, NBC had to offer both advertisers discounts and rebates so that they would move their shows. Their replacements were produced by NBC and carried as sustainers: that is, without advertising.

Pat Weaver

Even before the arrival of Pat Weaver in August 1949 as vice president in charge of television programming, considerable attention was being given to network-produced shows. In recognition of the need for central planning, a streamlined Television Program Department was created in the spring of 1949. As it would with Weaver, NBC reached into the ranks of the advertising agencies to pick Norman Blackburn of J. Walter Thompson as the national program director. Robert Sarnoff (David Sarnoff's son) was appointed production manager, Charles Prince was named manager of talent and procurement, and staff director Fred Coe was charged with creating new programs.

It was a much simpler arrangement for the network than the chaos of 1946–48. These four constituted the Program Board, which met regularly to discuss the schedule: Blackburn set the overall strategy, Sarnoff oversaw day-to-day productions (including the assignment of NBC personnel to agency shows), Prince looked for outside properties the network might wish to buy, and Coe, as the "idea man," developed new programming ventures. However, despite the rather grand plans envisioned by the network, the Program Department was hobbled by a small budget and practically no support staff. The majority of programs initiated by the department were news and public interest shows: in other words, sustainers. The board members—Coe in particular—spent most of their time servicing agency productions and not NBC-owned packages like *The Clock*.[21]

It was precisely this kind of dependence on Madison Avenue that galled Pat Weaver. If anything exemplifies Weaver's tenure at NBC, it was his relentless ambition to gain complete control of the schedule; almost every important executive action he took while at the network relates to it in some way (Kepley 1990b, 48–49). Upon arriving at NBC, he suggested that the network's television operation be streamlined by centralizing authority in his office. It was a bold move, one that Weaver was able to initiate primarily because NBC-TV's immature corporate structure was bereft of middle management personnel who might otherwise object to his power grab.[22]

Further, he was granted extraordinary leeway by RCA president David Sarnoff while the network was struggling to establish its program service. Sarnoff was, of course, vitally interested in NBC's activities—even to the point of making his son Robert a network executive—but at least until the mid-1950s he was much more focused on RCA's more technology-oriented production (see Douglas Gomery, chapter 9). Only when NBC's long-range planning shifted from expansion to stabilization as the television market leveled off did the elder Sarnoff wield the kind of whip hand he displayed at RCA (Kepley 1990b, 59; Dreher 1977, 173; Bilby 1986, 229–66; O'Connell 1986, 191).

Weaver also recommended that the network finance program development in part by farming out research, promotion, and legal work to outsiders. He admitted that his was a "spend money to make money" philosophy, but his single-minded insistence on control was grounded in the belief that NBC would maximize its profits only when it did not have to rely on outside sources, whether agencies or independent producers, for product. He reasoned that the network needed the flexibility to rearrange the schedule at will in order to both optimize audience flow and counterprogram the other networks; with this power NBC could attract the largest audiences. The promise of popular programming would encourage new stations to affiliate with NBC, and the subsequent expansion of NBC's coverage would allow the network to charge higher advertising rates as more people purchased television sets, preferably RCA sets, a rather consequential factor in the NBC game plan.

Weaver's approach met with some approval from the RCA board; between 1949 and 1951 the network absorbed $1.2 million in losses to produce ten programs in house. By 1953 those losses totaled $5.5 million, but the network was inching toward profitability. However, problems with one of NBC's most important sponsors prompted Weaver to make a major push for program control, one that would ultimately bring about the complete reorganization of the network's structure (Weaver 1994, 7; Kepley 1990b, 53).[23]

Colgate was sponsor of the *Colgate Comedy Hour*, a mainstay of NBC's powerful Sunday night lineup since 1950. In an unusual arrangement—and one Weaver never tired of criticizing—NBC produced the program, but Colgate owned the rights to the 8:00–9:00 p.m. time slot. Although Colgate occasionally complained about the show's content (especially when guest hosts Dean Martin and Jerry Lewis would make sly references to Colgate's competitors, what *Variety* called "cuffo plugs," after "fisticuffs"), neither network nor sponsor could argue with the program's popularity: it consistently beat Ed Sullivan and *Toast of the Town* on CBS (Weaver 1994, 214).[24]

Still, for the 1952–53 season, Colgate spent over $8 million in time and talent charges for the *Comedy Hour*, an escalation in cost that caused the company to reconsider if the expenditure was worth the return in increased sales. As owner of the time franchise, Colgate notified NBC in January 1953, through its agency Ted Bates, that it was thinking of replacing the *Comedy Hour* with another, less expensive program. Weaver was livid. He already had a very poor relationship with Colgate's chief executive officer Edward Little, but more importantly he believed that the loss of the program would be catastrophic to the entire Sunday night schedule. It angered Weaver that a program so vital to NBC's fortunes could be scuttled by a sponsor who did not own the show, only the time in which it aired.

The answer, Weaver contended, was for the network to produce the entire schedule top to bottom; NBC could then tinker with programming and audience flow to suit its institutional needs, not those of Madison Avenue. He freely acknowledged that the creation of huge new sales and production departments would be very expensive, but to saddle NBC with this debt now would pay off handsomely in the long term (Kepley 1990b, 52).

These ideas apparently got David Sarnoff's attention, for he asked Weaver to outline a strategy for the plan's implementation and its attendant costs. Weaver suggested streamlining the network in a way that would eliminate many of its promotional, research, and merchandising activities. More dramatic was his plan to reorganize NBC's middle management into a unit-producer system with himself as its leader.[25]

Concern on Madison Avenue

All Madison Avenue was alarmed by the skyrocketing costs of program production. From the agency perspective, the key to commercial television was to lower costs while increasing the number of viewers. Agencies and networks agreed that the only way to promote set circulation was to provide programming of sufficient popular interest to lure a wider audience. Costs could be contained in various ways. Almost every issue put out by television trade journals during the early 1950s contained at least one article on how to shave production expenses with new techniques, equipment, or approaches to planning.

Weaver believed that he had the answer—albeit an entirely self-serving one—for the advertiser concerned about the medium's rising cost: participation advertising, dubbed the "magazine concept." In participation advertising, advertisers purchased discrete segments of shows—typically one- or two-minute blocks—rather than entire programs. Like magazines, which featured advertisements for a variety of products, the participation show might, depending on its length, carry commercials from up to four different sponsors. Similarly, just as a magazine's editorial practice was presumably separate from its advertising content, the presence of multiple sponsors meant that no one advertiser could control the program. By Weaver's reckoning, the network would assume that responsibility.

As a veteran of Madison Avenue, Weaver recognized that this manner of advertising directly contradicted conventional agency wisdom concerning television. Although participations were becoming somewhat more commonplace at the local level (and had been common on local radio for years), most agencies and advertisers were reluctant to part with their faith in sponsor identification and the resulting gratitude factor. Many agencies were willing to reconsider their traditional insistence on production control but remained skeptical about participation at the national level.

Arguably, it was the sponsors and not the advertising agencies who thought they had the most to lose from the network's assumption of program control. In general, those advertisers who resisted the magazine concept—such as Kraft—were among the few who had a time franchise they wanted to keep. Agencies, however, sought to maximize advertising volume and their own profits by increasing the number of television advertisers and shifting the cost burdens of production elsewhere. Weaver and many agency executives were in accord that participation advertising promised greater profitability for both the networks and Madison Avenue. The networks could charge sponsors higher rates for shorter periods of airtime, and the agencies could gain clients and commissions if they were required to produce commercials for multiple advertisers during an hour of programming rather than just one.

Thompson, however, was slower to react to the changes within the advertising community, largely because of a firmly ingrained corporate philosophy personified by John Reber. For example, Kraft's advertising was the bailiwick of the Radio-

Television Department (*Kraft Television Theatre, Kraft Music Hall* on radio), the Copy Department (print advertising), the Art Department (commercial illustrations), and the Outdoor Department (billboards). These departments had a general idea of who was doing what for Kraft, but there was little coordination of effort. This reliance on specialists—phenomenally successful for the agency during radio's heyday—left Thompson with a cumbersome organization structure that often pitted one department against another.

Moreover, it was becoming increasingly clear that complete control of television production was unprofitable not just to clients but to the agency itself. *Kraft Television Theatre* was a tightly budgeted, well-managed program, but Thompson's costs in terms of salaries, research, overhead, and other expenses were not covered by the 15 percent commission. The money was in syndication, as the agency had discovered in 1951 when it purchased an independently produced show called *Foreign Intrigue*. However, other agencies had moved far more aggressively into syndication than Thompson, and with impressive results. Young & Rubicam in particular increased its television billings so dramatically throughout the 1950s that by 1954 they were the number one agency; Thompson was a distant third behind BBDO.[26]

Although Thompson was certainly amenable to signing production contracts with independent companies (for example, with Screen Gems for *Ford Theatre* and with Hal Roach for *Screen Directors Playhouse*), it remained the agency most strongly committed to in-house control of programming. Even as one agency after another stopped program production altogether, Thompson continued its work on *Kraft Television Theatre* and in 1950 introduced *Lux Video Theatre*, a half-hour live dramatic program on CBS.

Thompson further committed itself to production in October 1953, when it premiered a second *Kraft Television Theatre* on ABC, and again in the fall of 1955 with its *Ford Star Jubilee*, a once-a-month "spectacular" on CBS. The addition of a second *Kraft Television Theatre* surprised many industry observers who had expected Kraft, if anything, to pare down its television activities. NBC had tried to convince Kraft executives in the summer of 1953 to alternate *Kraft Television Theatre* with the *US Steel Theatre Guild*, but were rebuffed. Although the show cost Kraft almost $65,000 a week and consumed 40 percent of their advertising budget, the company remained pleased with the prestige and sales generated by the program. The original *Kraft Television Theatre* was never a ratings success, but Kraft apparently never expected it to be, consistently claiming that they measured the show's popularity by the number of recipe requests, not by its Nielsens.[27]

Thus the purchase of an hour on ABC on Thursday nights for another *Kraft Television Theatre* was made primarily on the basis of creating another advertising vehicle for Kraft's products, such as the new Cheez Whiz. The strain on the agency's television department was enormous, as each version had three episodes in development at any given time. Still, Thompson managed the programs with surprisingly few personnel—only nineteen people on the production staff in addition to the casting and script units. However, sales figures from products advertised on the ABC program did not justify the additional $2 million in costs, so Kraft pulled the show in January 1955. Even Thompson's expertise in production and the popularity of its programming did not solve the problem of profitability.[28]

By the end of the 1954–55 season, many agencies and sponsors felt constrained by their programming choices. Production was too expensive to try on one's own, yet the networks, independent producers, and talent agencies seemed to be unable to control costs either. A season-long mania for big-name, high-priced talent was maddening to agencies unwilling to pin their hopes on a single performer; the rapid descent of Arthur Godfrey, whose popularity plummeted after a spate of uncharacteristically churlish behavior, was frequently cited as an object lesson. Thompson— one of the few agencies still producing programs—set a firm ceiling on talent costs, turning down, for example, Gloria Swanson's demand of $7,500 to star in a *Lux Video Theatre* remake of *Sunset Boulevard*.[29]

An important new source of programming was the major Hollywood studios. Since the *Paramount* decision of 1948, the major studios had been seeking ways to recoup the revenues lost when they were forced to sell their theater chains. Paramount and Warner Bros. had at one time owned television stations, but they sold their licenses in 1950; others invested in subscription and/or theater television. Far from fearing the new medium, the majors tried to co-opt it. Failing that, by the mid-1950s, several studios had decided to invest heavily in television program production and to sell their backlog of feature films to syndication companies, who in turn leased them to television (Hilmes 1990; Anderson 1994). Whatever disagreements may have existed between the two major American entertainment industries thus came to an abrupt and profitable end, and on television's terms. Hollywood realized that television offered a means of stabilizing income (and an antidote to the blockbuster mentality), especially when syndication was thrown into the mix.[30]

Madison Avenue viewed these developments with alarm, convinced that the newfound coziness between the networks and the studios would come to dominate prime time. They complained that the networks were so wedded to ratings that they deliberately shunned any program they did not control in some fashion. Independent packagers also contended that they were being shut out of prime time. As one producer said, "We call what we're doing 'Operation Vulture.' We develop programs and then we wait for an existing show to drop dead. Then we'll jump in, and with any luck, we can sell one of ours." An advertising agent added, "They come in and tell us what shows we can have in what time periods, take it or leave it. I'm beginning to feel like a messenger boy with no other function than to carry word of the network's demands to the client."[31]

Network Hegemony

Agency-produced shows such as *Kraft Television Theatre* were very much the exception by the mid-1950s. Participating advertising was becoming the predominant form, catalyzed by the producers of small-ticket consumer goods, like Procter & Gamble and Lever Brothers. These companies were interested in circulation, or, in the parlance of the trade, "tonnage." In other words, they looked for programs with high viewer appeal; being completely uninterested in institutional advertising, they made their program purchase decisions almost entirely on the basis of ratings. By dispersing their advertising dollars throughout the schedule, these manufacturers ultimately strengthened network control of programming, for only the network could work with these companies to provide a multitude of participations in various programs, all of which were, in turn, network controlled (Boddy 1990, 158). The networks further embraced multiple sponsorship as a means of stabilizing their own income by avoiding the volatile swings of recession-sensitive durable-goods producers.[32]

By the fall of 1957, only three shows were wholly produced by an agency: *Kraft Television Theatre*, BBDO's *Your Hit Parade*, and McCann-Erickson's *Club Oasis*. *KTT* continued to drop in the ratings, and in April 1958 Kraft decided to sell the rights to the program to Talent Associates, a production company headed by David Susskind. Moving the program from agency to package production relieved much of Kraft's financial obligation to the show, as they could now split production costs with Susskind. Thompson personnel were kept on as creative consultants, but the main agency responsibility now lay with the commercials. *KTT* remained on the air only a few more months before it was completely reconfigured by Talent Associates as *Kraft Mystery Theatre*, which lasted until September 1958.

Although Thompson continued to supervise Kraft's subsequent television programs, its reign as the preeminent in-house production agency came to an end. The agency continued to encourage its clients to be associated with marquee names and event programming, but by the end of the decade it not only had completely converted from a specialist to an all-media approach but also had modified its entire promotional philosophy. No longer did it equate identification with single sponsorship; instead, the agency advised many of its customers to seek mass circulation through saturation advertising.[33]

In this, Thompson was very much in sync with Madison Avenue thinking. By the 1958–59 season, the agency withdrawal from direct production responsibility was essentially complete. No longer was sponsorship synonymous with control— it now merely meant the purchase of advertising time on somebody else's program. While sponsor identification remained important to such advertisers as Kraft and Revlon, most sponsors prized circulation over prestige; as a result, fewer agencies offered advertiser-licensed shows to the networks.

Thus, after little more than a decade of continually adjusting and redefining their relationship with sponsors and production companies, the networks were finally settling into a system of production that was cost effective yet flexible. The network role in this second phase of commercial television was essentially administrative— independent production companies generated programs, and sponsors paid the networks to advertise on their shows.

Conclusion

Throughout television's first decade, the agendas of NBC, J. Walter Thompson, and Thompson's clients increasingly diverged. Concerned that the expense of television programming far outstripped that of radio production, agency executives sought ways to develop television as a mass advertising medium while also seeking to avoid draining agency revenues with television program costs.

As part of this reassessment, Thompson and other agencies had to rethink their conception of single versus multiple sponsorship, which consequently influenced the industry's view of television as a marketing tool. Although Madison Avenue may have relinquished production responsibilities during the 1950s, the idea of sponsor identification remained an article of faith not easily denied. Single sponsorship was long equated with identification, but even this was subject to economic pressure.

For NBC, the shift from full to participating sponsorship also expanded the network's economic base by encouraging increasing numbers of smaller advertisers to buy nationwide markets while allowing large sponsors the opportunity to spread their messages efficiently throughout the schedule. The network continued to offer a variety of sponsorship packages throughout the 1950s to create a flexible advertising market, a strategy that paid off in substantial profits by the end of the decade. As the size of the television audience grew, so too did NBC's profits.

Of course, the changes in organizational behavior by NBC and J. Walter Thompson in the 1950s had a lasting impact on their business alliance. From the 1920s onward, NBC and Thompson had a mutually beneficial relationship that thrived despite the occasional disagreements. In the radio era this partnership was especially close, since Thompson served as a major program supplier for the network; in a very real sense, Thompson programming helped NBC achieve financial stability.

But by the time Thompson reorganized in the mid-1950s, the stakes had changed. Participation advertising marked the demise of the type of agency-network connection common in radio. Where once an agency like Thompson would establish a link with a specific network, as it did with NBC (and as Young & Rubicam did with CBS), by 1958 agencies were purchasing spots on all the networks, severing these kinds of long-standing ties. By the early 1960s, Thompson was purchasing more advertising time on CBS than NBC; it simply had no economic need to continue that relationship as the classic network system of the 1960s and 1970s took hold (Hilmes 2006, 217–18).

Notes

Abbreviations

JWT   J. Walter Thompson Archive, Duke University

Kraft   Kraft Foods Advertising History Collection, Center for Advertising History, Smithsonian Institution

LAB   Library of American Broadcasting, University of Maryland

NBC/WHS National Broadcasting Company Archives, Wisconsin Historical Society

1. Philip I. Merryman to Noran Kersta, March 15, 1946, Box 585, NBC/WHS.

2. "Television and the Sponsor Today," *Sponsor*, November 1946, 26.

3. John F. Royal, "Television Report," September 12, 1944, Box 113, NBC/WHS; RCA, *RCA: What It Is—What It Does*, 1947, 28, Pamphlet File, LAB.

4. Ted Mills to Noran E. Kersta, May 14, 1947, Box 585, NBC/WHS.

5. "Standard Brands' 'Hour Glass' Show," *Television*, October 1946, 12.

6. "Standard Brand's $105,000 Tele Experience with 'Hour Glass,'" *Televiser*, January–February 1947, 30–31.

7. Ibid.; Fran Holland (wife of Maury Holland, director of *KTT*), interview, n.d., Oral History Collection, Kraft.

8. "Standard Brands' 'Hour Glass' Show," 13–14; "Standard Brand's $105,000 Tele Experience," 30.

9. "The J.W.T. Weekly News," November 18, 1946, 2, JWT; "Standard Brand's $105,000 Tele Experience," 31.

10. "NBC Television Guide to Commercial Production Procedure, 1946," Box 103, NBC/WHS; "Tele Programs Falling into a Rut," *Televiser*, March–April 1947, 16; Al Durante, interview, n.d., Oral History Collection, Kraft; Warren Wade to Noran E. Kersta, July 29, 1946, Box 585, NBC/WHS.

11. John T. Williams to Noran E. Kersta, May 20, 1947, Box 585, NBC/WHS.

12. Editorial, *Televiser*, March–April 1947, 28.

13. "More Sponsor-Built Shows on the Air!" *Televiser*, May–June 1947, 21.

14. "TV's Crazy Quilt: Facilities Cost," *Sponsor*, February 11, 1952, 32–33, Sidney Bernstein file, Box 1B, Kraft; John H. Platt, speech to Television Council, May 21, 1952, Box 121, NBC/WHS.

15. "Kraft Theatre: A Television Epic," *Broadcasting*, June 15, 1953, 88.

16. "NBC Television Guide to Commercial Production Procedure," 1946, Box 105, NBC/WHS.

17. John F. Royal to Frank E. Mullen, October 22, 1947, Box 585, NBC/WHS; "Television NBC: A Nice Sunday Morning Subject," 1947, Box 105, NBC/WHS; "TV," *Sponsor*, November 1947, 36; "Who Is Responsible for What in TV?" *Sponsor*, January 1948, 52–54; "CBS Video," *Broadcasting*, February 23, 1948, 84.

18. "Weaver Scans the Way Ahead," *Broadcasting*, February 28, 1955, 38.

19. "The Hottest Trend in Radio—Block Programming," *Sponsor*, October 1947, 15–18; "Mr. Sponsor Asks," *Sponsor*, January 3, 1949, 44–46; "What Makes a TV Program Tick?" *Sponsor*, September 12, 1949, 64.

20. Linnea Nelson to George Frey, April 29, 1948, Box 403, NBC/WHS; Walter Scott to George Frey, May 17, 1949, Box 403, NBC/WHS.

21. Carleton Smith to Niles Trammell, July 21, 1949, Box 591, NBC/WHS.

22. "Memorandum Number One," September 26, 1949, Box 118, NBC/WHS.

23. "TV Breaks thru Barriers of Radio Orthodoxy," *Variety*, January 7, 1953, 93.

24. "Colgate's Friend or Producer?" *Variety*, April 23, 1952, 21, 27.

25. Pat Weaver to David W. Sarnoff, March 31, 1953, Box 121, NBC/WHS; Pat Weaver to J. M. Clifford, January 12, 1954, Box 123, NBC/WHS.

26. "The Top 20 Air Agencies," *Sponsor*, December 13, 1954, 31–33.

27. "Report to Sponsors," *Sponsor,* August 24, 1953, 2; "Kraft Theatre: A Television Epic," *Broadcasting,* June 15, 1953, 88–90.

28. "P.S.," *Sponsor,* September 21, 1953, 2; "The J.W.T. Weekly News," September 28, 1953, 1, JWT; "The Show Must Go On," *Pageant,* December 1953, 130–35; Marion Dougherty (casting director, *KTT*), interview, n.d., Oral History Collection, Kraft.

29. "Talent Agents: What's the Alternative to Paying Their Price?" *Sponsor,* February 1955, 36–37, 107.

30. "25,000 Films—How Will They Change TV?" *Television,* July 1956, 64–67.

31. "The Great Debate on Network Show Control," *Sponsor,* October 31, 1955, 92; "Sponsor Backstage," *Sponsor,* April 16, 1956, 30.

32. "Sponsor-Scope," *Sponsor,* February 16, 1957, 9; "Trends for Leading Advertisers," *Television,* April 1957, 54–55; "Sponsor-Scope," *Sponsor,* March 2, 1957, 9.

33. "Sponsor Hears," *Sponsor,* May 3, 1958, 68; "Dan Seymour: Guiding Genius of JWT's Air Strategy," *Sponsor,* July 19, 1958, 30–31; "Sponsor Hears," *Sponsor,* December 19, 1959, 58; "Will Media and Marketing Blend?" *Sponsor,* January 17, 1959, 29–31.

9

Talent Raids and Package Deals

NBC Loses Its Leadership in the 1950s

DOUGLAS GOMERY

In 1962, in his book *The Hungry Eye*, journalist Eugene Paul described the new television industry for a curious public. The title of chapter 4, "NBC First, Where It Really Isn't," reflected the changed realities of NBC's industry ranking since its heyday in the first decade of television—but for many observers it was hard to understand this sudden shift. Hadn't General David Sarnoff and his Radio Corporation of America and NBC network invented TV? Hadn't NBC been the top radio network for two generations? Hadn't Milton Berle been the king of television? Didn't Sarnoff bring color TV to the world? Paul's book confirmed for his readers NBC's surprising slide from first place, a position it had not held for almost a decade. By 1960 CBS-TV was the solidly established choice for the majority of viewers across the country. NBC-TV began the 1950s with thirteen of the top twenty highest-rated shows but fell behind CBS in 1952 and never succeeded in regaining its position. How could this have happened?

Paul blames poor management—but wasn't David Sarnoff the man who outmaneuvered corporate giants to create NBC in the first place? With more historical distance and more primary materials available, we can now clearly see what happened. NBC's fortunes declined in the 1950s when CBS used advice from top Hollywood talent agent Lew Wasserman, head of the Music Corporation of America (MCA), to raid the top stars, bringing CBS into the lead in television ratings and making MCA television's top production company. NBC managed to recover from its 1955 nadir by enlisting Wasserman's aid as CBS had done, but even with the top-rated show, MCA's *Wagon Train*, on its schedule it was unable to catch CBS. Not until the mid-1960s was Wasserman able to stabilize NBC and bring the network back as a serious competitor to CBS (Paul 1962, 43). In the first decade of the twenty-first century, history may have come full circle: Universal Pictures, which MCA purchased in 1962 to become MCA Universal, merged in 2003 with NBC (itself now a subsidiary of General Electric), forming NBC Universal. Lew Wasserman's hidden legacy had finally assumed front-page status.

The Hidden History of NBC in the 1950s

Though other historians have examined television networks in the 1950s, they have tended to focus on the industry's changing relationship with Hollywood, most notably the relationship of ABC and Disney,[1] or on the strategies of NBC's charismatic and well-publicized vice president of programming, Pat Weaver. Few note the spectacular reversal of fortune experienced by the oldest and most powerful network in the history of broadcasting, though it reveals much about how the nascent medium would develop. This essay argues that the decline in NBC's standing within the industry can be attributed primarily to the failure of David Sarnoff, still the primary power behind the scenes at NBC, to understand the changing nature of the television business. Sarnoff focused on the profits of electronics conglomerate RCA as a whole during this crucial period, neglecting NBC. Distracted by his efforts to make RCA a billion-dollar member of the twenty-five biggest military industrial corporations, Sarnoff opted for the easiest solution to the growing pains of the burgeoning television business: just keep on doing what had worked for radio. When that strategy failed disastrously, Sarnoff belatedly reversed course, initiated a new NBC strategy, and sought out the talents of Hollywood insider Lew Wasserman, as William Paley had done at CBS six years earlier.

Though Pat Weaver might have advocated for greater network control over production, as Michael Mashon argues in the previous chapter, NBC failed to take the necessary steps to ensure the strategic alliance with Hollywood studio production that Wasserman would broker. Throughout the 1950s David Sarnoff focused on making RCA an electronics giant rather than on furthering the growth of his television network, and his enormous influence over NBC's management prevented others from moving in innovative directions. It didn't help that during the most crucial years, 1953 to 1958, NBC's president was none other than the General's ineffective son, Robert Sarnoff. Grant Tinker (1994), working at NBC in the 1950s, wrote observantly that those who worked at NBC at the time were aware of the true situation: "the father, the son and the wholly-owned subsidiary" (212).

Talent Raids and Package Shows

As World War II ended, David Sarnoff, as the head of giant RCA and of the top-ranked radio network NBC, sat atop the broadcasting world. RCA had prospered during the war by manufacturing key military electronic technology. It dwarfed CBS in terms of total assets and sales. Sarnoff's experience as a leader during radio's early decades had persuaded him that the system of advertising agency production, with the network as time broker, worked very well. Sarnoff remained confident that RCA's lead in television technology could still drive its network profitability.[2]

Grant Tinker (1994), who started working at NBC in 1949, aptly summarized the situation forty-five years later in his autobiography: "NBC had been the most powerful company in radio ever since RCA's David Sarnoff founded it in 1926, and I was arriving just as the streak was ending. CBS's William Paley had picked off Jack Benny from the NBC schedule late in 1948 and in the following months was to take Red Skelton, George Burns and Gracie Allen, and Edgar Bergen. By the end of 1949, CBS [radio] would have 12 of the top 15 [radio] shows and NBC's era of radio dominance would be finished" (24). Had Tinker known that this same ratio of CBS to NBC television network winners would prevail in 1955, he might have considered employment elsewhere (Brooks and Marsh 2003, 1245).

In 1946, CBS's owner and CEO William Paley—frustrated by NBC's long-term top ratings status—sought a new business model for radio. During the spring of 1946, Paley and his newly appointed network president, Frank Stanton, raided advertising agency Young & Rubicam to hire Hubbell Robinson for a position that did not even exist at NBC: vice president for programming. Robinson, in turn, brought to CBS his deputy at Young & Rubicam, Harry Ackerman. These four— Paley, Stanton, Robinson, and Ackerman—formed, along with two more hires— Irving Mansfield and Cy Howard—the in-house programming unit of CBS radio. They met each Tuesday at 10:00 a.m., their agenda to remake the CBS radio network, to wrest control from the advertising agencies, and to pass NBC radio in the ratings.[3]

These experienced radio producers were used to dealing with talent agencies. They approached the most powerful agent in show business, MCA's Lew Wasserman, who developed a business strategy for CBS. With an income tax system wholly different from today's, in which individuals in the top bracket might pay up to 88 percent of their income in tax, Wasserman encouraged his clients to incorporate themselves and their programs as businesses. Rather than receive salaries, which would be taxed at the individual rate, as the heads of incorporated production companies they would benefit from paying the corporate tax rate, which was capped at 25 percent. This allowed Wasserman's clients to pay a fraction of the taxes they had owed formerly, and many of them became instant multimillionaires. Wasserman helped his star-clients to incorporate and sell their newly incorporated programs as "packages" to CBS. Paley was skeptical at first, but in May 1948, when Paley received a memorandum from an NBC vice president crowing over his network's dominance, he ordered his programmers to go on the offensive. Wasserman outlined his plan. Paley had found the lure with which he could tempt away the top NBC talent (Gomery 2005, 205–6).

Paley gave the go-ahead to this plan in the summer of 1948. Wasserman received Internal Revenue Service approval in September 1948, and a month later Paley triumphantly announced that the *Amos 'n' Andy* show had joined CBS after nineteen years on NBC. This first raid would never make CBS a great deal of money, but it did set off a stampede of NBC stars to CBS in the fall of 1948 (M. Ely 1991, 203–4). Thus began the "talent raids." Little did Paley or Wasserman realize that this new system would spill over and become the basis for the ascendancy of CBS-TV. Sarnoff was caught off guard when Wasserman suggested the same sort of deal for NBC's king of radio, Jack Benny. Wasserman's client Benny had felt for some time that Sarnoff took him for granted. When Wasserman proposed a deal worth $2.4 million to Paley, the owner of CBS personally flew to Hollywood and courted Benny. By the 1954–55 TV season *The Jack Benny Show* would rank seventh in the national Nielsen ratings and would remain at the core of CBS's programming during the two decades that the network led in prime-time ratings (Fein 1977, 106–9; S. Smith 1990, 260–64; McDougal 1998, 162–65).

On November 26, 1948, Paley announced the Benny defection. The news sent shock waves through the broadcasting industry. When asked about leaving NBC, Benny replied: "[Lew Wasserman] put me in a position where I could pay terrific taxes and still keep some money for myself. That was one of the attractions of MCA. They would call it giving an actor an 'estate.'" (McDougal 1998, 160). Contrary to his media image, Benny was a spendthrift, and Wasserman's deal made Benny able to afford anything he wanted. The Benny deal brought along almost all of the NBC comedians to CBS; it became commonplace during the spring of 1949 for a comedian to be broadcasting on NBC one week, then to turn up the next week on CBS. As Sally Bedell Smith (1990), Paley's biographer, neatly summarizes, this became the stuff of broadcasting legend, for most of NBC's top talent went to Wasserman and asked for the same deal as Benny. Here was Lew Wasserman's first masterstroke at changing broadcasting (261–64).[4]

Over at NBC, David Sarnoff held onto his expectation, based on long-standing radio practice, that major sponsors like Texaco, which had brought Milton Berle to the peacock pantheon, would provide competition to counter CBS's "new" radio stars starting their CBS-TV network shows. Sarnoff clung to his radio business model, thinking that Paley and Wasserman were crazy. NBC was staring down a radio ratings slide that would continue with television ratings. Even as Paley signed a contract with Desi Arnez at Desilu, Sarnoff was advising Pat Weaver to stick to the radio advertising agency model. Sarnoff ordered Weaver not to pay for star corporation productions even as CBS passed NBC, first in the radio network ratings (in 1950), and then in the television ratings (in 1953) (Murray 2005, 65–92; Weaver 1994, 4–9).

The General Looks to His Profits

The cover of *Newsweek* for December 5, 1949, featured a portrait of David Sarnoff over the caption "Besieged on Three Fronts." He didn't look worried. Smiling broadly, bright-eyed, even youthful at age fifty-nine, he seemed the very picture of corporate power. Yet *Newsweek* reported: "After a quarter of a century of almost unquestioned dominance, Sarnoff . . . is now waging a bitter, stubborn war on three fronts. In recordings [CBS's 33 1/3 long-playing records], radio broadcasting [CBS's leap over NBC], and television [CBS's likelihood of gaining FCC approval for its color TV as the industry standard], he is being challenged by organizations with spirit, flexibility, and dash."[5] David Sarnoff's primary broadcasting goal was to get FCC approval for RCA's color television as the industry standard. In 1950, CBS seemed to have won the FCC's approval; however, by 1953 Sarnoff had reversed that. Sarnoff was convinced, wrongly, as it turned out, that color TV would make NBC the top network. Fans would buy RCA sets and tune into NBC colorcasts. But although his technological strategy may have been in RCA's best interests, it did not prove to benefit NBC. CBS had the shows—albeit in black and white—that fans tuned into week after week (Bilby 1986, 176–228).

Yet RCA as a total corporation was making profits—big profits. A February 27, 1950, press release read: "Net earnings of Radio Corporation of America in 1949 amounted to $25,144,279, equivalent to $1.58 per share of Common stock."[6] The General began planning new directions for RCA. In October 1951, he announced that RCA would enter the air conditioner manufacturing business. It would not convert TV set assembly lines to produce air conditioners, nor would it erect additional factories. Instead, the air conditioners would be manufactured for RCA by Fedders, one of the largest independents in the industry. Initially they would be the familiar Fedders units, but in time they would be made to RCA's specifications with added electronics components. RCA's bottom line took a hit from this investment in Fedders, so when the news of RCA's fiscal health for 1951 was announced, the *Washington Post* reported, "RCA Gross Sets Record, Net Declines."[7]

Despite the investment, electronic air conditioners never appeared. Instead, RCA was about to enter new product areas with conventional offerings. In making the announcement, Sarnoff spoke of giving dealers an opportunity to "round out" their lines by adding air conditioners to radios, television sets, and phonographs and boldly proclaimed that if it worked out, more would follow—RCA refrigerators, RCA ranges, and RCA washing machines. The idea of expansion into related areas was alluring. Yet all that came of it was subcontracting deals in which RCA became the principal supplier of television sets to Sears Roebuck, sold under that retailer's Silvertone brand name, while Fedders supplied Sears with air conditioners (Sobel 1986, 168).

With Korean War orders, RCA was still in great shape, even as NBC languished. RCA had become a major war contractor. David Adams, longtime NBC executive, remembered being in the room when Weaver said, "General, you're not a broadcaster, you're a technician."[8] However, RCA did not dominate receiver manufacturing the way Sarnoff had hoped it would. In 1947 the company accounted for approximately 80 percent of the market; the following year its share had declined to 30 percent, as newcomers such as Admiral and GE took away sales from the leader. Thus, before the great television boom began, RCA's position in that industry had already begun to decline. Still RCA sold nearly a million sets a year in the early 1950s.[9]

Sarnoff became bolder. RCA made its initial entry into electronic data processing. It was done with a great deal of ballyhoo, complete with full-page ads in the more important newspapers and announcements on NBC-TV. Prospects were far more exciting than with air conditioners, and the business itself was as glamorous as television. Sarnoff hoped to remake RCA into the world's leading computer corporation, surpassing IBM (Sobel 1986, 177–78). As it turned out, Sarnoff's foray into computers, which pitted him against IBM's CEO Thomas Watson Jr., must be considered one of the major business blunders of all time. It almost destroyed RCA and certainly tarnished Sarnoff's reputation. When it was all over, many claimed that defeat had been inevitable, but Sarnoff's defenders saw this as another case of second-guessing and 20–20 hindsight. The latter view is more plausible. RCA had the assets to challenge IBM: indeed, during this period Thomas Watson Jr. considered RCA the greatest threat to IBM's hegemony in data processing (Sobel 1986, 169).

Sarnoff's other interest was in picking up government electronics contracts. In time, RCA would become a major government electronics supplier. [10] Sarnoff became more and more hawkish, siding with his former boss, Allied supreme commander and now U.S. president Dwight D. Eisenhower, in arguing for spending more to keep up with the Russians. Carefully and calculatingly, Sarnoff developed government contacts and business, volunteering in 1952 to head a Military Manpower study that found a "10% Waste in Defense [Spending]."[11] Sarnoff argued to his friends in the Eisenhower administration that electronics could help cut waste and beat the Russians with weapons powered by RCA "electronic brains." RCA government contracts doubled (Sobel 1986, 183). So while NBC was struggling, RCA was booming. In the annual report for 1955, corporate revenues from government contracts topped $1 billion, an increase of 320 percent since the Second World War had ended. To Wall Street RCA ranked first as an electronics manufacturer, then as a government contractor, and finally as a TV network.[12]

Yet with all the seeming success reflected on the RCA balance sheets, the General had a hard time defending NBC's slippage: the 1955 annual report stated that "[s]ales of the National Broadcasting Company in 1954 established a new record, 14.3 per cent higher than in 1953. Gross television network billings increased 30 per cent to a record high of $125,000,000." It did not mention that the CBS-TV network had passed NBC in the ratings or that NBC's profits were falling. As RCA grew, the General emphasized more and more that it was an electronics corporation—one of the top twenty-five in the world.[13]

Pat Weaver Fails

The General had not planned for NBC's profitability to shrink during the early 1950s. In 1949 he had hired ad agency executive Pat Weaver to build a television network using the same business strategies that had worked to make NBC radio network top ranked for twenty years. Weaver went on to become a mythologized figure in early television history, representing a more high-minded approach to television exemplified by such shows as *Today* and *Tonight* as well as his ambitious

"Operation Frontal Lobes"—a plan to make NBC the home of challenging, "serious" programming (Kepley 1990a). However, Weaver's ability to innovate in prime time at NBC was severely limited by the priorities and constraints set by David Sarnoff. Sarnoff demanded that Weaver stick to the ways that worked for radio. All Sarnoff asked that Weaver do was convert NBC radio—with advertising agencies buying blocks of time—to the NBC-TV network. He ordered Weaver not to copy the nonsense that William Paley was doing across town at CBS by making stars multimillionaires.

It was not that Weaver did not notice that CBS was flying past NBC-TV in the ratings. In a memorandum to his staff, Weaver proposed that NBC should move away from the radio model of single-sponsor programs and toward what he called a "magazine" style of advertising, with multiple advertisers purchasing time adjacent to NBC programming. Weaver was recommending that NBC copy the system CBS already had in place. The General quickly nixed that idea (Weaver 1994, 261–62).

When Weaver became NBC's president in 1953 he had big plans, and he encouraged his staff to think big too. But the General would not allow this experimentation in prime time. On September 11 of that year, Ted Mills announced plans for NBC's morning magazine show *Home* and stated Weaver's and NBC's positions clearly: "We need not, should not, rely on any outside individual packagers; if we hire properly, we can do as well—better than anybody in the field." In other words, outside prime time Weaver was able to copy what CBS was doing in prime time.[14]

Throughout the early 1950s, NBC's prime-time schedule remained filled with sponsor productions, creating schedules over which Weaver had little control. "NBC just sat there," recalled CBS president Frank Stanton. "They would take this or that program produced by the advertisers," since Sarnoff continued to believe that the network's stronger stations and greater reach were sufficient to attract the best programming and keep the stars in line.[15]

NBC's major effort to counter CBS was Weaver's "spectaculars," sold to a single advertiser, running anywhere from ninety minutes to three hours and costing up to $500,000 or more each. These supershows brought an excitement that neither TV nor radio had had before and helped to fuel Weaver's reputation. Weaver's philosophy of "enlightenment through exposure" combined competition with image building, a strategy that appealed to Sarnoff. NBC led in airing classics, current stage plays, ballets, operas, and documentaries. But they were costly one-shot deals that did not draw viewers to tune into NBC on a regular basis. Profits of NBC kept climbing as more U.S. homes filled with TV sets, but its prime-time schedule ratings continued to fall behind those of CBS.[16]

As early as 1952 Paley let the world know he had passed NBC. In its 1952 *Annual Report* CBS bragged: "During 1952 CBS Television maintained its reputation as pace setter of the networks."[17] *I Love Lucy* was a package program, produced by Desilu Studios and sold as a package to CBS. It delivered the largest audience ever won by a regularly scheduled program in the history of broadcasting—forty-one million viewers for a single broadcast. Moreover, program popularity studies in cities with more than two networks revealed that CBS television, during the 1952 fall season, dominated the top ten. Eight CBS television package programs appeared in the top ten sometime during the fall: *Arthur Godfrey and His Friends, Jack Benny, I Love Lucy, Life with Luigi, Our Miss Brooks, Talent Scouts, Toast of the Town,* and *What's My Line?*

The average audience rating in prime time on CBS, the crucial area of network competition, was 97 percent higher than NBC. CBS television's average nighttime audience was growing twice as fast as NBC's. CBS's average daytime audience rating increased 35 percent per annum, also ahead of NBC. On top of this, the CBS television network delivered viewing audiences at a lower cost than the others. This efficiency and effectiveness had a measurable effect on the acceptance of CBS television among advertisers. The annual reports failed to mention that it was Lew Wasserman who had brought these winning programs to Paley. Wasserman's agency packaged show after show that pushed CBS into the number one TV network position.[18]

Pat Weaver knew he would only get along at RCA and NBC if he did what the General wanted him to do and that he would last only until the General saw that Weaver had trained his son Robert Sarnoff. According to Weaver's autobiography, it first seemed as if that would take just three years. Weaver was hired in 1949 as vice president in charge of programming and head of the television network, with Robert under him. Just before Christmas 1951, David Sarnoff promoted finance expert Frank White above Weaver, chagrined with NBC's falling stature and Weaver's increasing resistance to the General's focus on technology over programming. But White grew ill, and in September 1953 Weaver was reinstated, now as president of NBC Television (Weaver 1994, 267–70).[19]

However, all industry insiders knew this promotion was temporary. The question was not "Will Robert Sarnoff become head of NBC?" but "When will it happen?" The General felt the pressure. CBS remained in first place. As its 1954 annual report summarized: "In this annual letter to you, we are gratified to report that 1953 was the most successful year in CBS history." CBS television won a nighttime average rating of 20.1 from January through December, compared to 16.9 for NBC. Eighteen different CBS television programs appeared among the Nielsen prime-time top ten at various times during the year. *I Love Lucy,* with a weekly audience averaging forty-four million, continued to be television's most popular show.[20]

For the 1953–54 TV season Weaver fought back by debuting big-budget, big-name comedy and drama spectaculars like *The All-Star Revue, The Comedy Hour, Producer's Showcase,* and *The Saturday Night Review,* which included *Your Show of Shows* starring Sid Caesar. These programs did little, however, to move NBC ahead in the prime-time ratings game. Industry observers watched Weaver attempting to break down the David Sarnoff–imposed radio strategic approach, but son Robert reported every proposed Weaver deviation to his father. The General grew more and more irritated as the 1955–56 TV season commenced. Weaver (1994) recalled: "After a flurry of rumors about changes in the executive structure . . . Bobby Sarnoff came into my office one day and told me exactly what was happening. His father had decided to make me [Weaver] chairman of the board because, he [David Sarnoff] said, it was about time for Bobby, after his long apprenticeship, to take the job he was destined to fill—the presidency of the NBC network" (268). In December 1955, Weaver stepped down as president of NBC and moved "up" to become chairman of the board of NBC. All industry observers and those broadcast experts on Wall Street knew who actually ran NBC: Robert Sarnoff, with his father's counsel. Robert Sarnoff took the post of president of NBC with explicit instructions to catch CBS. Only after his death did the *New York Times* feel safe in describing David Sarnoff's leadership style: "As a corporate chairman, surrounded by minions, press agents, lawyers and aides, he [was to all with whom he dealt] a cold unloved authoritative figure." The General was no corporate chieftain to be satisfied with second place (Weaver 1994, 269–70).[21]

Sorry, We Are Experiencing Succession Difficulties

The General's eldest son, Robert Sarnoff—Bobby to all—had joined NBC in 1948 as an account executive in the Sales Department. Over a period of seven years, he served his apprenticeship in a wide assortment of positions at the network. Sarnoff once remarked that for a time he was the in-house expert on the *Howdy Doody Show*. He played a lead role in commissioning NBC's much-acclaimed opera *Amahl and the Night Visitors*, by Gian Carlo Menotti, which in 1953 became the first commercial program broadcast in color. But everyone knew what the General was doing; he was grooming his boy to head NBC while he concentrated his duties to building up the bulk of RCA's businesses.[22]

As 1955 turned into 1956, Robert Sarnoff began crafting plans to revitalize NBC. He signed new stars. On Saturday nights, NBC's Perry Como gave CBS's Jackie Gleason competition. For Sunday nights he signed Steve Allen to run against CBS's Ed Sullivan. On Monday nights, Sarnoff introduced the new quiz show *Twenty-One* to chase CBS's *I Love Lucy*. Early in 1957, looking at the changes Robert Sarnoff made in 1956, *Business Week* concluded, "From now on, NBC is playing the rating game hard."[23]

In November, 1956, a year after his son became head of NBC, David Sarnoff brought the succession issue out in the open at a two-day meeting celebrating the creation of NBC. He said in part:

> I should like to say a word or two about Bob; pardon the pride which I naturally feel at his fine job. That is the fact that it is not always easy [for the son] of a father who is head of an organization to overcome all the roadblocks that attach to such a situation. I am not weeping for him, because I think that perhaps there is an advantage or two also, which might counterbalance these difficulties in a measure. . . . Sometimes fathers are criticized—particularly if they head public corporations as distin-

guished from private organizations—for having members of their own family in the same business in positions of responsibility. I have thought a good deal about this and have developed my own philosophy.[24]

He then went on to explain to *Business Week* three months later that "when a man stands in the way of his own son's progress, he is not thinking of the son, he is thinking of himself." This rare public defense demonstrated that the General was apprehensive that he would be criticized. He could read the ratings, and CBS was still on top—led by *I Love Lucy* and *The Ed Sullivan Show*. He continued:

> Now if what you do or fail to do is done in behalf of your son, I applaud it. If, however, what you do or fail to do is done to save yourself from possible criticism by some uninformed person who refuses to recognize that your son's ability had better be used for your company's benefit than that of a competitor, then I don't think you merit any applause. . . . I suggest that fathers have no more right to stand in the way of their sons' progress than the sons have to stand in the way of progress of their fathers. I am proud of the job that Bob and his associates in the NBC are doing and I wish them continued success.[25]

Yet insiders knew the General was defending his son's failure to catch CBS. Thus the Sarnoffs turned to the person who had helped put CBS on top—Lew Wasserman. After a series of meetings in February 1957, the General hired Robert Kintner, then an ex–ABC president and former Wasserman client, as TV network head. Kintner was a workaholic who would put in long hours to keep track of the details that seemed to make Robert Sarnoff's eyes glaze over. But even more important, Wasserman convinced the General that his television schedule needed a Wasserman makeover. David Sarnoff ordered Kintner to work with Wasserman to get the shows that could challenge CBS (McDougal 1998, 238–40).[26]

After all the failed moves by Weaver, the alliance with Wasserman caught the industry's attention. This was a very positive move, praised reluctantly even by Paley's chief aide Frank Stanton. As Stanton later recalled, Wasserman was not just any addition to NBC: "Anything you wanted in [Hollywood], [Wasserman] could get for you. He had all the connections."[27] Not surprisingly Robert Sarnoff grew to rely on Wasserman's man in New York, David Werblin, who became almost an NBC employee. Wasserman skillfully deferred to what David Sarnoff demanded, yet managed to convince the aging executive that new ways of scheduling and producing television were necessary. With his son in charge, and Wasserman whispering in his ear, the General was ready for changes he had resisted from Weaver. Industry headlines marveled in 1957 when the General approved a new NBC daytime show, *Queen for a Day,* and it became the top-rated adult show in the afternoon. This would never have happened without Wasserman's advice. By October 1957, that month's issue of *Television* magazine ranked Wasserman the third most powerful person in the television business—behind only Paley and the General himself.

For the 1957–58 season Wasserman produced and placed *Tales of Wells Fargo* against the long-running CBS Monday night hit *Arthur Godfrey's Talent Scouts,* and

FIG. **10** Lew Wasserman, NBC's secret weapon in its war against CBS for television ratings in the 1950s and 1960s. (Library of American Broadcasting)

by the end of the season Godfrey had fallen out of the top thirty while *Tales of Wells Fargo* ranked third, behind only CBS's *Gunsmoke* and *The Danny Thomas Show*. More importantly for NBC, in twenty-third place (in its first season) was another Wasserman western—*Wagon Train*. This one would rise to second place in the following season, 1958–59, with *Tales of Wells Fargo* at seventh place. NBC was back in the ball game (Brooks and Marsh 2003, 1245–46).

The General glowed as *Wagon Train* finished second only to *Gunsmoke* in the 1959 to 1961 TV seasons, then advanced to number 1 in the 1961–62 season. Wasserman had created the first NBC ratings blockbuster since Milton Berle. In retrospect, *Wagon Train* seems like a formulaic fusion of popular western genre conventions with a conventional narrative. It was created and filmed by a Wasserman company, MCA's Revue Television. It premiered on Wednesday night, 7:30–8:30 p.m., in September 1957. The show took its initial inspiration from John Ford's 1950 film *The Wagonmaster*. Each week, a star such as Ernest Borgnine, Shelly Winters, Lou Costello, or Jane Wyman (all Wasserman clients) would appear along with series regulars Ward Bond and Robert Horton. Filmed on location in California's San Fernando Valley, the show had an impressive budget of $100,000 per episode, at a time when competing westerns cost less than $70,000 to produce. Lew Wasserman knew how to merge the Hollywood star system and popular narrative and bring it to NBC; repeats and reruns would make everyone rich (Gomery 2005, 208–9; Perry 1983, x–xi, 110–11).

In a TV schedule full of westerns, *Wagon Train*, while fulfilling the genre's expectations, established a unique style reminiscent of the anthology drama. Wasserman knew if he created enough westerns one was bound to strike a popular chord. To critics and later historians it simply represents one of dozens of the TV westerns of the eras; for the history of NBC it meant a return to prime-time respectability (Brauer 1975; Cawelti 1984; MacDonald 1987).

The popular press gave all the credit to Robert Sarnoff and Robert Kintner, the executive faces of NBC. Wasserman and his MCA did all of their work behind closed doors. Wasserman himself was rarely interviewed, and only hints of his influence over NBC are available. Several historians have cited one example that did make it into the industry and business press. We know that one spring night in 1957 that Robert Sarnoff called a meeting of the network's programming executives. After they had assembled, the door opened and in walked MCA vice president David Werblin—carrying instructions from Wasserman. Without any preliminaries, Robert Sarnoff asked this representative of the MCA agency to look at the NBC schedule for next season, note the empty spots, and fill them in with MCA product. The rest of the evening the NBC executives—under orders from Robert Sarnoff—watched the MCA agent rearrange the NBC schedule and insert new shows brokered by Wasserman. When finished, the NBC schedule showed fourteen series (eight and a half hours a week) in prime time that MCA would produce for NBC—including *Wagon Train*.[28]

Yet Wasserman wanted the world to think that NBC was calling the shots. He was content to stay in the background as he worked at making deals behind the scenes. In the late 1950s, Wasserman's full client list was never made public. The company refused to say for publication which television film series it represented, even though a sign proclaiming "MCA TV, Exclusive Distributor" was prominently displayed on the screen at the end of each episode when these series were broadcast. Wasserman never went on the record to boast how many series he had created and produced. So while it seemed to most that the Sarnoffs were still programming NBC, they were nearly wholly dependent on Wasserman's deal making (Bruck 2003, 475-76).

Wasserman had his reasons for this secretiveness. For one thing, MCA had a fiduciary relationship with its clients and therefore did not discuss clients' affairs—or even reveal their names. For another, Lew Wasserman saw no good reason to disclose his methods to his competitors. No MCA "fiduciary relationships" were better hidden than those with the TV networks. MCA set up its own clients in the TV business, usually as equal partners. For example, one reporter for *Fortune* reported that the first three years of *Wagon Train*, which was budgeted at about $100,000 a week, somehow brought MCA $17 million a year when all was said and done.[29]

But Lew Wasserman did not work only for NBC. Wasserman placed clients wherever he could. Indeed, he was the chief agent for *The Ed Sullivan Show*, a hit for CBS. He packaged multiple hits through an MCA subsidiary, Revue, including *Leave It to Beaver* for CBS, the very same year he placed *Wagon Train* at NBC. (Both *Wagon Train* and *Leave It to Beaver* were nominated for the Emmy for Best New Program of 1957.) Wasserman and his clients were still supplying CBS with the popular *Alfred Hitchcock Presents*. And despite his many successes, Wasserman created an equal number of duds. For every *Wagon Train* came a one-season wonder such as *Buckskin* (1958-59).[30]

Bob Kintner played little role in all of this other than making sure that the trains ran on time. His love was news, and he gave the Sarnoffs some satisfaction with his invention of the policy of "CBS plus 30" for breaking stories—meaning NBC's news broadcast would stay on thirty minutes longer than CBS's any time there was breaking news. Paley and CBS may have had their Murrow, but in the late 1950s Murrow was gone and NBC news ranked at the top of both the ratings and the awards as best TV news. As Grant Tinker (1994) clearly lays out in his autobiography, as long as Robert Kintner played the loyal employee, a lieutenant to the General and his son Robert, all was fine. However, when the quiz show scandals broke the Sarnoffs disappeared. They let Kintner appear on *Time* magazine's cover to take the heat (69-73).[31]

1960: In Conclusion

Why have previous scholars ignored the crucial role played by Lew Wasserman in network television history? Wasserman saw to it that precious little record of his dominant role remains. He left a very scant paper trail. Yet a close reading of the trade press makes it clear that in the late 1940s Lew Wasserman changed broad-casting forever. His innovative use of the tax laws to drive the famous CBS "talent raids" empowered his agency, MCA, to spearhead the rise of packaged programs, which slowly but inevitably replaced the old single-sponsor advertising agency sys-tem clung to by David Sarnoff. Both William Paley at CBS and, belatedly, Sarnoff at NBC reaped the benefit of what Wasserman had wrought by selling ad time in small increments at ever higher prices. Maybe *Television* magazine had its rankings in the wrong order; Wasserman in historical analysis was the most powerful per-son in the TV business, with Paley and the Sarnoffs following (Brooks and Marsh 2003, 1246; McDougal 1998, 230).

Only rarely would anyone publicly expose the Sarnoff management mess as Eugene Paul did. Stars who complained risked never being seen on the network again. Most famously, over Labor Day weekend in 1960, movie star turned TV spe-cial producer Esther Williams was quoted as saying, "NBC management is a colos-sal mess." On August 8, 1960, her "Esther Williams at Cypress Gardens" spectac-ular drew half the nation's homes to NBC on that Monday night. Yet Williams would never be allowed to appear on NBC again, despite her superb ratings (E. Williams 1999, 324).[32] Had Lew Wasserman been her agent, she would have never made the mistake of going public with her complaints.

In the end, despite its Wasserman-inspired rally, NBC would pay the price of its earlier foot-dragging and enter the 1960s a perennial second-place network. Wasserman, on the other hand, would purchase Universal Studios and become the leading supplier of TV programs, particularly to NBC as long as a grateful Robert Sarnoff was in charge.

Lew Wasserman saved NBC but sought no credit. Loyalty to David Sarnoff and excellent PR staff work ensured that NBC's inept management never got much press. Pat Weaver became the darling of the critics and has remained the focus of much historical work. The Sarnoff mythmaking machinery concentrated on all the technological wonders that David Sarnoff had wrought and rarely spoke of his ig-nominious fall to second place in the TV ratings race. Lew Wasserman is barely mentioned in most network histories, with a few exceptions.[33] Yet no one played a more crucial role in the development of commercial network economics, estab-lished in the 1960s and still with us today, despite all the changes the last twenty years have brought.

Notes

Abbreviations

LAB   Library of American Broadcasting, University of Maryland
NBC/LC   Motion Picture, Broadcasting, and Recorded Sound Division, Library of Congress
NBC/WHS   National Broadcasting Company Archives, Wisconsin Historical Society

1. This essay is hardly the first to address NBC as a network during the 1950s. The standard and pioneering work is still William Boddy's *Fifties Television: The Industry and Its Critics* (1990). Boddy overlooks the role of Wasserman in formulating the long-term Hollywood–TV network relationship. Vance Kepley Jr.'s essay in Tino Balio's *Hollywood in the Age of Television* more directly addresses NBC in the 1950s but also fails to take Wasserman's key role into account.

2. See the annual reports of RCA for 1945, 1946, 1947, and 1948, NBC/LC.

3. Irving Mansfield (husband of novelist Jacqueline Susann) wrote of these meetings in detail in his autobiography *Life with Jackie* (1983, 72–73).

4. See NBC's year-end reports for 1945, 1946, 1947, and 1948, NBC/LC.

5. "Besieged on Three Fronts," *Newsweek*, December 5, 1949, 75.

6. Reprinted in RCA, *Annual Report*, 1950, NBC/LC.

7. "RCA Gross Sets Record, Net Declines," *Washington Post*, February 27, 1950, 17.

8. *Television Age*, June 1986, special issue on NBC's history.

9. NBC, *Year End Reports*, 1950, 1951, 1952, 1953, and 1954, NBC/LC.

10. Radio Corporation of America, *Annual Report*, 1956, NBC/LC.

11. *Washington Post*, November 26, 1952, and February 4 and 19, 1953. In time Sarnoff would take advantage of the 1957 launch to call for closing the missile gap with RCA electronics components. See "Urge Large US Role," *Washington Post*, January 14, 1958, A8. In 1961 he even predicted an RCA camp when men reached the moon. See "Today's Events in TV," *Washington Post*, January 29, 1961, C21.

12. Radio Corporation of America. *Annual Reports*, 1952–57, NBC/LC.

13. RCA, *Annual Report*, 1954, NBC/LC.

14. Ted Mills to Sylvester L. Weaver, September 11, 1953, Box 377, Folder 6, NBC/WHS.

15. Stanton is quoted in *Broadcasting*, October 18, 1971, 56.

16. See RCA's annual reports for 1950–60, NBC/LC.

17. CBS, *Annual Report*, 1952, LAB.

18. Ibid.

19. David Sarnoff memo file, NBC/LC.

20. CBS, *Annual Report*, 1954, LAB.

21. Jack Gould, "Sarnoff: Mr. Do-It of Broadcasting," *New York Times*, December 13, 1971.

22. Jack Gould, "TV: Changes at NBC," *New York Times*, December 9, 1955.

23. "TV Heart to Heart," *Business Week*, February 16, 1957, 90–92.

24. David Sarnoff memo file, NBC/LC.

25. "TV Heart to Heart."

26. "NBC Is Cutting Creative Staff," *New York Times*, April 26, 1957, 51.

27. *Broadcasting*, October 18, 1971, 56.

28. There are three versions of this story: "This Is MCA," *Television*, October 1957, 53–54; Edward T. Thompson, "There's No Business Like Show Business Like MCA's Business," *Fortune*, July 1960, 114–15; and the record of *U.S. v. MCA et al.* (1962). I have researched the small contradictions, and what I recount here seems to be the most plausible version.

29. Thompson, "There's No Business." C. Morrison, "Ward Bond and Wagon Train," *Look*, October 27, 1959, offers a detailed examination of this hit show.

30. "The Classic TV Archive: MCA's Revue Studios Series Guide, 1952–1964," www.geocities.com/TelevisionCity/Stage/2950.

31. *Time*, November 16, 1959. In a case where legend met fact, in Robert Redford's 1994

movie *Quiz Show* the Kintner character played the heavy while the Sarnoffs were wholly absent.

32. "Esther Williams Opines Wrong at NBC," *Washington Post*, September 7, 1960.

33. There has been precious little written about Robert Sarnoff, though the RCA PR department built up his father into a legend. Obituaries of Robert Sarnoff in the *Los Angeles Times* and the *New York Times*, February 23, 1997, however, describe the son's destruction of RCA—sold and broken up just ten years after his departure.

NBC and the Classic Network System 1960–85

Introduction to Part Three

NBC and the Classic Network System, 1960–85

MICHELE HILMES

By 1960, the three powerful national networks had already begun to advocate a new kind of relationship of sponsors to TV, led by NBC: the *magazine concept*, developed by NBC chief Pat Weaver after the style of women's daytime talk shows on radio, which substituted multiple sponsorship for single sponsors and made spot advertising the new order of the day. Seizing on the opportunity presented by the quiz show scandal and investigations in 1958 to 1959, the networks promised that from now on they would play a new, activist role in programming. Gone would be the dependence on corrupt, ratings-driven advertisers; here to stay would be a new era of centralized network responsibility and control. It was the blueprint for the classic network system to follow, marked by highly centralized network control over all phases of the industry: production, distribution, and exhibition. In return, especially after Kennedy-appointed FCC chair Newton Minow lambasted broadcasters at their annual convention with his condemnation of trivial, mindless programming, NBC and its competitors promised to improve dramatically in their provision of news and public affairs documentary programming. Michael Curtin discusses changes ushered in by Robert Kinter at NBC in the early 1960s in chapter 10, "NBC News Documentary: 'Intelligent Interpretation' in a Cold War Context."

The classic network system was a period of tight vertical integration, similar to that of the movie studios before 1947, and of oligopoly, with just three networks dominating the industry. Production control stemmed from a system of ownership interests, with multiple sponsorship limiting the influence of advertisers. As for production, networks either owned outright or owned an interest in most of their prime-time and daytime programming, and they controlled syndication rights as well. Distribution control reflected the ever-tightening relationship between networks and their affiliates, as network feed took over more of each station's total schedule. And exhibition control was due to the networks' increasing number of affiliate stations;

until the early 1980s, over 80 percent of U.S. television stations were either owned by or affiliated with one of the Big Three: ABC, CBS, or NBC.

By the late 1960s, the Big Three networks essentially held television production in thrall, purchasing shows for less than it cost to make them. As a result, independent producers in particular were dependent on network investment to stay afloat; they had essentially become production arms of the network. Hollywood studios increasingly resented the large cut that the networks took out of domestic syndication. Scheduling each evening's lineup became something of an art form, as the Big Three juggled shows and programmed against their competitors—with no sponsors to interfere with their decisions anymore. Sometimes this meant that they could afford to take unusual risks, as each network strove to build up its own audience and to differentiate its programming from competitors. In chapter 11, Jeffrey Miller traces NBC's use of innovative comedy programming in "What Closes on Saturday Night: NBC and Satire."

As with radio, centralized control increased along with homogeneity and standardization. The more producers jostled for change, the tighter the networks cracked down. One iconic product of American television, the *Star Trek* original series, got its start on NBC during this period, but, as authors Máire Messenger Davies and Roberta Pearson argue in chapter 12, "The Little Program That Could: The Relationship between NBC and *Star Trek*," it could not ultimately be sustained in the period of network dominance. Yet, another characteristic of the classic network system was the resistance building up from forces on the fringes of the television oligopoly—from independent producers and Hollywood studios; from critics of TV's homogeneity, racial policies, and violence; from the developing public television movement; and from its soon-to-be-archrival, cable TV. Chapter 12 demonstrates how differently the future generations of *Star Trek* would fare under these changing conditions.

The decades between 1960 and 1985 mark the emergence of what we, along with the rest of the world, now think of as American TV. But by the mid-1980s the tight network control that had been brought on by the quiz show scandals of the 1950s began to falter under a rhetoric that blamed the vertically integrated commercial network oligopoly for a host of problems. The emergence of PBS in 1967 pointed to all the things that the commercial networks failed or refused to do: educational programs for kids, serious public affairs and documentary series, coverage of art and culture, inclusion of racial minorities, and a host of other long-awaited program initiatives. The commercial networks responded by creating programming that attempted to capture youth audiences and win back others by pushing the boundaries of sexuality and violence. Elena Levine criticizes NBC's attempts to keep up with its competitors in chapter 13, "Sex as a Weapon: Programming Sexuality in the 1970s."

Pressures from reformist, political, and competing industry groups during the late 1960s and early 1970s created a groundswell of regulatory measures that would undermine the tight network cartel. The Financial Interest and Syndication Rule

(Fin-Syn) and the Prime Time Access Rules (PTAR), initiated in the early 1970s, pointed to places where the Big Three networks exercised excessive control. Government studies of the effects of television viewing on the child audience motivated the networks themselves to initiate a new approach to children's programming. In chapter 14, "Saturday Morning Children's Programs on NBC, 1975–2006: A Case Study of Self-Regulation," NBC executive Horst Stipp and consultant Karen Hill-Scott trace NBC's efforts to meet this new challenge. But by the early 1980s, under Ronald Reagan–appointed FCC chair Mark Fowler, this reformist philosophy would shift in a strong deregulatory direction, ushering the nation rapidly into the post-network period of the 1990s and beyond.

By 1985 the Big Three's affiliated share of the nation's television stations had declined dramatically: from a 1960 high of 96 percent, by 1985 only 69 percent of stations belonged to a network. The rest had begun to thrive on the favorable conditions for independent stations that cable had generated, with syndicated production reaching new heights as families, now that a majority of households owned multiple sets, separated into disparate demographic groups. The classic network system had all but collapsed. Through a combination of deregulation, the rise of cable and satellite technology, and proliferating channels and program forms, an era of competition, diversity, and choice eventually replaced scarcity, public interest obligations, and centralized control.

10

NBC News Documentary

"Intelligent Interpretation" in a Cold War Context

MICHAEL CURTIN

During the early 1960s, NBC Television, under president Robert Kintner, seized a leadership role in television news as it dramatically expanded its documentary news programming and launched the genre into prime-time viewing hours. A golden age of documentary ensued that remains to this day a singular moment in U.S. television history. Examining pressing social issues at home and abroad, the programs drew accolades from politicians and social critics and regularly attracted tens of millions of viewers. This remarkable public service was in part motivated by the internal dynamics of the television industry, but it was also a response to public debate, regulatory pressure, and the foreign policy interests of the U.S. government. NBC—with its expansive worldwide media ventures—was especially inclined to engage with the Cold War concerns of the Kennedy administration and consequently took the lead in news and public affairs programming. This chapter delineates the various forces that spurred NBC's documentary ventures and briefly analyzes an exemplary program, "Angola: Journey to a War," showing how it operated under a set of ideological assumptions that articulated the concerns of national politicians, network officials, and journalists.

In the mid-1950s, the three television networks dominated the market for the nation's most popular pastime and reaped some of the most fantastic profits in the history of the American economy. But this was also an era of public anxieties about social relations, contemporary morals, and the nation's sense of purpose. During the late 1950s, these anxieties would manifest themselves in a number of scandals that subjected the broadcasting and advertising industries to widespread criticism. But the single issue that evoked the greatest concern was the perceived threat posed by Soviet military advances. The detonation of a powerful hydrogen bomb in 1953 and the successful launch of the Sputnik satellite into outer space four years later showed that America's avowed Cold War adversary could now launch long-distance nuclear strikes against strategic targets and population centers in North America, and these developments spurred much discussion regarding the comparative status of U.S. science, schooling, and strategic preparedness. They also fueled concerns that the American public had grown soft, preferring backyard barbeques and TV comedies to a more serious engagement with public affairs. Accordingly, prominent social critics such as Edward R. Murrow and Arthur Schlesinger Jr.—both of whom would become key figures in the Kennedy administration—argued for the reform of television, claiming that the medium was increasingly dominated by rampant commercialism and mindless entertainment at a time when the nation was imperiled by a determined communist foe. These critics also suggested that television, because of its privileged access to the suburban family home, had an important role to play in educating the public for a protracted worldwide struggle. Such concerns culminated in the 1961 appointment of Newton Minow as chairman of the Federal Communications Commission (FCC), followed shortly thereafter by his first major speech to broadcasting executives in which he famously referred to network television as a "vast wasteland." Like other officials in the Kennedy administration, Minow explicitly put the TV industry on notice that he considered the medium a strategic weapon in the struggle against communism, and throughout his two-year term he prodded and cajoled network officials to expand their news departments and increase their coverage of international issues.

Yet the administration's priorities were not simply imposed on the industry. TV executives were generally sympathetic to the government's concerns, and news department staffers were especially receptive, hoping to see their profession restored to the prominence it had enjoyed during World War II. Immediately after the war, few imagined that television news would supersede its radio counterpart, and indeed most correspondents vied for plum *radio* assignments. NBC's initial TV news venture was hosted not by a journalist but by announcer John Cameron Swayze, whose *Camel Caravan of News* "hopscotched" the globe, delivering a mere fifteen-minute sampling of headline stories (Karnick 1988).[1] Because the transition from radio to television proved expensive, all three networks allocated most of their resources to entertainment programming during the medium's first decade, allowing only occasional opportunities for experimentation in news and information genres. At NBC that began to change in 1956, when Robert Kintner took charge as network president. An avowed "news junkie," Kintner expanded the scope and resources of the news division, creating a truly international news-gathering organization during his decade-long reign. Most immediately, Kintner parlayed Chet Huntley's and David Brinkley's adroit coverage of the 1956 Democratic and Republican conventions into the *Huntley-Brinkley Report*, a program that would dominate nightly news ratings until 1967. As the news division grew more active and prosperous and as government pressure increased, Kintner also became an advocate of news specials, often breaking away from regularly scheduled entertainment shows to provide live coverage of important events, such as spacecraft launches, congressional hearings, and the Cuban missile crisis. Kintner also nurtured the network's documentary efforts, overseeing the launch of the distinguished *NBC White Paper* series in 1960 and promoting a host of programs dedicated to news interpretation and analysis.

Kintner's efforts were motivated by more than pro bono professionalism, for he was the first network chief to stress the profit potential of TV news programming at a time when NBC's entertainment programming was lagging behind CBS and was threatened by the upstart ABC network. Just as importantly, Kintner, who would later serve in the Johnson administration, understood the public relations value of his news division at a time when government regulators were pressing for more informative prime-time fare, especially regarding world affairs. Here NBC's interests and government priorities dovetailed, since by the early 1960s the overseas operations of the network and its corporate parent, RCA, were emerging as important contributors to the corporate bottom line. Finally, Kintner supported the development of network documentary in part because it provided a morale boost to employees of the news division, many of whom felt slighted by the premium placed upon entertainment programming during the early years of TV. Journalists who filed stories from the battlefronts of World War II were, by the late 1950s, network executives and senior correspondents who perceived news as a crucial component of network programming. These employees therefore had professional reasons to support the expansion of news, since it would enhance their status and increase their visibility, and they were especially enthusiastic about documentary, seeing it as a genre that allowed them to examine important issues with a depth and complexity that might rival the work of their newsprint counterparts. Similar dynamics were at work at CBS and ABC: agitation from within combined with pressures from without prompted all three television networks to expand their news divisions during the early 1960s, with special emphasis on documentary.

In 1962 alone, the three commercial networks telecast close to four hundred documentaries, most of them during the evening hours (Carroll 1989). At a time when nightly newscasts were only fifteen minutes long and at the very moment when opinion polls showed that TV had overtaken newspapers as the public's preferred news source, the major networks touted documentary as an important vehicle of public education in an age of crisis and uncertainty. It was estimated that some 90 percent of all American homes viewed at least one documentary each month, and the increasing prominence of the genre was nurtured by critical acclaim (Carroll 1989, 415; Yellin 1973, 107).[2] *Variety* cited the documentary boom as the most exciting programming development of the early 1960s, and in 1962 the genre snagged three of the five Emmy Award nominations for program of the year.[3] One year later, a documentary succeeded for the first time in capturing the top honor: NBC's program about an escape from communist East Berlin entitled "The Tunnel" (Yellin 1973, 223; Brooks and Marsh 2003, 1208).[4] The genre was also promoted as an important new addition to the television syndication market, as all three networks now used documentaries to distinguish their overseas program catalogs. By 1962, NBC boasted that it was distributing informational fare to over fifty countries and that the programs were being used as a model for indigenous documentary

FIG. **11** Robert W. Kintner, NBC president and self-avowed "news junkie," who built up the news division and established the nightly *Huntley-Brinkley Report*. (Library of American Broadcasting)

efforts by broadcasters overseas. CBS and ABC made similar claims for similar reasons.[5]

But this era is also remarkable for other, seemingly contradictory milestones in television history. In 1962, *The Beverly Hillbillies,* one of the most popular entertainment programs of all time, premiered on Wednesday evenings, sandwiched between *The Many Loves of Dobie Gillis* and *The Dick Van Dyke Show.* Poking fun at the absurdities of modern suburban living, these shows regularly drew television's largest audiences, and opinion polls from the period showed that most Americans were primarily concerned with their immediate domestic surroundings. Yet at this very moment when Americans were looking inward, television began to expand its field of vision as never before. Documentaries about compelling national issues such as poverty, automation, and civil rights received prominent airplay, but the single issue that commanded the most network attention was the struggle to defend the "Free World" against the international challenge posed by communism. Consequently, NBC churned out dozens of prime-time documentaries such as "Red China," "Panama: Danger Zone," and "The Rise of Khrushchev."

The Importance of Going Global

As mentioned earlier, prime-time documentary became an important TV genre at the very moment when the major networks were anticipating the coming saturation of the domestic market and were therefore expanding overseas. In 1961, the United States Information Agency reported a 20 percent annual increase in overseas TV ownership, estimating that the medium reached fifty-five million households in foreign countries.[6] Not only was the worldwide audience for television growing, but many stations abroad were hungry for programming to fill their expanding broadcast schedules. The Television Program Export Association calculated $30 million in overseas sales by American syndicators in 1961, and three years later the figure more than doubled to $68 million in sales to more than eighty countries (Dizard 1964, 61). By the middle of the decade, foreign markets accounted for 60 percent of total syndication revenues, and industry analysts pointed to overseas operations as "the difference between profit and loss for the entire [syndication] industry" (Dizard 1964, 58).[7] They anticipated continuing growth as television receiver purchases escalated and as developing countries grew more prosperous. Consequently, all three networks showed increasing interest in international markets, but perhaps NBC and its parent company, the Radio Corporation of America, had an unparalleled stake in developments abroad.

With more than 11,700 products and services available in 120 countries and territories, RCA had its finger in nearly every pie, from satellite services in Canada to picture tube plants in Europe. Of its ninety thousand employees worldwide, more than 10 percent were stationed abroad. In 1963, RCA Italiana doubled its output of television receivers and projected an even brighter future with the anticipated adoption of color TV in Europe (Skornia 1964, 14–15). Besides manufacturing and marketing a full range of equipment—from transmitters to receivers to video tape recorders—NBC provided management services to new television stations around the world. Such contracts included administrative, technical, and personnel services as well as consultation regarding station construction and equipment installation. The typical contract ran five years, with NBC showing more interest in equipping and programming the station than owning it. In 1964, the Saudi government hired RCA to set up a thirteen-station network in what was the single largest television contract ever landed by an American network overseas.[8] Overall, the company claimed to provide programming and management services to three hundred stations in eighty countries, making it the undisputed leader in foreign markets.[9]

The impact of these growing international operations should not be underestimated. Although all three networks would later face reversals abroad, the early 1960s raised heady expectations for future growth overseas, auguring the prospect of Marshall McLuhan's "global village" in the not-too-distant future. Indeed, shortly before the 1962 launch of the first commercial communications satellite and well before McLuhan's writings captured the public imagination, RCA chairman David Sarnoff predicted: "Ten years hence—if vigorous foreign growth continues—there will be TV stations in virtually every nation on earth telecasting to some two hundred million receivers. An audience of a billion people might then be watching the same program at the same time, with simultaneous translation techniques making it understandable to all. In a world where nearly half of the population is illiterate, no other means of mass communication could equal television's reach and impact on the human mind."[10] Many government policy makers concurred, with FCC chairman Newton Minow remarking, "No one knows how long it will be until a broadcast from a studio in New York will be viewed in India as well as in Indiana, will be seen in the Congo as well as Chicago. But surely as we are meeting here today, that day will come—and once again our world will shrink" (Kahn 1984, 215). According to such projections, global television promised not only to speed communication and extend the diffusion of media messages but also to foster public dialogue and democratic politics. Just as regional trading pacts such as the European Common Market enhanced the free flow of goods, television would make possible, according to Minow (1984), an "uncommon market for the free exchange of ideas" (212). Such an exchange was important not only because of its utopian appeal: policy makers contended that better communication would lead to better understanding, not simply between nations, but between the world's peoples.

Shaped by liberal notions of noblesse oblige and tied to government development campaigns, New Frontier rhetoric envisioned a televisual campaign to open the eyes of the less fortunate to the possibilities of the modern world. As communication researcher Daniel Lerner (1958) contended at the time, social and economic development could take place only if people living in small, traditional villages expanded their vision so as to imagine themselves as part of a larger national, and even global, community. Television's capability of reaching illiterate populations worldwide made it an especially attractive medium for stimulating social change and held out the prospect of circumventing repressive political regimes by communicating directly with viewers at home. Richard N. Gardner, deputy assistant secretary of state, who was then deeply involved in planning the UN outer space program, explained that someday satellite TV signals would be beamed directly into households, forging "new bonds of mutual knowledge and understanding between nations" and bringing together the "family of man."[11]

Despite such enthusiasm, many foreign officials and opinion leaders expressed concern about the leadership of U.S. media industries, since Hollywood telefilm already represented 80 percent of all international syndication sales in 1962.[12] Many of these deals included action/adventure programming, giving Hollywood producers a reputation as purveyors of "blood, murder, mayhem, and sex," according to a leading trade publication.[13] As early as 1960, governments around the world were debating whether to impose import quotas on American programs, and by the following year restrictive legislation was pending in England, Mexico, Australia, Brazil, and Argentina.[14] At the very moment when U.S. TV executives were eagerly extending their reach, they confronted harsh criticism abroad as well as at home.[15] Interestingly, Mexican government officials cited Newton Minow's "vast wasteland" speech as justification for imposing import restrictions in 1961.[16] Network executives attempted to deflect such criticism by pointing with pride to the growing number of documentary offerings in their syndication catalogs. The genre therefore not only countered domestic criticisms but also proved useful overseas, where it enjoyed a high level of prestige. In countries where television was recently introduced, local station managers would generally shop for a "balanced" package of programs to import, touting the medium's educational wonders as well as its cornucopia of entertainment (Frappier 1969, 2; Skornia 1964, 19; Dizard 1964, 66–67).[17]

Network executives were therefore well aware of the documentary genre's allure, and NBC grossed over a million dollars in such exports as early as 1961.[18] Although global sales would continue to grow throughout the early 1960s, sheer dollar volume only begins to suggest the cultural significance of these programs. Documentary didn't just deflect criticism of TV; it also disseminated to tens of millions of viewers the U.S. administration's vision of the Free World, making the case for programmatic reform and modernization as opposed to violent, Marxist revolution. Shortly after President John F. Kennedy took office, ABC president Leonard Goldenson conveyed the sentiment of industry leaders when he declared: "In Cuba we have seen how the battle for democracy can be lost. We are in grave danger of losing it in many countries of Latin America, Asia, and Africa. We must get our message of democracy to the uncommitted countries as soon as possible, then let them see us as we are, not as the Russians paint us to be."[19]

NBC News Documentaries

After its 1956 premiere, the *Huntley-Brinkley Report* steadily grew in ratings and sponsor appeal, closing each broadcast with a signature tag line that became celebrated in American popular culture: "Good night, Chet," chirped Brinkley, to which Hunt-ley replied, "Good night, David, and good night for NBC News."[20] During the 1960 presidential campaign, NBC attracted more than half the audience for the nomi-nating conventions, and it expanded its coverage of breaking news events, provid-ing "unmistakable proof of the emergence of NBC News as broadcasting's fore-most news organization," according to NBC chairman Robert Sarnoff.[21] Locked in competition with CBS, the network launched a series of documentaries featur-ing solo performances by its star anchors, and in 1960 it established the prestigious *White Paper* series.[22] One year later, NBC announced that advertising time for all of its informational programming, including documentaries, was sold out for the upcoming season. It now claimed to be number one in sponsor appeal, with pro-jected revenues of $28.6 million, putting the news division several million dollars in the black.[23] This announcement was a marked departure from the sustaining tradition of network news organizations. Just as surprising, these profits were plowed back into *further* expansion of news, especially in the areas of interpretation and analysis.[24] But why would NBC make such an expansive commitment to documen-taries when nightly news was attracting its largest news audiences and generating most of the news division's profit?

First of all, NBC's claim to news leadership was more than a prestige issue. Net-work executives argued that news leadership had the potential to calm restless sta-tion managers who were growing impatient with the lackluster ratings performance of NBC's entertainment programming. By the late 1950s, the network's prime-time fare was running consistently behind CBS in the national Nielsen ratings, and in major cities, where it competed on equal terms with the other two networks, it often ran third. Moreover, NBC felt pressured by ABC's campaign to lure VHF affiliates away from the peacock network in markets where ABC had either no affiliate or an underperforming UHF affiliate. Even a few defections in key markets could un-dermine NBC's number two position in the national Nielsens and pave the way for further erosion of its ratings. NBC responded to ABC's challenge by distinguish-ing itself as a network with "balanced" programming and a tradition of significant public service. In a keynote speech to affiliates, NBC chairman Robert Sarnoff dis-missively referred to ABC as a "narrow gauge" network with little to offer beyond its action/adventure fare.[25]

NBC therefore countered ABC's inroads by touting the network's expanded com-mitment to news programming under the leadership of network president Robert Kintner. Yet Kintner was no stranger to the entertainment end of the business either. Indeed, during his earlier tenure as an ABC executive, he hatched that net-work's action/adventure formula, putting it on the road to commercial viability. His success at ABC attracted the attention of both NBC's Robert Sarnoff and CBS's Frank Stanton.[26] With offers from each, Kintner opted to join NBC in 1956 be-cause, according to one confidant, "He reasoned that CBS had too much execu-tive bench strength and that there was more opportunity at NBC for a new pitcher."[27] This perceived opportunity was also accompanied by complications, since the network's entertainment programming was not competitive with that of front-running CBS. Kintner therefore applied his action/adventure strategy soon after he arrived at NBC, creating a parade of profit makers such as *Wagon Train* and *Bonanza* at the expense of highbrow programs like *Omnibus* and *Wide World*. Such maneuvers earned Kintner the enmity of critics who referred to him as a "skillful and relentless peddler."[28] Indeed, he was characterized as something of a lowbrow who was known to chide his fellow executives by saying, "The trouble with you guys is you don't watch television."[29] Kintner, on the other hand, was a compulsive television viewer. In fact, he made a reputation for himself within the industry for having three television sets—tuned to each of the networks—running simultaneously in his office throughout the workday.[30] He claimed to watch every program on a competitor's schedule at least once each season.[31] Reportedly the same was true for Lucky, Kintner's collie and viewing companion during the boss's evening regimen. In fact, it was a standing joke among NBC executives to ask what Lucky thought of the program schedule last night. Whatever canine wisdom they may have divined from such banter, it took little imagination to decipher Kintner's thinking. "We're looking for shows we can sell," Kintner would snarl, unabashed.[32]

Yet it was this same "relentless peddler" who exploited the opening provided by Huntley's and Brinkley's convention coverage in 1956. At the same time that NBC was dishing up an expanded schedule of action/adventure entertainment, it was escalating its commitment to news. As *New York Times* critic Jack Gould observed: "The good night kids [Huntley-Brinkley] came along when [Kintner] needed them most. NBC was nursing a lackluster theatrical image, so Mr. Kintner directed attention to news and public affairs, gave [news vice president William] McAndrew more authority than any other network news head and established corporate morale that permeated all phases of NBC. In television, it may stand as the most striking instance of what can happen in the medium when the top officer has a sense of passionate commitment and uses his power. It's the occasional thing."[33] While Gould may have been right that Kintner exploited his advantage in news, it is not clear that Kintner's "passionate commitment" would have been so torrid without the ratings to back it up. Nevertheless Kintner seemed to understand enough about both news and entertainment to make his formula work. A newspaper reporter and columnist during the early part of his career, Kintner changed careers when he joined the War Department Bureau of Public Relations during World War II and then ABC Television in 1944 as vice president for programming, public relations, and advertising. Named network president in 1949, Kintner drew on his professional experience to bridge the worlds of news, public relations, and broadcast entertainment, but in his scramble to the top of the television trade he reportedly never lost his passion for news.[34] Fred Freed, one of NBC's top documentary producers, later lauded Kintner for the extensive resources he made available to his documentary producers and for the intangible moral support he lavished on his news employees.

The great thing about Bob Kintner was that he watched every documentary program that went on the air. And he told you about every program and whether he liked it or not. He didn't wait until the show was reviewed by Jack Gould in the *Times* to tell you. One of his eccentricities was about the supers that go up on the screen at the bottom of the pictures, telling who the people are. He called them "labels." He wanted them up over everybody. Any producer sitting in the studio as his show went on the air could count on calls from Bob Kintner growling, "Where the hell are the labels?" (Yellin 1973, 213–14)

Although NBC's news division made most of its money off its nightly news program, Kintner's appetite for a variety of news formats and expanded coverage was not quickly sated. Indeed, NBC management displayed an unequaled enthusiasm for informational programming, and with the news division's lock on advertiser commitments and its positive cash flow, there seemed no limit to what the future might hold. Thus the emergence of documentary as one of NBC's foremost genres of the early 1960s was animated by issues of prestige, programming strategy, affiliate loyalties, and a competitive battle for position in the growing arena of television news. Even though Bob Kintner was "looking for programs he could sell," he also expressed a passionate commitment to news interpretation and analysis. An ardent Democrat who later left NBC in 1966 to join Lyndon Johnson's White House staff, Kintner never lost faith in what he saw as the documentary's potential. "While I am opposed to editorializing on a network basis," he said, "I am convinced there must be more and more intelligent interpretation, for which a news department must take responsibility, so that complex local, national and international events may be better communicated to the public."[35]

"Angola: Journey to a War"

The quest to provide intelligent interpretation on television focused most centrally on foreign policy issues, especially regarding superpower struggle, and NBC took noteworthy leadership by providing extended critique of communism as part of its signature series, *NBC White Paper*. Shows about Marx, Stalin, Khrushchev, and "Red China" painted vivid images of totalitarian societies that provided a chilling contrast to the "American way of life." It is easy to look back at these programs and compare them to the incendiary rhetoric of World War II propaganda, such as the *Why We Fight* documentary series produced by Frank Capra Jr. NBC's "Red China," for example, conjures up images of a Yellow Peril much like the images of the fanatical Japanese masses in Capra's movies. Indeed, many documentaries of the early 1960s contended that both extremism of the right (fascism) and extremism of the left (communism) should be understood as varieties of totalitarianism, a form of absolute rule by the state that denies personal agency and human dignity. Communism was characterized as diametrically opposed to Western values and liberal democracy and as posing an undisputable threat to free societies much like that of fascism during the Second World War. As historian Erik Barnouw (1983, 227–28) has observed, network documentaries during this era seemed to express the official ideology of the military-industrial complex by reductively pitting East against West.

Such programs about communist countries provided dramatic testimony as to the core ideological dispositions of U.S. government officials and network executives, but documentaries that operated at a less explicitly rhetorical level were in many respects more potent, since, as we shall see, they seemed to be based on the dispassionate professional expertise of network news reporters. Programs about the Soviet Union explicitly foregrounded their anticommunist politics, but documentaries about countries occupying the middle ground between the two superpowers were far more complicated, partly because the politics of these countries fit less comfortably into Cold War dichotomies and partly because network news crews enjoyed greater access to these locales, so that they had to square their political rhetoric with the empirical data. The allegiances of countries such as India, Panama, and even France were much more uncertain, in large part because their histories, languages, and cultures complicated the reductive categories of East and West. In each instance, documentaries probed to understand distinctive local conditions, to ponder the country's political leanings, and to uncover any threats to stability that might be posed by outside forces. The programs seemed to ask: Should this particular country be considered a part of the Free World alliance? If not, might it be teetering toward the communist camp? And what, if any, action should the United States take? In other words, one of the primary purposes of these network documentaries was to comprehend and manage difference and to create a meaningful geography of the Free World. They also had to distinguish U.S. leadership from imperial dominance. If countries did not fit "naturally" into the Free World category, what might motivate them to cast their lot with the U.S.-led alliance?

NBC's "Angola: Journey to a War," for example, opens with a loosely framed shot of a missionary sitting on a riverbank speaking with a reporter about the system of labor exploitation in Angola.[36] The setting is tranquil and pastoral. Yet this tranquillity is disturbed not only by the missionary's graphic description of exploitation but also by the quiet intrusion of a black man paddling a white passenger downstream in the background of the frame. As the missionary continues to speak, the camera follows the canoe as it glides off into the distance. The image reminds us of a frequently expressed aphorism of this era: that communism is most attractive to people who live in societies that resist political reform and economic modernization and that such resistance makes societies ripe for infiltration and agitation by subversive agents from the Eastern Bloc. Angolan rebel leaders reject this presumption, claiming that their struggle against colonial oppression is a local matter, a civil war rather than part of the Cold War. Interviews with Portuguese colonial administrators suggest otherwise, yet the colonial government has steadfastly refused to allow a UN fact-finding mission into the country to verify such assertions. In fact, the Portuguese have kept strict control over the flow of information coming out of Angola, and the audience hook for this documentary is to offer a privileged view of a brushfire war that may have serious repercussions for the Free World. Moreover, the program implies a rough equivalence between the findings of the network's documentary and those of an independent international fact-finding commission, featuring footage of NBC's reporters testifying before a UN tribunal about the conditions they found during their travels on both sides of the battle lines. Their professional expertise and empirical research are represented as politically neutral and thus as a kind of substitute for a UN investigation.

As the narrative begins, reporter Robert Young slips across the border from a neighboring country and ventures behind rebel lines, traveling from village to village to inspect the traces of war. Speaking in the first person, Young introduces local residents and rebel warriors, observing the conditions of their daily existence. We hear first-person accounts of plantation life, labor exploitation, and the indignities of the colonial system. We learn that the odds are stacked against these villagers and come to understand the rationale for armed struggle. Cutting to footage of a motley brigade of guerrillas shouldering antique rifles, Young explains in voice-over that he found no signs of communist infiltration or Soviet military supplies. Instead, he describes an arduous guerrilla struggle against the Portuguese as villagers reenact enemy atrocities and escort us to gravesites of fallen comrades.

Young's sympathetic portrait presents these Angolans as gentle, even naive. We learn of their simple, subsistence lifestyle and their economic vulnerability. They welcome Young warmly almost everywhere he goes. As he enters one village, however, the chief seems guarded and skeptical. "But when he found out we were Americans," says Young, "everything changed." Much cheering, smiling, and handshaking ensues. The Americans seem to have a special status among the villagers, representing both political freedom and modern prosperity. "Charley and I found ourselves unwillingly becoming doctors," recounts Young. "Although we never had any previous training for the job, people looked to us to perform miracles. Almost everyone seemed to have some kind of illness." Thus the villagers—although living under dramatically different circumstances—seem to share core aspirations of citizens of the Free World, making them not so different from the viewers at home.

From the other side of the battle lines, Robert McCormick reports from Luanda as one of the first foreign correspondents allowed in by the Portuguese. In contrast to the villages visited by Young, with their images of poverty and warfare, the capital city appears prosperous and orderly. Broad modern boulevards bustle with traffic, and shops, schools, and public parks make Luanda appear to be a familiar Western metropolis in the heart of Africa. This island of progress, according to McCormick, was built upon a stable foundation provided by the Portuguese military, who have mediated among contending forces in a volatile situation. McCormick accompanies Portuguese soldiers into the bush as they attempt to flush out rebel forces, but his sympathetic portrayal of the colonizers is afforded considerably less airtime, and the program returns behind rebel lines for a concluding scene in one of the villages. Here Young observes teenagers drilling for battle and describes the devastation of local agriculture. Escorted back to the border, he bids farewell to a group of rebels, only to learn later that their village was destroyed the next day by Portuguese forces. "It's hard to understand," he reflects, "how good can come out of such evil."

Having looked at both sides and established the facts, the documentary comes to the uneasy conclusion that this is indeed an internal civil war and not a site of communist infiltration. The program therefore discourages U.S. involvement, but at the same time it legitimizes American inspection of local conflicts in such far-flung locales. It further reserves America's right to intervene should Soviet involvement be detected. Thus superpower struggle remains the fundamental narrative framework, even though the results of this investigation do not fit into conventional Cold War dichotomies. Indeed, the program comes to the uneasy conclusion that brushfire wars are not necessarily part of the Cold War and that colonialism, despite its ugly underside, is acceptable in the short term if it does not open the door to communist expansion. In the long term, however, the Portuguese must relinquish the colonial system. Despite the apparent progress in modern Luanda, villagers in the countryside are suffering and are being denied fundamental rights that societies of the Free World hold in common. If given the chance, the documentary suggests, Angolan villagers would aspire to the same goals and lifestyles as other citizens of the Free World.

The program legitimizes the authority of American television networks to ferret out facts about potential communist infiltration around the globe. Indeed, NBC promoted the documentary as a de facto substitute for a UN fact-finding mission, suggesting that journalistic methods could uncover and analyze facts in much the same way as a multinational panel of UN investigators. Cultural and political bias could seemingly be contained by objectively based procedures, providing access to knowledge that would transcend the interests of the U.S., Soviet, or Portuguese governments. This claim, of course, makes such documentaries even more ideologically powerful by obscuring the fact that the core conclusions coincide closely with the foreign policy of the Kennedy administration. Nevertheless, the program provides an uneasy sense of closure, since the viewers have been exposed to firsthand evidence that "brushfire wars" do not necessarily lead to a communist conflagration. Such evidence would reemerge in numerous other documentaries about such countries as Cambodia, Brazil, Italy, and even Vietnam. Moreover, the discourse of journalistic professionalism pressed news workers to seek out groups and cultures with ideas that were at odds with the "Free World" agenda of the New Frontier. Although dispatched to search for communist infiltration in foreign lands, many documentary crews returned with film footage and interviews that suggested substantial local resistance to "leadership" or domination by either superpower. The resulting documentaries often strained to contain these discontinuities within a Cold War narrative that divided the world into two opposing camps.

Conclusion

In all, documentary texts of this era remind us of sociologist Philip Schlesinger's (1991) contention that national cultures are ongoing sites of contestation over boundaries, dwelling upon notions of inclusion and exclusion. His argument can logically be extended to explain the ways these programs sought to define the community of the Free World during the post-Sputnik era, as the documentaries repeatedly move back and forth between concrete particularities and global abstractions in an effort to map the boundaries of belonging and the geography of superpower struggle. As we have seen, the fit between these various levels of analysis was often unstable if not contradictory, especially since the methodology of empirical documentation often clashed with the interpretive abstractions of New Frontier internationalism. Such conflicts point to tensions between the real and the ideal as well as between the local and the global. Even though prime-time documentary programming expanded dramatically as a result of the converging interests of NBC and the U.S. government, programs regarding countries of the middle ground were less predictable than anticipated.

Audience responses to the programs were also far more ambivalent than promoters of the genre had anticipated. Many viewers identified network documentaries with the reform agenda of a political and cultural elite. Some candidly expressed their opposition to the programs, while others simply avoided them (Curtin 1995, 216–45). This ambivalence caused internal struggles within the networks, since the programs consistently received lower audience ratings than other prime-time genres. Although pressured by government, corporate, and public opinion leaders to sustain the genre, news executives found it difficult to justify the programs within the context of a commercial entertainment medium. Attempts were made to tinker with the production values and stylistic qualities of network documentaries in order to broaden their appeal, but one of the fundamental problems with the programs was that they almost exclusively addressed themselves to a white, male elite. Although the "golden age" of network documentary resulted from the successful alignment of opinion leaders and national institutions behind a Cold War public education effort, this effort proved to be rife with contradiction, and by 1963 documentary began a slow, steady slide from its prominent position in prime-time commercial television.

News divisions also found that their awesome investigative powers could prove to be a liability. For although the networks claimed the authority to direct national attention at specific events and social concerns, documentaries about domestic issues tended to stir up controversy and counterattacks. Programs about the exploitation of migrant laborers angered farmers; criticism of public education worried parents; and investigations into lung cancer stirred resentment among cigarette companies, then the leading advertisers on network television. Perhaps most significantly, documentaries about civil rights elevated African Americans to a level of visibility they had never before enjoyed in the U.S. media. Sympathetic portrayals of the plight of black citizens stirred both righteous indignation and racist antipathy.

Likewise, as the war in Vietnam heated up, television news became a site of struggle between pro- and antiwar factions. During the early years of the war, Vietnam correspondents rarely challenged the U.S. government's rationale for intervention or its progress reports on the war effort. Yet President Johnson's decision to escalate troop commitments in 1965 greatly expanded the military draft, inciting resistance on American college campuses, within the government, and among military units in the field. Closely monitored by both sides, nightly news divisions juggled the competing claims of the administration and the antiwar movement as opposing viewpoints began to work their way into documentaries and regular news coverage. Now widely perceived as a news oligopoly, the networks both influenced public perceptions of key public issues and found themselves called to account for skewing political deliberation.

Despite these tensions, television would continue to prevail as the public's dominant news source into the 1970s, even though the prominence of documentary diminished throughout this period. After Kintner's departure in 1965, executives at NBC began to reassess his legacy of network news leadership. During the 1960s, RCA had accepted the costs of an extensive global news operation in large part because it had assumed that such programming helped to drive its international operations. By the 1970s, however, the sale of its television equipment in overseas markets began to taper off and criticism of U.S. media imperialism began to mount. RCA was also in the process of shifting its emphasis to computer, aerospace, and military product lines where government contracts played an important role. As White House administration criticisms of network news increased, RCA no longer relished the expansive ambitions of the Kintner era. Consequently, news interpretation and analysis—which had never strayed far from the mainstream—grew ever more timid, and the documentary genre faded from view, succeeded largely by network news magazines, such as *60 Minutes* and *NBC Dateline.*

Notes

Abbreviations

BRTC   Rose Theatre Collection, New York Public Library

NBC/WHS National Broadcasting Company Archives, Wisconsin Historical Society

1. Sponsored by Camel cigarettes, the program nevertheless pioneered the use of remote film footage that was shot, processed, and edited under daily deadline conditions.

2. *Broadcasting*, September 12, 1960, 27, and March 5, 1962, 52–53; *Business Week*, June 9, 1962, 50; *Printer's Ink*, December 23, 1960, 10; *Sponsor*, March 26, 1962, 29.

3. *Variety*, January 4, 1961, 21, and September 24, 1962, 35.

4. *Variety*, May 16, 1962, 62.

5. *Variety*, February 17, 1960, 22, and September 25, 1961, 31; NBC press release, November 10, 1961, *NBC White Paper* file, CBS News Library, New York; Don Meaney to Julian

Goodman, December 20, 1961, Reuven Frank Papers, NBC Collection, Box 292, File 20, NBC/WHS.

6. *Broadcasting,* May 14, 1962, 146.

7. *Variety,* November 21, 1962, 23.

8. NBC, *Year End Report, 1964,* NBC file, BRTC.

9. Ibid.

10. News release, Radio Corporation of America, April 5, 1961, Newton Minow Papers, Box 35, NBC/WHS. The utopian discourse of global television at the dawning of the satellite age is analyzed in Curtin (1993).

11. Richard N. Gardner, "Countdown at the UN," *Saturday Review,* March 17, 1962, 105. These notions of global community and mutual knowledge are also interesting in light of popular notions regarding "the family of man" during this period. For development theory suggests not only that all societies progress through similar stages of economic development but also that underneath our racial and cultural exteriors all humans are essentially the same. See the coffee-table picture book that was popular during the 1950s and early 1960s by Edward Steichen (1955). This book grew out of a museum show that traveled the globe during the 1950s, courtesy of the United States Information Agency.

12. *Business Week,* December 8, 1962, 58.

13. *Variety,* March 29, 1961, 23.

14. *Variety,* September 7, 1960, 27, and May 24, 1961, 21. Also, in Eastern Europe there reportedly was an effort to use the programs for propaganda campaigns against U.S. gangsterism, a development that drew pointed concern from the USIA. See *Broadcasting,* May 14, 1962, 146.

15. As program codes began to spread internationally, British television exports that eschewed violence began to pick up momentum. In response, the networks reportedly turned back more than a dozen television episodes for re-editing before they were made available for export. *Variety,* July 12, 1961, 30.

16. *Variety,* June 14, 1961, 29, and July 5, 1961, 27.

17. *Variety,* February 7, 1962, 33.

18. *Variety,* February 17, 1960, 22; March 29, 1961, 23; and October 25, 1961, 31.

19. *Variety,* March 1, 1961, 27.

20. Some notes from Eisenberg analysis of Edwards News and Huntley-Brinkley News, December 10, 1960, Mickelson Papers, Box 1, File 16, NBC/WHS.

21. Robert Kintner and Robert Sarnoff to "all NBC personnel," August 4, 1960, Harry Bannister Papers, Box 10, File 6, NBC/WHS.

22. *Variety,* September 21, 1960, 1.

23. *Variety,* May 31, 1961, 20, and June 14, 1961, 19.

24. *Variety,* December 13, 1961, 25.

25. Regarding Sarnoff's pitch to affiliates, see *Variety,* November 23, 1960, 24. One week later, NBC took out an ad in a trade magazine touting itself as the acknowledged leader in news and public affairs. See message to affiliates, *Variety,* November 30, 1960, 32.

26. *Newsweek,* December 20, 1965, Kintner file, BRTC.

27. *New York Times,* October 24, 1965, X:21.

28. *TV Guide,* February 9, 1963, 20.

29. *Variety,* December 24, 1980, Kintner file, BRTC.

30. *New York Times,* October 24, 1965, X:21. The Hollywood feature film *Network* later ap-

propriated this image as representative of the intense and seemingly mindless competition for ratings among leading executives of the three commercial networks.

31. *Newsweek*, December 20, 1965, Kintner file, BRTC.

32. *TV Guide*, February 9, 1963, 20–21.

33. *New York Times*, October 24, 1965, X:21.

34. "NBC Biography," July 11, 1958, Kintner file, BRTC.

35. *New York Times*, February 26, 1966, Kintner file, BRTC.

36. Broadcast, September 19, 1961.

11

What Closes on Saturday Night

NBC and Satire

JEFFREY S. MILLER

In *Television: The Business behind the Box*, his classic study of the three-network oligarchy at the height of its power, Les Brown (1971) refers to NBC as the most "venturesome" of the networks, with a particular slant toward sophisticated comedy (12). Nowhere are Brown's comments more evident than in the network's efforts to bring contemporary topical satire to a mainstream American audience. From the 1950s to the beginning of the 1980s, NBC took risks in the comedy it presented that CBS would either refuse or stifle and that ABC would only feebly imitate.

Of course, most of these attempts were not as successful as either the network or those involved with specific shows would have hoped. Early appearances by satiric comics on variety shows were notably watered down from what nightclub patrons or record buyers might hear. Before *Rowan and Martin's Laugh-In* became a cultural phenomenon in 1968, NBC's first efforts at prime-time satire, *The Bob Newhart Show* and *That Was the Week That Was*, met early cancellations, even with audiences devoted to each show. And *Laugh-In*, along with the more recent late-night hits *Saturday Night Live* and *SCTV Network 90*, demonstrated further difficulties in negotiating how a form of comedy defined by media scholars Steve Neale and Frank Krutnik (1991, 9) as working "to mock and attack social conventions" might be used by a powerful corporate entity vested in the very conventions being mocked and attacked.

The Greening of the Vast Wasteland

Though satire may have closed on Saturday nights when playwright George S. Kaufman and friends held court at the Algonquin Round Table, by the time of Kaufman's death in 1961, satire was opening doors at nightclubs and record stores for a number of comedians and their hip young fans. This boom in satirical comedy spoke not only to an incipient revolt against what historian Todd Gitlin (1987) calls the "tranquilized center" of American society during the Eisenhower years but to a new college-educated audience that valued intelligence and social awareness—reflecting its own, of course—in entertainment (29).

With a growing market of young adults both intellectually and financially disposed to satire, it would seem logical that the new medium of television would show some interest in the form. And to some extent, it did: by the time John F. Kennedy was elected president in 1960, Shelley Berman, Mort Sahl, and Mike Nichols and Elaine May had all become familiar to prime-time audiences through their appearances on variety shows on all three networks, as well as on NBC's pioneering late-night *Tonight*. Even the profane—and to many sacred—Lenny Bruce made a prime-time appearance on NBC's *Steve Allen Show*. Still, most evening television at the end of the 1950s dared to do little with a style of humor that mocked the verities of the society and culture it represented.

John F. Kennedy's election, however, moved the tectonic plates upon which network television rested. Young, attractive, and nominally liberal, with a Harvard education, a Pulitzer Prize, and a growing family, Kennedy and his wife Jackie were models of a particularly desirable audience. More importantly, the new president shared the attitude of critics of American "mass culture" who had come to the fore during the 1950s, hiring one of those critics as his special consultant on the arts. August Hecksher had served as principal author of a 1960 report for the Eisenhower Commission on National Goals entitled "The Quality of American Life," in which he argued that commercial network television was a prime offender in undercutting a cultural "standard of excellence" (Watson 1990, 38).

To ensure that this standard was maintained, Kennedy selected young lawyer Newton Minow as chair of the Federal Communications Commission (FCC). With Minow almost immediately excoriating the "vast wasteland" of television and convening an FCC inquiry into the rise of TV violence, networks and producers quickly had to consider ways to address his criticisms. NBC, with an organizational structure that allowed for risks and with close ties between its board members and the Kennedy administration, took the first leap, landing with both feet in a pool labeled satire (Brown 1971, 220). As it turned out, getting its feet wet also entailed a slip and a fall for the network.

Hi, Bob!

That NBC would choose genial young comic Bob Newhart to personify television satire in 1961 might have been a surprise to anyone familiar with Lenny Bruce or Mort Sahl. An itinerant white-collar worker in Chicago throughout the 1950s, Newhart in his spare time dabbled with a friend in improvised comic dialogues. After hearing tapes of that material done as monologues, executives of Warner Brothers Records immediately signed Newhart to a contract and recorded his first live solo club gig. The result, *The Button-Down Mind of Bob Newhart*, went to the top of the Billboard album charts in spring 1960; its follow-up, *The Button-Down Mind Strikes Back!*, did the same a few months later. His television breakthrough came at the

Emmy Awards show of June 20, 1960, at which he presented a monologue from *Button-Down Mind*, playing an aggrieved television producer trying to rehearse President Eisenhower's welcoming of Soviet Premier Nikita Khrushchev to Washington. After a deal between Newhart and CBS fell through a month later, NBC laid claim to the hottest young performer in the country, signing him to a contract for a series beginning in fall 1961 and promising him free rein over the show's content and style.[1] That promise, however, would come to be regretted by both parties to the deal.

In the year between his Emmy appearance and the start of production on his NBC series, Newhart found himself being feted as the kinder, gentler face of the satire boom in publications ranging from *Saturday Evening Post* to *Playboy*. NBC itself used satire as the peg from which the show would hang when it made its debut. *TV Guide*'s preview edition for the 1961–62 season quoted the NBC press release description of the show: "True satirical comedy, rather than slapstick, gags or patter. The comedy will spotlight topical sketches, comedy monologues and a series of weekly continuing features."[2] Producer and head writer Roland Kibbee raised the network's ante in a telegram to Newton Minow himself just before the show's debut: "Respectfully invite you to view the Bob Newhart Show premiering NBC 10 pm Wednesday, Oct. 11. We believe it to be adult, enlightened social satire, unprecedented on TV" (Watson 1990, 42).

Indeed, the only entity involved with *The Bob Newhart Show* who had any doubt about the star's status as a satirist was Bob Newhart himself. He had told *Newsweek* during the 1960 election debates that he had no intention of satirizing the campaign: "I don't go for the idea that comics should be social critics. . . . I don't see anything wrong with a routine that's funny, with no comment at all."[3] And while he was willing to go along with the notion that satire was a marketable television commodity by the time of his show's debut, he was still diffident about his own place in that market: "I don't slug people and institutions with a blackjack, but I'm not exactly bland, either."[4]

Unfortunately, the clash between what NBC and the show's producers hoped for and expected of the show and what the star thought he was most capable of doing resulted in *The Bob Newhart Show* not only avoiding blackjacks but embodying the very blandness Newhart himself feared. Thirty minutes in length, and with minimal production design, the show followed a standard comedy-variety format: opening monologue (frequently involving Newhart's trademark telephone), sketch, guest middle-of-the-road vocalist, longer sketch, optional second song, short sketch, and out. The self-conscious approach to topical satire taken by Newhart's show might best be exemplified by the opening monologue for the fourth episode: Newhart receives a call from a man trying to sell old magazines to people for whom current angst is too pressing. The caller demonstrates his product with a 1935 *Literary Digest* that includes articles entitled "Is There Too Much Violence and Sex on Radio?" and "Russia: Our Best Friend in Europe." An increasingly querulous Newhart finally tells the caller that he's not interested; he then listens for a moment and finally erupts with the catchphrase "Same to you, fella!"[5] Using the topicality not as source material but as gag lines, the routine, like many others on the show, presented a particularly thin broth of both satire and Newhart.

Critical responses to NBC's Newhart show were generally positive, though hardly adulatory. Ratings for the series also started well, and sponsor Sealtest was pleased with the number of young married viewers attracted to the program. By the time the show reached midseason, however, its identity crisis had careened out of control: Newhart tried to get out of his contract, which led Roland Kibbee and director Coby Ruskin to angrily leave the series, blaming the star for unprofessionalism and for cutting their most satirical material.[6] A new production staff pulled the show even more in the direction of standard TV variety material, without the budget to make that material come off well.[7] By the end of the year, the star and his writing staff were at such odds that one writer publicly threatened to beat Newhart up.[8] When Sealtest, responding to declining ratings, pulled its sponsorship in May 1962, NBC canceled its first prime-time venture into satire a few days later.

Ironically, however, while *The Bob Newhart Show* may not have turned out to be what its producers, its star, NBC, or its viewers might have wanted, it still managed to reflect glory on all those involved: the series won not only the 1961–62 Emmy for best comedy program but also a Peabody Award for outstanding achievement in television entertainment.

With those awards, *The Bob Newhart Show* represented a Pyrrhic victory in a quest to step outside the parameters of the vast wasteland. Now NBC would turn to the land of St. George himself to find satire willing to take on society's dragons.

That Was the Show That Was

The satire boom of the late 1950s and early 1960s was hardly confined to the United States.[9] In Great Britain a new generation of comedians, weaned on the BBC radio hit *The Goon Show* and nurtured by the theater clubs of Cambridge and Oxford universities, was also finding that mocking the vagaries of national politics, society, and culture could be rewarding both intellectually and financially. Four of those young comedians—Alan Bennett, Peter Cook, Jonathan Miller, and Dudley Moore—collaborated in 1960 to bring their best material to the Edinburgh Festival. Their show, *Beyond the Fringe,* included parodies of everything from Shakespeare to war films, jests at the upper class and at issues ranging from capital punishment to apartheid, all presented on a bare stage with no costumes. A cause célèbre in Edinburgh and then London, *Beyond the Fringe* made its way to the States in fall 1962, opening in New York on Saturday, October 27, and being proclaimed a smash by Monday, October 29.

With its success in theatrical venues, it was but a short time before television markets on both sides of the Atlantic would open up to this new British satire. BBC producer Ned Sherrin, responding to criticisms portraying BBC as a doddering "Auntie Beeb," began production of a *Beyond the Fringe*–styled topical revue in 1962.

To give the show the freshness of contemporary British satire, Sherrin hired primarily young performers and writers, headed by Cambridge graduate David Frost as moderator. Their collaboration, *That Was the Week That Was (TW3)*, made its debut in November 1962 to acclaim as loud as that received by its theatrical progenitor two years earlier. The response quickly made its way across the Atlantic; *Variety*, in a December 5, 1962, review, called the show "hardhitting, witty, pungent and brilliantly conceived."[10] Within months, NBC worked out a deal with the BBC to begin production of an American version of *TW3*.

The initial result of this special relationship was broadcast on November 10, 1963. The hour-long pilot copied much of what was notable about the British production: the live broadcast in an "open studio," with all cameras and technical crew visible; the opening musical number lampooning the events of the previous week; the sketches and songs dealing with all manner of topical issues and personalities. But although NBC had imitated the formal elements of the British series well, the satiric bite of much of the comedy itself was more an enfeebled gumming. Instead of the youthful David Frost, NBC's *TW3* had as its moderators veteran movie star Henry Fonda and equally veteran comedian/game show raconteur Henry Morgan. Sketches, like many on the Newhart show, seemed to uncomfortably straddle the fence between traditional TV variety shows and the provocative promise of satire.[11] Nonetheless, public and critical response was largely positive, and NBC proceeded to put the series into full production for a January debut.

That debut, however, was dramatically reshaped by an event that could be neither mocked nor parodied: the assassination of President John F. Kennedy. While American television ceased broadcasting its regular program schedule to follow the events of the assassination, the BBC moved its regular Sunday night presentation of *TW3* to Saturday, November 23. The show began with David Frost saying: "It was the least likely thing to happen in the whole world. . . . [T]hat Kennedy should go, well, we just didn't believe in assassination anymore, at least not in the civilized world." The twenty-two minutes that followed included spirituals, poetry, and tearful eulogies from other cast members.[12] NBC flew a tape of the program to the United States to run on Sunday, November 24. At its conclusion, some one thousand calls came into the network's New York switchboard praising the show and NBC for airing it.

NBC responded to that outpouring of praise when its *TW3* series began on January 10, 1964: gone was Henry Fonda, and in his place were Broadway performer Elliot Reid and, "by special arrangement with the British Broadcasting Corporation," David Frost, billed as "Our London Correspondent" and listed among the show's writers. Frost's youth and intelligence seemed to bring the American show the freshness it needed to function as legitimate television satire; still, that freshness was by and large absent from the first episodes of the NBC series, which again slipped into what *Time* called "nightclub material that would be tossed out of the thinnest of topical revues."[13] A later *TV Guide* article by Peter Bogdanovich on the series suggested that its problems reflected a clash among writers similar to the one

FIG. **12** Singer/songwriter Nancy Ames delivering the opening theme on *That Was the Week That Was*, from a 1964 broadcast. NBC produced its own version of the BBC hit, in which David Frost featured on both sides of the Atlantic. (Wisconsin Center for Film and Television Research)

that had dogged NBC's Newhart experiment, with Frost arguing for stronger satiric content against a staff concerned about inappropriate targets, racy language, and British jokes that would be lost on an American audience.[14]

Whatever internal strife may have existed, the American version of *TW3* faced two external concerns that further weakened the impact it might have had. First was the nature of American commercial television. Though the British series had run afoul of both politicians and BBC authorities, it had never had to satisfy sponsors who were supposed to pay for its existence. Companies that might sponsor a traditional American sitcom, however, were reluctant to spend money on a program that might make fun of their products. Sponsor Brown & Williamson proved the point when it pulled its ads from the third show in the series after writers and producers, acting against the tobacco company's request, decided to run a sketch about the health hazards of smoking.[15]

The second concern faced by the U.S. *TW3* was the network system of which it was a part. Despite the scathing early reviews and a continued problem with content weaker than its British version, the still relatively innovative and topical show developed a devoted following over its first season, one that made the program competitive in the Friday night ratings. Given that modicum of success, NBC's decision to move the show for the 1964–65 season to Tuesday night seemed peculiar, to say the least: for a series called *That Was the Week That Was*, Friday night was certainly a more logical choice than Tuesday. And as it turned out, in 1964, an election year, Tuesday nights would carry an additional risk.

However watery *TW3*'s satire may have seemed to some, those at whom the jokes were directed were even less amused. Among the most frequent targets in the show's first season were the Republican Party and its then-presumed presidential nominee, Barry Goldwater. Those involved with the series found it more than ironic, then, when they found themselves watching a paid political program for Goldwater and the Republicans at 9:30 p.m. on Tuesday, September 22, when their first show of the season was to be broadcast. In the first seven weeks of the 1964–65 season, NBC's topical satire ran twice, with Republican infomercials and election coverage consuming the remaining five weeks. An angry David Frost, now sole moderator of the series, confronted an NBC official about the political preemptions and was told that the *TW3* spot was one of only three half-hours that could be sold to political parties. By the time *TW3* returned full time to the fall schedule, ABC's competing soap opera *Peyton Place* had become the surprise hit of the season. The final NBC *TW3*, victim of partisan politics, commercial interests, and network management, was broadcast on May 4, 1965.[16]

From London to Beautiful Downtown Burbank

After the cancellation of *TW3*, it would ironically be the staid CBS, not the "venturesome" NBC, that would take television satire to a different level in 1967 with *The Smothers Brothers Comedy Hour*. Tom and Dick Smothers were West Coast ver-

sions of Bob Newhart: comedians whose brother act and folk music credentials provided humor that was both timely and gently satiric but hardly stuff to keep them
off prime-time television. The quiet politics of the show's first season, which was
surprisingly successful in the ratings, became more and more hard-edged in its second and third years, however, as the United States went through the assassinations,
riots, and political instability of 1968 (Bodrogkhozy 2001, 128–34; Marc 1997,
120–22). Leftist political jabs, drug jokes, and musical commentary from controversial singers including Joan Baez, Harry Belafonte, and Pete Seeger increasingly
infuriated CBS censors and their bosses. As the series became overtly antiauthor-
itarian, ratings started to decline, which allowed CBS to become overtly intrusive,
cutting entire segments, refusing to air a show because of comedian David Steinberg's satiric monologue about religion, and finally canceling the series on the flimsy
pretext that a tape of an episode had been delivered late.

Though CBS's corporate culture and its ties to the Johnson administration (via
network president Frank Stanton) made the end to the Smothers Brothers' quixotic
adventure in television satire a foregone conclusion, the youthful audience the series spoke to could be ignored only at the peril of any network. NBC managed to
tap into that audience—and a much larger one beyond it—through circumstances
as loopy as the show that evolved out of them.

Rowan and Martin's Laugh-In was, at first glance, an impossibly incongruous concept. Vegas-soaked comedy duo Dan Rowan and Dick Martin could hardly have
been more antithetic to the comic coolness of the Smothers Brothers. NBC had given
the comedians a summer replacement series for Dean Martin in 1965 but had been
unsuccessful in putting together another series around them. With their contract
about to expire, NBC's West Coast programming head Herb Schlosser asked producers George Schlatter and Digby Wolfe to take a shot at a new format for the
team. Schlatter, who had previously produced CBS's *Judy Garland Show*, and Wolfe,
a British satiric comedian who had come to the States following television successes
on the BBC and in Australia, had met via an agent in 1966 and had come up with
a topical variety series that was, in Wolfe's words, "a barrage of jokes—no singers,
absolutely balls-out nothing but comedy."[17] They took the idea to NBC, where executives, still sensitive after the collapse of *TW3*, told them that American audiences
were too slow for what they were doing and that satire didn't sell in the States.

Schlosser, however, was intrigued with the concept and wanted to see how it
would look on tape. Schlatter and Wolfe tailored their idea to fit Rowan and Martin's comedy style and then hired a troupe of virtually unknown performers to bring
their jokes and sketches to life. The initial result, according to Wolfe, was "an absolute disaster. Everything NBC said was true: There was no focus; it was too irreverent." After their initial response, however, Schlatter took the tape back to the
editing room, cutting everything in half. What he and Wolfe saw the next day and
took back to the network was an incredibly fast-paced collection of one-liners, sight
gags, and short sketches, many of them addressing current political and social events,
that was indeed the verbal and visual barrage for which they had hoped.

NBC broadcast the *Laugh-In* pilot on September 9, 1967; the response was so strong that it was brought back as a midyear replacement on Mondays in January 1968. Almost immediately, it became the top-rated program in prime time. *Laugh-In* was not satiric television in the way that those responsible for *The Bob Newhart Show* or *That Was the Week That Was* had envisioned—though it certainly owed a debt to the latter, most specifically for its regular "*Laugh-In* Looks at the News" feature, which simply took David Frost's format and added jazzy music and dancing. But even *TW3*'s open studio couldn't come close to the complete deconstruction of the television comedy-variety genre that *Laugh-In* accomplished. Instead of laboriously overwritten sketches and overproduced musical numbers, *Laugh-In* employed lightning-quick cuts and zooms to shatter any expectations viewers of traditional television might have had. In that fragmented format, the topical one-liners thrown about—"All the kids at my school really admire the astronauts. Imagine staying high that long"; "Perhaps the reason more women don't run for the Senate is because every six years their seat is up for grabs"—garnered more immediate attention but then were more quickly lost in the continuing barrage than the longer jokes and sketches of *Newhart*, *TW3*, and *The Smothers Brothers Comedy Hour*.[18]

It also helped that NBC censors were considerably looser than their colleagues at CBS. Drug jokes were rarely challenged, and while sex gags were more closely screened there was greater leeway with *Laugh-In* than with the Smothers Brothers' show. Still, even though one-liners about the Vietnam War were surprisingly acceptable early on—"You know, we went into Vietnam as advisors. Last week we dropped 400,000 tons of advice"—when punch lines were brought back to specific markets at home, such as one comparing the 1968 Soviet invasion of Prague to the Chicago Democratic Convention, NBC's censors got busy. As the Nixon administration's battles against the "nattering nabobs of [media] negativism" heated up, and after Paul Keyes, a mutual friend of both Nixon and Rowan and Martin, left the *Laugh-In* writing staff, political gags became even more closely scrutinized: by 1971, according to Wolfe, NBC had dispatched an emissary from New York to Burbank to tell its producers that *Laugh-In* could no longer make political references of any sort in its humor.

Whether the Nixon administration put pressure on NBC to curb *Laugh-In* and whether the network capitulated to that pressure are in the final analysis secondary to the fact that the *Laugh-In* concept had largely run its course. The show simply couldn't take either its satiric content or its radical form any further in the directions it had staked out from the start; most of its stars had left, to be replaced by far less memorable performers. Rowan and Martin and crew soldiered on through declining ratings until *Laugh-In* finally wore out its welcome in 1973, after an improbable five-and-a-half-year run.[19] With satire, particularly in the zippy, zappy form of *Laugh-In*, losing its viability as prime-time fare for NBC, it would be pushed to the margins—an area in which the network had always found success and was about to do so again.

What Closes on Saturday Night

As the popularity of *Laugh-In* declined in the early 1970s, so did all of NBC's prime-time programs, overwhelmed by the topical sitcoms of Norman Lear and the MTM studios—and, more importantly, of CBS. The comedy-variety genre, a final refuge for prime-time satire, was also accelerating its decline—NBC's once-popular *Flip Wilson Show* was gone by fall 1974, following the long-running *Dean Martin Show* by a year. By the time *Laugh-In* left the air in 1973, the only major hits the network had were the Lear-produced *Sanford and Son* and the rotating *Columbo/MacMillan and Wife/McCloud* Sunday night mystery series, a situation that would only worsen over the next several years.

With the 1974 arrival on American airwaves of the British show *Monty Python's Flying Circus*, however, prospects for a new kind of comedy show suddenly opened up. Viewers of local PBS broadcasts of the sketch comedy series in places as disparate as Manhattan, Dallas, Sacramento, and What Cheer, Iowa, responded with a fanatical devotion far surpassing anything offered to network shows. As the five-year time gap between the original BBC broadcasts and its American airings indicates, *Monty Python* did not deal in specific topical gags, as did *TW3* and *Laugh-In*. Instead, authority in all its institutional guises—government, police, education, religion—was the broad target. And television itself, in both content and form, was the institutional authority most frequently attacked throughout the series. American television, parodies and mocking one-liners aside, had neither seen nor produced anything approaching what *Monty Python* could do with television to comment on television. The popularity of the British import suggested to some that maybe American TV could do the same.

NBC's opportunity to pursue that thinking came in summer 1974. Johnny Carson, the network's biggest star, informed executives that he no longer wanted his *Best of Carson* reruns of *The Tonight Show* optioned to local stations for weekend late nights. With the network facing lost revenue from ad sales on the repeats, new NBC president Herb Schlosser—the same Herb Schlosser who had given *Laugh-In* its green light eight years earlier—decided to risk creating a new show for the time slot. In August 1974, Schlosser gave Dick Ebersol, a young ABC sports executive to whom he was about to offer a job as head of late-night weekend programming, the task of creating a show that would indeed close Saturday nights, one based on the traditional comedy-variety series but doing something at least slightly, if not completely, different. None of the ideas floated for the series seemed connected to anything contemporary in comedy, topical or otherwise, until Ebersol met with writer Lorne Michaels in Hollywood late in 1974. A writer for *Laugh-In* during that show's first season, Michaels and comedy partner Hart Pomerantz returned to their native Canada to front a comedy-variety show on CBC in 1969, at about the time that *Monty Python* also showed up. "It was miraculous to me, a revelation," Michaels later said about the British series (Hill and Winegrad 1987, 38). Michaels headed back to the States in 1972, hoping to develop a show that would do for American TV what *Python* had done for the BBC. Ebersol decided to give him the chance.

NBC's Saturday Night, as it was then called, melded the old with the new. Its home, Studio 8H in Rockefeller Center, had been used in the 1950s for broadcasts of the NBC Symphony Orchestra and had been almost unused since. And, following Schlosser's initial wishes, the program was live, hearkening back to *Your Show of Shows* and the dramas of TV's golden age. But the sketch comedy Michaels envisioned and the performers and writers who would purvey it were of a different generation entirely. The debut, which broadcast on October 11, 1975, with king of hip comedy George Carlin as host, opened with a sketch in which writer Michael O'Donoghue plays an English teacher helping an Eastern European immigrant (John Belushi) learn how to speak via sentences like "I would like to feed your fingertips to the wolverines" before collapsing of a heart attack—which his pupil promptly emulates. "It seemed to me that, whatever else happened, there would never have been anything like this on television," Michaels later said of the opening (Shales and Miller 2002, 62).

Response to the first *Saturday Night* episode was mixed, both within NBC and without. Overall ratings for the first few shows were nothing more than what *Best of Carson* had provided, and for a lot more money; the demographic breakdown, however, showed that *Saturday Night* was attracting a higher percentage of viewers in the all-important eighteen-to-forty-nine age group—the "television generation"—than any other program on the air. With Schlosser's support, some important critical raves, and key demographic numbers backing him up, Michaels was able to take *Saturday Night* further in the direction he wanted than he had dared hope.

As had been the case for *Laugh-In*, the heart of *Saturday Night* was its ensemble of young, unknown sketch performers, the Not Ready for Prime Time Players. Downplayed at the series' inception in favor of demographically appropriate guest hosts (Carlin, Candice Bergen, Richard Pryor), the troupe was brought more to the fore by the middle of the first season, adding a topicality to the show's comic attacks on society and culture owing more to *TW3* than to *Monty Python*.[20] The centerpiece of *Saturday Night* was "Weekend Update," a virtual clone of the *TW3* format with Chevy Chase instead of David Frost as the host. As "Update" skewered the week's headlines, the show's sketches in turn took shots at political, social, and media issues that became increasingly more direct than anything even *Laugh-In* had done. Whether an exchange of racial insults between Chase and Richard Pryor ("Junglebunny." "Honkey!" "Spade." "*Honkey* honkey!" "Nigger!" "*Dead* honkey!"), Dan Aykroyd's alarmingly accurate mocking of Richard Nixon and Jimmy Carter, Gilda Radner's equally deflating portrayal of news diva Barbara Walters, or any of the show's takes on television, past and present, *Saturday Night* presented an awareness of and a willingness to comment on the world around it that no show, prime time or otherwise, had ever exhibited on American television.[21] The four Emmies it won its first season, including best comedy-variety series, validated its importance. And despite low-to-middling ratings and attitudes ranging from concern to outright hostility about both the show's content and its costs among many NBC executives, *Saturday Night* would not go the way of *The Bob Newhart Show:* it was renewed for a second season, and then a third, and a fourth, and a fifth.

While *Saturday Night* appeared to be very, very good for satire and for NBC, the inevitable creative and financial clashes took a heavy toll on both the show and the network. The antagonism felt by many at NBC toward *Saturday Night* and its creators was hardly one-sided. Lorne Michaels had "NBC's" removed from the show's name in ads for its second season; he and others involved on the creative side continually sniped at the network's efforts to rein in spending, as well as what they saw as the disrespect it showed in every area from promotion to censorship. When Herb Schlosser, taking the fall for NBC's decline over the previous five years, was replaced as president in 1978 by Fred Silverman, Michaels's relations with the network grew even worse. Between corporate battles and problems with actors and writers, ranging from rampant egomania to rampant substance abuse, what was by then *Saturday Night Live* was left slowly twisting in the wind by the end of its fifth season. The show's remaining stars—Chase, Aykroyd, and Belushi had already left—were preparing to depart, and Michaels, who had been noncommittal about returning, found himself replaced by associate producer Jean Doumanian after the season ended. It was a decision all would soon regret: the performers and writers she chose to replace the originals were notably weaker, and she could exert little control over either the day-to-day production or the overall quality of the series. Critics turned against the series before the public did, but ratings dropped throughout the 1980–81 season. NBC decided then, for safety's sake, to produce an additional satire program, this time by turning to one of the genre's key American predecessors.

Greetings from Melonville

The Second City revue opened its doors in Chicago late in 1959. Within a year, its reputation for hilarious takes on contemporary society and mores was attracting both huge local audiences and celebrities passing through Chicago. Within a decade, Second City had mounted a long-running show in New York, made several tours around the States and to Toronto, and watched its alumni become increasingly familiar faces in television and film. Those early Canadian contacts, which included a short series for the CBC in 1964, came to full fruition in 1973, when Second City opened a theater in Toronto. In the original players were Dan Aykroyd and Gilda Radner, who, with John Belushi from the coterminous Chicago company, would be core members of the original *Saturday Night* cast. With those ties to the burgeoning NBC hit, producers and writers from the Second City theaters on both sides of the border met in Toronto early in 1976 to discuss the possibility of a Canadian Second City television venture. What emerged was the idea of a half-hour show— there was barely enough money for even that—representing the programming day of a local TV station in the town of Melonville. In addition to parodies of commercials, television shows, and bad movies, the show would allow viewers to meet the station's personnel, both in front of and behind the cameras.[22]

Like *Monty Python* before it, *Second City Television (SCTV)* surreptitiously made its way into the States after its 1976 Canadian premiere. In a slowly but steadily increasing number of U.S. markets, *SCTV* was broadcast by NBC affiliates in a late-night slot on either Friday or Saturday, after the rock concert show *Midnight Special* or *Saturday Night Live*. Both NBC programming head Brandon Tartikoff and vice president Irv Wilson had been paying attention to the ratings and the quiet buzz the Canadian import was getting—at exactly the same time that *Midnight Special* was faltering and that *Saturday Night Live* was going through its implosion after the departure of Lorne Michaels and the original troupe. Wilson, campaigning to get Michaels's replacement Jean Doumanian fired, hoped that her departure might lead to the demise of the series as a whole—and what better to take its place than an already established, hip, satirical, ensemble sketch comedy show? At the same time Tartikoff was trying to get Dick Ebersol, now executive producer of *Midnight Special,* to return to *Saturday Night Live* to save the series. Meanwhile, John Candy and Joe Flaherty of *SCTV* had each contacted NBC to ask if the network would be interested in the show. In the end, if all parties didn't get quite what they wanted, they all got what they needed: *Midnight Special* was canceled, allowing Ebersol to take over *Saturday Night Live* and making room for *SCTV,* expanded to ninety minutes and retitled *SCTV Network 90,* to follow Carson reruns Friday nights.

Because of the suddenness with which the show needed to air, given the quick cancellation of *Midnight Special,* the first few episodes of *Network 90* are little more than greatest-hits compilations from the half-hour series, with wraparounds familiarizing the show's new audience with the characters running the SCTV Network: stingy network president Guy Caballero (Flaherty), bawdy programming chief Edith Prickley (Andrea Martin), blowhard producer/star Johnny LaRue (Candy), incompetent newscaster Earl Camembert (Eugene Levy), irascible commentator Bill Needle (Dave Thomas), and many others.

What was also quickly apparent was that the show's premise continued to be based more on parody than on topical satire—although, with the subject being television itself, parody often was topical satire. As the show came into its own, however, it willfully went beyond parody, particularly in the Emmy-winning "Moral Majority" episode, in which the wraparound sketches feature network boss Caballero handing over SCTV programming to advertisers and pressure groups for financial gain—both the network's and his.[23] Though brilliant in concept and in execution, the "Moral Majority" sketches represent a brand of satire that, while particularly direct, is also relatively safe: very few in network television would have disagreed with its ultimate point. And while *SCTV* occasionally took shots at other social and political topics—the U.S.-Soviet contretemps, feminism, religion—its focus on TV itself and the hermetic way that focus was addressed made it less prone to content questions from the network than *Saturday Night Live*—even when the network itself was mocked by *SCTV* for its obsession with ratings or its propensity for cheap re-

runs and "best-of" shows. Conflict between *SCTV* and NBC came more from organizational issues, specifically the network's insistence upon installing its own producers, over the objections of the cast, to oversee the creative process. Indeed, some
of the cruelest comedy on *SCTV Network 90* was the unflattering representation of
NBC producers and executives in some of the sketches.

It was, in the end, not the show's content but simple business arithmetic that led
to the end of the relationship between *SCTV* and NBC. *Network 90* (and, in its second and final season, simply *Network*) never had the ratings boost that *Saturday Night*
had had in its first two seasons. NBC even tried running *SCTV* in the *Saturday Night
Live* slot three times in 1981–82—the first slow year of rebuilding under Ebersol—
with disappointing results. With mounting production costs and license fees, NBC
found itself working into the same debts that it had had with *Saturday Night Live*,
without the returns in ratings or advertising. On March 18, 1983, and despite the
loud protests of its fans, *SCTV* made its NBC signoff.[24] Rarely as edgy as its predecessors but usually more successful in nailing its comedic target, *SCTV Network 90*
served as another example of a star-crossed relationship between those working in
a genre devoted to mocking social norms and a business wanting to distribute their
work to broader audiences—but with those very social norms defining how they
might distribute it.

Update

By the time *SCTV Network* departed, NBC was well on its way to its "must-see TV"
dominance of the 1990s, with *The Cosby Show* and *Cheers* reviving its sitcom heritage
and paving the way for *Seinfeld* and *Friends*, and with the "quality" MTM dramas
Hill Street Blues and *St. Elsewhere* clearing the ground from which *L.A. Law*, *E.R.*, and
The West Wing (as well as *Miami Vice* and *Law and Order*) would grow. Satire played
little role in the prime-time renaissance, with the network revisiting the genre only
briefly with Lorne Michaels's 1984 *New Show* and Michael Moore's 1994 "docu-
comic" *TV Nation*. Both experiments were short-lived.[25] The upstart Fox network,
meanwhile, made edgy sketch comedy one of its early hallmarks in *The Tracey Ull-
man Show* and *In Living Color;* its animated sitcoms, from *The Simpsons* to *Family Guy*,
are arguably the last bastion of satire on American prime-time network television.
And cable television, from HBO's early *Not Necessarily the News* to Comedy Central's
TW3 descendants *The Daily Show* and *The Colbert Report* (to say nothing of *South Park*
and *Chappelle's Show*), has been an ever-expanding market for comedians trading
in social and topical humor.

Satire always offered more risks than rewards for the networks during the pre-
cable era. The audience it attracted, particularly in prime time, was an ideal one—
young, educated, upwardly mobile—but to be successful by the standards of
A. C. Nielsen it had to reach beyond that audience into the masses—a difficult propo-
sition, given that so much satiric material made fun of the everyday assumptions
and rituals of those masses. With the fears of sponsors and the concerns of network

programmers and censors devoted to eliminating content that might be objection-able, prime-time commercial television satire could never approach what was available in other venues. Given that, *The Bob Newhart Show* and *TW3* should be seen less as inevitable failures than as noble, if flawed, experiments by both the creative and the business elements behind them. That the truly experimental *Rowan and Martin's Laugh-In* should even have been broadcast, much less become a definitive landmark in prime-time history, again owes as much to NBC's willingness to take a business risk as it does to the creativity of the show's writers and producers.

NBC's true legacy with satire, however, lies not in prime time but in late night. *Saturday Night Live* and *SCTV Network 90* both built on the freedom of *The Tonight Show;* whether under the auspices of Steve Allen, Jack Paar, or Johnny Carson, it always provided for comics trafficking in attacks on social norms. Indeed, despite his furious battles with management, Lorne Michaels has assumed the role with NBC that Johnny Carson had at the birth of *NBC's Saturday Night* in 1975: that of the network's sine qua non. *Saturday Night Live* in its thirty years has become as definitive of NBC as *Today, Tonight,* or *Meet the Press;* Michaels's repackaging of the show's sketches as "Best of . . ." specials keeps satire at least a minor NBC prime-time concern. And it was Michaels who, when David Letterman left *Late Night* and NBC in 1993, convinced the network to hire the virtually unknown Conan O'Brien to re-place him and took over as the show's executive producer. O'Brien's biography, however, reads like a pilgrim's progress through contemporary American satire: writer for the *Harvard Lampoon* and *Not Necessarily the News;* performer with the Groundlings, L.A.'s equivalent to Second City; writer for *Saturday Night Live;* writer/producer for *The Simpsons;* liner notes writer for the DVD box set of *SCTV Network 90.*

In 2004, NBC announced that in 2009 O'Brien would replace Jay Leno as host of *The Tonight Show,* a decision that gives Lorne Michaels at least a creative share in NBC late-night programming six nights a week. For all the difficulties it has had in its several incarnations on the network, satire in some form, it appears, will close for NBC on every night but Sunday, when both God and the network decree that it deserves a rest.

The title for this chapter is taken from playwright George S. Kaufman's bon mot, "Satire is what closes on Saturday night." Many thanks to Alissa Denke for her help in researching and editing this chapter, and to Digby Wolfe for his time in sharing his experience and insight on Rowan and Martin's Laugh-In.

Notes

1. CBS pulled the offer after Ed Sullivan informed the network that he already had an exclusive agreement with Newhart for four shows in 1960–61.

2. "Wednesday: If It's Laughter You're After," *TV Guide,* September 16, 1961, 23.

3. "Button-Down Benchley," *Newsweek,* October 10, 1960, 96.

4. Pete Martin, "Backstage with Bob Newhart," *Saturday Evening Post,* October 14, 1961, 118.

5. *The Bob Newhart Show*, November 8, 1961, produced and written by Roland Kibbee, directed by Coby Ruskin, NBC. Transcript from the Museum of Broadcasting, Chicago.

6. "Newhart Troubles," *Variety*, January 24, 1962, 27.

7. According to *Variety*, the estimated budget for a single episode of *The Bob Newhart Show* was $52,000, compared to the $68,000 budgeted for an episode of CBS's *Red Skelton Show*. "Estimated Weekly Network TV Program Costs," *Variety*, January 10, 1962, 113.

8. "Newhart's Writing Emmy Nomination Starts a Rumble," *Variety*, May 16, 1962, 26.

9. Much of the material in this section is taken from the author's *Something Completely Different: British Television and American Culture* (Minneapolis: University of Minnesota Press, 2000), 113–23.

10. Review of *That Was the Week That Was*, *Variety*, December 5, 1962, 28.

11. *That Was the Week That Was* (American version), premiere episode, November 10, 1963, produced by Leland Hayward, written by Earl Doud, Robert Emmett, and Gerald Gardner, directed by Hal Gurnee and Marshall Jamison, performed by Nancy Ames, Henry Fonda, Henry Morgan, et al., NBC. Transcript from the Museum of Broadcasting, Chicago.

12. *That Was the Week That Was* (British version), November 23, 1963 (U.S. broadcast, November 24), produced by Ned Sherrin, written by Christopher Booker, Caryl Brahms, David Frost, Herbert Kretzmer, David Lee, and Bernard Levin, performed by David Frost, Roy Kinnear, Millicent Martin, et al., NBC. Transcript from the National Broadcasting Company Collection, Motion Picture, Broadcasting, and Recorded Sound Division, Library of Congress.

13. "That Was Weak, That Was," *Time*, January 17, 1964, 76.

14. Peter Bogdanovich, "That Was the Week That Was for TWTWTW," *TV Guide*, April 4, 1964, 24–28.

15. See "'TW3' Smoking Spoof Gets in Sponsor's Eye," *New York Times*, January 24, 1964, 57; Jack Gould, "TV: Finding the Target," *New York Times*, January 25, 1964, 49.

16. The BBC's *TW3* itself ended because of industrial and national politics: its attacks on the Tory government during and after the Profumo scandal of 1963 led to an outcry that caused the BBC Board of Governors, responsible for maintaining the political neutrality mandated by the corporation's charter, to end the series prior to the elections of 1964.

17. Digby Wolfe, interview, January 17, 2005. All quotes attributed to Wolfe are from the same interview.

18. See Richard Warren Lewis, "Crazy George and Friends Run Wild in Downtown Burbank," *TV Guide*, March 8, 1969; also Bodroghkozy (2001, 148–50) and Marc (1997, 124–27).

19. Schlatter and NBC tried to revisit the show's success four years later with a series of specials under the *Laugh-In* name. As might have been expected, all the specials did, aside from introducing young comic Robin Williams to a national audience, was prove that you can't go home to beautiful downtown Burbank again.

20. Pryor's hosting stint was marred by the network's fear that Pryor would use the language of his live shows and albums, which caused NBC to add a five-second delay to that "live" broadcast. Still, the network retained an interest in Pryor and sought to build a prime-time show around him. The 1977 comedy-variety *Richard Pryor Show* crashed and burned, however, since the network and star clashed from the first sketch of the first show (of only five) on appropriate material. See Hill and Winegrad (1987, 116–17) and Louie Robinson, "Richard Pryor Talks," *Ebony*, January 1978, 116–22.

21. *NBC's Saturday Night*, December 13, 1975, with guest host Richard Pryor, produced by Lorne Michaels, directed by Dave Wilson, written by Anne Beatts, James Downey, Michael

O'Donoghue, et al., performed by John Belushi, Chevy Chase, Jane Curtin, et al., NBC. Transcript from the author's private collection.

22. Global TV in Toronto provided a studio and crew; producer Len Stuart fronted $35,000 to get the first seven episodes made. See Patinkin (2000, 119).

23. *SCTV Network 90*, July 10, 1981, produced by Andrew Alexander, Doug Holtby, and Len Stuart, directed by John Blanchard, written by Dick Blassucci, Paul Flaherty, Bob Dolman, et al., and performed by John Candy, Joe Flaherty, Eugene Levy, et al. *SCTV Disc 1: On the Town / Polynesiantown Episodes,* Shout! Factory, DVD 33469, released June 7, 2005.

24. Brandon Tartikoff told the cast that the network wanted to keep the show running— at 7:00 p.m. Sunday night, opposite ratings juggernaut *60 Minutes,* and with network approval of all material so that it wouldn't offend the children watching at that hour. It was an offer that *SCTV* could refuse. See Thomas (1996).

25. *The New Show* starred *Saturday Night Live*'s frequent guest Buck Henry, *SCTV*'s Dave Thomas, and Valri Bromfield, a Second City Toronto veteran who had made her network TV debut doing a stand-up routine on the first episode of *NBC's Saturday Night.*

12

The Little Program That Could

The Relationship between NBC and *Star Trek*

MÁIRE MESSENGER DAVIES AND ROBERTA PEARSON

Star Trek in its various incarnations is one of the most successful television franchises ever produced and one of the longest-running. It is also a cultural phenomenon that goes far beyond television. For this the world has NBC to thank. Yet, also thanks to NBC, it nearly did not become so. In an ironic twist of fate, the current (in 2005) franchise owners, Paramount Network Television and UPN, announced in February 2005 that the most recent *Trek* series—the fifth, *Star Trek: Enterprise*—would be canceled that May, after four seasons, because of falling ratings. This could be seen as history repeating itself. It recalls what happened to the very first *Star Trek* series in 1969, when after three struggling seasons it was finally canceled by NBC.

However, the cancellation of *Enterprise* is not quite history repeating itself. There are marked differences between the current cancellation and the way the original series of *Star Trek: The Original Series (TOS)* slipped out of the airwaves in 1969. These differences reflect historical changes in the television industry and its relationship with audiences that enabled the *Trek* franchise to reinvent itself and to turn failure into spectacular success in the 1980s and 1990s. The differences also reflect the more straightforward economic imperatives that governed network decisions in the 1960s. As Herb Solow, the executive who sold *TOS* to NBC, and co-author of *Star Trek: The Continuing Story,* put it in an interview with us: "In the final season, NBC gave 'a short order' of twenty-four episodes; NBC went out on a limb [with *Star Trek*] and it ended up losing money. . . . *Star Trek* was not a big deal to NBC."[1]

By contrast, in 2005 *Star Trek: Enterprise* (2001) was a very big deal to Paramount. As a press release stated in February 2005: "All of us at Paramount warmly bid goodbye to *Enterprise* and we all look forward to a new chapter of this enduring franchise in the future."[2] In other words, in 2005, unlike in 1969, this massive, money-spinning, multimedia cultural phenomenon was not going to be allowed to stop producing profits for its owners, whether through television, through other media, or through spin-off merchandising. Rewards like these were evidently not anticipated by NBC when they canceled the original show in 1969, even though, as Gary Westfahl (1996) has pointed out, a busy unofficial trade in *Trek* souvenirs and memorabilia had already started among fans. We can be sure that, learning from its history, *Star Trek*'s owners will go on exploring ways of reinventing and rebranding the product so that it continues "to boldly go" where no media products have gone before. *Star Trek* celebrated its fortieth anniversary in 2006, and, with four seasons— the minimum for profitable syndication—safely in the can, *Enterprise* joined the four earlier TV series that continue to be rerun on TV stations around the world and will continue to make profits for its owners.

It was NBC that brought *Star Trek* to its first mass audience, and the network surely deserves some reflected glory from the phenomenon that the series became. Yet the NBC/Universal Web site does not mention the 1966 launching of *Star Trek* as one of the significant events in its history; in contrast, "television's longest running program," *Meet the Press*, is featured for meeting its "half-century mark" in 1997. But, as an example of NBC programs and policies under the classic network system, *TOS*—canceled in 1969 after seventy-nine episodes—offers a useful case study. It illustrates the adventurousness of the NBC network, as Herb Solow has claimed, but it also offers a case study of how a program that failed under the traditional network system was able to do better under a different system, twenty years later.

We argue here that *Star Trek* was a program that could have thrived had it been aired after the shift to demographically differentiated ratings in the 1970s and 1980s, which was prompted by the relative fragmentation of the audience due to cable and satellite channels. *Star Trek: The Next Generation* (*TNG*, 1987) did indeed thrive on that basis. Yet even in the 1960s, the original *Trek* presaged a new era, for those who cared to notice, because of its relationship with fans and its special demographic appeal to young viewers—an appeal that the network failed to exploit because of the industry's perceived need in the 1960s to appeal to large, general audiences rather than to smaller niche ones. *Star Trek* was a series ahead of its time. In 1987, *TNG* became the first episodic series drama to go straight to syndication, thus bypassing the networks altogether, as the new world of cable made possible. And more recently, when the network concept was reinvented in the 1990s under the control of Hollywood studios, the flagship show on Paramount's new network UPN was *Star Trek: Voyager*. Our case study of *Star Trek* in its various incarnations illustrates the major structural developments in American television across its forty-year history.

In describing the relationship of the original series with NBC, *Star Trek* scholars are fortunate that people like Solow and his co-author Robert Justman are still very much alive, articulate, and writing and speaking in the public domain. Such TV veterans' accounts of past events, though often contrasting, illuminate working practices and relationships within the industry that have now been superseded by new technological and industrial processes and that are too rarely documented in detail. *Star Trek* is an exception: even before we were able to conduct interviews, much of the inside story of NBC's dealings with the show had been reported in Solow and Justman's *Inside Star Trek: The Real Story* (1996) and in Stephen Whitfield and Gene Roddenberry's *The Making of Star Trek* (1968). *Star Trek: The Next Generation— The Continuing Mission*, by Judith Reeves-Stevens and Garfield Reeves-Stevens (1997), is also a source of much valuable inside information about the resurrection of *Star Trek* as a television series, including the decision in 1987 not to sell it to a major network. These insider accounts—often (understandably) self-promoting—are all authorized by the production company. Thus we can assume that some information that scholars might find illuminating is not covered, including some of the more forthright personal remarks about individuals that some of our interviewees made to us. Nevertheless, to the extent that original production materials, such as memos and scripts, are reproduced, scholars and readers are free to draw their own conclusions.

In contrast, most other television programs of the past have not been so well documented in published form, whether authorized or not, or indeed documented at all. The original internal memos between producers and network, letters, pitches, diagrams, models, scripts, and plans that have survived thanks to *Star Trek*'s status as a cultural phenomenon with a huge fan following can be accessed through their marketing in these "insider" books. The authorized published accounts are well known in the *Trek* community, whether of fans or of *Trek* scholars, but this essay may perhaps introduce them to media scholars interested more generally in network histories and in television. This essay also reflects on the relationship between documented history, mythmaking, direct primary information (such as our interviews), and secondary sources such as the authorized accounts in discussing the meaning and significance of television shows over time.

Star Trek as Television:
The American Classic Network System

But we must begin at the beginning: the original network environment within which *Star Trek* was launched. The person primarily responsible for selling *Trek* to NBC, a former head of daytime programming at the network, was our interviewee Herb Solow. In 1964 Solow was director of program development at the independent studio Desilu, run by Lucille Ball and her husband, Desi Arnaz. There had been a failed attempt by *Trek*'s originator, Gene Roddenberry, to sell the series to CBS, but Solow's insider knowledge of NBC suggested to him that NBC would be a more desirable client: "I took *Star Trek* to NBC for various reasons, one being that no advertising agency would spend the development money needed, another being that the advertising agencies chose to stay put in New York and Chicago. NBC welcomed me; I had left on good terms with them." Solow was very defensive of NBC, claiming that the network had been unfairly denigrated within the *Star Trek* mythos. To him, the network was "the hero." As he put it, "NBC gave us its all": "NBC should be applauded. . . . I feel that NBC has been totally misjudged and maligned by *Star Trek* fans. Since I had worked twice for NBC prior to *Star Trek* [director of network daytime programs and program director for the NBC film division], I was very close to all the key NBC executives, Grant Tinker, Herb Schlosser, Mort Werner, Jerry Stanley, Paul Klein [vice president of research and a very influential person], Bobby Sarnoff [David Sarnoff's son]. I was aware of the network's always-present station, sponsor, and government problems."

For Solow, Gene Roddenberry was not "the hero" of the *Star Trek* story, and certainly not "the Great Bird of the Galaxy," as producer Robert Justman dubbed him, to the network's annoyance. During our research for our book (Pearson and Davies, forthcoming) it has been illuminating to see how very differently our various interviewees spoke about him. Some appeared to idolize him; many respected his talents. But Solow, the astute company man, producer, negotiator, and deal maker, portrays the "visionary" as something of a nuisance in the deal-making process with NBC:

> I only took him to a meeting with me once. Once was enough. . . . Gene set about making NBC the heavy, the villain with regard to everything: schedule, ratings, programs practices (censor), publicity, etc., thus playing to the fans. He felt that the fans were more important than the network. He cast himself as the god and NBC as some demonic force from the other side. . . . The networks (I use the plural as they all speak to each other) felt differently. . . . Gene went ahead and created a villain (NBC) with the help of fans—people with a financial interest in fandom.

In the 1950s and 1960s the networks were synonymous with television: anyone wanting to broadcast a commercial program to the American public had to do so via NBC, CBS, or ABC or not at all. Herb Solow approached his former colleagues at NBC directly on behalf of the Desilu studio, which had agreed to shoot a pilot episode for *Trek*. He described the "ordering pattern" at the time:

> If the network likes the pilot . . . [it] orders the series; in the case of *Star Trek*, NBC ordered a total of sixteen new episodes (seventeen including the pilot). The early episodes did fairly well, so they exercised their option and extended the order to twenty-six new episodes for the first season. The two-parter (first pilot recut, etc.) and the second pilot film make up the total of twenty-nine episodes ordered for the first season. In season 1 the ratings were slowly falling. Remember, the networks must order additional episodes for the second season while the first season episodes are still being broadcast. NBC was not sure what it wanted to do. . . . Their choice was twenty-six new episodes or cancel the series. Much to their (and stations') financial regret, they went for a second year. Remember, stations get paid by the networks based on sponsorship of the series they carry. So with few sponsors, it's the local stations who suffer financially along with NBC.

Networks also exerted control over content through their broadcast standards departments, and they exerted almost universal control over audiences and distribution; 98 percent of all TV audiences in the 1960s watched the big three networks.

As well as interviewing Herb Solow in 2005, we were able to interview (in 2002) his co-author, Robert (Bob) Justman, a meticulous chronicler of his own career, who has kept his letters and memos to and from Roddenberry, Desilu, NBC, and other parties. In contrast to Solow, he was less complimentary about some of the network's judgments: "NBC was considerably appalled by the pilot we made ['The Cage']. So much so that they called Herb [Solow] in and Gene and said, 'Look, we like what you did, but there's some things we want to change, especially in the areas of casting, and especially in the areas of *Don't be so smart*.' They didn't say the word *smart*. They just mentioned things like: our concepts were too intricate for the normal television human mind. . . . Well I thought it wasn't that way at all. I felt that we could barely keep up with people." Justman was referring to the multiethnic cast, including the alien "Vulcan," Mr. Spock, played by Leonard Nimoy, which was proposed for the first series and the then-daring idea of having a female first officer. (This was dropped—but the series was eventually to pioneer a woman captain in *Star Trek: Voyager* [1995–2001] and a black captain in *Star Trek: Deep Space Nine* [1993–99].) He was also referring to the kinds of political and ideological debates prompted by the series, which, according to him, were deemed "too smart" for the 1960s mass audience.

We were also able to interview William Shatner (Captain Kirk), the star of the original series—a man who came across as impatient with *Trek* mythology. Shatner commented on the original *TOS* pitch, praising Roddenberry's "genius" (even though he had not always seen eye to eye with him): "It takes a certain genius to do that, to sell a series, to come up with a commercial enough theme, and a kind of concept that speaks to these network executives, who are [either] very bright and are there because they're conducting a network, or very stupid because there's no place else for them to have gone."[3] It seemed that Roddenberry (and Shatner) were lucky enough to meet some bright executives—at NBC. One was Jerry Stanley; the other was Grant Tinker, who was described by Herb Solow as "an outstanding person" and by Todd Gitlin (1985) as the "most liked man in Hollywood" (125) and who would later become a legendarily successful president of the network. Solow and Justman (1996) described in their book their first meeting with Tinker and Stanley at NBC Burbank in May 1964: "It was like most network meetings: fifty percent small talk, twenty-five percent network gossip and twenty-five percent business" (19). Tinker and Stanley were not convinced the show would be commercial and did not believe there was "enough of an audience out there to support this mixture of science fiction and fantasy" (19). Solow and Roddenberry asked NBC for a commitment for a ninety-minute pilot script that could run as a TV special if the show did not sell as a series.

Tinker and Stanley agreed, and the first pilot episode, "The Cage," written by Roddenberry, went into production at Desilu. This episode featured James T. Kirk's predecessor, Captain Christopher Pike, played by Jeffrey Hunter, who leaves the *U.S.S. Enterprise* with a landing party in response to a distress signal from a planet, Talos IV. The Talosians, strange-looking monklike creatures with translucent heads, have lured Pike and his colleagues there in an attempt to use them as breeding stock to create a race of slaves that will repopulate their ravaged planet. They encourage Pike to breed with a beautiful human female captive, Vina. He is attracted to her, but her beauty turns out to be an illusion—in fact, she is disfigured from an earlier crash landing. The humans refuse to be used in this way (a classic motif to be used again and again), and the Talosians give in and let them return to their ship.

"The Cage" was piloted to NBC in 1964, and according to the insider accounts (Solow and Justman 1996; Whitfield and Roddenberry 1968) Mort Werner, head of programming for NBC, "loved it." Nevertheless the network decided not to commission it because, so Robert Justman told us, it was "too cerebral." However, in their book, Solow and Justman (1996) drew attention to "[t]he unspoken reason, [which] dealt more with the manners and morals of mid 1960s America." The network broadcast standards office was concerned about the perceived eroticism of the pilot and what it foreshadowed for the ensuing series. NBC's Sales Department worried that the Mr. Spock character, with his pointed ears and slanting eyes, would be seen as "demonic" by "Bible Belt affiliate station owners and important advertisers." It was at this point that *Star Trek* received its next stroke of luck from NBC; as Solow and Justman put it, "Mort Werner did not forsake us" and unusually allowed Desilu to produce another pilot, "Where No Man Has Gone Before" (60–61). According to Whitfield and Roddenberry (1968), for a network to commission a second pilot "shattered all television precedent" (126). This seems to have resulted from the good and mutually respectful relationship between Solow and Werner, with Roddenberry, the loose cannon, being diplomatically kept out of, or in, the picture as Solow thought fit.

There were many negotiations with NBC about the diversity of casting. Roddenberry had wanted a female first officer, which the network did not accept—according to Solow in our interview, partly because Majel Barrett (later to be Nurse Chappell in *TOS*, and Lwaxana Troi in *TNG*, as well as the second Mrs. Roddenberry) did not work in the part. Nevertheless, NBC had a policy of encouraging a degree of diversity from which *TOS* benefited. The series still looks exceptional in the multiculturalism of its cast. In May 1965, NBC's Mort Werner had sent out a directive to all network series producers to hire more actors from diverse racial backgrounds; the regular *Star Trek* crew had African American Nichelle Nichols, Japanese American George Takei, Walter Koenig as the Russian Chekov, and of course, Leonard Nimoy as Mr. Spock, the Vulcan, providing a regular commentary on the nature of otherness that was to become a major theme in all the *Trek* series and movies and the subject of a still-proliferating flow of scholarly comment.

Daniel Bernardi (1998) points out the social and political context of *Star Trek*'s production in the 1960s, when "the civil rights and antiwar movements accelerated the fight against a separate and unequal reality in the hopes of achieving a more egalitarian ideal" (26).[4] He suggests that NBC was exceptional in allowing a series with such aspirations on the air: "While the majority of network programming remained white, *Star Trek* was among the few series that embraced and consistently spoke to the shifting meaning of race that contextualized its production and initial

FIG. **13** Captain Kirk (William Shatner), Dr. McCoy (DeForest Kelley), and Mr. Spock (Leonard Nimoy) on the set of *Star Trek: The Original Series* in 1966. (Library of American Broadcasting)

reception" (34). Bernardi attributes much of the source of this "liberal humanist" discourse of racial equality to Gene Roddenberry and, like all *Star Trek* scholars, freely draws on the mass of secondary material about Roddenberry, such as a published interview with him in 1991 (see Alexander 1991). Although Roddenberry is now deceased, we found that "Gene's vision"—that is, the discourse of liberal humanism—was still pervasive among production staff in the very different production and historical circumstances of 2002 when we visited Paramount. Contrasting the durability of the Roddenberry "vision" with some of the negative firsthand accounts of the man has been one of the many illuminating insights of our primary research on *Star Trek:* however irritating Roddenberry may have been to the network in the 1960s, as Solow and others describe, both he and they appear to have gotten hold of something culturally important, almost despite themselves.

Back in January 1966, as Bernardi writes, negotiations with the network about casting and story resulted in the unprecedented second pilot. This pilot, extensively recast, dropped the female first officer, replaced Jeffrey Hunter as Captain Pike with William Shatner as Captain Kirk, and, just managing to preserve Mr. Spock, was sent to NBC in New York. The series was commissioned, due to air the following September. In his interview with us, Shatner—an extremely astute commentator on the relationship between the economic and institutional requirements of television and the role of the "creatives"—explained the difference between himself and Hunter: "The character [Kirk] was a leading man. The·shirt comes off and this goes on, and the girl comes in, and the fight starts, and it's all leading-man stuff. So when people would ask me, Did you suffer from being typecast, my standard answer is: I wouldn't know whether someone in a boardroom somewhere said, Let's not hire him. I only know the people who said, Let's hire him. Because he dashes and jumps and kisses the girl."[5]

Critical Responses to *TOS*

NBC accepted the series, but the beginnings of *Star Trek* did not augur well. *Variety* wrote that the series "needs to be shaken up and given more life than death."[6] Despite the *Hollywood Reporter*'s contrary opinion that the show "should be a winner," within three months it was in danger of cancellation.[7] The insider accounts give an impression of constant difficulties, as well as what Justman told us was "enormous fun."

There were regular clashes with network overseers. As Solow and Justman (1996) point out, series with standard formats are "network damage proof," but sci fi/fantasy is an exception: "It needed an NBC program manager with experience, good taste, an appreciation for the written word, lack of ego and absence of involvement in private lives of personnel who could represent the interests of the sponsor and the network regarding series and story content and timely delivery of the product" (140). Stan Robertson became the program manager, and there were many disagreements between him and Gene Roddenberry. Network censors—the Broadcast Standards and Practices Department—also had the power of veto over content. According to Solow and Justman, the first broadcast standards official they had to deal with, Jean Messerschmidt, was "firm and reasonable." But, as Justman told us in our interview, there were many occasions when censors were not, and he and Solow frequently used the censors' focus on eroticism to slip more controversial material past them. Solow and Justman recount in their book how by drawing the Broadcast Standards Department's attention to a sexual issue they could incorporate ideological questions into the story line without being noticed. An example was the second-season episode "A Private Little War," in which the issue of whether Captain Kirk and his crew were right to intervene in maintaining the balance of power between warring factions on an alien planet was obviously a thinly veiled reference to the Vietnam War. In their book, Solow and Justman describe an exchange of memos about this episode with the network, which objected to a scene that included "an open mouth kiss" between a half-naked woman and Kirk. The network apparently did not notice that the story was about "the police action" in Vietnam. Solow and Justman observed: "But the audience did. We got letters. Lots of them" (356). In his later interview with us, Solow defended the network on this score: "You have to understand the time. NBC were not conservative; they were following the broadcasting codes set by the NAB [National Association of Broadcasters] (following the Hays Office). For instance, Lucy was not allowed to say *pregnant*."

In his interview, Justman, a production perfectionist who had learned his trade in Hollywood with Robert Aldrich and King Vidor, expressed unhappiness with the lack of technical control in his dealings with the network:

> It was much better before it went on [the TV screen]. . . . What got lost is some of the richness of the color image and the shadows and the lighting. When you give your show, that you worked on so hard to bring it to as close to perfection as you can, and you give it to the network, and the network puts it on in their machine room, and they just blast a light through that print and wash it out. . . . I was kvetching on the phone to NBC, saying, Wait a second, what are you doing to our show? It doesn't need that much light.[8]

There is again a difference of emphasis between Solow and Justman, indicative of the way in which histories and mythologies are built up and revised, on the technical point about "the richness of the color image and the shadows and the lighting." Whereas Justman complained about the network "washing it out," Solow in his interview voiced a more pragmatic attitude and pointed out that broadcast color was in its early days and "TV color was different." His view was, "We needed to trust the people who worked for RCA and NBC—they were the experts." He also put a gloss on the account given in his and Justman's book: "Color projected in a screening room was not the color seen on the air. The conversion to electronic broadcasting played havoc with film color. NBC had a color specialist named Alex Quroga who worked with *Star Trek* and *Bonanza* to try to come close. Justman's only complaint that is valid is that no one told the NBC broadcast color technician that Spock's skin was supposed to be yellow, so when the first episode was broadcast, the color technician overrode the film and removed some of the yellow color and replaced it with a pinkish skin-tone. That's early television."

While these tussles were going on, *Star Trek*'s corporate status changed. In July 1967, Desilu was bought by Gulf+Western, which had just (in 1966) bought Paramount Pictures. Thus Paramount, the show's present owners and beneficiaries, became the (then not very enthusiastic) owners of the *Trek* franchise. Later, in 1989, Gulf+Western was renamed Paramount Communications Inc., and in 1994 Viacom, an independent company that spun off from the CBS broadcasting network when CBS sold its syndication divisions in 1971, merged with Paramount. So, in one of the ironic turns of corporate fate that can be so fascinating to historians of the industry, *Star Trek* finally ended up in a relationship with the network, CBS, that had refused it initially.[9] According to Solow in his interview, when Paramount bought Desilu they didn't want *Star Trek:* "Paramount didn't want *Star Trek* because it was losing too much money each week and didn't have enough episodes to syndicate successfully. That was a wise business decision at the time. They did not have the Kaiser Television figures available, as it hadn't happened yet [see below]. Recall that Roddenberry was also offered a chance to buy all of Paramount's equity in *Star Trek*. He passed at a price of $150,000. Who knew the property would gross near $3 billion?"

Despite its lukewarm reception by some critics and its unimpressive ratings, the original *Star Trek* began to attract the enthusiasts who would eventually be the saving of it and who would help provide a foundation for its renaissance twenty years later, in the new, postnetwork, demographically targeted era, with *TNG. TOS* had its fans—and they were thoughtful, argumentative, and determined fans. According to an NBC booklet issued in August 1967, twenty-nine thousand pieces of fan mail were received in the first season—only *The Monkees* drew more fan response. This booklet described the *Trek* audience as "decision makers," people who would be attractive to potential sponsors. But despite this acknowledgment of the kind of audience the program was likely to attract, it was still scheduled in a slot on Friday night, 8:30 to 9:30, where it was likely to miss the young audience of high school and college students to whom it most appealed. By December 1967 the series was again in trouble; fans John and Bjo Trimble drew up an advice sheet, "How to Write Effective Letters to Save *Star Trek*," for fans to circulate. These were sent to the presidents of NBC, NBC affiliates, TV columnists, and *TV Guide*. In an updated version of its 1967 *Mailcall* pamphlet about fan mail, NBC reported that 115,893 letters had been received as a result of the fan campaign, 52,358 during the month of February. Roddenberry himself was involved in this letter campaign.[10]

The show was renewed—but was placed in an even worse scheduling slot, Fridays at 10:00. This would kill it. In our interview, Herb Solow commented on audience figures now, compared with the "death" of the original series:

The average audience for *TOS* networkwise was five million. Not spectacular. *Mission Impossible* [which was broadcast by CBS, not NBC] was getting twenty million viewers. . . . If *Enterprise* were on NBC today as a network show and it attracted five million viewers it would be considered viable. If *TOS* were on now and attracted five million, NBC would keep it on the air. There's so much competition—if you get five million now that would be doing darned good. . . . Another reason *TOS* would have been renewed is that the fan demographics indicated a quality buyer mentality, which is music to sponsor's ears.

Solow and Justman (1996) also attributed the demise of the original series to a fundamental clash of values: "Late summer 1967 . . . the creatives ran into corporate America" (367). This interpretation was to recur in the accounts of the *Star Trek* production personnel we interviewed ourselves. Solow and Justman were scornful of corporate America, with what they called its "disease of MBA-ism" and its jargon. They objected to being asked about the "product line" and the "return on investment." Justman said, "We don't manufacture widgets here, this is show business, the whole thing is fucking gobbledegook" (Solow and Justman 1996, 367). Nevertheless, their show *was* a commodity and was never going to be saved, or reproduced, unless some corporation could be convinced that there was money in it. At that point, nobody could see any money in it.

In his interview, Solow contrasted the new "MBA-ism" with how things had operated at Desilu:

> Not like the old system at Desilu that I used to run. It was like a family. Anyone could come into the office if they had an idea and we'd listen to it. [There was] a group of Desilu studio people who loved their work and did more than expected of them. To this day crew people and executives alike will tell me it was the best years of their lives. TV is an interesting animal in that it put together the broadcasting industry and the movie industry. The death of the motion picture business was linked with the rise of the TV business. Their old way of doing business suddenly (within a few years) changed. They were no longer alone in supplying visual entertainment to the world. A new guy was on the block, and, at first, they tried to ignore him and failed. They finally joined up and television film production became a major industry. Today, of course, these very same unwilling players own networks, cable stations, publishing companies, media outlets around the world.[11]

On January 9, 1969, *TOS* in its NBC incarnation was over. The show's ratings had dropped by 50 percent. Production of the seventy-ninth episode, "Turnabout Intruder," had run one day over schedule and $6,000 over budget. Properties of the show, which would be worth a small fortune today, were dispersed and disappeared. "Tribbles" (little furry creatures who featured in one of the most famous episodes of the whole five series, "The Trouble with Tribbles"), props, and costumes were stolen. There were also not enough episodes to make a standard syndication package, which usually requires four seasons, as in the case of *Enterprise*.

Nevertheless, another stroke of luck occurred. In 1967, while the original series was still on the air but struggling, Paramount Television struck a syndication deal with Kaiser Broadcasting. Kaiser owned a number of major-market UHF stations— Philadelphia, Boston, Cleveland, Detroit, and San Francisco. Knowing that the series was popular with young males, Kaiser had the bright idea of scheduling the show every night against the 6:00 p.m. newscasts of their competitors, "gambling that young males were not heavy viewers of television news programs," as Solow and Justman (1996, 418) put it. Thus began *Star Trek*'s afterlife in syndicated sales, including international sales.

A year after the demise of the show, Gene Roddenberry asked Paramount for control of the rights so he could do something with it himself. They agreed to sell all rights, title, and equity position to Roddenberry for $150,000, but, as Solow pointed out to us, he could not afford it. Under the terms of the original deal, Desilu and Norway Productions, Roddenberry's company, and the studio (Paramount) retained overall control of the property. However, net profits were to be shared among Desilu, Norway, William Shatner, and NBC. The original series had lasted only three seasons, and it would seem that, in devising such a formula, Roddenberry and his studio had not hit on a commercial winner but had in fact miscalculated quite badly.

Audiences: From Mass Ratings to Demographics

What the network had failed to calculate, although Kaiser Broadcasting apparently had, was the effect that the series would have on key demographic groups of educated young men and women. These included the students at MIT who attributed their desire for space careers to *Star Trek* (see Tulloch and Jenkins 1995) and the young Whoopi Goldberg, who was inspired in her career by the presence of a black woman playing an officer, not a maid or a comic, as a regular star of an adult series drama on TV—Nichelle Nichols as Lieutenant Uhura. *TOS* appealed to young men with disposable income. In *TV Week*'s second Annual Poll of Favorites by Age Group, *Star Trek* was at the top in both the twenty-to-thirty and thirty-to-forty age groups (Solow and Justman 1996, 356). But in the 1960s, with its emphasis on the mass audience, this was not enough to rescue the series for the networks.

When *TOS* originally aired, the three commercial networks had a 98 percent share of the whole audience and the simple goal of each network was to get a bigger share, especially in prime-time evening programming, than the other two. Times changed; in 2002, as Mike Mellon, vice president for research at Paramount Pictures, Television, pointed out to us in an interview, the three big networks' *combined* share was only 33 percent. He described the May sweep of 2001, when, for the first time, non-network output got a larger share of the audience than network programs. (Non-network output includes cable and basic cable, plus VCRs.) *Star Trek* had to reinvent itself to take account of these larger changes taking place in the industry as a whole, including changes in audience measurement.

When *TNG* came on the air in 1987 within a rapidly developing multichannel television landscape, including cable, satellite and VCR use, audience impact was being assessed differently. As Michael Mellon told us: "Households are shrinking, and the demographics become that much more important. . . . Why is the Superbowl always the highest cost spot in prime time television every single year, and not necessarily an efficient one? Because you're looking at the most men of any spot that will ever run that year. . . . And they set up a spot for more money than any spot they have because it's a valuable spot."[12]

In 1970 the Federal Communications Commission (FCC) prohibited networks from receiving profit participation in series licensed for broadcast and also outlawed network participation in syndication rights, although existing agreements were allowed to stand. As Les Brown (1971) pointed out, these new rules (Financial Interest and Syndication Rule—"Fin-Syn") "were a boon to Hollywood studios which came to realize enormous profits from their network hits, because they owned the shows entirely and because they were able to sell the re-runs in syndication while the new episodes on the networks were at the peak of their popularity. . . . [T]he syndication market flourished" (157).[13] Such an arrangement—the selling of "front-end" (original) material and "back-end" (repeat) material at the same time—by the Hollywood studios, turned out to be tailor-made for the deal leading to *Star Trek*'s eventual revival with *TNG*.

Star Trek as television was fully reborn in 1987.[14] The rebirth was announced in September 1986; the first twenty-two-page "bible" is dated November 16, 1986, and it resulted in what many people argue is the finest and most successful product of the whole franchise: *Star Trek: The Next Generation*. Thanks to the relative box-office success of the *Star Trek* films, of which there were by now five, and also to the existence of a loyal audience for *TOS* in syndication, Paramount decided that it would be worth attempting to produce a completely new television series. This provoked considerable controversy among both fans and *Trek* insiders, who felt that Kirk and company could never be replaced. Nevertheless, it was thanks to Kirk and company that *TNG* was ever considered feasible at all. Another of our interviewees in 2002 was then the head of Paramount Television, Kerry McCluggage. As he put it, "The original *Star Trek* . . . became a hit and a phenomenon when it was sold into syndication. There were only seventy-nine episodes, but they were stripping it five days a week, and it became immensely popular. And it was the popularity of that show in off-network syndication that spawned *The Next Generation*."[15] *TNG* would be produced and distributed under very different conditions than the earlier series. Paramount decided to avoid the networks and go straight to syndication—in other words, to sell the new series directly to local stations. This made economic sense to the studio because it cost more to produce an hour-long episode of a TV series (particularly an expensive one like *Star Trek*) than the network would be willing to pay for it. The shortfall had to come from syndication— repeat sales—and, as McCluggage pointed out, *TOS* already had a guaranteed market for these. The value of the back catalog—a value always recognized by fans but

only now belatedly by the legal owners of the product (the studio)—could be exploited. The deal for selling the untried *TNG*, with its bald "unknown Shakespearean
actor"[16] as captain, to the local stations was cautious and extremely ingenious.

TNG took advantage of the strategy of barter syndication. In exchange for running the new show for free, local stations were required to allow Paramount seven
minutes of commercial time in each episode to sell to national advertisers. The station could sell the remaining five minutes of commercial time for themselves. This
income from advertising still would not cover the cost of production, but Paramount
was already making $1 million per episode through repeats of *TOS* in syndication.
The clinching ingredient of the deal was that Paramount would sell the profitable
TOS only to stations that took *TNG* too. Mel Harris, the Paramount executive who
announced the deal to the press, explained this by saying, "We came to the conclusion that nobody was going to give it the same kind of attention and care that we
could give it" (Alexander 1996, 501). In 1995 Paramount formed its own network—
UPN—and on the strength of the existing franchise and a new series, *Star Trek: Voyager* was created in 1995. Ever since *TNG*, *Star Trek* as television has gone out either
as a syndicated show or on Paramount's own "netlet": *Deep Space 9* (1993), *Voyager*
(1995), and *Enterprise* (2001) have never been broadcast as first-run shows on the big
three American broadcast networks.

In his interview with us, Bob Justman described how it felt producing a show
not for network but for syndication in the new post–Fin-Syn studio-dominated television universe:

> *TNG* was a totally different experience. It was totally different, and totally the same.
> But the big difference was, and this, this is heaven, this is heaven for a film producer.
> [whisper] *There was no network.* [then louder] There was no network, folks, no network.
> There was no Broadcast Standards Department. There were no censors. We censored
> ourselves, so to speak. We did not have to submit one of our stories to the network
> for approval by programming and that same script to broadcast standards for approval
> by the broadcast censors. Nothing. Nada. You know, once Paramount tried to step in
> and get involved in the cutting of an episode, and Gene Roddenberry blew them away
> and told them, "Don't come back again," you know, "*We'll* take care of the creative
> end of everything."

So the little program that could became the big program that did. And despite the
current setback with the end of *Enterprise*, it is likely to continue to be the huge franchise that will. It seems a pity for NBC that they are unlikely to be able to claim
credit for it. *Star Trek's* fortieth birthday in 2006 will almost certainly involve individuals and organizations across the media industries, from publishing, to models,
to computer games, to movies, to special DVDs, to Web sites, both authorized and
unauthorized, in its celebrations. Let us hope that it will earn at least a mention on
the Web site belonging to the organization—NBC—that originally gave it to the
world and that, according to Herb Solow, the loyal ex-employee, was the original
"hero" of the continuing story.

Notes

1. Herb Solow, interview by Davies and Pearson and e-mail exchanges with both authors, April 2005.

2. Paramount/UPN press release, February 2, 2005.

3. William Shatner, interview by Davies and Pearson, January 16, 2002.

4. On race in *Star Trek*, see also Harrison et al. (1996) and Pounds (1999).

5. William Shatner, interview by Davies and Pearson, January 16, 2002.

6. *Variety*, September 8, 1966, 9.

7. Bill Ornstein, "Star Trek," *Hollywood Reporter*, September 9, 1966, 4.

8. Robert Justman, interview by Davies and Pearson, 2002.

9. In another twist of fate, the rights to *Star Trek* television now reside with CBS Paramount, the new company created when Sumner Redstone split Paramount/Viacom into two separate entities. The splitting of Paramount/Viacom and the subsequent merger of the WB and UPN networks came as this chapter was in the final stages of revision.

10. See the account of Roddenberry's enthusiastic and Machiavellian operations in Solow and Justman (1996).

11. Herb Solow, interview by Davies and Pearson, 2005. It is interesting that the word *family* was also used by the people we interviewed in 2002, working on *Enterprise*, such as line producer Merri Howard, postproduction producer Wendy Neuss, and actor/director Jonathan Frakes.

12. Michael Mellon, Paramount Studios, interview by Davies and Pearson, January 16, 2002.

13. The Fin-Syn rules were repealed in 1995, allowing much greater concentration of ownership between networks and production companies. The trend for networks and studios to become part of the same conglomerates, as in the case of Paramount/Viacom in 1994, is discussed in Holt (2004).

14. We refer to "television" for the purposes of this chapter as live action. In 1973 in the United States there was an unsuccessful animated series made by Filmation for NBC on Saturday mornings, which folded after twenty-two episodes.

15. Kerry McCluggage, interview with Davies and Pearson, 2002.

16. This was the notice on Patrick Stewart's dressing room door during the first season of *TNG*.

13

Sex as a Weapon

Programming Sexuality in the 1970s

ELANA LEVINE

In both popular memory and scholarly accounts, U.S. television in the 1970s is a series of puzzling contradictions. Groundbreaking sitcoms such as *All in the Family* (CBS, 1971–83) and *M*A*S*H* (CBS, 1972–83) took on the social issues of the day, from race relations to the war in Vietnam. As Todd Gitlin and others have argued, CBS in particular turned to "relevance" as a means of attracting an upscale audience and the advertiser dollars that came with it (Gitlin 1985, 207–9; Bodroghkozy 2001, 205). Yet 1970s TV is also remembered as a morass of silly, mindless, exploitative fare, from the hokey nostalgia of the hit sitcom *Happy Days* (ABC, 1974–84), to the absurd shenanigans of the roommates in *Three's Company* (ABC, 1977–84), to the glamorously coiffed beauties of *Charlie's Angels* (ABC, 1976–81). This flipside of the 1970s turn to relevance is often conceived as a turn to "irrelevance," an embrace of escapist, juvenile entertainment meant to appeal to a not especially discriminating mass audience. Much of the "irrelevant" 1970s programming aired on ABC, the historically third-place network that quickly rose to number one on the popularity of this very material. While historians of the intersection of TV industry tactics and American culture have found both CBS's and ABC's strategies significant, NBC has received little attention in their narratives.

Further, the 1970s have received little attention in most narratives of NBC's history. Scholarly histories of broadcasting, such as Erik Barnouw's *Tube of Plenty* (1990) and J. Fred MacDonald's *One Nation under Television* (1990), dwell on NBC's dominance in radio, its formative role in the development of television technology (through its owner, RCA), and its revitalization of the family sitcom in the 1980s. The network's public celebration of its own past, as in the May 20, 2002 special, *Twenty Years of Must See TV,* typically begins in the 1980s, when a continuous roster of ratings successes made it a notable network once again. But the 1970s (and much of the 1960s) drop off the historical radar in both scholarly and popular accounts.[1]

Clearly, the 1970s were not NBC's decade, and NBC programming was not the defining element of 1970s TV.

Just because the television industry lives and dies by Nielsen ratings data, however, does not mean that television historians must do the same. Despite NBC's third place in the ratings, millions of people watched NBC programming in the 1970s, making it relevant to histories of television as a component of everyday life. An exploration of NBC's efforts in the late 1970s in particular can be exceptionally revealing of TV industry strategizing at the height of the network era. NBC's late-1970s programming choices can help us to see which genres, themes, and representations were considered valuable and how each network tried to position itself in relation to the others.

Examining the network's efforts in the late 1970s can also illustrate the different ways that U.S. television was representing sex in the wake of the sexual revolution, a time of great change in sexual mores and practices. Elsewhere, I argue that U.S. television of the 1970s referenced, discussed, and represented sex to an extent previously unseen on television (Levine 2006). Although CBS's attention to sex-themed social issues in its hit sitcoms and ABC's use of sexually suggestive humor and female sex symbols in its successful shows are the best-known examples of this trend, some of NBC's offerings provided yet another perspective on the sexually charged times, an alternative to the other networks' efforts. In well-publicized statements, NBC executives criticized ABC in particular, disparaging the new ratings leader for its exploitative use of sex to attract viewers. Alongside these denunciations, however, were NBC's own attempts to use sex-themed programming to climb out of its ratings slump. In this chapter, I analyze NBC's attempt to use sex as a weapon in the battle for network supremacy in the 1970s. I argue that NBC managed to critique ABC's use of sex while carving out its own brand of sex-themed programming. In attempting—and failing—to beat its competition, NBC employed a version of sex both sensational and moralizing, a version slightly, but significantly, different from that offered by the other networks. The representation of sexuality in NBC's dramas and made-for-TV movies in particular offered moralizing takes on contemporary sexual issues that tried to exploit risqué subjects while still playing it safe in an era of intensified network competition and regulatory scrutiny of TV content.

Network Identities in the 1970s: What NBC Lacked

Despite the network's once foundational status in American broadcasting, NBC in the 1970s lingered outside the more popular world dominated by CBS and ABC. In certain respects, the network lacked the clear identity that its competitors had attained; it was much like the middle child lost between a popular older sibling and a scrappy, resilient younger one. A joke circulating in the TV industry of the time aptly illustrates the three networks' relative reputations as well as characterizing those reputations in sexual terms, thereby demonstrating the looming importance of sexual material in the networks' standings. The joke went like this: the three networks were marooned on an island, deserted except for a beautiful girl with whom the networks agreed they should all have sex. ABC was the first to volunteer and proceeded "to ravish the beauty unashamedly in plain view of the other two networks." Though CBS declared he did not like being second to anyone, particularly to ABC, he told the girl, "I'll be next, but come with me to the other side of the island where we can have privacy." Then it was NBC's turn. Though anxious to have sex with the girl, NBC said, "First, I've got to call New York and see what they say" (Quinlan 1979, 173). While the joke's sexism is indicative of the gendered power dynamics in the TV industry at this time, its characterization of the three networks is also quite indicative of the *kind* of masculine potency each was imagined to have. ABC was the impetuous adolescent, quick to jump into bed with any attractive offer, unconcerned with how it looked to the others. CBS, long an industry leader, was ever the gentleman, perfectly willing to debase itself but only away from judgmental gazes. Finally, NBC was the regular fellow, excited by the prospect of an illicit romp but nervous about the ramifications and hesitant about forging ahead. As a result, NBC was last to get the girl, coming across as overly cautious and tentative, not the "real man" that the other networks proved themselves to be. The feminizing of NBC in this joke demonstrates the network's problematic reputation within the industry, a reputation that would carry over to its public image. In fact, one might argue that NBC's willingness to exploit sexually suggestive material later in the decade was a response to this reputation; the timid fellow seeking to prove his prowess went overboard in his macho one-upmanship.

NBC had so much to prove in the 1970s because industry and public attention was fixed on the upstart ABC and its substantial challenge to the venerable CBS. At the start of the 1970s, CBS's leadership and ABC's also-ran status were firmly entrenched. CBS extended its longtime number one standing with a revamp of its prime-time schedule. Recognizing that highly rated series such as *Mayberry R.F.D.* (1968–71) and *Family Affair* (1966–71) tended to draw viewers in middle-American small towns instead of the major cities where the network's owned-and-operated stations fed directly into its earnings, CBS set about replacing such series with a different sort of programming meant to appeal to upscale viewers in major urban centers. By the start of the 1972–73 season the network had found three sitcom anchors—*All in the Family, The Mary Tyler Moore Show* (1970–77), and *M*A*S*H*— that spoke to the changing social worlds of the young and urban while not alienating older, more traditional viewers. Among the contemporary social issues up for comedic treatment in these shows were the changes inspired by the sexual revolution, including a new openness about homosexuality, a greater acceptance of premarital sex and promiscuity, and a wider awareness of women's sexual desires and needs.

CBS's use of sexual subjects in its new programming would be taken in a very different direction by ABC, which overtook CBS as the number one–rated network in the mid-1970s and shook up the standings and reputations of the Big Three in the process. ABC began its slow rise to parity with its competitors in the early 1970s and then outrated NBC in the 1975–76 season and CBS in 1976–77. At that point, not only had it bested its better-established competitors, but it also achieved the highest season average rating in the history of television.[2] ABC held onto this position throughout the remainder of the 1970s, allowing it a degree of industry power it had never before experienced.

ABC rose to prominence through a number of economic and regulatory shifts working in its favor, but the most publicly recognized element in its success was its programming, especially that developed by the new president of ABC Entertainment, Fred Silverman.[3] Silverman was typically characterized as someone who was closely in tune with public tastes and who just knew what would or would not work on a television schedule. The lineups he built at ABC counterprogrammed CBS by offering shows with no overt discussion of social issues, no apparent political message, and no pretensions to artistry. Silverman believed in appealing to the mass audience's common denominator—they had all been kids at one time or another— so he made broad, simple comedy and comedy-action-fantasy hybrids the foundations of the ABC schedule. This approach carried over into ABC's take on sex. By combining kid-oriented comedy with innuendo-laden sexual humor, Silverman's ABC was able to engage with the sexually changing culture without taking too radical a stance on sexual matters. ABC's shows specialized in delivering a barrage of innuendo, double entendres, and suggestive jokes and displaying sexy young women in revealing clothing. In its *Movie of the Week* series ABC also engaged sexual subjects, sometimes comedically, and in distinct contrast to NBC's *World Premiere* movies, which tended toward the action-adventure and suspense genres.[4]

As CBS was debuting its slate of socially "relevant" sitcoms and then scrambling to match ABC's ratings, and as ABC was basking in the profitable, if culturally disparaged, status it had attained, NBC was in trouble. Across the 1970s, NBC had few hit series and even less cultural buzz. Alongside the threatened dominance of CBS and the unexpected power of ABC, NBC held fast to its few successes. As the decade began, *Rowan and Martin's Laugh-In* (1968–73) was still number one and network standby *Bonanza* (1959–73) remained in the top ten. In the early years of the decade, the comedic talents of African American performers Flip Wilson (*The Flip Wilson Show*, 1970–74) and Redd Foxx (*Sanford and Son*, 1972–77) kept the network on the Nielsen charts. Although *Chico and the Man* (1974–78) joined *Sanford and Son* in the top five shows for the 1974–75 season, *Sanford* was the only NBC series to remain in the top ten consistently through the 1975–76 season (during which it was the only NBC series to place in the top *twenty*).[5] The second half of the 1970s was especially disappointing for the network's prime-time schedule (although NBC late night experienced a popular resurgence with the new *Saturday Night Live* in 1975). Most seasons, only movie nights and *Little House on the Prairie* (1974–82) made it to the prime-time Nielsen top twenty. Although the network aired the prestigious miniseries *Holocaust* in 1978, even it was no match for the commercial and critical success of ABC's *Roots* the previous year. Without any breakout hits, NBC prime time in the late 1970s was unable to build an audience substantial enough to compete with either CBS or ABC. NBC's programming seemed unable to achieve the popular cultural status of the other networks or to establish a clear identity within the television industry.

NBC's Response: "Adult Porn" versus "Kiddie Porn"

Although NBC was in certain respects a nonentity in 1970s television's industrial and cultural history, we can write an identity for NBC back into the historical record by exploring the network's attempt to use sexual material to compete with the other networks, and especially with ABC. NBC's construction of sex in the 1970s was often more sensational, and more moralizing, than the representations of sex and changes in sexual mores offered by the other networks. In this respect, the history of NBC in the 1970s shows us the importance of sexual material in programming during this decade, as well as pointing out the different ways the broadcast networks constructed sex in the wake of the sexual revolution.

NBC's two main strategies in its attempt to establish a place for itself amid the CBS-ABC rivalry of the late 1970s were seemingly contradictory, but they were actually a careful combination of efforts meant to siphon off a portion of ABC's audience. The network's strategies were first, to publicly criticize and condemn ABC for its pandering use of sex to draw audiences and, second, to try to best ABC by being even more explicit, sensational, and controversial about sex than its competitors. Although both strategies were more reactive than proactive, more products of desperation than attempts to contribute something new, they helped define ABC's approach to sex—and the approach to sex of 1970s TV—in ways that influenced the networks' reputations and cultural statuses at the time and in our historical memory. NBC's efforts helped establish ABC's lowbrow reputation in the 1970s—and helped develop an ultimately quite narrow, quite conservative construction of sex on television during a time of potentially radical sexual change.

NBC's efforts to disparage ABC and to offer even riskier sexual material were particularly significant because of the ongoing pressure on all of the networks to "clean up" their content. Early in the decade, much of the pressure centered on representations of violence and their impact on young viewers, an issue that drew the attention of the U.S. Congress. Increasingly risqué sexual fare was also of concern, and worries about sexual and violent content led to the ill-fated Family Viewing Hour policy instituted by the industry's self-regulating body, the National Association of Broadcasters, in 1975. As the decade progressed, citizens' groups, professional societies, and religious leaders, as well as the government, attacked television content as morally objectionable. For the network and their affiliates, the most troubling such protest came from advertisers, who demanded the reformation of programming perceived to be beyond the boundaries of taste and acceptability. Much of this pressure was directed at ABC, where shows such as *Three's*

Company and *Charlie's Angels* regularly made it to the top of "most objectionable TV" lists. NBC's efforts to disparage its competitor contributed to the lead network's troubled reputation and deflected attention from the even *more* risqué material that NBC would soon program.

NBC made its most significant assault on ABC's ratings and respectability in the late 1970s, when it slipped from second to third place in the Nielsen ratings. This indignity may have been the instigating factor, but, as we have seen, NBC had been struggling throughout the decade to establish an identity for itself. When ABC's number one schedule began to draw harsh criticism from advertisers, politicians, and citizens' groups for offending standards of taste, corrupting young viewers' innocence, and objectifying women, NBC executives seemed to recognize an opportunity and joined in the criticism. For example, in 1977, NBC research vice president William S. Rubens spoke to the Association for Consumer Research about sex on television and slyly mentioned "one network [that appeared] to be giving viewers more cheesecake and making greater use of sexual overtones."[6] But Rubens's thinly veiled allusion to ABC was a minor jab in comparison to the ongoing disparagement of the number one network from NBC programming executive Paul Klein. Klein was notorious for his impolitic pronouncements on industry workings and audience habits, but his critique of ABC in the late 1970s was perhaps his most infamous declaration.

Klein coined the terms *kid porn* and *jiggle television* to describe the ABC strategy, terms that have had great resonance in historical accounts of this era. As Klein explained, *kid porn* described programs "that make kids squeal and close their eyes," while *jiggle TV* applied "when you have a young, attractive television personality running at top speed wearing a limited amount of underwear" (Bedell 1981, 204). Klein was fond of comparing ABC's fare to pornography, tapping into contemporaneous anxieties about the spread of pornographic culture throughout mainstream America. As he commented regarding ABC's sex-heavy soap opera parody *Soap* (1977–81), "[Silverman's] doing Lady Chatterley, making it look like a work of art, when what it really is, is a Marilyn Chambers [the 1970s porn star]."[7] Klein was particularly disdainful of how juvenile ABC's sexual content was—the fact that most of it was presented comedically and was designed to inspire tittering and giggles of intrigued embarrassment from the sex-crazed adolescent in all of us. It is doubtful that Klein's disdain came from any serious moral stance or deeply held principles about television's public service mission. Klein was a shrewd businessman and was well aware of the controversies over sex on television in the 1970s. By disparaging ABC's juvenile use of sex as a ratings-grabbing strategy, he was trying to shape public opinion about the first-place network, presenting it as a low-class exploiter of the audience's vulnerabilities. Given the controversies about not only sex on TV but also the impact of the sexual revolution on American family life, Klein's tactic was smart—even if it did not have the hoped-for effect of lessening ABC's lead.

Klein's comments did have the effect of categorizing ABC's hit programs in such

FIG. **14** Paul Klein, vice president in charge of programming at NBC from 1976 to 1979, creator and practitioner of the concept of "least objectionable programming." (Library of American Broadcasting)

a way as to trivialize their perspectives on the sexual revolution and their place in television history. By placing the focus on ABC in this way, Klein was able to take some risks in NBC's programming, risks that were little remarked upon at the time and that have received even less attention since. In certain respects, NBC tried out some of the same strategies as did ABC, offering action series with sexy women leads, weekly dramas in which characters grappled with sexual choices, and made-for-TV movies about sex-related social issues. But by the late 1970s, NBC took chances with these program formats that went beyond ABC's use of sex. With little to lose, NBC offered a take on sex a bit more explicit and sensational but also more moralizing than that offered by the other networks. As Klein flamboyantly put it, "If ABC is doing kiddie porn, NBC will give the audience adult porn."[8]

When he spoke in less sensationalistic terms, Klein explained that NBC hoped to appeal to the older segment of ABC's audience by offering more sophisticated programming. His plan for NBC was "Don't get the kids, be a little more sophisticated than that, and skim off the top [of the audience scale]." The end goal was to "do a job on ABC, enough to lower their ratings points, and pick up the most salable part of their audience" (Klein 1979, 18). Klein thus set out to trip up ABC by criticizing its reputation, but his underlying aim was to segment the lead network's audience by counterprogramming with "adult" fare that offered a different take on sexuality. Three NBC programs from the late 1970s that illustrate Klein's strategy are discussed below: a failed pilot for a *Charlie's Angels* clone, a controversial story line from a weekly drama series, and a made-for-TV movie that referenced gay male sexuality. In each of these cases, we can see how NBC attempted to capitalize on ABC's winning formulas while trying to offer up "adult" representations of sex. In these cases, *adult* meant both more explicit and, often, more moralizing, especially when it came to young people's sexual experimentation.

Cover Girls: Cloning *Charlie's Angels,* with a Twist

When *Charlie's Angels* became a big hit for ABC in the 1976–77 season, both ABC and its competitors quickly sought to "clone" the *Angels* formula with programming featuring sexy young women, often in action-oriented roles. NBC's efforts in this regard included picking up *The Bionic Woman* for the 1977–78 season after ABC decided not to renew it and revamping two existing series (*Baa Baa Black Sheep/ Black Sheep Squadron* and *B.J. and the Bear*) by adding more sex in the form of attractive young women. NBC also aired some short-lived new series with sex symbol stars— *Quark*, *Rollergirls*, and *Legs*, all in 1978—as well as pilots for several *Charlie's Angels*–like series, among them *Cover Girls* (May 18, 1977), *The Hunted Lady* (November 28, 1977), and *The Secret War of Jackie's Girls* (November 29, 1980). *Cover Girls* told the story of two female spies, Linda and Monique, who also happened to be fashion models. While it seemed to have all the right ingredients—beautiful stars, glamorous clothing and settings, undercover work, car chases, guns, and even some humor—the pilot took for granted the women's status as fashion model spies. Viewers received no explanation for how Linda and Monique got into the spy business (which came first—modeling or spying?), and thus the characters seemed equally at home on display as sexual objects and on the go as crime fighters. The effect of this equalization of roles was to suggest that the women's status as sex objects was as important to their lives as was their more "liberated" occupation.

This aspect of *Cover Girls* made the potential series even more overtly invested in the leads' sex symbol potential than was ABC's *Charlie's Angels*. Despite the publicity and the criticism around the ABC hit that figured the female leads as sex objects, the Angels were private detectives first and foremost, and they participated in sexual objectification (admittedly, without much protest) as an aid to their detective work, not as an equally significant occupation. While *Charlie's Angels* showed the women in their undercover work, highlighting their bodies, faces, clothes, and hair, the narrative also made clear that the Angels had more "serious" purposes. In contrast, *Cover Girls* featured extended scenes of Linda and Monique modeling, even when their modeling had no function as a cover for their spying. In one seven-minute sequence, Linda and Monique model in front of a fountain, then are photographed dancing in a disco amid a crowd of admirers. The fashion model spies are not engaged in any particular mission during these events. They are simply doing (and enjoying) their modeling work, with momentary interruptions from their spying duties (such as eyeing a suspicious car in the distance). In this respect, *Cover Girls* made its main characters' sexiness foundational to their identities, thereby becoming even more blatant than *Charlie's Angels* in its attempt to portray its leads as sex symbols.

Cover Girls also moved beyond its predecessor's sexualized displays of the female body by attempting to titillate viewers with the suggestion of erotic involvement between the two leads. An early scene in their apartment features Monique lying on the sofa on her stomach, seemingly naked, with Linda perched next to her, massaging her shoulders and arms. When Linda turns Monique over, we see she is draped in a towel. Their conversation proceeds through shots of each woman over the other's shoulder, with Linda still hovering above the reclining Monique, in keeping with the love scene coding. This scene is followed by what might have read as a postcoital dressing scene, with Monique slowly pulling her nylons up around her thighs and a sweater over her head before zipping up her jeans. This obvious attempt at titillation was not completely foreign to *Charlie's Angels*. The infamous first-season episode "Angels in Chains" (October 20, 1976) put the three women in prison, where a leering guard ordered them to open their towels so she could spray their naked bodies. But "Angels in Chains" was the exception rather than the rule for the program; the characters were rarely put in situations so blatantly exploitative. In contrast, *Cover Girls* made a point of emphasizing the erotic connection between Linda and Monique in the pilot episode and thus of making that connection a premise of the potential series. In these subtle but significant ways, *Cover Girls* illustrates NBC's efforts to "out-sex" ABC by offering a more "sophisticated" take on sexuality, in this case by insinuating an erotic involvement between the two women leads.

James at 15: Representing Teen Sex

Charlie's Angels imitations were one component of NBC's efforts in the late 1970s to siphon off a segment of ABC's audience and establish an identity for itself. Another such component was the representation of young people's sexuality as a sensational audience draw. Because NBC's programming tended toward references to and representations of teenage sexuality more overt and explicit than ABC's typically suggestive allusions, this programming offered the more "sophisticated," "adult" take on sex that Klein saw as NBC's mark of distinction. The network's willingness to represent sex in risky ways was central to its plan to gain some competitive ground by distinguishing itself from the other networks, perhaps appealing to young viewers as well.

One of Paul Klein's more widely publicized attempts to step up NBC's sexual explicitness was his effort to influence the narrative development of the network's continuing teen drama *James at 15* (1977–78, retitled *James at 16* partway through the run). Klein asked the show's producers to create a special episode for the February 1978 ratings sweeps period. He asked that James lose his virginity at a local brothel as a "gift" from his uncle for his sixteenth birthday. The idea was not a completely foreign imposition on the program, as other episodes had dealt with James's sexual curiosity. But series creator Dan Wakefield thought the idea of James going to a brothel was outdated, so he wrote a script in which James's trip there is a comedic disaster. He followed through with Klein's request for James to lose his virginity, however, by planning for him to have sex with a Swedish exchange student with whom he had fallen in love. Important to Wakefield's script was the fact that James and his girlfriend, Gun, truly cared for each other and that they acted "responsibly" by using birth control. Wakefield was willing to play the birth control discussion scene vaguely, with nothing more specific than the kids talking about being responsible. But NBC rejected the idea. They insisted that the teens *not* use birth control, that "[i]f they have sex at all, it must be in a moment of spontaneous passion." They also insisted that Gun have a pregnancy scare afterward (though she would not, in fact, be pregnant) so that she and James would regret their actions.[9] NBC's preferred version aired along with a follow-up episode in which James fears he has contracted a venereal disease. But NBC's interference led Wakefield to resign from the show, and the series was canceled just a few months later.

The *James at 15* incident demonstrates some of the controversy around television's handling of sex in the 1970s, but it also suggests the particular parameters of Klein's vision of the network's "sophisticated," "adult" take on sex. For Klein and NBC, *sophisticated* and *adult* meant the opposite of ABC's handling of sex; it meant allowing characters to have sex, instead of just suggestively referencing it, but it also meant punishing those same characters for their actions. In NBC's fictional on-screen world, birth control could not be condoned, but teens engaging in sex could be condemned. In this way, NBC managed to be more sensational than its chief rival but also to seem morally superior. The network could exploit the plot development of teens having sex and at the same time come off as disapproving of teen sex. In developing the story of James's sexual experience, and especially in avoiding mention of birth control while dangling the threats of pregnancy and venereal disease, NBC managed to extend the boundaries of conventional TV content acceptability while reinforcing the boundaries of conventional sexual morality.

Alexander: Gay Sexuality Exposed

Alongside NBC's efforts to outdo ABC by displaying female sex symbols and representing sexually active teens were the network's contributions to the made-for-TV movie form, contributions that exploited sexual themes, including gay male sexuality. By the 1974–75 season, ABC and NBC, significantly more than CBS, were regularly airing TV movies treating sex as a social issue. At NBC this resulted in two movies, *Dawn: Portrait of a Teenage Runaway* (September 27, 1976) and its sequel, *Alexander: The Other Side of Dawn* (May 16, 1977), along with a host of other made-for-TV movies and miniseries with ostensibly "adult" treatments of sex. Although all three networks placed young people in sexual danger in their telefilms, NBC was the only one to take on young, gay male sexuality. In this respect, *Alexander* fit NBC's tendency to push the boundaries of television acceptability a step further than its competitors. In the ways that the film represents Alexander's sexuality, however, we find the moralizing element also typical of NBC's efforts. Much like *James at 15*, *Alexander* demonstrates the conflict inherent in NBC's attempt to offer sensational, risqué, "adult" material without seeming to condone or promote nontraditional sexuality. *Alexander* (like *James*) ends up reinforcing the sexual status quo despite its seemingly radical subject matter.

The story of teenage Alexander Duncan, who is thrown out of his small-town home and ends up on the streets of Hollywood, was originally envisioned as a parallel tale to that of young Dawn, who runs away to Hollywood and becomes a prostitute. When writer Dalene Young was first researching and outlining the project for producer Douglas Cramer, it was one movie, titled *Dawn and Alexander: The Story of Two Teenage Runaways*. The process whereby this initial project developed into two TV movies reveals a gradual deemphasis of Alex's non-normative sexuality, resulting in an ambiguous representation in the actual film. In an early outline of *Dawn and Alexander*, Alex is explicitly identified as a male hustler who "parades peacock-like" on the street seeking customers. Indeed, the description of his character explains that "[h]e has come to believe he's a homosexual," a belief that Dawn affirms when she discovers Alex's hidden "male muscle magazine." Alex, despite his "homosexual tendencies," falls in love with Dawn, and the two determine that they will begin a new life together.[10] This proposed story allows that Alex has some same-sex desires, even while it resolves the narrative—and Alex's sexuality—with a conventional heterosexual happy ending.

But in a second version of this outline, one labeled as a "presentation" (presumably for NBC executives), all explicit references to Alex as gay—or even as a male hustler—have been removed. Instead, the outline explains that Alex never forces more than "an embrace, a puppy-dog's kiss" upon Dawn, setting the character up as definitively heterosexual, if sensitive, from the outset. Alex's "well-paid week of the 'good life' with a Pasadena man" from the earlier outline becomes "a well-paid week, 'a bonus at the liquor store'" in this new version.[11] The outline suggested that Alex's "bonus at the liquor store" is a cover story (note the scare quotes), but the lack of any even slightly overt reference to Alex engaging in same-sex sexual activity makes this euphemism so broad a signifier as to be meaningless. With even the merest suggestion of Alex's occupation excised, any suggestion of his gay desires is also missing. In addition, this version has been retitled to focus only on Dawn, even though the plot is little changed. Clearly, Cramer and his colleagues felt that framing the tale as the story of a teenage girl prostitute, whose true love also works the street but in a vague, undefined way, would be more palatable to NBC. Indeed, the version of *Dawn* that NBC eventually broadcast continued this obfuscation of Alex's "work" and of his sexual orientation. But a clear sense of Alex's situation was not so easily avoided in the sequel to *Dawn* that NBC soon commissioned.

Although NBC wanted to air Alex's story, the network and Cramer struggled over exactly what story to tell about Alex's background and his experiences in Hollywood before and after his involvement with Dawn. *Dawn* had already established that Alex had some heterosexual desires; after all, he had fallen in love with Dawn. But everyone involved seemed to want to acknowledge Alex's sex for hire with men while upholding the Alex and Dawn love story. For NBC, a tale of male teen hustling was an ideal way to "out-sex" ABC. ABC telefilms such as *Hustling* (February 22, 1975) and *Little Ladies of the Night* (January 16, 1977) had represented the seedy world of female prostitution; *Alexander* could be the "sophisticated" take on the subject NBC needed to differentiate itself. In telling the story of how Alex had gotten to this point, however, NBC and the film's producers had to address *why* Alex had engaged in same-sex sexual activity. And this raised questions about sexual identity with which American television of the 1970s was not ready to grapple. Was same-sex sexual activity only a product of desperation, something a young man like Alex engaged in when he had no other viable means of economic support? Was it a product of an immature state, one that Alex overcame through his relationship with Dawn? Or could sexuality actually be as fluid as Alex's experience might suggest, swaying along a continuum of same- and opposite-sex desires? With pressure from multiple sources to clean up TV content, and with widespread cultural controversy over sexuality in the wake of the gay rights movement and its detractors, figuring out how to tell Alex's story was a significant challenge.

As a result, writer Young, producer Cramer, and executives at NBC considered various approaches to the film. An early version centered on Alex's struggle to understand his sexual identity. In this version, Alex gets involved in same-sex prostitution after his father throws him out, suspecting that he is gay because of his close relationship with his older, male tutor (the relationship is platonic, but the tutor admits his feelings for Alex).[12] In a later version of the story, Alex's father throws him out because his interest in art and books keeps him from taking on his expected "man's" role at the family ranch.[13] This version contains less suggestion that Alex may be gay and less of a struggle over his "true" identity. But the version of the story that was ultimately filmed and broadcast did not make Alex's sexuality, or even his masculinity, a factor in his leaving home. Instead, it recounted that Alex's parents just couldn't afford to support him anymore, especially since he was more interested in his art than in working on the family farm. As the progression of Alex's story through these different versions indicates, the final film deliberately sidesteps the question of Alex's sexuality.

The decision to avoid answering the question of Alex's sexual identity seems to have guided the final choices made by Cramer and NBC in many respects. For instance, Alex's relationship with a closeted gay football player, Charles Selby, is represented ambiguously in the final film. There is no doubt of Charles's sexuality; however, there is doubt as to what Alex does or does not do to incur Charles's generosity and hospitality. (In early script outlines, their relationship was much more clearly sexual.)[14] Throughout, the film refuses to confirm anything about Alex's sexuality, including the extent of his sexual activity with other men, leaving only hints and ambiguities that may have been read in very different ways. Because these hints and ambiguities are presented within the larger narrative of Alex pining away for Dawn and doing all he can to reunite with her, the film ultimately codes Alex as heterosexual. Indeed, the final product ends up suggesting that any nonheterosexual identity is outside the realm of possibility for Alex, that any same-sex sexual activity he might have engaged in was what he had to do to survive, that sexuality is neither fluid nor flexible, and that the happy ending can come only when the heterosexual couple reunites and heads toward marriage.

Ultimately, Cramer and NBC's deliberations between two versions of the story, one that would "[go] after the situation with no holds barred" and one that would have "wider public acceptance and [would] . . . find the same audience as *Dawn*," helped shape not only this project but NBC's contribution to discourses of sex in 1970s television.[15] Clearly, NBC was more invested in the latter version, so that was the version that was ultimately produced and aired. This sort of approach, one that handled an "adult" subject but did so without validating a non-normative sexuality, was most in keeping with NBC's interests and current competitive strategy. But it is important to remember that the film might have told a different story, one that more fully explored the fluidity of sexual identity. As Cramer asserted to NBC's vice president in charge of TV movies, even after agreeing that the "wider public acceptance" route was the right choice, he "still [believed it was] very possible to approach another variation of the story of Alexander, with taste and dignity."[16] As Cramer's comment reveals, NBC's choices in this matter contributed to a particular, limited, conventional, even old-fashioned representation of sex, despite the network's plan to offer a "sophisticated" and "adult" take on the changing times.

The Failure of NBC's Strategy

Paul Klein's efforts to differentiate NBC's approach to sex from ABC's ultimately failed to establish any clear identity or improve upon the ratings for the third-place network. In trying to "out-sex" ABC, NBC took a chance in a climate of increased scrutiny of TV content, although the network also attempted to minimize the risks of such an endeavor by helping direct public, government, and advertiser attention toward ABC's use of sex. Even while some of NBC's programs were more explicit and more willing to address sexual themes overtly than were programs on the other networks, they did not produce especially new or progressive material. In fact, as in the case of *Cover Girls*, they sometimes failed to generate the audience interest necessary to justify a continuing series, and, as in the case of *James*, they sometimes led to the downfall of a formerly well-regarded show. As television critic John J. O'Connor argued of *Alexander*, "The producers want to have their sexual dabblings and, at the same time, retain their innocence." O'Connor pointed out that this made Alex himself into "something of a socio-cultural zombie . . . [walking] through his bisexual adventures in a state of boyish confusion."[17] One might make a similar point about NBC prime time in the 1970s—working overtime to seem current but ultimately seeming rather out of touch with the surrounding world. During a time of radical change in sexual mores, experiences, and politics, a time of women's liberation, gay liberation, increasingly sexually active youth, and rising divorce rates, NBC's "adult" fare remained boyishly confused. Though claiming that its programming was more sophisticated and serious than that offered by the other networks, NBC failed to offer a truly mature treatment of the sexually changed and changing times.

As valuable as it is to consider the ways that internetwork competition shaped network reputations and, in this case, shaped the definitions of sex on offer through America's most mass medium, in many respects there was very little difference between the three broadcast networks. This is best illustrated by Fred Silverman's journey across all three. In the early part of the decade, he contributed to CBS's turn to social relevance; mid-decade, he helped make ABC number one; and in 1978, he joined NBC as its president. With his arrival at the third-place network, Silverman trumpeted his new attitude toward programming, pledging to take NBC in a direction very different from that proposed and executed by Klein. In fact, in Silverman's first speech to NBC's annual convention, he announced: "True leadership requires responsibility—programming that does not violate general standards of taste. We must avoid material that would alienate significant elements of the audience, and we must continue steadfastly to make the difficult and delicate judgments that draw the line between the offensive and the acceptable."[18] Silverman sought to make NBC a "class act" with "a more intelligent approach to comedy" than he had developed at ABC.[19] Whether to revise his image, to disprove Klein, or to respond to pressure groups, he strove to limit the number of overtly sexual shows on the NBC schedule and to seek out more typically wholesome family fare.

Though he found a few new hits this way, his efforts at NBC were ultimately rather inconsequential. He was unable to have the same impact on this network as he had had on the other two. NBC would remain in third place until Grant Tinker took over from Silverman in 1981. Neither the "adult porn" promised by Paul Klein nor the "kiddie porn" associated with Fred Silverman would ultimately define NBC in the 1970s. But only by seeking to understand such labels and their impact on the medium's construction of sex during tumultuous times can we begin to grasp the historical import of television's failures alongside its successes.

Notes

Abbreviations

AHC   Douglas S. Cramer Collection, American Heritage Center, University of Wyoming

GMTF   Gay Media Task Force Collection, Carl A. Kroch Library, Cornell University

1. This is not to say that the 1970s at NBC have received no historical treatment. See, for example, Jeffrey Miller (2000), as well as Miller's contribution to this volume.

2. "ABC-TV Wins in Prime Time and in a Big Way," *Broadcasting*, April 25, 1977, 38–39.

3. Among the regulatory and economic shifts working in ABC's favor were the Prime Time Access Rule (PTAR) and the acquisition of new affiliates. PTAR benefited ABC over the other two networks. ABC was happy to eliminate its lowest-rated 3 1/2 hours from its prime-time schedule (the rule made the networks return the 7:00–8:00 p.m. eastern hour to the affiliates), since this time was costing ABC money instead of turning a profit. In addition, ABC gained thirty new, affiliated stations between 1968 and 1973 (in comparison to CBS's two and NBC's eleven) by offering those stations higher-than-normal payments to switch their affiliation. See "Halcyon Days for ABC—and All TV," *Business Week*, August 18, 1973, 47–48.

4. Judith Crist, "Tailored for Television," *TV Guide*, August 30, 1969, 8–9.

5. NBC's success with programming featuring people of color may help explain the network's running the controversial *Richard Pryor Show* (though for just four episodes) in 1977.

6. William S. Rubens, "Sex on Television, More or Less," speech to the Association for Consumer Research, Chicago, October 14, 1977.

7. Dwight Whitney, "What Uproar over 'Soap'?" *TV Guide*, November 26, 1977, 9.

8. J. Dempsey, "NBC Discovers the (Ratings) Joy of Sex," *Variety*, December 14, 1977, 37.

9. Richard M. Levine, "Cotton Mather's Last Stand," *New Times*, February 20, 1978, 66–67.

10. "Writer's Outline, *Dawn and Alexander*," May 21, 1975, Box 23, Writer's First Draft, January 18, 1974, AHC.

11. *Dawn—Portrait of a Teenage Runaway*, May 28, 1975, Box 22, Presentation, May 28, 1975, AHC.

12. "*Alexander* Outline," June 11, 1976, Box 10, Writer's Outline, April 7, 1976, AHC.

13. *Alexander: Portrait of a Teenage Throwout*, First Draft, November 16, 1976, Box 14–5, GMTF.

14. "*Alexander* Outline," June 11, 1976.

15. Douglas S. Cramer to Joe Taritero, September 10, 1976, Box 5, AHC.

16. Ibid.

17. John J. O'Connor, "TV: 'Alexander,' Effective Story of Male Hustler," *New York Times*, May 16, 1977, 43.

18. David Blum, "King of the Tube," *New Republic*, October 28, 1978, 13.

19. Sally Bedell, "Silverman Outlines Strategy for Making NBC 'The Class Act,'" *TV Guide*, September 30, 1978, A5–A6.

14

Saturday Morning Children's Programs on NBC, 1975–2006

A Case Study of Self-Regulation

KAREN HILL-SCOTT AND HORST STIPP

In 1975, there were three broadcast networks—ABC, CBS, and NBC—that between them virtually owned the viewing audience. Even though *Sesame Street* on PBS had started to attract a large portion of the audience segment made up of the youngest children, most children and adults chose between three channels. Those days are over. There are now hundreds of channels and multiple technologies for receiving television signals, resulting in constantly increasing audience segmentation. In addition, viewers are using the television screen for alternate entertainment technologies such as VHS and DVDs, digital video recording (DVR), and video gaming.

Where three broadcasters once offered a children's day part consisting of three variations on the Saturday morning block, by 2006 there were six broadcast networks available to virtually every American TV viewer[1] and several cable channels with family and children's programming. Consumers with digital cable access could choose between as many as ten cable channels devoted solely to children's entertainment.[2] An increasing number of children can now choose to watch programming from twenty different sources, compared to three just thirty years ago.

This chapter focuses on one specific aspect of the history of children's programming at NBC: a unique self-regulation process that began in 1975 and became known as the NBC Social Science Advisory Panel. This process relied largely on academic and other consultants with expertise in relevant fields. Not only did it shape NBC's children's programming in a time when that network often reached almost half of all children during one Saturday morning, but it also encouraged the use of advisors at other networks and affected the way writers, producers, and program executives approached the creative process of children's programming. Finally, this panel process influenced the way academic advisors thought about children and television and their ability to affect programming in a competitive commercial television system.

Over several years, the process evolved in its role, size, function, and composition. For the first ten years it consisted of a single panel of advisors selected from universities around the country. As the competitive and regulatory climate changed, the panel evolved into a set of network-initiated consulting relationships with experts based in Los Angeles who worked on an as-needed basis to assist writers and producers in meeting regulatory requirements.

The Origins of NBC's Social Science Advisory Process

NBC's efforts at self-regulation began in 1975, when NBC's head of social research, Ron Milavsky, proposed that the network use consultants to provide a social science perspective regarding the content of its Saturday morning programs and the possible effects on children.[3] He believed that children were a special audience and that programming directed at them would benefit from a process designed to enhance understanding and consideration of their needs. Milavsky suggested that management recruit a panel of scholars with theoretical and research expertise in television and its effects on children. These consultants would meet a number of times a year to recommend improvements to the network's Saturday morning program content. The proposal was accepted, and four highly respected scholars were recruited to the panel.[4] Its members were George Comstock, a social psychologist and communications scholar, professor at the S. I. Newhouse School for Public Communications, Syracuse University, and author of several books on television effects; William McGuire, a professor of psychology at Yale University and a leading authority on attitude change and television effects; Paul Mussen, a professor of psychology at the University of California, Berkeley, who had written several leading texts on child development; and Percy Tannenbaum, a social psychologist and professor of public policy at the University of California, Berkeley, whose work in communications and meaning extended to television, entertainment, and the impact of violence on children. The NBC Research Department felt that if the academics could bring their knowledge to bear on enhancing existing and proposed programming, the schedule could only improve and criticisms would subsequently diminish. The panel NBC assembled was called the Social Science Advisory Panel, and its first meeting was held on December 17, 1975.

The Panel Process

The story behind NBC's Social Science Advisory Panel must begin with an understanding of the conditions at the time. In 1975 the three commercial networks still captured between them the majority of television advertising dollars, including those spent on reaching children, so that it was economically viable for the three networks to purchase and air children's programming in tight competition with each other. As is the case today, the mainstay of children's programming was animation, and the bread and butter of animation was the comedic adventure caper full of gag strings and pratfalls. Stories served the action, not the other way around. The primary pressure felt by the networks at this time concerned decreasing violent content in children's programs.

During the 1960s, Congress, the Federal Communications Commission (FCC), and the Federal Trade Commission (FTC) had initiated investigations into children's television, particularly the perceived high levels of violence on television directed at children. NBC had responded by establishing a Social Research Department that conducted a large panel study on the relationship between children's TV exposure and aggression (Milavsky et al. 1982). Congressional and regulatory agency pressure on the networks played some role in the formation of the panel. However, the panel was deliberately designed to work without political pressure or publicity and was not a result of any mandate. In fact, the panel's role and scope of activities at the network were greatest during periods of reduced regulatory pressure.

The most important catalyst for the creation of the panel was the fact that the companies that supplied commercial Saturday morning programs rarely employed social scientists as consultants. Only at the publicly funded Children's Television Workshop (CTW) did producers, writers, academic experts, and researchers collaborate. CTW's corporate mission was to achieve educational goals through television, specifically via *Sesame Street*. NBC believed that without such advisors' input content might not improve or conform to the new standards that were emerging as important for children's programming.

The panel needed to be organized in a way that most effectively meshed its activities with the nine-month work cycle of program production. NBC's goal was to ensure that the panel met at appropriate times to weigh in on executive decisions about programming choices, that it met again to discuss issues and problems while changes in the programming could still be made, and that it then convened at least one more time to discuss how the series were shaping up and what might be considered for a future year. Through three or four well-timed meetings per year, the panel could become a collaborative effort that brought research, child development theory, and creative expertise to bear on the goal of producing entertaining children's programming with prosocial content.

Around the beginning of each calendar year, independent production companies offered program ideas to the network, and NBC in turn suggested program ideas to production companies. On the basis of these discussions, the network could pick up the option to develop a show, at which point the show's creative team would develop a "series bible." The "bible" contained a narrative description of a series concept, an explanation of each character's personality and purpose within the show, some story ideas, and drawings of characters and settings. New series were chosen, old series were renewed, and the fall schedule was announced around April.

Once choices were made, the NBC Children's Programming Department worked with production companies to transform concepts into actual animated programs. During this development process, the "bible" was often changed to accommodate not only the programmers but also the Broadcast Standards and Practices Department, NBC's arbiter of appropriateness, taste, and propriety.

Development proceeded from half-page story premises to outlines to a complete script to a storyboard with rough drawings. Finally, the audio was recorded and the animation pictures were drawn. At each point, the Children's Programming and Broadcast Standards Departments could request changes, and the Broadcast Standards Department screened each episode for final clearance before airing. Broadcasting of the episodes usually began in October.

The Expansion of the Panel Process

Starting around 1980, the process expanded because the Children's Programming Department became interested in using the panel more regularly and for more diverse tasks. They also wanted to expand the panel's charge and membership to address issues regarding ethnic and gender stereotypes.

In 1980, Aimee Dorr, a professor of education at UCLA and a psychologist who specialized in research on children and television, joined the panel. In 1983 Karen Hill-Scott, a child development expert, became a panel member, and she later played an increasingly important role in consulting. Hill-Scott was an adjunct associate professor of urban planning at UCLA and the founder and executive director of Crystal Stairs, California's largest private nonprofit child development agency. Her appointment reflected NBC's desire to add racial diversity to the panel and to increase the number of its members who had practical experience working with parents and children.

With the addition of these new members and an increasing interest in using academic expertise, NBC executives made further plans to invite other professionals to panel meetings depending on the issues at hand. In 1984, the new vice president of children's programming determined to focus on eradicating negative stereotypes of minorities and females in children's programming. To this end, she recognized a need for the participation of panelists who could bring multiethnic expertise to the table. She and her staff organized the panel's first public symposium, "The Effects of Stereotypes on Minority Child Development." Originally intended for a cross-departmental team of NBC executives, the symposium proved so successful that it was replicated for the program suppliers, taken public with a presentation at the Directors Guild, and reformatted twice so that the vice president of community affairs could present a program to special interest groups in Los Angeles and New York on the network's efforts to reduce racism and stereotyping in children's *and* prime-time programs.

Horst Stipp, NBC's director of social research, built on these activities with numerous meetings and extensive correspondence with various academics, commissioning further research on specific children's issues. These contacts led to creating a larger pool of experts to draw from for panel activities or special presentations.

Because of the sensitivity of producers regarding requests for changes in scripts and other elements of production, the children's programming staff usually communicated panel comments to the production companies' producers and writers.

Program creators sometimes participated in meetings with panel members. But for the most part, results of the periodic meetings were conveyed to creative personnel by network staff and not by the panel members themselves.

The panel members began to have more involvement in reviewing specific shows during this period. They reviewed concepts, story premises, outlines, and scripts for programs needing special care. This work was completed within the network's time frame, and reactions were conveyed to the program executive and, in some cases, to the Broadcast Standards Department.

Another characteristic of the Social Science Advisory Panel process during the 1980s was that research was sometimes requested to explore children's understanding or perceptions of crucial program elements. Under the direction of the Social Research Department, small studies would be commissioned to find out if programs were successful at communicating prosocial messages to children or to explore other issues directly related to programming. A portion of most regular panel meetings was typically given to a social scientist's presentation of his or her own research. This practice not only increased the base of participation in the panel but also kept those involved in children's programming up to date on research about children and television.

Memos from 1982 to 1988 show that the panel met about five times a year during this period, as contrasted with three to four meetings a year in the first stage of development. NBC vice presidents and/or staff from the Social Research, Children's Programming, Broadcast Standards, and Program Research Departments attended these meetings, most of which were held in Los Angeles. This geographic pull toward the West Coast presaged a change in how the advisor role would evolve as competitive and regulatory pressures increased.

The Results of the Panel Process

As described above, the panel process turned out to be very successful. Some of those involved in children's programming at NBC, along with most of the writers and producers at the production companies that developed the shows, initially had some reservations about outside advisors, especially regarding their ability to make programs more prosocial without making them less entertaining and therefore less competitive. However, as the panel evolved, these concerns decreased, especially within NBC. In fact, the panel process demonstrated that academic advisors in the network environment could be useful not only from a regulatory and prosocial point of view but also from a commercial perspective: the advisors and broadcasters learned how to make programs better and, at the same time, more popular.

There are several reasons for the success of the panel. First, panel members' knowledge of child development, family life, and societal trends turned out to be very useful to programmers. Second, some of the programs chosen or modified along lines suggested by panel members turned out to be very successful. *The Smurfs*, which ran from 1981 until 1990 and established NBC's Saturday morning dominance for several years, is an example. Third, the panel members' sophistication and sensitivity in interacting with the network increased as the process developed. Fourth, the network's staff learned the implications of social science findings for children's programs and started to apply that knowledge to their activities. Finally, the Social Research Department management team, which had originated and continued to supervise the process, learned how to conduct successful panel meetings and improve the process.

A similar evolution took place in the area of regulating commercials directed toward children. As standards and practices editors became aware of the expertise of the consultants and of the helpful role they could play, panel members started to take on an expanded function in this area as well. This aspect of the panel's work is not discussed in any detail here, but it included helping to present toys more accurately to reflect how they could be used in reality.

As the panel process evolved, it became apparent that the academics' theoretical insights were only as effective as their skill in translating abstract generalizations into ideas that the NBC staff could understand and apply to a specific program concept or episode. To accomplish this, the group worked on developing methods for communicating the differing institutional perspectives held by the panel members and the creative executives. The expanded use of panel members to do interactive script review, along with the addition to the panel of new people with specialized expertise, broadened both the network's and the producers' insights about how outside advisors could work. Finally, on a more practical level, it was clearly more convenient if those most actively involved in the panel resided near Los Angeles, where most of the work on children's programming took place.

Nevertheless, some problems encountered during the first years never disappeared completely. While all participants in the panel process agreed that children were a special audience who should be exposed to socially responsible programs, there were continuing snags in the panel process.[5] One source of difficulty was that the groups involved in the panel process had some different goals and priorities. Panel members hoped to apply their scientific knowledge to improve the prosocial content of shows. Broadcast Standards Department staff wanted to avoid program content that violated standards of taste and propriety or that might have negative effects. Programmers wanted to act responsibly, but they needed to entertain, attract large audiences, operate economically, and receive programming on schedule. Program producers wanted creative freedom and financial success. These differing goals were not necessarily incompatible, but they were often hard to achieve simultaneously. They required discussion and compromise—and that took time, which is in very short supply in the typical production schedule.

Another source of difficulty was the widely varied backgrounds and skills of social scientists, network staff, and the creative community. The advice of social scientists had to be implemented by members of the creative community and those at the network who knew how to conceptualize, develop, market, and schedule programming. They felt that they had delivered many entertaining, even prosocial, shows to children over the years, and it is understandable that they sometimes resented being told how to do their jobs or felt that it was being suggested that they had not done their jobs well. The academics, on the other hand, were sometimes impatient with those who purported to understand the psychology and needs of children simply because they had provided programming attractive to the child audience.

From the panel's inception, NBC and panel members tried to develop mechanisms to minimize difficulties inherent in working together. Though the panel had an advisory function, authority to adopt panel suggestions rested with the Children's Programming and/or Broadcast Standards Departments. At the same time, it was understood that panel members were free to say whatever they liked without influence or pressure and that they would clarify when they were speaking as social scientists, on the basis of research, or expressing opinions as parents, citizens, or activists. (Obviously, decisions about prosocial values involve value choices themselves, and in a pluralistic society not everyone agrees on the same causes and sees the same priorities.) Further, on those occasions when the network made a programming decision that ran counter to panel advice, members understood that they needed to accept that decision and move on to the next matter. It was important to make clear that the interests and goals of the various groups involved in the panel process were to be recognized and respected.

Several mechanisms were developed to promote better interaction. Panel members usually met first with members of NBC's Social Research Department, who were themselves social scientists and researchers. This meeting provided a good opportunity for panel members to debate issues and talk about research issues that might be a bit boring to others from the network or the creative community. As a result, the researchers avoided confusing the programmers about an appropriate course of action on an issue. In general, comments about programming were given to network staff at a panel meeting, over the telephone, or in writing. The staff then relayed these comments, with editorial license, to the production company. A meeting between panel members and the creative community *never* occurred without prior meetings of the panel and network staff.

Key Issues Addressed during the 1980s

Over the years, the panel discussed and monitored many issues during its work on NBC Saturday morning programs. An analysis of corporate documents, including meetings, reports, memoranda, letters, papers, and written comments on program "bibles," concepts, premises, scripts, and storyboards shows four major issues: violence, stereotyping, developmental appropriateness, and prosocial content. An analysis of memos on panel activities mentioned earlier confirms this: in the 101 memos analyzed for the year 1982, violence was still a major topic, even though the total pool of memos dealt with a variety of issues. In 1985 and 1988, however, most of the memos dealt with other topics and the preoccupation with violence decreased.

Violence

Because of regulatory and social pressures, the panel had to address violent and aggressive program content first. They drew on existing research to formulate written suggestions about how to depict violence and aggression so as to decrease possible negative effects on child viewers. On the basis of research by Bandura (1977), for example, they recommended the use of unrealistic settings and fantasy weapons and the portrayal of superhuman feats rather than fistfights to diminish the potential for imitation. By this process and others, programmers and broadcast standards editors were sensitized to the kinds of portrayals that are worrisome.

Even before the panel process started, NBC programmers had rejected program concepts they considered too violent. After a few years of the panel, the network placed increasing emphasis on the development of "softer" program concepts. Thus in the early 1980s NBC's Saturday morning hits became *Smurfs* and *Alvin and the Chipmunks*, two series that deemphasized action and aggressive interpersonal conflict themes. However, action programs were occasionally produced against panel recommendations (e.g., *The Incredible Hulk*, *Lazer Tag*). In these instances, the panel urged that natural catastrophe and jeopardy situations replace interpersonal conflicts as often as possible. At the same time, the panel was wary of catastrophe and jeopardy situations because their violence or threat of violence might frighten children. Panel members also had occasion to ask the network to reject script ideas for particular episodes or to change them substantially because of violence concerns. These recommendations were often accepted, although writers sometimes resisted, believing that aggressive interpersonal conflict was inherently interesting.

Surprisingly, however, another action program, *The Mr. T Show*, turned out to be responsive to a positive restructuring of the content. In fact, with information from children's focus groups and abundant public relations, Mr. T became redefined as a friend to children, a direct contrast to his prime-time persona as a violent nightclub bouncer and professional wrestler. Overall, violence became a rather infrequent concern of panel members after scripts had been through the review process. In other words, after the process had been established and this issue had been addressed, violence became one issue among several, not the panel's top concern.

Stereotyping

Negative stereotypes, especially of females and minorities, became a dominant issue during the 1980s. Panel members alerted NBC early on that the underrepresentation of females on Saturday morning could suggest to young viewers that women were not as important or interesting as men. In addition, the panel felt that many programs depicted females according to negative stereotypes. They pointed out that female characters in the programs tended to be depicted as weak and in peril (to be rescued by a male character) or as coquettish flirts. (It is worth mentioning that practically every writer of Saturday morning programs in the early 1980s was a

FIG. **15** Phyllis Tucker Vinson, vice president of children's programming, worked with the Social Science Advisory Panel in the 1980s to bring awareness of negative social stereotypes to NBC's program strategies. (Library of American Broadcasting)

young white male. In contrast, NBC employed many women in the Children's Programming Department, including the head of the department.) NBC programmers were sympathetic to the panel's concern not only for personal reasons but also because they suspected that the girls watching Saturday morning programs would prefer female characters in a variety of roles. Thus the panel mechanism resulted in considerable progress in eliminating those problems from NBC's Saturday morning schedule starting in the 1980s.

Concerns about the underrepresentation and stereotyping of ethnic, racial, and other (e.g., physically challenged) minorities were similar to those about women. This issue became a major concern when Phyllis Tucker Vinson, an African American woman, became NBC's vice president of children's programming in 1983. She wanted to increase the number of nonstereotypical, ethnically diverse characters in Saturday morning programs and asked the panel for information that would help achieve that goal.

Addressing this issue was a huge challenge because not a single production company that supplied NBC with programming had even one writer from an ethnic minority group, and few had any women. It was no wonder that stereotypes permeated children's cartoons. It appeared that awareness of the potential for negative impacts from stereotypical program content was very low. Therefore, to make a real difference, it was necessary to reach the producers and writers. Special seminars were held at which guest social scientists specializing in social attitudes, stereo-typing, race relations, minority cultures, and minority child development shared their knowledge with panel members and NBC staff. The first was held in December 1982 and was attended by about forty producers and writers who were involved in supplying programs to NBC and also the other networks. Among the many points emphasized at the symposia were that problems of stereotyping are greatly reduced when more than one representative of a minority group is included in a show and when writers and producers are knowledgeable about the variety of lifestyles and personal characteristics within minority groups. The network made a continuing effort to follow these recommendations, but putting them into practice was not always easy (as detailed by Stipp, Hill-Scott, and Dorr 1987). Another symposium took place eight years later, in February 1990. There had been relatively few man-agement changes in children's programming at NBC, but most of the audience who had attended the 1982 symposium were no longer working on children's pro-grams. Thus it was the purpose of the 1990 symposium to impart these lessons to a new generation of writers and producers (who were somewhat more gender di-verse) and to increase their sensitivity toward these issues.[6]

Developmental Appropriateness

Writers are understandably interested in stories they themselves find exciting or funny, and they sometimes lack awareness of children's developmental limits and needs. As a result, children's misunderstanding of programs or program elements was a recurring issue for the panel. Members repeatedly identified instances where the language or plot seemed beyond the grasp of most two- to five-year-olds and even many six- to eleven-year-olds, the main audience for Saturday morning pro-grams. This was not an issue that NBC and the panel focused on initially, but it turned out to be very important. Social science researchers were able to make valu-able contributions that, in the view of most participants, made programs not only better but also more popular.

Prosocial Program Content and Learning

The panel and programmers did not always agree on whether or how to encour-age prosocial content within a show. The gap was caused primarily by different em-phases on entertainment versus prosocial content, even though both sides eventu-ally agreed that the two goals were compatible. Panel members complained that NBC's Saturday morning schedule did not include the kind of prosocial, learning-oriented series one would find on PBS. The network responded that series origi-nating from such a perspective had continually failed in the ratings in competition with more entertainment-oriented series shown on other networks at the same time.[7]

Research, however, did help find ways to deal with the tension between proso-cial content and ratings: they showed that children responded positively to messages about prosocial behaviors and themes embedded in series whose primary emphasis was entertainment. This made the panel members more comfortable working on entertainment-oriented programs, and they routinely offered suggestions about possible prosocial content. Across the entire schedule, the programming staff encouraged writers to develop scripts around important or sensitive issues, and stories were developed on topics such as the death of a pet, adoption, disabilities, and drug abuse. One *Smurf* episode, "The Lure of the Orb," won the coveted Humanitas Prize for covering how children can be drawn into and should resist drug use.

In a different vein, the network had direct control over the promotional time that was sandwiched between commercials during program breaks. The panel weighed in on whether short-form interstitial programming (also called "drop-ins") could be used to fortify the schedule with informational or prosocial messages. Skeptical at first, panel members doubted that drop-ins could be effective. However, one panel member, Aimee Dorr, had conducted some research that showed children do pay attention to these types of messages (Dorr et. al. 1981).

The programming executives then decided to develop a series of interstitial segments on topics of interest to children and use the talent from prime-time programming to present the messages to the audience. Called *One to Grow On*, these sixty- to ninety-second spots covered topics as wide ranging as personal safety, being home alone, dealing with bullies, honesty, peer pressure, honoring commitments, and establishing priorities. In the course of two years, 120 *One to Grow On* drop-ins were aired, and NBC received an Emmy for the programming in 1987. More important were the letters from parents, children, and public officials recounting how children had used the content, particularly the segments on safety and first aid.

Ultimately, the panel conceded that the "drop-ins" were a good way to reach millions of children with social and educational messages; certainly they were more effective than well-intentioned long-form "educational" programming that got canceled for lack of an audience. Nonetheless, the panel continued to express frustration over the entertainment focus of Saturday morning programming and persisted in believing that neither the network nor the creative suppliers of children's programming were motivated to focus sufficiently on prosocial and educational goals. They could not be completely convinced by the network's researchers, who, in contrast, felt they had established beyond any doubt that most children over six or seven would not turn on the TV on a Saturday morning to learn more of what they were taught in school all week. The researchers contended that children would accept prosocial messages only if they were wrapped in "fun" content.

To meet the panel's objectives and NBC's own desire to be innovative, several attempts to insert information into entertainment programs were made. But sometimes this proved to be harder than anticipated because of the nature of most children's programming. Animated shows typically contained factual as well as fantasy elements, so it was often difficult to portray facts in such a way that young viewers would recognize them as facts. In addition, the educational content had to be woven into a narrative story line, and that probably involved more interaction with an educator than the panel provided. Thus both NBC and the advisors gained some interesting and sometimes unanticipated insights during the years of the panel process.

As a network "first," the panel made contributions that ultimately reached almost half of all children during the course of one Saturday morning. It also encouraged the use of advisors at other networks and influenced the way writers, producers, and program executives approached the creative process of children's programming. The panel contributed to shifts in programming toward more prosocial content, and working with the network taught panel members that creating and embedding educational content into entertainment programming was easier said than done.

The Advisory Process during the 1990s

The audience for the networks' offerings of children's television programs began shrinking during the 1980s as local stations started airing more and more children's programs during weekday afternoons. Its decline continued in the face of increasing competition from cable networks. The erosion of Saturday morning network audiences was so substantial that more children watched prime-time family shows at 8:00 p.m. than watched the Saturday morning block. Phyllis Tucker Vinson, then vice president of children's programming, commented in a 1985 *Los Angeles Times* article that even though NBC was number one in the ratings it was having difficulty selling advertising for the upcoming season.[8]

In 1988, NBC made a strategic decision to shift programming to a new audience demographic. All the networks and most of the cable channels were oriented to the 6:00–11:00 audience segment, while PBS had a monopoly on the preschool audience. Teens, especially young teens, were a neglected sector. NBC started a trend to target programming to different subsets of the previously broadly defined "children's market." This would lead to the development of now-classic shows, anchored by *Saved by the Bell*, on a lineup that later paved the way for cable channels to enter what is now called the "tween" market.

In 1989, when *Saved by the Bell* went on the air, NBC had made several big shifts in programming. They had moved not only from a children's to a teen audience but also from outsourced to network-owned and produced content and from animation to live action. In addition, despite audience segmentation and erosion, federal policy regarding children's television caused a shift toward greater regulation of content with the passage of the Children's Television Act of 1990 (P.L. 101–437).

The Children's Television Act requires commercial broadcasters to air regular programming for children ages two to sixteen, with content that has a *core* purpose of educating and informing the audience. According to many of its advocates, the act compelled broadcasters to serve the public interest in exchange for the right to use the publicly owned airwaves (Kunkel 1998). However, when broadcasters began filing their compliance reports, both advocates and the FCC noted that patently noneducational shows were being counted as qualifying for broadcast under the act (Kunkel and Canepa 1994). Fortunately, *Saved by the Bell* was not among the listed offenders, but NBC executives decided to act aggressively to vet their content while it was in production and to use an interactive consulting process to ensure compliance.

In 1993, the network engaged Karen Hill-Scott, EdD, a Social Science Panel member who had worked closely with producers on the *One to Grow On* interstitials and some of the more challenging animated programs during the 1980s *(Mr. T, Lazer Tag)* as the primary educational consultant. Hill-Scott began reviewing the existing inventory of programs on the air to discern the extent to which each show on the schedule would be likely to qualify for the required FCC icon "E/I" (educational/informational programming). A review process was developed with the network executives and support from the NBC Research Department. This process evolved from the panel process of the 1980s but was more intensive, better documented, and marked by daily feedback loops as a story idea made its way from concept to a final-cut videotape.

In 1996, when the FCC passed the Children's Television Rules, commonly known as "the Rules" (Vol. 73.671), every broadcaster in the country was required to offer a three-hour weekly children's block with specifically designed children's educational programming for a target age group. Each program had to be a minimum of thirty minutes long; short-form and interstitial content would not be credited toward the minimum. Programs had to be identified as educational/informational with an E/I icon at the beginning of each episode, and the shows had to air in a regular time slot between the hours of 7:00 a.m. and 10:00 p.m. Each network was also required to document the process of content development and file reports (FCC Form 398) summarizing the educational objective of each episode of every show aired during the preceding quarter for public access and review. The rules also limited advertising on shows to 12 minutes on weekdays and 10.5 minutes on weekends (except for programming for children over age twelve) and limited preemptions by other programs (such as live news and sports events). In the event of a preemption, the programming block had to have a regular second home, and viewers had to be notified in advance of the program and the time it was scheduled to air.

Generally speaking, the Rules served notice that the FCC was serious about content, airtime, and fines for noncompliance. Fortunately, NBC programming had been cited as an example of the kind of programming that would qualify, but the network was going to have to increase the amount of content from two hours to three hours per Saturday.

In 1996, Hill-Scott and the NBC Research Department decided to anchor the consulting process with a Writer's Seminar.[9] This seminar would heighten awareness of the seriousness of the requirements for the network, the affiliates, and producers of children's content. Just as important, the seminar had the potential of bringing everyone together to work toward achieving a strong season with exemplary content. It began with a review of ten criteria that defined a qualifying show.

Three were set by the FCC—having a target audience, having core educational/informational content, and having core content that was cognitive or socioemotional. The others were:

- The content had to move audience knowledge from one level to another.
- The development of the core message had to be present throughout the episode.
- The episode had to refrain from promoting negative stereotypes of ethnic, religious, disabled, or other groups.
- The core content had to be of interest to the target group or had to be information adults felt was important for children to know.
- The content had to be handled in a way that was appropriate to the program format (drama, comedy, reality, or documentary).
- The content had to be presented in a comprehensible, consistent manner.
- The content had to be accurate (when factual) and faithful to the character (when based on personalities).

The writers were also given several writing strategies to support their efforts at merging the core educational message of each story with central plot development. The full consulting process now had six documented and measurable components—the Writer's Seminar, story conferences, script analysis, content tracking (through script revisions), verification of educational content on final cuts, and preparation of the FCC report.

The Writer's Seminar took place before production and included the creative teams from NBC Productions, NBC Executives, NBC Research, and outside consultants, who included two high school principals familiar with the pressures and problems of teens. This one-day working meeting contained a half-day of presentations from the Research Department, guest researchers or topic experts, and the high school principals, whose rich anecdotal material gave the writers a lot of content to use as the basis for story content. The second half of the day focused on developing prototypical story ideas from the anecdotes, from the content of the research presented, or from ideas the writers had already formulated. The main purpose of the meeting was to demonstrate, in real time, how a typical teen problem-solving situation could be developed within a humorous and entertaining story framework.

Immediately after the seminar, all the shows went into production; the four components of the process would run in sequence on each episode of each show. These consisted of additional story conferences, script analysis, educational content tracking, and verification of educational content on the producer's cut of the taped program. As the season's production neared completion, the quarterly reports for the FCC were prepared. The entire process was documented in writing to substantiate the level of effort and the amount of care taken to develop core educational and informational content for the audience.

After the first year of this process, a content analysis was prepared of themes covered during the prior year for each of the shows. For example, in 1999 almost half the shows aired dealt with life skills, about a third focused on personal development, and only 17 percent focused on teen relationships and romance. Of these, 36 percent were in the socioemotional domain, 30 percent were in the cognitive domain, and 34 percent combined both to tell a story. All of the stories in the cognitive domain focused on developing life skills, such as making good decisions, knowing what to do in an emergency, and getting help for a friend in trouble. Of those stories in the socioemotional domain, 64 percent were mainly about personal development, being true to your values, not growing up too fast, or refusing to change who you are to please another person.

The main outcome of the process for the writers and consultants was the creation of complementary contributions to the end product. For example, the consultant would stress how children digest material and perceive the message or lesson from story content. The writers would illustrate how the story elements needed to build in order to draw in audience interest to embrace the material.

From 1990 to 2000 almost six hundred original episodes of educational content were produced through this process, and episodes won the Gracie, Prism, Humanitas, and Parent's Choice awards.[10] Further, in the reviews of the Annenberg School of Communications and Public Policy from 1996 to 1999 (Woodard 1999), the NBC-produced shows made the grade for educational content. The self-regulation processes the network had designed were having the desired effect on content, program quality, and compliance with federal regulations. They were not enough, however, to make a dent in market pressures from competitors who did not have to meet the same regulatory requirements.

Change: The Signature of the Millennium

At the end of the century, market pressures continued to erode the audience base for the network's children's programs. The "tween" audience was no longer an NBC monopoly as Nickelodeon and Disney began their incursion into this audience segment. Further, these competitors were reaching larger children's audiences than the networks because they became "destinations" for entertainment at any time, weekday or weekend. NBC had to consider alternative ways to bring an audience back to the day part. The situation was similar at all of the major networks. Amy Jordan (1998), a noted researcher who put together the Annenberg annual ratings on E/I programming, commented that were it not for the Children's Television Act networks probably would have discontinued children's television altogether.

NBC explored the possibility of partnering with a content provider who could fulfill the FCC obligations. In 2002, Discovery Communications, a cable provider with a reputation for high-quality documentary and nonfiction programming that appealed to kids, entered into a multiyear agreement with NBC to take responsibility for the children's day part. The content developed for NBC would also air on their home channel, Discovery Kids. Discovery and NBC wanted to continue the process of ensuring compliance with the Children's Television Act, especially since NBC was still responsible for the quarterly reporting. The consulting process continued, but without the Writer's Seminar, in part because the shows were produced all over the world. Individual conferences were held with producing/writing teams, and the script review process and reporting remained the same.

In an interesting confluence of regulatory pressures and market recomposition, the lines between cable and broadcast television became blurred. Legally there was a difference between the two, but in the eyes of the end user it was all television. Audiences went to the programming they enjoyed and made little differentiation in who provided the content. Given this new television context, the business relationship that brought educational television to the air on NBC was a behind-the-scenes issue.

In 2006, the relationship between NBC and Discovery Kids was not renewed, and the network decided to manage the day part directly and improve synergies with its own family-oriented cable outlet. However, the process of external review and self-regulation, begun in 1975, will continue. Children's television at NBC will follow the same high road, but the business side of delivering quality content for children's viewing will be dynamic and responsive to an ever-changing competitive landscape.

Notes

Abbreviations
SRD NBC Social Research Department Files

1. In February 2006, CBS and Warner Bros. Entertainment announced a joint venture that would reduce the number of networks from six to five: the CW (which consolidated The WB and UPN), Fox, NBC, CBS, and ABC.

2. The eleven children's cable channels were Disney, TOON Disney, Discovery Kids, Nickelodeon, Noggin, PBS Kids, the Cartoon Network, Boomerang, TV Land, Nick Toons, and Sprout (PBS). The five family cable channels were ABC Family, ION (which was PAX until February 2006), the Hallmark Channel, HBO Family, and SHO Family.

3. Ron Milavsky to William S. Rubens, December 11, 1975, memo proposing a pilot project using social science consultant for Saturday morning programs, SRD.

4. For additional detail, see Stipp, Hill-Scott, and Dorr (1987).

5. A discussion about similar problems at PBS (Ettema, 1982) suggests that such difficulties may be a necessary part of this kind of process.

6. Research by Calvert, Stolkin, and Lee (1997) indicates that NBC's work in this area had a continuing positive impact on diversity in children's programming.

7. As discussed by Entman and Wildman (1992), the debate about content and ratings was not limited to the NBC consulting process; rather, it is typical of consulting in this field.

8. Lee Margulies, "Explosion in Children's Films and TV Programs," *Los Angeles Times*, August 1, 1985, 6:1.

9. Each year, a Writer's Seminar Handbook was produced that included the ten re-

quirements for developing educational content, strategies for meeting the intent of the Children's Television Act, and presentations from speakers and the NBC Social Research Department on current issues of importance to children in the target age group.

10. The Gracie Award is for realistic portrayals of women in a host of venues, including news and feature programming; the Prism Award recognizes accurate depictions of drug, alcohol, and tobacco use and addiction in television, feature film, video, music, and comic book entertainment; the Humanitas Award honors excellence in television and film writing that celebrates human dignity and the human spirit; and the Parent's Choice Award honors the best material for children—books, toys, music and storytelling, magazines, software, video games, television, and Web sites.

PART FOUR

NBC in the Digital Age
1985 to the Present

Introduction to Part Four

NBC in the Digital Age, 1985 to the Present

MICHELE HILMES

The late 1980s ushered in the current period of decentralization, deregulation, audience fragmentation, merger mania, globalization, new programming strategies, and the rise of digital media. The creation of three new over-the-air networks—Fox in 1986, UPN and The WB in 1995—brought attention to minority audiences and led to an emphasis on quality programs led by producer-auteurs on the Big Three nets. Cable television became a mature medium, offering competition and alternatives to the networks. Deregulation continued, and both the Fairness Doctrine and the Fin-Syn and PTAR rules were phased out. A greater concentration of ownership developed, predicated on the notion of synergy and vertical integration. In one of the biggest moves, electronics giant General Electric acquired RCA and with it NBC in 1986. NBC would experience its dramatic rise to first place in the ratings during this period, as Amanda Lotz describes in chapter 15, "Must-See TV: NBC's Dominant Decades." It would lose this momentum by 1990, then roar back during the mid-1990s in an overall context of the continuing network loss of audience share.

The decades after 1985 saw the growth, beyond all former anticipations, of both the promises and the threats of globalized digital and corporate convergence. The insular national scope of the media began to change as convergence technologies, legislation, and industries expanded globally, inevitably drawing the whole world into the same arguments, conflicts, and utopian potentials, and media conglomeration became the globalized norm. Christopher Anderson uses the 2003 merger of NBC and Universal Studios, which formed NBC Universal under the leadership of the General Electric Corporation, to analyze the effects of corporate ownership on the fortunes of a television network in chapter 16, "Creating the Twenty-first-Century Television Network: NBC in the Age of Media Conglomerates." Conglomeration often resulted in a blurring of the lines that had shaped older forms: between content and advertising, news and entertainment, print and video, cable and broadcast, public and private, commercial and nonprofit, U.S. media and global media, audience segmentation and conglomeration. It also represented many more opportunities for profit—and for bypassing the profit system altogether. Kevin Sandler looks at NBC's use of innovative promotion, programming, and scheduling techniques in chapter 17, "Life without *Friends*: NBC's Programming Strategies in an Age of Media Clutter, Media Conglomeration, and TiVo."

What does the new millennium hold for the television network? NBC, from its former position of first and dominant player in a field of only two entrants, later expanded to three, now competes in a world of hundreds of channels. Its status as an over-the-air network, an enormous advantage in the previous century, now seems almost a handicap in an age dominated by cable and satellite delivery; its roster of local stations placed, in accordance with the American compromise, in cities and towns across the land increasingly inhibits the network itself in an age of nonterrestrial delivery. Stations and networks now compete with each other in a cluttered landscape. Advertising as a sole means of support becomes insufficient, so that new revenue streams must be delivered. A return to integrated advertising seems imminent, bringing network programming operations full circle. Viewers born after 1980 can barely distinguish the Big Three networks—now expanded to the Big Four with Fox—from cable channels, as original production on both basic and pay cable becomes more and more prevalent, often resulting in shows that attract considerable critical attention and high ratings. From its customary 35 percent audience share in the early 1950s, NBC's typical audience amounts to no more than 10 percent of the public on most nights. Yet as a media producer and distributor it too has expanded, comprising a constellation of cable and satellite networks, along with many related media properties, that reach viewers across a number of demographic, geographical, and linguistic divides.

The historical role that NBC has played in the formation of our nation's culture cannot be denied. In chapter 18, "Network Nation: Writing Broadcasting History as Cultural History," Michele Hilmes and Shawn VanCour review the rise of broadcasting history as a field of study, now that globalization has allowed us to perceive clearly the unique nation-building role that broadcasting networks played in the twentieth century. The importance of preserving historical materials, ranging from recordings to scripts to in-house memos to letters from viewers, has become ever more acute in the age of electronic data. NBC, alone among the major U.S. networks, had the foresight to donate its archives to the Wisconsin Historical Society in the late 1950s, and more to the Library of Congress and the Museum of Television and Radio in the 1990s. Thanks to the vision of a few executives, the history of American broadcasting, one of the most influential and successful in the world, has not been entirely lost, and this chapter assesses the other sources for broadcasting history research still available to scholars and public alike. It is doubtful that we will see again a broadcasting institution with NBC's dominance over the developments of its times.

15

Must-See TV

NBC's Dominant Decades

AMANDA D. LOTZ

Popular coverage of the horse race among U.S. broadcast networks throughout the 1990s and early 2000s advanced a perception of NBC as an invincible champion. The duration of NBC's late-century success suggested to many a perpetual domination dating back to the dawn of television, but a more historically informed examination reveals that NBC's supremacy—while long uncontested—did not always exist. Until the late 1980s NBC was often a distant competitor in the network household ratings race, and ABC, a comparative newcomer, surpassed NBC in the 1970s as both networks tried to obtain the ratings title controlled by CBS since the late 1950s. The dominance of NBC from the mid-1980s through the early twenty-first century is indeed astonishing given the years of effort required to accomplish it.

NBC's programming dominance in the late twentieth century is not a simple matter of dogged persistence or even veteran's luck. It illustrates the shifting strategies required by a host of significant changes in the broadcasting industry during a period of transition from the "classic network era" to the "postnetwork era." And it ended just as the U.S. television industry was teetering on the precipice of new adjustments of an unprecedented scale. The future of NBC is tied closely to the future of broadcast networks in general, regardless of the legacy and history borne within the Peacock's plumage.

There are many ways to evaluate the success of a commercial television network. Given networks' location within a commercial system, their bottom line probably provides the most tenable measure of performance, and chapters 16 and 17 of this book chronicle NBC's economic position in this era in detail. But given that TV is a cultural industry, networks can also be evaluated by quality measures. Though many perceive the mid-1980s through early 2000s as a time of unbroken NBC dominance with regard to highly acclaimed, "quality" programming, this was not actually the case. NBC experienced two distinct phases of rising and falling in both critical and popular evaluations of its programming between 1985 and 2005: the peak of the first phase was in the mid-1980s and the peak of the second in the mid-1990s. A complex range of programming approaches (besides just the famed lineup on Thursday night) led to these successes. Examining how NBC gained both popular success and critical acclaim during its ratings peaks provides valuable insight into the changing nature of U.S. television programming and its audiences in this era of industry upheavals.

NBC's winning strategy in the mid-1980s was to schedule shows that relied on universal themes and stories of family, friendship, and mystery and that drew on underrepresented demographic groups in casting. In the mid-1990s its winning strategy was to schedule programs that featured characters reflecting, and themes targeted to, a narrower demographic, namely a younger and more affluent urban audience. This aided the network in establishing a distinctive brand, which it leveraged in promotional slogans such as "the quality shows on NBC" and "must-see TV," and simultaneously drawing a distinctive brand of audience member. In the early 2000s, as the mid-1990s shows aged, the network in some ways returned to the classic "broadcast" programming strategy that had been successful in the 1980s, but this time the approach was not effective because of the significant industrial changes introduced by audience fragmentation and the rise of niche network competitors in the intervening years.

The industrial context of both NBC and the larger televisual competitive environment is key to understanding the significance of NBC's success and strategies. Classic network-era practices still dominated in 1985. Characteristics of that era include fairly limited programming choices and very little viewer control over programming. But in the mid- to late 1980s, technological and competitive advancements were combining to redefine the television landscape in significant ways. Viewer choice expanded as the result of additional networks such as broadcasters Fox in 1986 and UPN and The WB in 1995. Likewise, cable significantly expanded the network options available. Only 19 percent of television households had access to thirty or more networks in 1985, whereas 76 percent of television homes could access more than thirty channels and 52 percent could access sixty channels or more by 1999 (Nielsen Media Research 2000, 17). As a result, the Big Three networks saw their share of the prime-time audience decrease from 74 percent in the 1984–85 season to 54 percent in 1998–99 (Nielsen Media Research 2000, 17).[1] And at the same time that choices for viewers expanded, remote control devices and videocassette recorders entered most U.S. television households, providing viewers with unprecedented control over how and when they viewed. Whereas in 1985 just 23.5 percent of homes had VCRs, VCRs were nearly universally available—found in 97.6 percent of homes—by 2002 (Quigley 2004, 17).

This increased choice and control had significant consequences for broadcasters who had enjoyed an oligopoly over the business for decades. The accumulated rating of the Big Three broadcasters slipped from 50 in 1983–84 to just over 21 in 2004–5 (Nielsen Media Research 2000, 17; Steiner 2005, 2). Not only did the traditional networks lose viewers to other program outlets, but the new networks (both broadcast and cable) implemented strategies of targeting specific niche audience groups that made many of the Big Three's traditional competitive strategies less viable. Niche networks could more precisely cater to individual tastes of groups who had long been underserved by the more generalized programming of the broadcast networks. Broadcast economics required these networks to pursue a large and broad audience, and as niche program providers targeted specific groups such as teens, women, African Americans, and Spanish speakers the broadcasters could do little to compete with their focused address. This changing competitive environment, along with the changes in network ownership and the rise of conglomeration discussed in chapters 16 and 17 of this book, required broadcasters to make substantial adjustments.

Part of the perception of NBC as a dominant network that developed during the 1980s and 1990s resulted from its success in other day parts that do not receive detailed examination here. In its 2003 upfront (meeting with major advertisers to announce fall programming and sell airtime several months before the season begins), NBC was able to claim itself as the number one network among eighteen- to forty-nine-year-olds not only in prime time but in morning, Sunday morning, daytime, news, and late-night slots, marking the second consecutive year it was able to claim first place in all day parts.[2] Success in these other components of the schedule, particularly in the morning with *Today,* and success in obtaining the rights to broadcast the Olympics significantly contributed to awareness of NBC's dominance and its brand. At the peak of its success, NBC presented a well-rounded schedule of regular and special programming that achieved both critical success and as large a popular audience as any network achieved in this era. The network's success in nonprime hours made its reputation in this era more unassailable, but prime-time dominance affords the most cultural cachet, despite lower production costs that allow others to be more lucrative.

NBC Programming during the Decline of the Network Era

By some accounts, the late 1970s and early 1980s mark the low point in NBC's programming history (Anderson 2004, 1608). The talented Fred Silverman, who had brought fortune to CBS with his program schedules from the mid-1960s through the early 1970s and to ABC in the mid-1970s, was unable to score a similar coup at NBC during his tenure there as president and chief executive officer from 1978 to 1981. Silverman arrived to a schedule that was heavy on special events and movies of the week and included few shows that remain a part of the collective television memory. The critically acclaimed *Rockford Files* was arguably the creative pinnacle of the schedule, and *Little House on the Prairie, CHiPS, Diff'rent Strokes,* and *Real People* were the only regularly scheduled series to break into the Nielsen top thirty during Silverman's reign (Brooks and Marsh 2003, 1464–65).[3]

Silverman's departure from NBC in 1981 allowed for the arrival of Grant Tinker. Television historians have attributed Tinker's success in producing top-rated and critically lauded television to his reputation for nurturing creative talent and protecting creative minds from business concerns and network pressures (Feuer, Kerr and Vahimagi 1984; McLeland 2004, 2340). The NBC of Grant Tinker would presumably bear little resemblance to the NBC that had featured shows such as *B.J. and the Bear* under Silverman's direction.

The presence of Brandon Tartikoff was a constant during the Silverman/Tinker transition. Tartikoff moved from vice president of programs to president in 1980, a position he would hold for an unprecedented ten years (surpassed only recently by Les Moonves at CBS) (Tartikoff and Leerhsen 1992, xi). Despite the arrival in 1981 of critically lauded *Hill Street Blues* (which Silverman had developed), the network's ratings were slow to respond. Tartikoff recalls his 1983 schedule as the September Train Wreck of 1983, in which not one of nine new series survived long enough to "make the cold weather" (Tartikoff and Leerhsen 1992, 12).

Yet *Hill Street Blues*, in conjunction with Tinker's presence, was symbolic of a shift at the network that did not appear immediately. Silverman's strategy at NBC had been simply one of seeking to get hits on the schedule (Tartikoff and Leerhsen 1992, 9). His strategy at CBS and ABC may have been similar, but there a coherence of hits created an early prototype of network branding. At NBC, however, Silverman's hits varied from *Hello, Larry* and *B.J. and the Bear* to *Real People* and *Hill Street Blues* (9). Tartikoff understood the need for greater consistency in tone among a network's programs and compared his task to shifting NBC's brand from "Kmart" to "Saks Fifth Avenue" (9).

Despite its place in the history of television criticism, *Hill Street Blues* never achieved broad popular success. It ranked only twenty-first among households in its second season and thirtieth in its fourth season despite critical applause, Emmy and Peabody awards, and a well-established place in television aesthetic and narrative history. Nonetheless, the show in many ways marks the beginning of Tartikoff's efforts to turn NBC into the Saks Fifth Avenue network.

Rather than emphasize NBC series well known among television critics and scholars, this chapter focuses upon shows that achieved broad popular and occasionally critical success. The program rankings that I use to indicate NBC's competitive position are those of total household viewing rather than the also common ranking among viewers ages eighteen to forty-nine. The eighteen- to forty-nine-year-old ranking (which NBC emphasized in the late 1990s and early 2000s because of CBS's dominance in households that resulted from its older audience) is unquestionably important, particularly as the currency guaranteed to many of the nation's television advertisers. But here I address NBC's role in reaching the culture defined by parameters broader than those preferred by advertisers. NBC's ability to deliver the viewers most highly prized by advertisers was closely tied to its ability to create distinctive programming and to take certain content and scheduling risks, and it remained a key determinant of the network's cultural production. The programming NBC produced in this era, however, circulated cultural forms

FIG. **16** Brandon Tartikoff, president of NBC's entertainment division from 1980 to 1990, on stage with comedian Bill Cosby in 1985. Tartikoff brought the network into first place in the prime-time ratings, with help from *The Cosby Show*'s key spot on Thursday nights. (Library of American Broadcasting)

and meanings beyond the demographic group most valued by advertisers and networks, so that Nielsen household ratings are the more relevant measure. Further, NBC's first wave of success marked the end of the era of broadcasting in which top shows reached at least 30 percent of that night's audience. Although television continues to be the dominant storytelling medium in U.S. culture, it now tells stories to far more diffuse and fragmented audiences in a way that fundamentally alters its ability to produce a generalized "cultural forum" (Newcomb and Hirsch 2004, 503). Household ratings are a more inclusive index of this broadly conceived image of the nation's audiences than measures of a narrower demographic group.

The First Wave

NBC's first wave of success occurred from roughly 1985 to 1991. The network went from placing just one show in the Nielsen top ten in 1983–84 to placing three shows in 1984–85 and five shows in 1985–86.[4] Moreover, it increased its number of series ranking in the top thirty from six, to eleven, to fourteen over these three program seasons.

Many attribute this mounting success to *The Cosby Show*, and certainly the comedy series played an important role in changing the network's fortunes. Beginning with its launch in the fall of 1984, *The Cosby Show* surged to a third-place finish in its first season, while leading off a Thursday night schedule that had formerly begun with *Gimme a Break* and *Mama's Family* and counted only *Hill Street Blues* in the top thirty (where it ranked thirty). The thematic coherence of *The Cosby Show* with *Family Ties*, a two-year-old series that had never ranked in the top thirty, strengthened both shows and drew audiences to the also previously unranked *Cheers*. By the 1985–86 season, all of the shows in the 8:00 to 9:30 block ranked in the top five, with *Night Court* ranking eleventh at 9:30.

The Cosby Show and the Thursday night schedule were not the only shows that drew both critical praise and sizable audiences. In 1985 and 1986, NBC introduced shows that each became main draws on other nights. *Golden Girls* launched in 1985 at 9:00 on Saturday night—a night whose schedule had undergone many changes on all the networks ever since it had featured blockbuster programming on CBS in the early 1970s. Like *The Cosby Show*, *Golden Girls* achieved top ten status in its first season on the air without a strong show in the preceding time slot to build upon or significant existing viewership on the night. Reproducing NBC's success on Thursday evening, *Golden Girls* pulled the shows immediately before and after it (blackcast comedies *227* and *Amen*) into the top fifteen in its second season. When NBC scheduled *Empty Nest* after *Golden Girls* in 1988, both shows ranked in the top ten and drew audiences into the 10:00 drama *Hunter*.

The trend continued similarly on Tuesday nights. In 1986, NBC replaced *The A-Team* (the series ranked in the top ten its first three seasons) with the folksy lawyer drama *Matlock*. *Matlock* was not as immediately successful as the comedies, but it debuted at fifteen and rose to fourteen in its second year. Midway through its second season, NBC paired *Matlock* with *In the Heat of the Night*, and both shows remained ranked in the top twenty until *Matlock* ended its run in 1991.[5] These shows were not as high ranking as the Thursday and Saturday comedies, but their stability helped supplement the NBC schedule. (*Unsolved Mysteries* provided a similarly unheralded function by leading off Wednesday nights beginning in 1988 and was the second and third highest-ranking show on NBC in 1991–92 and 1992–93 respectively.)

The crest of this wave of success was the 1987–88 season, during which NBC aired six shows that ranked in the top ten and nineteen that ranked in the top thirty. The Thursday night schedule was the most successful, with *The Cosby Show* (1), *A Different World* (2), *Cheers* (3), *Night Court* (7), and *LA Law* (12). Significantly, despite the acclaim of the 10:00 dramas that preceded it (*Hill Street Blues*, *St. Elsewhere*), only *LA Law* maintained the audience drawn by the comedies to the degree necessary to achieve a top fifteen ranking. *Golden Girls* remained strong on Saturday, scoring an impressive ranking of fourth despite its less coherent placement among *227* and *Amen*. *Matlock* and *In the Heat of the Night* began their run on Tuesdays at midseason, and a new series featuring a puppet from outer space named *Alf* garnered a top ten rating on Mondays.

In addition to the popular success of these series, many shows were honored with awards recognizing their excellence. NBC won Peabody awards in 1985 for its movie *An Early Frost* and for *The Cosby Show* (1986) and *LA Law* (1987), while the Television Critics Association honored *The Cosby Show* as outstanding comedy in 1985 and 1986 and awarded outstanding drama recognition to *LA Law* in 1987 and *St. Elsewhere* in 1988. The network also accumulated awards given by those in the industry by winning outstanding comedy Emmys for *The Cosby Show* (1985), *Golden Girls* (1986, 1987), and *Cheers* (1989, 1991) and an outstanding drama Emmy for *LA Law* (1987, 1989, 1990, 1991). These awards were certainly significant, but other than in Emmys NBC did not win a disproportionate percentage of awards relative to other broadcasters.[6] (CBS drew recognition in this era for *Murphy Brown*, *Frank's Place*, *Cagney and Lacey*, *Northern Exposure*, and *Picket Fences*, while ABC was honored for *Wonder Years*, *thirtysomething*, *Twin Peaks*, and *Roseanne*.)

No one event ended this period of dominance. Many of the shows that contributed to NBC's success in this era launched and aged together. By the late 1980s the network was struggling to develop new hits and consequently keeping some shows on the schedule beyond their creative prime, with the result that many key hits were lost at the same time. NBC's decline was precipitous. The network dropped from having five shows in the top ten in 1990–91 to having only one the following season.[7] Likewise, its shows ranking in the top thirty declined from nineteen in 1987–88, to ten in 1990–91, to just six in 1993–94.

Although NBC's dismal performance in 1991 correlated with Warren Littlefield's first year as president of programming, it was attributable not so much to him as to predecessors who had left several series on the air too long and had neglected to find or nurture replacements. Tinker had left NBC in 1986 shortly after General

Electric purchased the network, and GE CEO Jack Welch installed longtime GE executive Bob Wright to replace him. According to the network's self-produced history book, Wright came to NBC with the goals of streamlining costs and moving NBC into cable (M. Robinson 2002, 177). Such cost considerations probably contributed to the lackluster program development that resulted in NBC's rapid reversal of fortune. But *Seinfeld* launched in 1990 (after a 1989 pilot), and NBC's patience in the trough years of 1991–93 would eventually be well rewarded. Likewise, *Law & Order* premiered in 1990, though it would require seven seasons before breaking into the top twenty and ten before reaching the top ten.

Many aspects of the comprehensive success NBC achieved during its first wave are particularly striking, especially from the vantage point of 2005. In 1985, the broadcast networks (still just the Big Three) drew 75 percent of the audience (Nielsen Media Research 2000, 17). The fear of audience fragmentation was certainly beginning, but it was by no means as evident as in 1995, when broadcasters (including Fox) reached 66 percent of the audience, or in 2005, when aggregate cable networks drew more viewers than aggregate broadcasters and twice as many networks split the broadcast share (17). Nonetheless, the successful programs of the first wave exhibit a remarkable blend of niche and broad appeal. The NBC schedule of 1987 was far more demographically diverse than that of any year to follow. (After achieving success with four predominantly black-cast comedies—*The Cosby Show, A Different World, 227, Amen*—the network decreased its minority representation to the point that in the mid-1990s it earned the dubious distinction of standing for "Nothing But Caucasians.") Similarly, the age range of the characters appearing on NBC in the 1980s exhibited a diversity that would seem impossible twenty years later.

In the competitive situation of the era, NBC achieved broad-based success with series cast with African Americans and people over fifty. The quality of the writing and execution of the shows accounts for part of this success, but the competitive environment was equally important. Shows such as *The Cosby Show* and *Golden Girls* debuted before many narrowcasters joined the industry and began targeting younger and African American viewers without attempting broad-based appeal. *The Cosby Show* fell from first to eighteenth ranking in just three seasons. Although the series had covered much creative terrain by this point and adjusted its cast, the slip in rankings occurred in the first season Fox scheduled programming on Thursday night. Premiering *The Simpsons* (launched the previous December on Sundays) and *Beverly Hills, 90210*, Fox offered a new option to younger viewers with its youthful and irreverent programming brand.

NBC achieved a delicate balance with shows such as *The Cosby Show* and *Golden Girls*. Both were noteworthy, even in their time, for including images of people not typically represented on U.S. television. Despite their uncommon casting, both shows also told stories with broad-based appeal. *The Cosby Show* explored stories many families could relate or aspire to, while the *Golden Girls* provided an unprecedented opportunity to explore women's friendships and varied perspectives (a theme successfully repeated with women of a more common television age in *Designing Women* and *Sex and the City*). *Cheers* and *Night Court* advanced the workplace comedy with distinctive and intricately drawn characters, while *Matlock* provided a slightly different version of the procedural at a time when the form was not nearly as abundant as it was during the 1970s or late 1990s. *In the Heat of the Night* took the uncommon risk of dealing more openly with issues of ethnicity and racial conflict as well as exploring stories located outside an urban environment. The next wave of successful NBC programming emerged after the network eliminated many of the uncommon faces and stories that had appeared in this era.

The Second Wave

NBC suffered through three inglorious years of ratings from 1991 to 1994 but then rose again to top ratings as quickly as it had fallen. By 1994–95, the components of the second wave of success were in place, with *Seinfeld* ranking first, *Friends* eighth, and the new *ER* second. The network returned to its dominant position in 1995–96 and reached a new peak with seven top ten hits in 1996–97 and a total of sixteen series in the top thirty.[8] Fully evaluating the downward trajectory from that point is complicated by the two years during which ABC programmers aired three installments of *Who Wants to Be a Millionaire* each week in 1999–2000 and four in 2000–2001, all of which ranked in the top ten. Ignoring the blip of *Millionaire*, we can see that NBC gradually lost strength, "slipping" to only five or six shows in the top ten (the remaining shows were broadcasts of *Millionaire*) in 1997–2002. The network then declined significantly: it had only three top ten series in 2002–4 and scheduled no series that ranked higher than thirteenth in 2004–5.[9] Again, its rapid decline seems closely linked to a heavy reliance on existing hits that overstayed their creative capacity and an inability to develop new hits (particularly in the case of comedy).

This second cycle differed considerably from the first. In this cycle, NBC's dominance on Thursday reached an unprecedented level—what might be identified as an ability to induce audiences to watch anything it scheduled on Thursday night. The popular and critical success the network achieved with *ER* provided a draw in the 10:00 hour that the network was unable to establish during the first wave. Although the audience seemed content to spend three hours each Thursday with the network, the schedule never developed the coherence it had in the first cycle. *Friends, Seinfeld, Frasier,* and *Will & Grace* all existed as bona fide hits on Thursday but never formed an ensemble in the way that *The Cosby Show, Family Ties/A Different World, Cheers,* and *Night Court* achieved. NBC reprogrammed the 8:30 time slot in most years, with no show developing strong enough interest to thrive outside the Thursday night environment.[10] Notably, it is somewhat false to say the network had seven top ten hits in 1996–97, as three of these shows occupied the same Thursday time slot (*Suddenly Susan* began the season at 9:30, *The Naked Truth* held the slot from January to April, and *Fired Up* ran April through May). This might be viewed as exceptional strength in that shows such as *Friends, Seinfeld,* and *ER* were so phenomenally powerful that viewers remained tuned to NBC regardless of what aired between them.

At the same time, this phenomenon indicates the lack of depth in the network's schedule even at its peak of popularity, and thus the network's rapid decline once it lost these key components of its schedule.

NBC's Thursday programs illustrate another phenomenon addressed more thoroughly in chapter 17 of this book but deserving of some discussion here. Between NBC's first and second periods of success, the FCC eliminated the remaining vestiges of the Financial Interest and Syndication (Fin-Syn) rules that prevented networks from owning a share in the programming that they aired. Perhaps no set of program choices provides better evidence of the degree to which networks attempted to gain an interest in their programming in the post Fin-Syn competitive environment and the negative consequences that could result. Consider the series NBC scheduled in the valued 8:30 Thursday time slot from its establishment between *Friends* and *Seinfeld* in 1995 (coincidentally concurrent with the elimination of Fin-Syn rules) until 2002.[11] Five series occupied the slot in seven seasons: *The Single Guy* (1995, 1996), *Union Square* (1997), *Jesse* (1998, 1999), *Cursed* (2000), and *Inside Schwartz* (2001). Four of these series (airing in five of the seasons) featured partial ownership by NBC Studios (all but *Jesse*). Arguably, this example illustrates how the greed of maximizing ownership opportunities may lead networks to be their own worst enemy. Each of these series was a popular and critical failure, with none shooting enough episodes for full syndication.[12] Although the short-term benefit of aiding a new series with a scheduling position guaranteed to bring in viewers may appear to be in the conglomerate's best interest, wasting a valuable site for exposure on mediocre products unquestionably hurts the network in the long-term search for successful series.

Another key component of NBC's second-wave ratings success was the newfound strength it developed in the 10:00 hour. Until *ER*, no 10:00 show placed in the top ten and few even placed in the top twenty (*Miami Vice, Hunter, LA Law*). Beginning in 1996, NBC added another 10:00 night into the top twenty each year until 1998, when it counted *ER* (1) in the top ten and *Law & Order* (13), *Providence* (16), *Dateline-Tuesday* (19), and *Dateline-Monday* (19) in the top twenty. Strength in the 10:00 hour is particularly valuable to affiliates, who experience gains in sampling of 11:00 newscasts as a result, and strong performance in this hour can also increase viewership of *The Tonight Show*. The *Dateline* and *Law & Order* franchises were particularly helpful in maintaining NBC's ratings lead throughout the late 1990s. By 2001, *Law & Order* also had achieved a top ten ranking, while *Crossing Jordan, Law & Order: SVU*, and *Medium* also ranked in the top twenty by 2005.

NBC achieved and maintained its second successful ratings cycle differently from the first. During these years NBC more openly branded itself as the network of "upscale," college-educated, eighteen- to forty-nine-year-old viewers. Serving as president of entertainment from 1991 to 1998, Warren Littlefield was particularly responsible for the brand of entertainment that came to be known as "must-see TV." The network's demographic specificity is most apparent in the various series scheduled in the Thursday sitcom block during the second cycle. With varying success, the network repeatedly told stories about young, affluent, white urbanites who lived in worlds curiously devoid of people different from themselves.

NBC also received a fair amount of praise from critics in these years, in some cases for the same series that achieved popularity in Nielsen households. Well before a sizable audience found it, *Seinfeld* won a Peabody award in 1992. Peabodys were also given to *Homicide: Life on the Street* (1993, 1995, 1997),[13] *Frasier* (1994), *Mad about You* (1994), *ER* (1994), *Law & Order* (1996), *Dateline* (1998, 2000), *The West Wing* (1998, 2000), and *Boomtown* (2002). NBC comedies *Seinfeld* (1992, 1993) and *Frasier* (1994, 1995, 1996) were given outstanding comedy honors from the Television Critics Association, which also bestowed outstanding drama awards on *I'll Fly Away* (1992, 1993), *Homicide: Life on the Street* (1995, 1996, 1997), *The West Wing* (2000, 2001), and *Boomtown* (2003). NBC experienced similar Emmy award victories, with *Frasier* winning the outstanding comedy award for five consecutive years between 1993 and 1998 (*Seinfeld* won in 1992). Subsequently *Will & Grace* won in 2000 and *Friends* in 2002. NBC received awards in the outstanding drama category for *ER* (1996), *Law & Order* (1997), and *The West Wing* (2000, 2001, 2002, 2003).

Littlefield left NBC at the end of 1998, and although NBC remained dominant when measured by Nielsen household viewing levels, subsequent leadership did not appreciate the importance of nurturing critically acclaimed niche shows as Tartikoff had done with *Hill Street Blues* and *St. Elsewhere* and Littlefield had done with *I'll Fly Away* and *Homicide: Life on the Street*. Much of the critical favor NBC earned during the second cycle resulted from its willingness to continue and support some artistically sophisticated shows even when they were not strong ratings performers. Littlefield's replacements, first Scott Sassa (who quickly canceled *Homicide*), from October 1998 until he became president of West Coast operations in June 1999, and then Garth Ancier, from May 1999 until December 2000, failed to develop series achieving popular or critical success (except for adding to the *Law & Order* franchise). Far more success was expected from Ancier, who had begun his career under Tartikoff in the early 1980s and had developed a successful record at Fox and The WB. In a somewhat surprising move, Wright then named Jeff Zucker, previously executive producer of *Today*, NBC's president of programming. Although Zucker continued to climb the NBC executive ranks following the NBC-Universal merger in 2004, his accomplishments in developing new programming were limited. Isolated hits such as *American Dreams*, *Las Vegas*, *The Apprentice*, and *Fear Factor* were launched under his watch, but his legacy was the way these shows dismantled the NBC brand established by Tartikoff and Littlefield. Kevin Reilly replaced Zucker in May 2005 after Zucker completed development on what turned out to be a dismal 2004–5 season.

As competitors increased throughout the latter half of the 1990s, NBC, like the other Big Three broadcasters, struggled to find its place. The WB and UPN networks siphoned away younger viewers, while Fox achieved the status of a Big Four network that could compete on par with the others, particularly in the lucrative eighteen- to forty-nine-year-old demographic. Simultaneously, many of the stronger cable networks began developing original series programming that matched the quality offered by broadcasters. Networks such as HBO, Fox, and USA basked in the popular and critical attention afforded to their series that broke established boundaries and provided uncommon stories. The broadcast networks' grasp on valued upwardly mobile, young, urban audience members (those Ron Becker [2001, 36–47] terms "Slumpies," or socially liberal, urban-minded professionals) weakened as cable competition mounted. Broadcasters faced the dilemma of maintaining the status quo that led to the Slumpies' exodus to cable or more narrowly targeting their programming to win back Slumpies while potentially sacrificing their "broadcast" base. The fate of the broadcaster is uncertain in a narrowcast era.

Broadcasters' Challenge: Finding a Brand

With compelling advertising tag lines such as "where the quality shows" (and the programming to support them), NBC established itself as the network of Slumpies in the mid-1990s. *The West Wing* and *Frasier,* while not ranking as highly with households, were quintessential shows for reaching NBC's target of upscale eighteen- to forty-nine-year-olds. Such shows constructed too narrow an identity for broadcast economics and scheduling practices, challenging broadcasters who competed with each other and cable networks that could draw acclaim by programming only one or two new hours of niche-focused content per week. After Littlefield's departure, NBC had difficulty filling its schedule with programs that supported the established brand. The new shows that succeeded on NBC lacked coherence with each other or the existing NBC brand and contributed greatly to the network's marked decline. In each of the seasons from 2000 through 2004 the network successfully launched a new drama, while it developed only one successful comedy in all five years.[14] NBC also began competing in the genre of "reality" or unscripted programming at this time, earning its most significant success with *Fear Factor* (2001) and *The Apprentice* (2003) but also achieving moderate success with *Average Joe* (2003) and *The Biggest Loser* (2004).

Given the challenges of development, this is not a terrible record of accomplishment (except in comedy), but the lack of coherence among the shows that succeeded and their lack of fit with what had been established as the NBC brand dismantled the identity created under the leadership of Tartikoff and Littlefield. In 2001, an ever self-assured Jeff Zucker appeared before the Television Critics Association wearing a bulletproof vest to theme music of "Hit Me with Your Best Shot" in response to their critiques that the recently launched summer series *Fear Factor* violated the network's "quality" identity (M. Robinson 2002, 205). Zucker reminded the critics that the network was a "broadcaster," so that it could not air "twenty-two hours of *The West Wing*" (205). Rather than acknowledge the valid assessment of how this show did not fit with the programming identity NBC had established, Zucker moved *Fear Factor* from a summer replacement series to a regularly scheduled program. The network then developed a successful companion with *Las Vegas,* the network's only bona fide hit in 2003. The series's casino setting enabled opportunities to include scantily clad showgirls and pool goers, and while the series fit well with the show preceding it, *Las Vegas* was not a show for the *Frasier/ The West Wing* audience. *Fear Factor* performed well for its first few seasons and provided economy to a network license fee schedule bloated by the expense of *Friends* and *ER*. But license fees are not the only way a series can "cost" a network. The series garnered a considerable amount of critique and negative publicity as *Fear Factor* became the show that symbolically represented many of the excesses of the genre, with its regular feature of nearly naked beauties forced to eat disgusting items never intended as food.

By 2003, NBC appeared to be a schizophrenic mix lacking coherence across the week and even within the schedule on most evenings. The legacy of Tartikoff had been forgotten, and the network's programmers had returned to trying to stick a few hits on the schedule regardless of whether they fit a common identity. The irony, of course, is that network identity was more important in 2005 than in it was in Tartikoff's days.

NBC's ignominious fall from glory in the early years of the twenty-first century was possible only because of the extraordinary accomplishment of the network over the preceding two decades. All of the networks experienced ebbs and flows in ratings positions throughout their long histories. The adjustment that occurred in the middle years of the first decade of the twenty-first century is just one of many transitions that occur in countless cycles throughout broadcast history. Yet the substantial changes in the business of U.S. television during these years make the variant strategies NBC used to achieve this success and their outcome particularly informative of how the broadcasting business was changing in more permanent ways.

NBC rose to dominance by using a range of programming strategies that expertly adapted to the changing competitive situation during a time of pronounced industrial change and uncertainty. At moments of creative and commercial excellence, NBC managed to meet the demands of the diverse array of masters common within cultural industries. The network produced a programming brand of distinction by delicately balancing the need for popular success with the need for artistic innovation and critical excellence. Many of the NBC shows produced in this era serve as cultural and generational touchstones and lived on long after their time on the NBC airwaves, while some of the less popular shows endure as examples of the finest achievements in television storytelling. During a period in which U.S. audiences shared fewer and fewer stories via the televisual hearth in their homes, NBC regularly brought audiences together on Thursday nights in the waning years during which the medium could offer stories characterized as "must-see TV."

Notes

1. Share includes only ABC, CBS, NBC, and Fox.
2. Notably, these claims were made in a presentation that did not feature the typical

caveats regarding method that one normally finds in printed reports. The presentation was a bit unclear about what audience group the network placed first with, during what period of time, and by whose measure.

3. Unless otherwise noted, information about Nielsen top thirty ratings and program schedules come from Brooks and Marsh (2003).

4. In 1983–84, *The A-Team* (4); in 1984–85, *The Cosby Show* (3), *Family Ties* (5), and *The A-Team* (6); and in 1985–86, *The Cosby Show* (1), *Family Ties* (2), *Cheers* (5), *Golden Girls* (7), and *Miami Vice* (9).

5. Both shows were produced by the Fred Silverman Company, with Silverman (perhaps proving himself after all) serving in the capacity of executive producer.

6. I include the Emmys because they are perhaps the best-known television award, but their status as an award that industry workers give themselves makes them questionable in their partiality. Both the Peabody awards and those given by the Television Critics Association have historically honored television shows that exemplify creative excellence and are free from industry self-interest.

7. In 1990–91, *The Cosby Show* (1), *Cheers* (3), *A Different World* (4), *Golden Girls* (6), and *Empty Nest* (9); in 1991–92, *Cheers* (4).

8. These seven hits in the top ten were *ER* (1), *Seinfeld* (2), *Suddenly Susan* (3), *Friends* (4), *The Naked Truth* (5), *Fired Up* (6), and *The Single Guy* (8).

9. In 2002, *Friends* (2), *ER* (4), and *Law & Order* (9); in 2003, *The Apprentice* (4), *Friends* (6), and *ER* (9); in 2004, *The Apprentice 2* (13).

10. *Frasier* did perform solidly outside the Thursday time slot. Its audiences were smaller, but this also owes to the more niche sensibility of the show.

11. In 2002–4, NBC scheduled *Scrubs*, in which it shared an ownership interest with Touchstone. *Scrubs* broke the 8:30 curse to survive on Tuesday nights. After moving *Scrubs*, NBC scheduled established show *Will & Grace* in the time slot, a show that is incidentally produced by NBC Studios.

12. Some cable stations (particularly USA) offered limited syndication runs for short-lived series, including some listed here. Although some additional profits were made possible, by no means did they come close to those available from a full syndication run.

13. This is an unprecedented and unsurpassed number of awards for a scripted series.

14. The dramas were, for 2000, *Ed;* for 2001, *Law & Order: Criminal Intent* and *Crossing Jordan;* for 2002, *American Dreams;* for 2003, *Las Vegas;* and for 2004, *Medium* (midseason). The one comedy was *Scrubs* in 2001. "Success" here means a series that lasts two full seasons. *Boomtown* returned for the beginning of a second season but was pulled from the schedule by winter. By some counts *Good Morning Miami* might rank as a success, but it limped through a second season after losing its valued Thursday time slot and was preempted so frequently that nine episodes remain unaired. At the time of writing, *Joey* has somewhat unexplainably been picked up for a second season, although chances for the series to ever be a hit look slim.

16

Creating the Twenty-first-Century Television Network

NBC in the Age of Media Conglomerates

CHRISTOPHER ANDERSON

The first three decades of network television in the United States were a period of remarkable stability for the television industry. Once the basic structure of the industry had been established, the television seasons rolled past with comforting familiarity. The three networks filled their schedules with daily and weekly series that made it possible to deliver a consistent and relatively predictable number of viewers to advertisers. New series debuted each fall. Some found an audience and survived; most were canceled. And the cycle started all over again. The three networks battled one another for ratings supremacy, because each ratings point translated into millions of dollars in advertising revenue, but little happened to challenge the fundamental logic of the television business. Under these conditions, the networks were among the most durable corporations in the media industries. Founded as radio networks in the 1920s, NBC and CBS survived six decades without a change in ownership; ABC changed hands once, in 1953. The end of this era in network television occurred gradually, and then suddenly, in the 1980s.

By the middle of that decade, the tremendous early success of cable TV and home video had disturbed the balance of power in the television industry. The three networks still shared more than 80 percent of the television audience and collected a secure income from advertising, but, for the first time in decades, their long-term viability was open to debate. Corporate legacies burnished over decades of prosperity faded quickly in the glare cast by dazzling new technologies and fierce new competitors. Stock analysts questioned their prospects for future growth, investors lost confidence, and the price of shares began to drop. In the 1980s, any company with an unsteady stock price and a reliable cash flow soon found itself, like a wounded gazelle in the Serengeti, encircled by predators. Over a period of six months beginning in 1985, each of the three networks changed owners. In the parlance of Wall Street, these were friendly takeovers, not the handiwork of corporate raiders who would eviscerate a company and sell off its parts for quick profit.

But these were still the first new owners of an American television network in more than thirty years. It was the end of a familiar era in American television and a time of apprehension and opportunity in the television industry.

For more than a half-century NBC had been secure in the patronage of its corporate parent, but in 1986 the RCA board accepted a $6.28 billion bid to join General Electric, paving the way for what at the time was the largest nonoil merger in U.S. history.[1] Employees of NBC and many observers of the media industries were dubious. General Electric was a vast conglomerate based in Fairfield, Connecticut, an easy commute to New York but a world apart from network television, which turns on an axis of its own, stretched between network headquarters in midtown Manhattan and the studios in Hollywood. General Electric manufactured lighting, appliances, and electronics for consumers and plastics, power turbines, jet engines, locomotives, and medical equipment for industry and government. From its origin in manufacturing, GE also had diversified into service industries, becoming a leader in commercial and consumer loans, insurance, commercial real estate, and corporate leasing (a division in which GE has owned the world's largest fleet of automobiles and trucks, more airplanes than any airline, and more railcars than any railroad).[2] What role would a television network play within a conglomerate that had accumulated an almost unfathomable array of subsidiaries but lacked any significant investments in the media industries? And why purchase a television network at precisely the moment when the networks had begun to lose viewers — a trend that many believed to be irreversible? Why acquire a broadcast network at the moment when cable, satellites, and home video threatened to end the supremacy of over-the-air broadcasting?

By virtually any measure, NBC has prospered since becoming a subsidiary of General Electric, reaching heights never seen during the RCA years and serving as a model of stability in an otherwise turbulent business. Since conglomerates first acquired the television networks in the mid-1980s, both ABC and CBS have changed owners again — twice in the case of CBS. Meanwhile, NBC chairman Robert (Bob) Wright, who rose through the ranks at GE, learning the ropes in the plastics and credit divisions before taking over the network in 1986, has achieved a historic tenure surpassed only by such industry legends as William S. Paley of CBS and Leonard Goldenson of ABC. The landscape of American television has changed more dramatically during Wright's tenure than in all the preceding years. Companies have responded by growing ever larger, continuing the pattern of mergers and acquisitions begun in the 1980s. During much of this period, however, NBC remained the anomaly in network television: GE stood alone in choosing not to diversify into other media businesses besides television.

This changed in May 2004, when GE acquired 80 percent of Vivendi Universal Entertainment in a deal valued at $14 billion. By adding Vivendi's additional cable channels and Universal studios to NBC and its cable networks, GE created NBC Universal, a twenty-first-century media corporation operating in a television landscape for which the term *national broadcasting* is but a quaint reminder of a

FIG. **17** Robert C. Wright, in front of historic NBC and RCA logos, 1995. Wright became president and chief executive officer of NBC when General Electric acquired the network in 1986. (Library of American Broadcasting)

bygone era. The name Universal has its own history and brand-name recognition, dating back to the earliest days of Hollywood, but it also makes NBC Universal a suitably descriptive name for a company determined to reinvent itself as a global media titan.

To approach the history of NBC since 1986, I have chosen to begin by asking how a television network functions within a conglomerate like General Electric. It's a simple question, but one not easily answered. Those who criticize consolidation in the media industries provide many powerful insights into the organization and influence of conglomerates, but the model of conglomerate ownership that emerges from this work too often overlooks the differences among the networks and their parent corporations, particularly in the tensions and contradictions that arise within and between a conglomerate's subsidiaries. What does it mean for a television network to operate as one subsidiary among many in a diversified conglomerate? How are networks influenced by the larger agendas of parent corporations? These questions are not answered by simply following the spreading tentacles of ownership that lead from corporate headquarters to the far-flung outposts of its empire. Once you've traced the six degrees of separation that link *NBC Nightly News* to a GE-made nuclear reactor in Kazakhstan, you certainly know something about NBC, but what exactly is it that you know?

This essay will focus on the changing role and status of NBC within General Electric. Although there are many valuable questions that one might pose, for the purposes of the present volume I will ask the following: What role has NBC played for GE, and how has its role changed over time? How has the network's status as a subsidiary of GE shaped the programs that it delivers to our TV sets or those that we may encounter on a range of other computer and video screens? Does NBC bear a detectable stamp of GE ownership? Does it share a common corporate culture, operating procedures, or management strategies with other GE businesses? Has the network maintained a degree of autonomy—perhaps due to the peculiar conditions of the television industry or the real challenges of attempting to coordinate the disparate and far-flung enterprises in a conglomerate? Finally, how has GE attempted to convert NBC into a television network for the twenty-first century?

Looking for the Conglomerate behind the Television Screen

Critics of the media industries use a variety of metaphors to explain the critical enterprise. They "reveal" patterns or underlying structures that are invisible to the casual observer. Or they "shed light" on activities and relationships that are otherwise obscured. The case of NBC and General Electric poses a new variation of this methodological challenge, because they are anything but hidden. Both companies operate in plain sight and, through their products, are deeply woven into the fabric of daily life. General Electric is a publicly traded company, required by law to provide open access to a staggering amount of corporate information, and

NBC may have the highest public profile of any GE business. Yet the size and complexity of General Electric, which provides only brief and carefully managed glimpses of its inner workings, makes it difficult to comprehend the company in any but the most abstract terms or to answer questions about it with any degree of certainty. At the same time, NBC now operates on a scale that dwarfs that of a mid-century Hollywood studio or a network in the first four decades of television, yet it is merely one enterprise in a corporation that conducts business in every corner of the globe. And the television network—a major national institution in the United States—accounts for just 5 percent of that company's annual worldwide revenue.[3]

Depending upon the vagaries of its stock price, General Electric is one of the world's two or three most valuable corporations, a globe-straddling colossus with hundreds of separate businesses in dozens of countries, more than four hundred thousand employees worldwide, and combined annual revenues of $134 billion. GE's portfolio of businesses changes several times each year as it acquires companies that appear poised for growth and discards others whose profits have fallen. At the time of its 2004 *Annual Report*, these subsidiaries were organized into eleven separate business units: Advanced Materials (plastics, chemical- and silicon-based products), Consumer and Industrial (appliances and other manufactured goods), Infrastructure (technical systems for water purification, security, etc.), NBC, Commercial Finance, Consumer Finance, Energy, Healthcare, Transportation, Equipment Services, and Insurance.[4] For those who think of NBC as a giant of the media industries, a glimpse of the network among these disparate businesses provides a useful perspective on its status within the company.

It is a challenge even to conceive of a company as large as General Electric, much less to determine from the outside how one business functions within the larger organization. In financial markets shaken by the high-profile corporate scandals of Enron and MCI Worldcom, the complexity of conglomerates worries investment bankers as much as it troubles critics of media consolidation. "Perhaps GE is just too large and diverse a company to understand," one stock analyst has lamented. "Who can comprehend the aircraft industry, plastics, medical technology, insurance, mortgages, and derivative markets all at once? There could not possibly be a company more difficult to analyze than GE."[5] General Electric may seem more comprehensible if one assumes that a single business strategy governs all corridors of the conglomerate, but that isn't how the company actually operates. "GE is simply too big and diverse to have a strategy per se," one business reporter writes. "Rather, it has something closer to a domestic policy—a set of ideas and initiatives that the CEO promotes throughout the company's businesses."[6] To make sense of GE, in other words, one must occasionally set aside the language of business and resort to terms normally reserved for the affairs of nation-states.

For GE, the long-term value of NBC may not have been immediately apparent, but it soon fit the pattern of a new business model. In recent years, GE has made a concerted effort to shift "away from the steady, industrial businesses that have dominated it for decades, and into riskier, high-growth new areas that GE executives hope will redefine the company."[7] As a company committed to double-digit earnings, GE has looked increasingly to the high profit margins delivered by information- and service-oriented businesses. GE has transformed itself over the past twenty-five years from a company that in 1980 earned 85 percent of its profits from manufacturing to one that in 1999 earned 75 percent from information and services.[8] Unlike a traditional GE industrial business that manufactures *things*, NBC delivers profits by making and circulating *information, images*, and *stories*. In this, NBC is more closely related than one might at first imagine to other rapidly expanding businesses, including biotechnology and diagnostic medical imaging, which are intended to create and manage intellectual property controlled by GE. As a result, the television network that seemed vaguely superfluous when acquired twenty years ago now serves as a paradigm for the future of the conglomerate.

Finding the Conglomerate within the Network

In the publicity that surrounds high-profile mergers and acquisitions—not to mention the fears of media critics—conglomerates perform with orchestral grace, each distinct business blended in concert under the baton of a charismatic chief executive. The reality is quite different: companies brought together by investment capital are frequently torn asunder; mergers that make sense on paper dissolve once people from different professional backgrounds lock horns over strategic decisions. Cautionary tales abound in the media industries, where ill-fated unions like AOL Time Warner disintegrate on the front pages of the business press. In fact, the incorporation of diverse businesses into a functional conglomerate is an extraordinary social and cultural achievement that cannot be explained solely in economic terms. How does a conglomerate such as General Electric knit together its subsidiaries? How has this process of incorporation influenced NBC over the years?

In most cases, a conglomerate "generates returns by trading in and out of businesses; it's basically a giant mutual fund."[9] General Electric has bought and sold hundreds of businesses over the last twenty years, yet it operates as something more than a giant mutual fund due to a robust corporate culture actively created and carefully sustained by management. Credit for this generally goes to CEO Jack Welch, who directed the company from 1981 until 2001. Welch earned a reputation for ruthless cost efficiency, gaining notoriety initially for closing down plants in the United States and cutting GE payrolls by more than 120,000 employees in the first half-dozen years of his tenure.[10] From the perspective of Wall Street, Welch's success was beyond question. He inherited a company with a $14 billion market value and left his successors one worth more than $400 billion.[11] Under Welch, GE recorded a growth rate that few companies ever have matched—even in the superheated markets of the 1990s. In that decade, while becoming the first company ever to post $10 billion in annual earnings, GE rocketed past its longtime rival, Westinghouse, whose 30 percent drop in stock value over the period looks even worse when compared with GE's 400 percent increase.[12]

GE may not be capable of producing the direct synergy promised by media con-glomerates like Disney and News Corporation, but it is still much more than the sum of its parts. GE's great size gives its individual businesses the ability to domi-nate capital-intensive industries where size is a clear advantage. In developing the GE90 jet engine, for example, GE spent $1 million a day for almost five years.[13] "GE generates returns," a reporter has observed, "by undertaking projects that only it has the wherewithal to undertake: the biggest, the most difficult, the longest term. Scale is one of GE's strengths."[14] This is a particular advantage in industries such as high technology and media, where initial costs—research and development, in-stallation of technical infrastructure, the production of content—can be enormous, while the cost of reaching each additional customer is relatively small. Such econ-omies of scale encourage corporate consolidation by rewarding companies with the financial resources to sustain enormous initial costs and the years that often pass before an investment pays off.

Of course, size also can be a handicap, particularly when it comes to building a functional corporation from a collection of diverse businesses. Welch was par-ticularly skilled at knitting together companies that initially had little in common except a corporate parent. He extolled the value of a common corporate culture and dismissed those who didn't conform. He set clear goals for the entire company and publicized them widely—identifying globalization, digitization, and a shift to information- and service-oriented businesses as the keys to growth. He established internal channels for communicating information and ideas, making it possible to transfer knowledge and expertise across widely dispersed businesses.

GE most directly transfers knowledge through its practice of rotating managers from one business to another. By circulating among the subsidiaries, managers ac-quire experience and share knowledge; collectively, they help to foster a common corporate culture. In this manner, for instance, Bob Wright gained valuable expe-rience in several areas of GE before becoming chairman of NBC. Much of the additional coordination and sharing of knowledge takes place in seminars and work-shops at GE's renowned management-training center in Crotonville, New York, which has been described as "the glue holding the parts of GE together."[15] As a result, GE has created a distinctive corporate culture, famed for having a language of its own, as in its proprietary quality control system, known as "Six Sigma," which is widely admired in the business press.[16]

NBC came to dominate network television during the latter half of the 1990s because Bob Wright succeeded in adapting certain GE management principles to the business of television. Success was never a foregone conclusion, however. By the early 1990s, GE's foray into television looked as if it was about to become another cautionary tale of the conglomerate era. For the first few years under GE, the network coasted on the momentum of its existing hits until viewers began to desert and NBC dropped into third place for the first time in over a decade. Net-work profits plunged from $603 million in 1989 to $204 million in 1992.[17] Rumors spread that GE was prepared to bail out of television, at one time or another entertaining offers from Paramount, Time Warner, Disney, and even a syndicate headed by former network star Bill Cosby.

During this time, GE management, and Wright in particular, came under harsh criticism for cost-cutting measures and a pressure to develop new revenue streams; many thought these tactics had damaged network operations, particularly in the news division, where GE was accused of undermining NBC's news-gathering ability—not to mention its journalistic integrity—by closing down foreign bureaus and eliminating thousands of jobs. The network suffered one public relations debacle after another during this period. The CNBC cable channel, which NBC had launched as a joint venture with cable operator Cablevision in 1989, lost $60 million in its first two years, forcing Cablevision to withdraw from the partnership. Wright's appointment of newspaper executive Michael Gartner to head NBC News ended in a highly publicized scandal over a fraudulent news report on the prime-time news magazine *Dateline*. Attempts to name a successor to the retiring Johnny Carson as host of *The Tonight Show* turned into a public brouhaha as network executives wavered between Jay Leno and David Letterman. Leno eventually ended up in Carson's seat, while Letterman fled to CBS.[18]

The turning point in Wright's tenure at NBC came in 1993—the year GE finally ended speculation by announcing that NBC was not for sale.[19] On the surface this statement may seem rather banal, but it changed everything at NBC. Until this time, industry observers and many network employees had questioned whether GE was committed to operating a television network or simply slashing costs to bolster the network's value in an inevitable sale. As *New York Times* reporter Bill Carter noted, "[T]he failures at the network were partly attributed to the inattention of G.E. corporate management, which was said to be more interested in deal-making than in broadcasting."[20] Wright remained in charge following the announcement, and he gradually instilled a direction and purpose that had been lacking in earlier years. He began by hiring two new executives who would play key roles in revitalizing the network.

Andrew Lack, a veteran producer at CBS News, was appointed president of the NBC news division, where he revamped *The Nightly News* with Tom Brokaw and *The Today Show*. As an experienced network news producer, Lack shared the values of the professional journalists in the news division, but his competitive nature also gave him a knack for speaking the language of a corporation that measured success in ratings points and earnings. Critics complained that *The Nightly News* replaced hard news with pandering "news you can use" features on topics such as health care and personal finance, but the newscast surged into first place in the ratings. *The Today Show*—outfitted with a new street-level studio, padded with attention-grabbing stunts, and expanded to three hours under the guidance of rising star Jeff Zucker—became firmly entrenched as the number one morning show and the most lucrative program in network television, responsible for $200 million a year in profits.[21] Lack gained stature within the corporation as he transformed the news division into a profit center.

Wright also convinced veteran sports producer Don Ohlmeyer to accept a newly created position as president of NBC's West Coast operations, a move that effectively placed Ohlmeyer in charge of all entertainment at the network. Two aspects of Ohlmeyer's hiring stand out as signs of Wright's leadership. First, Ohlmeyer was an unusual and brave choice for the position. He had earned his reputation as a producer and director at ABC Sports in the 1970s before moving on to become an independent producer. In the business of network programming, executives are normally promoted from within the ranks, but Ohlmeyer had no experience as a programmer and little experience in entertainment. Second, Wright brought Ohlmeyer into a new position above entertainment president Warren Littlefield but kept Littlefield in place. The easy solution—repeated endlessly over the history of network television—would have been to fire Littlefield, making him the scapegoat for the network's plunge in the ratings. But this unorthodox decision—really a kind of experiment in management—gave Ohlmeyer responsibility for running the entertainment division while allowing Littlefield to return to his strength in program development, where he soon earned credit for developing such subsequent hits as *Frasier, Friends,* and *ER.* Ohlmeyer quickly placed his stamp on NBC's prime-time schedule. By rearranging the schedule, changing the flow of programs, and creating new promotions such as the "Must-See TV" slogan for the Thursday night lineup, he crafted an identity for the network—just as cable channels like MTV or Nickelodeon had learned to build identifiable network brands that superseded individual programs.

Given the uncertainty of audience tastes and the challenge of developing hit series, any network's success from one season to the next may be fleeting, but Wright and his executives at NBC brought a consistency to the network that resembled the sober management style of its corporate parent more than the usual tumult of showbiz. In contrast with other networks, where executive suites are equipped with revolving doors, NBC had remarkably consistent leadership during the 1990s, as represented most evidently in the long career of Wright himself. Once in place, NBC executives dissected audience demographics and measured the advertising potential of each program developed for the network, carefully weighing program costs against advertising revenue for each portion of the schedule.

GE has been willing to write big checks for programming when its deep pockets provide a true competitive advantage or when the programming serves a strategic goal for the conglomerate. The Olympics are a case in point. In an effort to forge its identity as the network of the Olympics, NBC has locked up Olympics rights until at least 2012. NBC has spent more than $6 billion on the Olympics since capturing rights to the 1996 Atlanta games. To win the rights for 2010 and 2012 alone, GE paid $2 billion and agreed to spend an additional $200 million to become a worldwide Olympics sponsor.[22] The investment makes sense for GE because, unlike any other form of television programming, the Olympics serve several purposes at once.

As a form of sports programming, the Olympics still have a unique aura, a value that cannot be duplicated and has not yet been diminished in the multichannel television universe. Unlike other types of sports programming, NBC has a contractual monopoly on television coverage of the Olympic events. Under the guidance of Dick Ebersol, who has run NBC Sports since 1989, NBC has shifted away from live coverage of the events by using recorded coverage edited to enhance drama and to suit the desired flow of network programming and commercials. The Olympics are one of the few remaining forms of television programming capable of uniting the fragmented TV audience. As such, they serve as signature programming for NBC, helping to create a brand identity for the network and awarding a social stature that broadcast networks once routinely claimed. While providing a valuable platform for the promotion of NBC's other programs, the Olympics continue to be profitable from advertising sales alone. Finally, NBC has used the Olympics to launch additional programming services beyond broadcast television. For instance, the network offered the incentive of Olympic coverage on its cable channels, CNBC and MSNBC, to convince cable system operators to add the channels to their services.

NBC achieved an unmatched record of success in network television in the second half of the 1990s by adapting to the diminished opportunities available for a broadcast network, mastering the heightened competition for an audience that grew ever smaller, even as program costs continued to rise. For Bob Wright, however, this left NBC facing a larger challenge. "We have to be bigger than broadcasting," he told a reporter in 1997.[23] While NBC routinely surpassed the ratings of its competitors, the other networks had begun to participate in a reinvention of the television business by aligning themselves with major Hollywood studios through ambitious mergers. Wright expressed interest in several potential acquisitions that would have diversified NBC. He explored deals with Ted Turner before Turner sold his assets to Time Warner and with Sony when the Japanese manufacturer considered unloading its Hollywood studio. But the corporate calculus that produced NBC's success in prime time also served as a restraint on the network's growth. GE chairman Jack Welch had engineered the deal that brought NBC into General Electric, but he was wary about expanding in the media business, which he perceived as being too unpredictable for a company that needed to meet quarterly profit projections. He was reluctant to support any expansion of NBC that might dilute earnings. Due to the volatility of the movie business, he was particularly dubious about acquiring a studio.[24]

When GE acquired NBC in 1986, the National Broadcasting Company was still much as its name described—a *broadcasting* company with programs directed almost exclusively at a *national* market in the United States. NBC had grown substantially since its origins as a radio network six decades earlier—and had expanded into international markets under GE—but its approach to earning profits hadn't changed much over the years. As the twentieth century came to an end, NBC still derived more than 90 percent of its revenue from the sale of commercial time to advertisers.[25] With the emergence of new technologies such as digital video recorders, Internet-based distribution, and video on demand, however, industry observers wondered how much longer the advertising-based economics of television would survive.

From National Broadcasting to Universal Television

On September 7, 2001, Jeffrey Immelt succeeded Jack Welch as chairman and chief executive officer of General Electric. The events that led to the NBC Universal merger began to fall into place following this changing of the guard. Immelt, a twenty-year veteran of the company who rose to the top of GE Healthcare, has accelerated GE's shift away from traditional industrial businesses and toward high technology, information, and services. He may have been inclined in this direction by temperament and experience, but the GE board also received a strong push from investors after GE's earnings in 2001 dipped below double digits for the first time in years. Investment analysts pointed out that earnings had stagnated in GE's industrial businesses.[26] A faltering stock price gave GE a strong incentive to pick up the pace of its transition to growth-oriented information and service businesses.

The watershed week in Immelt's tenure occurred in October 2003, when GE reached agreement or closed on three massive deals, totaling $25 billion in acquisitions. On Wednesday of that week, the company signed a $14 billion agreement to acquire 80 percent of Vivendi Universal Entertainment. On Thursday, it completed a $2.3 billion deal to buy Instrumentarium, a Finnish medical-device maker. The week ended with a $9.5 billion agreement to acquire Amersham, a British medical diagnostic and bioscience company.[27] The agreements with Vivendi and Amersham were two of the three biggest deals in the company's 111-year history (the 1986 RCA deal is the third).

The Vivendi merger should be viewed in the context of these other major deals because together they represent the company's movement toward high-tech information and communication systems. General Electric appears to be increasingly committed to the development, management, and exploitation of various forms of intellectual property—from biotechnology patents to television series.[28] This notable shift into riskier, high-growth areas recognizes that networked digital technologies are transforming global economies and cultures. According to NBC chairman Bob Wright, the merger that created NBC Universal resulted from a sense that NBC needed a broader base "to make the transition from an analog consumer world to a digital consumer world."[29]

The question facing General Electric was how to transform a television network that had been built to meet the historical conditions of the twentieth century into one capable of thriving in the twenty-first. GE's acquisition of Vivendi's Universal properties follows as a logical step in the pattern of consolidation that emerged across the media industries in the 1990s, as conglomerates gathered broadcast networks, cable channels, and studios under a single roof. By combining broadcast and cable networks, a media conglomerate diversifies its revenue streams, increases its bargaining leverage when negotiating transmission fees with cable and satellite service providers, and offers greater value to advertisers by spreading commercials across a range of networks that can provide access to different sorts of viewers, both in the United States and around the globe. The acquisition of Vivendi Universal's entertainment properties gave NBC Universal several additional cable channels in the United States, Europe, and Asia (including the USA Network, the Sci Fi Channel, and Trio), along with the Universal movie and television studios, Universal Studio theme parks, and a library consisting of five thousand movies and over thirty-four thousand hours of television programs. Like the other media conglomerates, NBC Universal is capable of producing programs for its own broadcast network and its cable channels in the United States and around the world, while also preparing for new modes of distribution, such as broadband Internet and video on demand, that will emerge in the coming years. The immediate goal of the merger is to create new revenue streams that will reduce the company's reliance on advertising. NBC Universal plans to reduce its dependence on income from advertising, which eventually will account for only half its annual revenue (with the rest coming from sources such as retail sales and license fees).[30]

With the merger NBC also acquired the studio responsible for producing its most valuable television programs: the *Law & Order* franchise. Nothing reveals the new economics of the television industry better than the negotiations that began in summer 2003 over the renewal of the three *Law & Order* series (*Law & Order, Law & Order: Special Victims Unit*, and *Law & Order: Criminal Intent*). Universal and producer Dick Wolf offered to bundle the three series together in a new three-year contract at a cost of $550 million per year; at $1.6 billion this would have been the largest series programming commitment in television history.

While the three *Law & Order* series don't attract as many viewers in the eighteen- to forty-nine-year-old demographic as *ER* or *Fear Factor*, they "repeat well." In other words, unlike the ongoing stories of *ER* and *The West Wing*, or the immediate sensation of a contestant eating worms on *Fear Factor*, the self-contained stories of *Law & Order* draw large numbers of viewers even in reruns. Over the past few years NBC has used repeats of the three *Law & Order* series to plug holes in its schedule, even filling entire nights with back-to-back episodes. In summer 2003, for instance, 20 percent of NBC's entire prime-time schedule consisted of one version or another of *Law & Order*. One industry analyst estimated that the *Law & Order* franchise accounted for 25 percent ($180 million) of the network's prime-time profits in 2001–2. The twenty-five- to fifty-four-year-old demographic most attracted to *Law & Order* at 10:00 p.m. also works in NBC's favor because it provides an ideal audience leading in to the local news and *The Tonight Show*, both of which appeal to slightly older viewers and are enormous profit centers for the network and its owned-and-operated stations. Clearly, NBC could not afford to lose *Law & Order*. Nor could it afford to be held hostage in renegotiations. It made more sense simply to buy the studio.[31]

NBC now owns the *Law & Order* franchise (including new editions, such as the unsuccessful *Law & Order: Trial by Jury*). Ownership reduces many of the headaches involved in negotiating license renewals and cuts the network in on the riches of the syndication and retail markets (though it creates new concerns about potential conflicts of interest that arise when the network is also the producer). Over the last half-decade it has often seemed as if an episode of *Law & Order* was always on the air, with originals and repeats on NBC or syndicated reruns appearing on A&E, TNT, and USA at virtually any hour of the day. Of course, NBC Universal ultimately wants *Law & Order* to appear only on its own channels. With a studio library that contains not only *Law & Order* but also thirty-four thousand hours of television and five thousand movies, NBC Universal has the content to fill any number of specialized cable channels.

The studio's intellectual property—the movies and TV programs stored in the vaults—proved to be a crucial incentive for the merger. The television network of the twentieth century possessed a unique ability to gather a synchronous mass audience for a single broadcast, but the network of the twenty-first century will also function as a repository for content that will be available for individual use through video on demand or some other mode of access. In conversations with journalists, network chairman Bob Wright has said that the television network of the future will resemble "a lending library," where users make individual selections according to their particular interests. Unlike a public library, however, it will make this material available only for those willing to pay some sort of fee.[32]

Consider how an event like the Olympics will change to suit this vision. Instead of being doled out gradually over a period of time to a single mass audience, the events of the Olympics will become a repertoire of choices that exist simultaneously, with selection determined not by the network but by individual users. "I think the Olympics are a sort of proxy of what being a big content company is going to mean in the future," NBC's Randy Falco has said. "Think of the Olympics as being a content library. It's about identifying what your assets are and then cross-selling and cross-promoting them."[33] NBC offered a glimpse of this future in its coverage of the 2004 Athens Olympics, in which the network spread an astonishing 1,200 hours of coverage across its many television outlets: NBC, CNBC, MSNBC, USA Network, Bravo, and Telemundo. (By comparison, NBC offered 400 hours of events from the 2000 Sydney Olympics.) Video highlights were available on the network's Olympics Web site—free, but only available to Visa credit cardholders.[34]

As with any networked digital media, the real dilemma is not how the corporation will store and distribute digital content but how it will protect its intellectual property from unauthorized duplication and distribution. As NBC Universal attempts to find technological solutions for this problem, Wright has taken up a new crusade in Washington, joining other industry leaders in lobbying for intellectual property laws that favor corporate interests. All of this suggests that the television network of the twenty-first century may resemble a publisher, but it does little to clarify the future of commercial broadcasting. The goal for NBC Universal is to develop new revenue streams that, in the short term, begin to redefine the economics of a television network. The larger challenge will be to determine how the conventional broadcast network—with its dependence on local affiliates and advertising revenue—will adapt to survive in the twenty-first century.

Conclusion: How to View NBC

There is an inherent problem in writing the history of current events: everything is fluid, nothing settled. By the time this essay appears in print, NBC Universal will have changed several times. Perhaps General Electric will have acquired additional businesses to be integrated into the NBC division. Under the right circumstances, GE may even have sold NBC. The only certainty is that GE cannot stand still; financial markets and competition in the media industries will not allow it. "As rivals become larger and more powerful," a reporter has written since the merger, "the definition of a 'major scale' media business keeps changing. NBC Universal is going to have to keep expanding if it wants to keep pace."[35] The next round of mergers may involve the consolidation of content providers with companies that control the technological systems for digital distribution. News Corporation, with its satellite systems, and Time Warner, which owns cable systems, offer precedents for this form of consolidation, and it wouldn't be a surprise to see a media company like NBC join forces with a cable company like Comcast (which already has tried and failed to acquire Disney), a satellite company like Echostar, or one of the many telecom companies interested in entering the content-delivery business.

Regardless of how things change in the coming years, it will be possible to write the history of NBC in the conglomerate era only as long as particular events are viewed from a perspective that makes visible both NBC and General Electric. Crucial questions have yet to be answered about the role played by a television network in the conglomerate era. What is it like to work in the different divisions of a network under conglomerate ownership? How do managers coordinate the activities of employees or communicate the parent company's strategies and values? How do those who work within these companies experience and make sense of the company on a daily basis? How do they think of their professional identities? Do they see themselves as being primarily independent of the corporation or in service to it? From the perspective of an employee, how does one conglomerate differ from another?

Finding an answer to any of these questions poses a challenge for the historian. On the one hand, there is an almost overwhelming surplus of public information about these companies because of the reporting requirements demanded of publicly traded corporations and the constant drumbeat of corporate PR. But the internal deliberations and decision making—not to mention the day-to-day routines of individuals working for a TV network—take place out of sight. When companies like NBC and GE allow reporters to peek inside, they usually offer brief, stage-managed glimpses designed to serve a public relations goal. The historian writing about these companies must depend upon public records and industry reporting, while inspecting each document carefully to see through the glaze of corporate self-promotion that tends to envelop most accounts of the corporation.

Finally, it is important to remember that even a company as large as NBC Universal must respond to external conditions. No matter how deep the pockets of General Electric, NBC has not been able to dictate the changes that have taken place in the television industry, much less the actions of people who use television. Regardless of what NBC executives think people will be doing with television in the years to come, it is likely to be something that hasn't been anticipated. And NBC will respond—even if NBC has become something entirely different from the television network that we have come to recognize over the past half-century.

Notes

1. J.J. Davis, "Did RCA Have to Be Sold?" *New York Times Magazine*, September 20, 1987, 23.

2. John Curran, "GE Capital: Jack Welch's Secret Weapon," *Fortune*, November 10, 1997, 116.

3. GE, *Annual Report*, January 2004.

4. Ibid.; Jerry Useem, "Another Boss, Another Revolution," *Fortune*, April 5, 2004, 112.

5. Melanie Warner, "Can GE Light Up the Market Again?" *Fortune*, November 11, 2002, 108.

6. Jerry Useem, "It's All Yours, Jeff. Now What?" *Fortune*, September 17, 2001, 64.

7. Ken Brown and Kathryn Kranhold, "GE's Immelt Faces Hurdles after Acquisitions," *Wall Street Journal*, October 13, 2003, C1.

8. "The House That Jack Built," *Economist*, September 18, 1999, 23.

9. Useem, "Another Boss," 112.

10. Edwin A. Finn, "General Electric Acquisitions Changing Corporate Focus," *Forbes*, March 23, 1987, 74.

11. Marc Gunther, "Money and Morals at GE," *Fortune*, November 15, 2004, 176.

12. "The House That Jack Built"; John Curran, "GE Capital: Jack Welch's Secret Weapon," *Fortune*, November 10, 1997, 116.

13. "The House That Jack Built."

14. Useem, "Another Boss," 112.

15. Ibid.; Useem, "It's All Yours," 64.

16. Laura M. Holson, "Six Sigma: A Hollywood Studio Learns the GE Way," *New York Times*, September 27, 2004, C1.

17. John H. Taylor and Kathryn Harris, "Whither NBC's Peacock?" *Forbes*, March 4, 1991, 40; Geraldine Fabrikant, "For NBC, Hard Times and Miscues," *New York Times*, December 13, 1992, C1.

18. Fabrikant, "For NBC"; Bill Carter, "The Peacock Preens Again," *New York Times*, April 14, 1996, C1.

19. Carter, "Peacock Preens Again."

20. Bill Carter, "A Peacock on Phoenix Wings," *New York Times*, May 22, 1995, D1.

21. Bill Carter, "Anchor Aweigh," *New York Times*, November 14, 2004, 2:1.

22. Richard Sandomir, "When It Comes to Sports on Television, NBC Favors a Small Ball," *New York Times*, March 4, 2005, D1.

23. Marc Gunther, "How GE Made NBC No. 1," *Fortune*, February 3, 1997, 92.

24. Bill Carter, "NBC Sticks to Solo Strategy as Media Rivals Consolidate," *New York Times*, September 13, 1998, C1.

25. Ken Brown, "Will GE Be Enjoying the Movie?" *Wall Street Journal*, September 2, 2003, C1.

26. "The Jack and Jeff Show Loses Its Luster," *Economist*, May 4, 2002, 69; "Solving GE's Big Problem," *Economist*, October 26, 2002, 77.

27. Kathryn Kranhold, "GE's Pricey Deals Prompt Questions," *Wall Street Journal*, December 2, 2004, C1; Brown and Kranhold, "GE's Immelt Faces Hurdles."

28. Diane Brady, "Will Jeff Immelt's New Push Pay Off for GE?" *Business Week*, October 13, 2003, 94.

29. Diane Mermigas, "NBC's Diller Dilemma," *Mermigas on Media*, January 21, 2004.

30. Brown, "Will GE Be Enjoying the Movie?" C1; Tim Burt, "After the Acquisition of Studio and Entertainment Assets from Vivendi," *Financial Times*, November 30, 2004, 17.

31. Bill Carter, "*Law and Order*, a Hot Franchise, Seeks a Rich Deal Early from NBC," *New York Times*, June 2, 2003, C1; Michele Greppi, "NBC Finds Wolf at Door," *Television Week*, June 16, 2003, 6.

32. Diane Mermigas, "NBC Universal Takes Shape," *Mermigas on Media*, January 14, 2004.

33. Pamela McClintock, "Getting to Know U," *Variety*, November 1–7, 2004, 1.

34. Katie DeWitt, "NBC's Marathon of Coverage," *Business Week*, August 9, 2004, 35.

35. Steve Rosenbush, "Can NBC Universal Measure Up?" *Business Week Online*, January 18, 2005, www.businessweek.com/technology/content/jan2005/tc20050118_9579_tc024.htm.

17

Life without *Friends*

NBC's Programming Strategies in an Age of Media Clutter, Media Conglomeration, and TiVo

KEVIN S. SANDLER

Anybody who says or believes that the network television business isn't under siege has their head stuck firmly in the sand.

SANDY GRUSHOW, chair, Fox Television Entertainment Group, quoted in Josef Adalian, "Primetime Pickle," *Daily Variety,* January 2, 2004

Will CBS's near-guaranteed new hit, *CSI: New York,* really take down NBC's mighty *Law and Order* on Wednesday night at 10? Will NBC be able to retain its two-decade hold on television's most lucrative night, Thursday, having lost its last great comedy hit, *Friends?* Will NBC also maintain its long claim to being the most successful network, fighting off challenges from CBS and Fox network?

BILL CARTER, "As Season Begins, Networks Struggle in Cable's Shadow," *New York Times,* September 19, 2004

Sandy Grushow's statement at the end of the fall 2003 season and Bill Carter's query at the start of the 2004 fall season surely mirrored the uncertainty felt by NBC executives over their new prime-time lineup after the network lost two of its most profitable shows in May 2004—*Friends* (which ended its ten-year run) and *Frasier* (which lasted eleven years)—and saw *The West Wing*'s audience drop by 31 percent between 2002 and 2004.[1] *ER, Will & Grace,* and *American Dreams* have experienced losses in audience as well. Nevertheless, NBC still raked in $2.9 billion in advertising commitments for the 2004–5 season in the May upfronts (meetings with major advertisers to introduce fall programming and sell airtime), about $500 million more than second-place CBS.[2] The 2003 corporate merger between General Electric (GE) and Vivendi Universal Entertainment (VUE) and its broadcast of the Athens Olympics in August could not have come at a more opportune time for NBC to promote its new and returning shows. NBC was optimistic that over 1,200 hours of Olympic coverage across NBC Universal's terrestrial and cable networks (NBC, Telemundo, CNBC, MSNBC, NBC HDTV, Universal HD, USA Network, Bravo,

Sci Fi Channel, and of course, NBC itself) would have a halo effect on the fall season, helping the broadcaster maintain its dominance as the most coveted destination for the eighteen- to forty-nine-year-old audience, the most affluent demographic for advertisers.

However, it became apparent during the first six weeks of the fall 2004 season that NBC's rating supremacy had come to an end. For this period, NBC's ratings were down 11.6 percent in the eighteen- to forty-nine-year-old demographic and down 10.8 percent in households.[3] The numbers slightly improved during November sweeps, but by the end of the season NBC had lost 9 percent of its much-sought-after eighteen- to forty-nine-year-old demographic from the previous year.[4] *Joey*, with Matthew LeBlanc reprising his role from *Friends*, fell 43 percent among adults aged eighteen to forty-nine (9.4 rating to 5.3) from the previous year in the same 8:00 p.m. Thursday time slot.[5] Also, on this most lucrative night in television advertising, *The Apprentice* was down almost three ratings points, at 7.8 in the eighteen- to forty-nine-year-old demographic despite being the no. 5 show among this coveted audience.[6] Ratings for two of the three *Law & Order* series (the flagship original and *Criminal Intent*) declined by 20 percent and 11 percent, respectively. None of NBC's shows were breakout hits; only *Joey* and *Medical Investigation* got picked up for the entire year, and *The Biggest Loser* earned a second season. In the end, it was the first time since February 1994 that NBC finished third in any sweeps period. On NBC's fall season of 2004, Peter Olson, director of national broadcast buying at Grey Global's MediaCom unit, said, "This is more than we were thinking they would fall in the post-*Friends* and *Frasier* environment. But this is a changing of the guard. NBC had a nice long run."[7]

The 2004 November sweeps marked "the end of an era," stated Jack Wakshlag, the chief research officer of Turner Broadcasting System Inc.[8] Cable held more than a five-share advantage over broadcast networks, posting a total 51.7 share of households (up 3.4 from the previous year) while broadcasters registered a 46.3 (down 2.6).[9] Eight of the top ten cable networks experienced year-to-year growth, while ABC, thanks to the breakthrough top ten hits *Desperate Housewives* and *Lost* and a fourth-place finish in the previous year, was the only broadcast network to actually increase viewers during November sweeps.[10] "We're in a single television world now," said MTV Networks' vice president Betsy Frank about broadcast viewer erosion and cable's siphoning of its viewers. "People aren't making distinctions between the broadcast networks and the cable networks anymore."[11]

Ironically, at this watershed moment in television history, the sweeps themselves were becoming an anachronism of audience measurement for networks and advertisers. Because of cable, television programming no longer conveniently fits into three artificially competitive periods (February, May, and November). The economic model that formed the basis of broadcast television—fall premiere week, original programming and stunts in sweeps months, and summer reruns—does not apply to a 365-day-a-year cable schedule. As a result, stated Fox Entertainment president Gail Berman, broadcasters need to change their business strategies. "With the choices that exist in the marketplace today, we have to compete for our viewers. The way to compete with them is to provide them with vital programming 52 weeks a year. There is no more free lunch in this game."[12]

Year-round programming is just one of the many challenges that the broadcast networks face in an increasingly fragmented, cluttered, and consolidated media environment. Alternative media competition, increasing production costs, a declining international marketplace, a weak off-net syndication landscape, and digital video recorders (DVRs) like TiVo have fundamentally rewritten broadcast television rules. Situated in a context of falling ratings, a growing cultural conservatism under a Bush White House, and fears of Federal Communication Commission (FCC) indecency fines in the wake of the Janet Jackson/Justin Timberlake Super Bowl incident, bottom-line-obsessed and risk-adverse media conglomerates have forced their broadcast subsidiaries to rethink their methods for doing business.

Broadcast programming is not the only sector affected by these industrial developments; so is advertising. For what is the nation's largest national medium, only CBS and UPN posted revenue gains, and very marginal ones, at the 2004–5 upfronts. Marketers, in fact, took their advertising dollars to the top-tier cable outlets before negotiating with broadcasters. Broadcasters are also seeing more of their ad dollars expended on newer media platforms (Internet, video games, cell phones). These numbers reveal a growing disenchantment with broadcast television's cost and value. Even though the combined prime-time ratings for NBC, CBS and ABC fell 19 percent between the 1999–2000 and 2003–4 seasons, the three networks' prime-time advertising revenue rose 18 percent, a differential that Sandy Grushow believes will no longer be tolerated.[13] "Undoubtedly, advertisers at some point are going to be unwilling to pay more for less. Networks have to figure out a way to open an alternative revenue stream."[14] The revenue streams currently exploited by the broadcast networks and their parent companies—DVDs, product integration, sponsorship, subscription-based video on demand (SVOD)—reflect not only viewer erosion but a growing skepticism over the effectiveness of the thirty-second commercial. By 2009, researchers say that 44 percent of American households will have some form of DVR that allows viewers to fast-forward through commercials.[15] It is only a matter of time, many suggest, before the thirty-second spot is dead.

While not completely successful without *Friends* and *Frasier* on the schedule in fall 2004, NBC's programming strategies and practices reflected a network acclimating itself to a cluttered, conglomerated media landscape. To illustrate NBC's attempts to respond to a new broadcast model, this essay analyzes twelve series aired on the network in the fall of 2004: *American Dreams, The Apprentice, The Biggest Loser, Dateline: NBC, Father of the Pride, Hawaii, Joey, LAX, Las Vegas, Medical Investigation, Scrubs,* and *Will & Grace.* This mix of scripted comedies and dramas, reality shows, and news magazines reveals the increasingly murky blend of entertainment and advertising, news and marketing, first-runs and repeats that characterizes American television in the twenty-first century. Cross-promotion of talent within the corporate family, new launching, scheduling, and repurposing strategies, and the development of new revenue streams are just some of the techniques NBC used in this competitive media marketplace. Ultimately, these innovations could neither resurrect floundering shows nor forge hit ones on NBC.

Synergy and Cross-Promotion

Any discussion of NBC's most recent programming practices must begin with the corporate-dominated marketplace of U.S. television. Its vertically and horizontally integrated media empires and their television subsidiaries include Viacom (CBS, UPN), Disney (ABC), News Corporation (Fox), Time Warner (The WB), and NBC Universal. According to David Croteau and William Hoynes (2001, 109–10), such media giants pursue three core business strategies. First, they look to maximize profits from their vast media holdings. Second, they seek to lower costs by improving efficiency and streamlining departments. And third, they reduce risk by fully utilizing and combining their assets into an integrated media strategy. With access to tremendous amounts of investment capital and numerous distribution channels and exhibition sites, these conglomerates can develop predictable and profitable economies of scale.

With the merger of GE and VUE, NBC became the last commercial broadcast network to affiliate with a major Hollywood film studio (Universal Studios and its art house subsidiary, Focus Features). Like its corporate brethren, NBC Universal's holdings extend to other media outlets. It owns cable networks (USA, Bravo, Trio, CNBC, MSNBC, Sci Fi Channel, Telemundo, and Mun2), television production companies (NBC and Universal), television stations (NBC and Telemundo O&Os), amusement parks and attractions (Universal Studios parks in California, Florida, Japan, and Spain and the family entertainment complex City Walk), Universal Home Entertainment, Universal Music Group, and Vivendi Universal video games. When NBC Universal synergistically cross-promotes and cross-pollinates a single product across these once-unrelated business entities, it increases the scope and reach of a product and reduces its economic risk. "The theory behind media conglomeration," states Robert McChesney (2004), "is the profit whole is greater than the sum of the profit parts" (184–85).

Synergies of cross-promotion and cross-pollination drove a lot of the media activity in NBC's fall lineup. Across NBC's sitcoms, dramas, reality shows, news magazines, and specials, extensive cross-promotion of NBC's and NBC Universal's products was deployed to attract attention. Sometimes cross-promotions are simple intertextualities, as in the *Joey* episode "Joey and the Nemesis," which refers back to Drake Ramoray, Joey's fictional character in *Days of Our Lives* (an NBC daytime soap opera) from the second season of *Friends*.[16] More often, NBC directly integrates already-existing NBC Universal properties into the narratives of their shows. *The Apprentice* features various cross-promotions, some subtle, others blatant. John McEnroe's appearance at Arthur Ashe Stadium to play tennis with the task-winning team in "Lights! Camera! Transaction!" made no mention of his talk show on CNBC (the now-canceled *McEnroe Show*).[17] However, boxer Sugar Ray Leonard openly promoted his upcoming NBC boxing reality series *The Contender* (with Sylvester Stallone) to the Lincoln Center Alice Tully Hall audience on the final three-hour "Decision Time" episode of *The Apprentice*, even though his appearance had nothing to with determining the winner.[18]

Other than the typical promotional spots for NBC's shows, cross-pollination in advertising included commercials for Bravo's *Project Runway* and Sci Fi Channel's *Ghost Hunters* during NBC shows[19] as well as an "NBC DVD Spotlight" of *Eternal Sunshine of the Spotless Mind* situated within "The Longest Day" episode of *LAX*.[20] Marketing the following day's release of the Focus Features film with clips and interviews of stars Jim Carrey, Kate Winslet, and Kirsten Dunst, the ad's claim of "highlighting this week's best DVD" exemplifies the current trend of blurring the distinction between the entertainment and commercial sectors that formerly was the practice mainly of MTV or E! Disguising its synergistic practices more surreptitiously is the "Montecito Lancers" episode of *Las Vegas*. Upon seeing the arrival of A&M recording artists Black Eyed Peas before their performance at the casino, the casino's head of security, Josh Duhamel (Danny McCoy), proclaims, "I love them."[21] In this case, synergy supersedes storytelling as characterization and narrative take a back seat to the cross-promotion of these Universal Music Group artists. Non–NBC Universal properties also perform in concert on *Las Vegas* (Clint Black, The Polyphonic Spree, Michael Bublé) and are given a similarly flattering reception, but seeing James Caan, who plays president of operations, bounce up and down to the Black Eyed Peas' "Let's Get It Started" might be taking synergy just a little too far.

However, the most prominent examples of cross-pollination in NBC prime time take place on *Dateline: NBC*. Masquerading as news reports, "advertorials," which blend editorials and advertisements, serve as promotional vehicles for NBC Universal's properties. Entire programs or program segments are devoted to interviews with media celebrities who play some role in the NBC Universal empire. *Dateline* devoted five hours of programming to the season finale of *The Apprentice* and series finales of *Friends* and *Frasier* during the May 2004 sweeps. The following fall, these advertorials continued with stories focusing on Ellen Degeneres, whose syndicated talk show, *The Ellen Degeneres Show*, airs on NBC's owned-and-operated stations; Carolyn Kepcher, Donald Trump's right-hand woman on *The Apprentice* and author of the new book *Carolyn 101: Lessons from "The Apprentice's" Straight Shooter;* and Jane Pauley, ex-*Dateline* and *Today* anchor and host of her new syndicated talk show produced and distributed by NBC Universal Television. Even the program on tiger-mauled Roy Horn (of Siegfried and Roy fame)—one of many *Dateline* stories covering more sensationalized topics like Princess Diana's secret tapes or Michael Jackson's pedophilia charges[22]—was itself a cross-promotion for *Father of the Pride*, an animated series about the magicians and their lions.[23]

Narrated by NBC News reporter Maria Shriver under the banner of NBC Entertainment rather than NBC News, *Siegfried and Roy: The Miracle* symbolizes the blurring of news and entertainment programs in an age of media conglomeration. No longer autonomous loss leaders within a television company, news divisions are now a logical and lucrative outcome of a corporate commitment to synergy (McChesney 2004, 85). The news, according to Leonard Downie Jr. and Robert G. Kaiser in *The News about the News: American Journalism in Peril*, is now "an extension of [a conglomerate's] entertainment businesses and a way to promote them. . . . 'Infotainment' [is] a better prime-time product than old-fashioned entertainment—much cheaper to produce, easy for a network to control and attractive to advertisers" (25). Fluff pieces like *The Miracle* or the *Friends* special often outrate typical *Dateline* episodes featuring hard news or investigative journalism.[24] The adjustments made to *Dateline* in fall 2004 to produce even more celebrity interviews and cross-promotions made the newsmagazine not much different from its entertainment counterparts: *Today*, *The Tonight Show with Jay Leno*, *Late Night with Conan O'Brien*, and *Last Call with Carson Daly*.[25]

Programming and Scheduling Strategies

While synergy creates unique promotional and programming opportunities among a conglomerate's various media properties, the practice alone cannot help NBC or any broadcast network break through the media clutter. Greater competitive pressures from cable television and other viewing options have forced NBC to rethink the marketing, launching, and scheduling of its shows just to stop people from switching the channel. In fall 2004, NBC borrowed many long-standing programming strategies from the cable industry while exploiting the more traditional broadcast means of attracting and keeping viewers.

NBC premiered many of its new series shortly after the conclusion of the Olympics in late August and early September. Although not as early in the season as Fox's successful summer launch of *The O.C.* in 2003, NBC's new shows—*Father of the Pride* (August 31), *Hawaii* (September 1), *Medical Investigation* (September 10), and *LAX* (September 13)—all aired ahead of the traditional fall premiere weeks (late September). Returning shows like *Scrubs* (August 31), *The Apprentice* (September 9), and *Will & Grace* (September 16) also premiered outside this period, and *The West Wing*'s season opened an entire two months later (November 10).

After NBC canceled three of its new series (*Hawaii*, *LAX*, and *Father of the Pride*), the network did not simply fill these time slots with reruns of current shows. Recent industry research showed that viewers were simply ignoring network reruns in favor of sampling other original series, many increasingly coming from the cable networks. When *The Sports Illustrated Swimsuit Model Search* took over the time slot in January 2005, the unscripted swimsuit competition was already part of a larger NBC programming strategy to premiere original, short-run reality series after the cancellation of new scripted dramas and comedies. *The $25 Million Dollar Hoax* replaced *LAX* in November, and *The Biggest Loser* succeeded another short-run reality series, *Last Comic Standing*, in October. Less costly than their scripted counterparts, these reality shows were basically low-risk, easily marketable shows waiting in the wings at NBC to be conveniently inserted anywhere into an open spot in the fall lineup.

These intermittent and often unforeseen scheduling strategies reflected a larger shift in NBC's programming model away from one that bundled premieres inside a two-week window toward a more flexible, year-round cable model. The November bow of the three-episode *$25 Million Dollar Hoax* and the October bow of the twelve-episode *The Biggest Loser* mirrored networks like FX and HBO, which often randomly or unorthodoxly unveiled new seasons of their shows throughout the year. For instance, in 2004, FX premiered *The Shield* in March, *Nip/Tuck* in June, and *Rescue Me* in July. NBC's two mid-fall replacements even replicated cable's series orders. Every season of *The Sopranos* lasts only thirteen episodes, while FX's shows range from thirteen to sixteen, far fewer than the broadcast network's commitment of twenty-two to twenty-four episodes per season.

Like *The Sopranos*, NBC aired the entire run of *The Biggest Loser* over thirteen uninterrupted weeks (except for a week break during Christmas) rather than spreading the show out over a thirty-five-week season like most broadcast series. For reality shows, including *The Apprentice* and *Fear Factor*, this is quite common, since many unscripted dramas are limited-run, half-season orders of episodes in which individuals or teams compete for a prize (a job with Donald Trump or $50,000). Broadcasters, though, are increasingly adopting the practice for their scripted dramas in order to attract viewers. Most notably, ABC in the past few years has consecutively aired original episodes of its thirteen-week miniseries *Kingdom Hospital* as well as its long-running show *NYPD Blue*. In fall 2004, NBC employed this strategy in a limited sense, advertising "the first of six all-new episodes of *ER*" during an episode of *Joey*.

This shift certainly does not suggest that reruns of scripted dramas and comedies on the broadcast networks are disappearing; they still make up of the bulk of nonsweeps and summer months. However, as NBC moves toward a year-round schedule, the network has recycled and recrafted its rerun programming in more immediate and imaginative ways to amortize the high costs of its television shows. NBC's practice of "repurposing" its programming under corporate parent NBC Universal comes in many forms. The network has been gradually adopting cable's economic model for repeats by playing second and third runs of the episodes the same week. These repeats aired primarily on Saturday, the least-watched night of television and one for which the networks have almost completely abandoned original programming except for stunts, sports, and theatrical films. Reruns of just-aired episodes from *The Apprentice* and the *Law & Order* franchise frequently played on this evening, competing against other network hits like CBS's *Survivor: Vanuatu* and ABC's *Lost* and *Desperate Housewives*.

For *The Apprentice* on Saturday, NBC reedited the show to include more "boardroom" footage than its Thursday airing, but the network shortly disbanded this unique but low-rated strategy after only six episodes. Even so, NBC Universal maximized its investment in *The Apprentice* by repurposing the show across its other media platforms: NBC.com offered exclusive video footage, ex-contestant commentaries, and clips from that week's episodes; MSNBC aired encores of Thursday's *The Apprentice* later that week, a repurposing strategy shared by USA Network with regard to *Law and Order: Criminal Intent* and *Law & Order: Special Victims Unit.*

Often NBC ran ninety-minute episodes of *The Apprentice* as one of the many other scheduling and programming tactics that the network employed to prevent channel surfing and curb viewer erosion in fall 2004. NBC had first offered expanded versions of episodes in February 2001 when it "supersized" *Friends* to forty minutes to counter CBS's ploy of moving the second season of *Survivor* to 8:00 p.m. on Thursday to compete with *Friends*. In fall 2004, NBC occasionally supersized that same time slot, as in the September 16 "Must-See TV" airings of *Joey* (thirty-five minutes), *Will & Grace* (forty-four minutes), and *The Apprentice* (one hour and one minute). However, NBC more commonly expands episodes for "unscripted" shows like *The Apprentice*. With hours of extra footage on hand, reality producers, unlike scripted comedy or drama producers, can easily expand existing episodes at minimal cost to NBC and at no cost to the narrative flow of the show. Certain episodes of *The Biggest Loser, Last Comic Standing,* and *Fear Factor* were expanded to ninety-minute or two-hour lengths, or, as was the case with the finale of *The Apprentice* (as well as CBS's *Survivor* and Fox's *American Idol*), to three hours. Conversely, NBC started shows a little before or after the half and ended them early or late without alerting viewers. "Off-the-clock" programming allows for the insertion of more commercials into a hit show and forces viewers to watch shows live rather than on TiVo if they want to catch the entire episodes.

New Revenue Streams

Cable television is just one of the many competitive pressures that networks like NBC encounter in a cluttered media landscape. Broadcasters have had to accept not only smaller audience shares but smaller audiences, due to viewers' migration to other forms of entertainment (Internet, video games, cell phones). "There's no question lower numbers are more acceptable now," stated Fox Entertainment president Gail Berman. "[In the past], a 20 share was just unacceptable—that's abject failure. And now a 20 share for us is a huge success. The business has changed, no question about it."[26] As a result, the networks have had to seek out alternative sources of revenue and advertising opportunities to make up for viewer erosion and rising production costs.

DVD sales have proven to be one such windfall, a strategy that the networks' corporate parents quickly learned from the theatrical film business. "There's not a sector of the entertainment industry," says Scott Hettrick, editor-in-chief of *Video Business*, "to which DVD is not a significant, if not the dominant contributor of revenue."[27] In 2004, only 21 percent of studio feature-film revenues came from the box office while 63 percent came from movies sold to retail stores, a majority of that from DVDs. The discs generated a 66 percent profit margin for the studios and $15 billion in sales in the United States alone.[28] To rise above the noise and clutter in the marketplace, the studios now spend comparable amounts of money on marketing DVD and theatrical films. The creation and implementation of DVD "extras" or supplemental features has become a driving force in these campaigns and a cottage industry in itself, often generating multiple editions of the same film (e.g., the *Lord of the Rings* trilogy).

While PriceWaterhouseCoopers estimates that DVD sales growth will drop to mid-single digits by 2007–8, the firm expects continued growth in TV DVDs.[29] Sales for TV DVDs in 2004 skyrocketed to $2.3 billion, a 62 percent increase from the previous year, helping to offset weak off-net syndication revenue and international sales as production costs continued to increase.[30] Television series, once released on video four to five years after a show's airing, are now regularly available on DVD before the next season premiere. And as with films, consumers are purchasing second and third versions of the same television shows: *The "Mad about You" Collection* and *Family Guy: The Freakin' Sweet Collection* are best-of episodes—many previously compiled in earlier DVDS—now filled with extras that were handpicked by its cast and creator.[31] It is not surprising, then, that NBC Universal would take advantage of this revenue stream and market this medium alongside NBC's programming lineup. Previous seasons of *The Apprentice, Will & Grace,* and all three *Law & Order* series were promoted during the Olympics and released a few weeks before the their fall premieres. *Boomtown,* an NBC-produced series that only lasted the 2003–4 season, was released on DVD shortly after its cancellation and was subsequently advertised on NBC. *The Seinfeld Story,* which aired on Thanksgiving Day during November sweeps, was specifically designed around the show's DVD's debut. Part documentary, part nostalgia as the stars, creators, and executives reminisced about the series that had anchored NBC's Thursday night lineup from 1993 to 1998, *The Seinfeld Story* was no more than an hour-long infomercial for the Sony DVD release of the series two days earlier.

Digital video recorders (DVRs) or personal video recorders (PVRs), like TiVo, may cut into DVD sales and rentals, since consumers can store all their favorite shows on a hard drive and play them at their convenience. Yet it is the consumer's ability to fast-forward or "TiVo" through commercials using DVRs that poses a grave threat to the economic basis of ad-supported television: the value of an advertising spot. Research shows that consumers watch 20 percent to 30 percent more television after getting a DVR but use it to skip about 70 percent of ads.[32] With DVR penetration expected to reach 44 percent by 2009, networks have recently had to figure out new ways to finance their programs and market the products of advertisers. "The 30-second business is still robust," remarked Bill Abbot, executive vice president of national ad sales for the Hallmark Channel, in August 2004, "but we're very much in the game of trying to provide solutions to advertisers beyond that."[33]

To recapture ad dollars lost to alternative forms of media content, the broadcast networks now look for ways that companies can develop a consistent and recognizable presence in the shows themselves. "Embedded advertising" has become a new revenue stream for the networks, one that NBC gainfully utilized in the fall 2004 season. Two of its strategies date back to beginning of television: sponsorship and product placement. Sponsorship, once the medium's predominant advertising model for shows like *Texaco Star Theater* or *Pepsi Cola Playhouse,* had been phased out of commercial television by the mid-1960s in the wake of the *Twenty-One* quiz show scandals when networks succeeded in wresting scheduling and production control away from advertisers, initiating the practice of spot advertising. Four decades and a deregulatory climate later, sponsorship has sneaked back onto prime time, sometimes in name (WB's *Pepsi Smash*) but more often in a bumper following a show's credits. Its positioning provides advertisers a greater degree of control of the media environment than traditional thirty-second spots, creating visibility of the product free from other advertising clutter and TiVo fast-forwarding. On NBC, the "Two of a Kind" episode of *Las Vegas* was "sponsored in part by Mazda." And Toyota sponsored *Father of the Pride*'s premiere ("What's Black and White and Depressed All Over?") commercial-free, receiving an on-screen identification in behind-the-scenes segments bracketing both ends of the show.

Product placement, in its most basic form, also appeared on NBC. A list of advertisers often surfaces during a show's credits, preceded with "furnished by," whether or not you notice the products in the shows themselves. GMC trucks can be seen in *Medical Investigation,* Hewlett-Packard products are omnipresent in *Las Vegas,* and Tempur-Pedic mattress systems are visible in *The West Wing.* However, the few seconds these products appear on screen are hardly an alternative to a thirty-second spot, especially in an age of DVRs, remote controls, and multichannel viewing options. "Advertisers want to be on the front end figuring out how best to integrate their products into programming," stated Laura Caracciolo-Davis, senior vice president at the Starcom Entertainment media agency. "At the same time, the networks are getting smarter about owning the space between the commercials. They want to commoditize product placement."[34]

Enter instead "branded entertainment," the fusion of entertainment content and brand marketing that CBS chair Les Moonves predicts will be carried in some form in 75 percent of all prime-time scripted shows by the end of the decade.[35] Branded entertainment immerses a product into the content of a show, weaving its message within the script and scenery of that show. These in-program opportunities have grown alongside reality shows over the past few years due to the genre's limited rerun value and its need for real-world products. On one hand, Coca Cola's involvement with Fox's *American Idol* in 2002 clearly established the huge payout possibilities of branded entertainment, which, except for a few of the big hits, still does not have the development and production costs of scripted programming. On the other hand, American Express's participation in NBC's *The Restaurant* in 2003 demonstrated its pitfalls. For branded entertainment to work, it must feel organic to the show without being too obvious. Product placement on *The Restaurant,* however, according to *Advertising Age* editor Scott Donaton, was "aggressive, intrusive, and clunky": instead of seamlessly integrating American Express into the narrative of the opening of a New York eatery, it felt "crass and phony" in a way that would undermine viewers' trust in the show.[36]

Mark Burnett, the creator of *The Restaurant* as well as *Survivor*, did not repeat this mistake with *The Apprentice*. A touchstone in symbiosis between entertainment and advertising, *The Apprentice* perfectly integrates corporate America into the tasks performed by the contestants, who are each vying for a $250,000-a-year job working for Donald Trump. "*The Apprentice* is supposed to be about business so it's very appropriate to have these big companies with name brands testing these young guns who want to make it big."[37] For season two of *The Apprentice* in fall 2004, companies like Procter & Gamble, QVC, Petco, Levi Strauss, and Pepsi paid $1 million each (for season three in Spring 2005, that number reached $2–3 million) to have their products displayed prominently in the episode.[38] Instead of employing a traditional product placement, the show had contestants spend many on-air minutes during a single episode discussing the marketing or development of a corporate product. For example, in "The Pepsi Challenged," that week's task was to design a bottle as well as a campaign for Pepsi's new soft drink, Pepsi Edge.[39] Throughout the episode, the teams were shown manufacturing the prototype, discussing marketing slogans, selling their idea to executives, and of course, drinking tons of Pepsi products.

It is not quite clear how much money, if any, NBC received from the product integration on *The Apprentice*—Mark Burnett produced the show and sold all the brand extensions himself.[40] The success of such reality shows has led the major broadcast and cable networks to assert more control over branded entertainment deals, battling producers over integration rights, coveted ad inventory, and license fees.[41] For branded entertainment to be most profitable for the networks, the shows must be produced in house, opening up another valuable revenue stream for their corporate parents. NBC pursued this course most successfully in fall 2004 with *The Biggest Loser*, a joint venture between 3 Ball productions, 25/7 Productions, and Reveille LLC, an independent studio that was also responsible for *The Restaurant* and Bravo's *Blow Dry*. *The Biggest Loser* pitted teams of obese contestants against each other to see which one could drop the greatest percentage of weight and body fat. Incorporated into the series was the gym franchise 24 Hour Fitness, whose circular logo showed up during training, competitions, and weigh-ins. Although *The Biggest Loser* was not what Randy Falco, group president of NBC, called "upscale reality"—attracting an affluent audience profile like *The Apprentice*—it still doubled the rating in adults aged eighteen through forty-nine that NBC had been averaging in the Tuesday time period a year earlier.[42]

More upscale was NBC's brand partnership with Campbell's Soup Co. and Scholastic magazine to promote *American Dreams*. The companies sponsored an essay contest—which offered a grand prize of a $100,000 college scholarship and walk-on roles for the winner and a friend—that was mirrored by a similar essay contest on the show. Campbell's advertised the series on forty-two million tomato soup cans and in print, radio, and television advertising, while NBC integrated the soup into numerous episodes of the series.[43] Integrated advertising like this, said series creator Jonathan Prince, "present[ed] an opportunity for us to stay on the air in a way unlike any other show."[44] Another sophisticated product integration in *American Dreams* was Ford Motor Co.'s commercial-free sponsorship of "Tidings of Comfort and Joy" to advertise the new 2005 Mustang.[45] A two-minute introduction (featuring a 1966 Ford Mustang morphing into the newer model) and a few product placements were not nearly as elaborate as the four-minute "movie" that followed the episode. Both the movie and the just-seen conclusion of the episode featured a soldier returning from war and, upon his homecoming, receiving a Ford Mustang (2005 vs. 1966) from his father. "Product placement is nothing new, but what Ford has done is unique," said Vipe Desai, president of the marketing agency Propaganda HQ. "We're going to see more of it. It's a sign of creativity—you've got brands now that need to expose their consumers to their product in a different way."[46]

The between-show entertainments that Desai speaks of are referred to as micromovies, situation commercials, or "situ-mercials," a burgeoning form of product integration that place shows within products rather than products within shows. These ads may reflect the story lines, play off the aesthetics, or feature characters from a series in their pitch. Ford had already twice bookended two season premieres of Fox's *24* with action-packed spots featuring a character named Mr. Bauer (though not played by Kiefer Sutherland).[47] NBC utilized this form of brand partnership in the aforementioned "Pepsi Challenged" episode of *The Apprentice*. In this situ-mercial, just-fired Andy Litinsky sits in a taxicab, holding a can of Pepsi Edge, and proclaims, "I can't believe he fired me, in front of millions of people. I'll never get a job again." The camera then cuts to reveal the driver as Raj Bhakta, an already-fired contestant, replying, "Yes, you will." The ad promoted an online sweepstakes for a chance to win one of a hundred limited-edition replicas of the winning Pepsi Edge bottle from the show and a grand prize of two tickets to *The Apprentice* finale in New York City.[48] Earlier in the season, Procter & Gamble offered the same first-place prize in a similar interactive marketing spot during "Send in the Crowns" for its new Crest toothpaste flavor, mint-vanilla.[49] The ad featured P & G executives asking viewers to go to crest.com and enter an essay contest about how they would have promoted the new Crest flavor, a project just undertaken by the *Apprentice* contestants.[50] Almost fifty thousand consumers logged on to each corporation's Web site. Such response suggests that situ-mercials can break through the media clutter and neutralize, to some extent, TiVo technology, providing television networks like NBC a unique, new advertising form.

Conclusion

At the Television Critics Association winter press tour in January 2005, Kevin Reilly, NBC's president of entertainment, wryly pronounced his assessment of the network's fall 2004 season: "Let me jump into the newsflash of the day: This Fall was challenging for NBC. Things did get tougher and maybe even a little tougher than we expected."[51] It only got worse for NBC in spring 2005. By the end of May sweeps, NBC's prime-time ratings fell 17 percent among eighteen- to forty-nine-year-olds, dropping the network from first to fourth place in total viewers in this demographic from the same time the previous year.[52] As a result, NBC was forced to cut its CPM rates—the rates it charges to reach one thousand viewers—by 2 to 3 percent and was the only network to do so.[53] Advertising sales for NBC correspondingly decreased 30 percent at the upfront market, translating into a $900 million shortfall from the previous year's $2.9 billion. Except for the moderate success of the mid-season replacement drama *Medium,* none of NBC's new shows in 2004–5 proved to be hits. Along with *Medium,* the only returning shows in the 2005–6 lineup were *Joey, The Biggest Loser,* and the midseason entry *The Office,* the American remake of the hit BBC series.

However, NBC still retained its spot at the top of *Broadcasting and Cable*'s annual ranking of the twenty-five largest TV networks. Network revenue totaled $5.1 billion, an increase of $600 million, or 13.5 percent, over the previous year.[54] Being without *Friends* for only four months of the year and accruing $900 million in ad sales for the Olympics certainly inflated these numbers, suggesting that the network would decline further in 2005. Even so, NBC's other day parts remain immensely lucrative, helping to provide a third of parent NBC Universal's $2.6 billion in operating profit in 2004, $860 million of that earned in the fourth quarter.[55] NBC Universal chair and CEO Bob Wright elaborates:

> To have dipped by only a single-digit percentage post-*Friends* is actually fairly impressive, and don't forget, we still deliver the most affluent and difficult to reach audience, which is extremely important to advertisers. Our primetime planning for this season took into account that *Friends* and *Frasier* had left our schedule, and as a result we remain profitable. Primetime is important, but it's also balanced by the *Today* show and late-night, which are extraordinarily strong performers. Our competitors don't have that kind of balance. The network is now balanced by all the NBC Universal businesses—film, cable, production, home entertainment, international distribution, the theme parks, and more—so the impact of a cycle like this one is less than it would have been a year ago.[56]

Despite a disappointing 2004–5 season, NBC still possessed the highest-indexing drama *(The West Wing),* comedy *(Will & Grace),* and reality show *(The Apprentice)* for adults aged eighteen to forty-nine with an income of $75,000-plus and four years of college, a demographic that fetches top dollars from advertisers like American Express and Volvo. The *Today* show generates nearly $300 million in profit,[57] and NBC's *Nightly News* remains in first place with an average audience of 10.21 million viewers, even with the transition from Tom Brokaw to Brian Williams as its anchor.[58] These figures, viewed alongside strong worldwide box office for Universal's *Meet the Fockers, The Bourne Supremacy,* and *Van Helsing,* as well as the DVD releases of the latter two films, suggest that NBC can weather any fluctuations in audience ratings and television advertising.

The seemingly endless array of synergies and product integrations that currently pervade broadcast and cable television, however, is not celebrated by those outside the industry. In January 2005, Democratic commissioner Michael Copps of the FCC addressed the National Association of Television Program Executives conference about the stifling of creativity and loss of public interest protection on the television airwaves under media conglomeration.[59] "Years ago," Copps stated, "some of the experts told us not to worry because the rapidly-expanding multi-channel universe of cable TV would save independent programming. It didn't happen. Instead, 90% of the top cable channels are owned by the same companies that own the TV networks and the cable distribution systems." He added, "More channels are great, but when they're all owned by the same people, we're not doing justice to diversity and localism and competition." Copps made a plea against media deregulation with an appeal to the FCC to set aside a certain number of prime-time hours for programming from independent producers.

Current debates over broadcast indecency in the wake of the Janet Jackson/ Justin Timberlake Super Bowl and *Monday Night Football/Desperate Housewives* incidents cloud these very concerns when they should be at the forefront of public debate. The new programming and advertising models employed by media conglomerates like NBC Universal to combat clutter, channel proliferation, and viewer erosion are primarily intended to benefit shareholders, not the public interest. Increased in-house production does not tend to breed competition. Cross-promotion and brand partnership do not constitute diversity. Viewers now witness between eighteen and twenty-one minutes of nonprogramming (commercials, public service announcements, promos) in a broadcast hour; twenty years ago it was nine-and-a half minutes per hour. And these figures do not even include product integration. Television is a "very special industry," said Michael Copps. It is not just a commodity traded between corporations and advertisers, it is "the people's business, too." The growth of Internet blogs in the first half of the decade and the bipartisan public outcry over the FCC's loosening of the remaining media ownership restrictions suggest that Americans are deeply concerned about how the airwaves are being used for entertainment, advertising, and news. NBC once boasted its network as "Where the Quality Shows." Now the network is brought to you in living "clutter." If NBC hopes to return to its glory years of the 1980s, it must once again observe the credo of its legendary chair and CEO Grant Tinker during that time: "First be good. Then be first."[60]

Notes

1. Bill Keveney, "*West Wing* in a New Campaign for Ratings, Respect," *USA Today*, October 20, 2004, 4D.

2. Brooks Barnes, "Less Seen TV: NBC Viewership Takes a Tumble," *Wall Street Journal*, October 13, 2004.

3. Compare NBC's ratings to those of CBS, which was down 1.2 percent in households but up 11.1 percent in the eighteen- to forty-nine-year-old demographic. Claire Atkinson, "NBC's Grip on Prime Time Slips as Young Viewers Flee," *Advertising Age*, November 2004, 4.

4. NBC was down from a 4.4/12 average in November 2003 to a 4.0/10 average in adults aged eighteen to forty-nine in November 2004. Also during this time frame, NBC lost 11 percent of its adults aged eighteen through thirty-four, 8 percent of its adults aged twenty-five to fifty-four, and 11 percent of teens. See Christopher Lisotta, "Sweeps Youth Elixir for CBS," *Television Week*, December 6, 2004, 1.

5. Claire Atkinson, "A Closer Look at Must-See TV," *Broadcasting and Cable*, November 29, 2004, 12.

6. Verne Gay, "Apprentice Getting Old?" *Newsday*, December 16, 2004, C1+.

7. Leon Lazaroff, "NBC Ratings Plummet in Wake of *Friends, Frasier* Curtain Calls," *Chicago Tribune*, December 2, 2004.

8. Denise Martin, "Cable's Neat Sweep," *Daily Variety*, December 2004, 6.

9. Ibid. The Cabletelevision Advertising Bureau put these numbers at 51.6 for cable and 46.7 for broadcast. See Mike Reynolds, "Cable Sweeps Up," *Multichannel News*, December 6, 2004, 1+.

10. Martin, "Cable's Neat Sweep"; Reynolds, "Cable Sweeps Up."

11. John Dempsey, "Cable Snares Webs," *Daily Variety*, December 27, 2004, 5.

12. Rob Owen, "The World of TV is in State of Flux," *Pittsburgh Post-Gazette*, January 22, 2004, B1+.

13. "NBC Ratings Fall Good for Buyers," *Advertising Age*, November 15, 2004, 24.

14. Josef Adalian, "Primetime Pickle," *Daily Variety*, January 2, 2004.

15. Mary McNamara, "All Alone, off the Beaten Wavelength," *Los Angeles Times* September 5, 2004.

16. *Joey*, "Joey and the Nemesis," air date October 14, 2004.

17. *The Apprentice*, "Lights! Camera! Transaction!" air date October 7, 2004.

18. *The Apprentice*, "Decision Time," air date December 16, 2004.

19. *Las Vegas*, "Silver Star," air date November 29, 2004; *Medical Investigation*, "Progeny," air date October 1, 2004

20. *LAX*, "The Longest Day," air date September 27, 2004.

21. *Las Vegas*, "Montecito Lancers," air date November 1, 2004.

22. *Dateline NBC*, air date September 2, 2004.

23. *Siegfried & Roy: The Miracle*, air date September 15, 2004.

24. David Bauder, "NBC Dismisses Criticism for Run of *Dateline* Entertainment Shows," *Associated Press*, May 28, 2004.

25. See Michelle Grippi, " Season of Change at Newsmags," *Television Week*, September 20, 2004, 1+.

26. Owen, "World of TV," B1+.

27. Sharon Waxman, "Studios Rush to Cash in on DVD Boom," *New York Times*, April 20, 2004, B1.

28. Jon Gertner, "Box Office in a Box," *New York Times Magazine*, November 14, 2004, sec. 6, 104+.

29. Merissa Marr and Joe Flint, "DVDs Are Finally Paramount," *Wall Street Journal*, February 23, 2005, B2.

30. Jennifer Netherby and Scott Hettrick, "Disc Bliss for Biz," *Daily Variety*, January 5, 2005, 1+.

31. Susanne Ault, "TV Titles Now Packed with Extra Features," *DVD Exclusive*, February 2005, 6.

32. Anthony Bianco et al., "The Vanishing Mass Market: New Technology. Product Proliferation. Fragmented Media. Get Ready: It's a Whole New World," *Business Week*, July 12, 2004, 18.

33. T. L. Stanley, "Networks Bet Big on Mini Movies," *Advertising Age*, August 9, 2004, 19.

34. Leon Lazaroff, "Brought to You by . . . ," *Chicago Tribune*, June 25, 2004.

35. Lianne George, "Is Kiefer Sutherland Trying to Sell You Something?" *Maclean's*, February 21, 2005, 30+.

36. Scott Donaton, "*Restaurant* Serves up Lesson in How Not to Integrate Brands," *Advertising Age*, August 11, 2003, 14.

37. Meg James, "Products Are Stars in New Ad Strategy," *Los Angeles Times*, December 2, 2004, C1+.

38. Wayne Friedman, "Placement Bonanza Remains Elusive," *Television Week*, October 11, 2004, 22.

39. *The Apprentice*, "The Pepsi Challenged," air date November 25, 2004.

40. Claire Atkinson, "New Reality Dawns for TV Economics," *Advertising Age*, September 2004, 75; Claire Atkinson, "Marketers Dive into *Apprentice 3*," *Advertising Age*, November 29, 2004, 1+.

41. Gail Schiller, "Television," *Hollywood Reporter*, Feb 10, 2005, www.hollywoodreporter.com.

42. Bill Carter, "Reality Intrudes on a Spring Rite of Network Television," *New York Times*, April 19, 2004, C1.

43. Gail Schiller, "Television," *Hollywood Reporter*, September 1, 2004, www.hollywoodreporter.com.

44. Adalian, "*Dreams* Cut Short in NBC Sweeps Shift," *Daily Variety*, February 2005, 6.

45. *American Dreams*, "Tidings of Comfort and Joy," air date November 21, 2004. See Liz Halloran, "Mini-Movies Sneak past Ad Zappers," *Hartford Courant*, November 23, 2004, A1; Wayne Friedman, "Ford Inks NBC's *Dreams* Deal," *Television Week*, October 2004, 1A.

46. Halloran, "Mini-Movies."

47. Brian Steinberg, "Newest TV Spinoffs: 'Situ-mercials,'" *Wall Street Journal*, March 2, 2004, B11.

48. Stuart Elliot, "Fired on Trump Show; Hired for a Pepsi Ad," *New York Times*, November 29, 2004, C1; Amy Johannes, "Pepsi Sweeps Sends Winner to *Apprentice* Finale," *Promo Magazine.com*, December 8, 2004.

49. *The Apprentice*, "Send in the Crowns," air date September 23, 2004.

50. Patricia Odell, "*The Apprentice* Sparks Record Interest in Crest Toothpaste," *Promo Magazine.com*, September 30, 2004.

51. Rob Owen, "NBC Acknowledges Troubles but Shows Hope for Future," *Pittsburgh Post-Gazette*, January 22, 2005, C8.

52. Josef Adalian and Michael Schneider, "Peacock Feathers Ruffled," *Daily Variety*, July 25, 2005, 1+.

53. Michael Learmonth, "NBC Upfront Falls 30%," *Daily Variety*, June 21, 2005, 5.

54. John M. Higgins, "Still Strutting after All These Years," *Broadcasting and Cable*, December 13, 2004, 20+.

55. Meg James, "The Peacock Network Seeks to Reverse Slide," *Los Angeles Times*, November 1, 2004, C1; Pamela McClintock and Ben Fritz, "NBC U Drives Record GE Earnings in 4th Q," *Daily Variety*, January 24, 2005, 12.

56. Brooks Barnes, "Wright's Hollywood Script," *Wall Street Journal*, December 22, 2004, B4.

57. John M. Higgins, "Early-Morning Drama; NBC's *Today* Show Slips, ABC's GMA Gains," *Broadcasting and Cable*, January 31, 2005, 8; Scott Collins, "Networks' New Wave of News," *Los Angeles Times*, December 2, 2004.

58. Michael Learmonth, "Network News in Tight Ratings Race," *Daily Variety*, February 16, 2005, 26.

59. Copps's speech is available at the FCC Web site, http://hraunfoss.fcc.gov/edocs_public/attachmatch/DOC-256292A1.doc.

60. Andrew Wallenstein, "NBC Vows It'll Be 'Stronger in September,'" *Hollywood Reporter*, March 18, 2005, hollywoodreporter.com.

18

Network Nation

Writing Broadcasting History as Cultural History

MICHELE HILMES AND SHAWN VANCOUR

When the editors at Oxford University Press in 1959 commissioned Columbia University professor Erik Barnouw to write a history of broadcasting in the United States, they were building on their recent experience in England. There, the press, with the cooperation of the British Broadcasting Corporation, had persuaded noted historian Asa Briggs to take on a similar task of social historiography. Briggs became the semiofficial chronicler of the nation's broadcasting system over the first seven decades of its existence, producing five volumes between 1961 and 1995, none less than four hundred pages long—and this despite the fact that British broadcasting consisted for most of this period of a single state-chartered corporation. At his disposal was the entire BBC Written Archives, a magnificent collection of materials documenting the BBC's internal and external communications from before its formation in 1922 up to the present time, staffed by formidably competent professional archivists (Kavanagh 2004). Briggs finished his first volume in 1961 and went on to write four more over a forty-year period. His project has been picked up by historian Jean Seaton, and a sixth volume on the history of the BBC should appear sometime soon.

Erik Barnouw faced a considerably different task. Broadcasting in the United States had no central national broadcasters, no public archive, and no established historian willing to take on the task of chronicling the chaotic, commercial, only semirespectable radio and television industry. U.S. broadcasting consisted of three major national networks, several smaller or regional ones, hundreds of local stations, and thousands of program producers, along with a host of ancillary businesses such as ratings measurement firms, advertising agencies, and a lively trade press, as well as a fairly tumultuous and complicated regulatory situation. Barnouw himself was not a trained historian but had started out as a scriptwriter for an advertising agency, moving to Columbia to teach radio but keeping his hand in as writer for prestigious shows such as *The Cavalcade of America* and *Theatre Guild of the Air.* During World War II he served with the Armed Forces Radio Service, returning to Columbia at war's end and publishing several books on radio and television. This background gave him an insider's edge, with a basic working knowledge of how the industry operated and what doors might be knocked on and sources consulted.

But where was U.S. broadcasting's archive? Or, more relevantly, *what* was U.S. broadcasting's archive? On what materials might a historian such as Barnouw draw, given the scope and complexity of his project? No centralized library preselected by the broadcaster itself awaited his attentions. In the introduction to his first volume, *A Tower in Babel* (1961), Barnouw affirmed radio and television's importance as vital forms of both American industry and American culture but stressed that the history of these media was one of struggles waged by numerous individuals within a broad range of social institutions. His task, he explained, was to trace "how the broadcast media have grown, both as instruments of expression and as industries; who has risen to leadership in them, and how; what these media have told us, and not told us, about ourselves and our world; what struggles have been fought, open and hidden, for their control. . . . Our chronicle will involve statesmen, mountebanks, teachers, salesmen, artists, wheeler-dealers, soldiers, saints, reporters, propagandists—and others" (5).

How does the historian begin to address this imposing collection of characters and questions? What sources does one consult, and where does one find them? Barnouw himself enjoyed access to a number of resources unavailable to earlier historians—resources that have continued to expand and multiply since his inaugural study of 1961. This chapter offers a necessarily brief survey of some of the key resources available to today's historians, with an eye toward fostering further study of a subject that has received insufficient elaboration in existing histories. While its status in today's media environment seems increasingly uncertain, the network played a central role in giving American broadcasting its form and substance over the course of the past century. The present chapter thus prefaces its survey of historical resources with a consideration of the subject that has formed the organizing axis for the essays included within this volume: the network as an object of historical analysis and dominant culture-producing mechanism within the national system of American broadcasting.

Broadcasting, Culture, and the Nation

Asa Briggs had no doubt as to where to look to find the heart of broadcasting in Great Britain: the BBC occupied that space preemptively. U.S. broadcasting offered no similar unified focus, and it is telling that the only comprehensive scholarly network history yet published recounts the story of the innovative but short-lived DuMont operation (Weinstein 2004).[1] Barnouw set himself the task of writing a history that spanned existing institutions, the networks among them, as the title of his second volume, *The Golden Web* (1968), indicates. Yet his three volumes also visit the

more powerful stations scattered across the country, the meeting rooms of advertising agencies, the halls of regulators, the production lots of Hollywood, and the
propaganda centers of the U.S. Information Agency and move outward to the society at large: its political centers, courtrooms, sporting events, battlefields, living
rooms, and every other place where radio and television made their presence felt.
Moreover, as his later book, *The Sponsor: Notes on a Modern Potentate* (1978), made clear,
for Barnouw it was ultimately the sponsors who drove the machine of American
broadcasting. All other institutions, the network included, functioned in his view as
either symptoms or supports of a market-based system that lurked behind or be-
neath American broadcasting's forms of cultural expression, with the sponsor as
their principal "author" and advertising their primary message. Here the network
fades into the middle distance as a broker or organizer and is rarely shown as a creative agent in its own right.

Such scholarly neglect of the network's centrifugal role in U.S. broadcasting's
overwhelmingly centripetal eighty-year history has affected the way in which American national culture has been understood. In nations such as Great Britain, the
national broadcasting system evolved into a powerful engine of national cultural
production (often in resistance to, among other things, the spread of market-driven
"American" culture) with a deliberate and well-thought-out mission of promoting
national identity and encouraging indigenous creativity. Not only did organizations
such as the BBC themselves produce programs that reflected and celebrated national cultural traditions, but they served as national conduits and promoters for a
wide range of other social and cultural rituals and events that brought the nation
together and created a common unifying experience of national solidarity for citizens across the land: major sporting events, addresses by central political figures,
celebrations of national holidays, the best of artistic performance, news about the
entire nation (Scannell and Cardiff 1991). They did this under a national mandate,
spelled out in official documents, supported by public funds, and reviewed by public
bodies. Often they relied on the "brute force of monopoly," in BBC head John
Reith's famous term, to compel a public to assemble around these devices and ex-
pressions of homogenous, centralized national culture. Nonindigenous cultural
products (as defined by the powers of the day) were limited by quota or fended off
altogether. Even when the introduction of competing systems (such as commercial
networks, cable, or satellite services) opened up the national imagination to outside
productions, state-sponsored broadcasters remained strong in most nations, taking
an active role as central institutions in their national cultures.

In the United States, broadcasting networks certainly provided programming
and infrastructure that served all of these same purposes, yet they did it under a
system that provided no clear national mandate or public funding, that based itself
(as described in chapter 1) on a highly dispersed system of private commercial stations, and that relied less on a centralized definition of what constituted American
culture than on the same principles of diversity and hybridity that underpinned
the society more generally: a de facto definition of American culture that matched

its heterogeneous and creole identity far better than any homogenizing definition or institution ever could. No wonder, however, that it was hard for outsiders to grasp its outlines—or even for insiders to do so, given the immense debates over what might more properly constitute the American system that have raged unabated since the medium's inception.

Yet there the American system stood, with the major networks at the heart of it, as rambling and chaotic a media system as any nation had managed to produce, yet one with remarkable staying power. And it produced a truly *popular* culture unique to the United States, but with tremendous appeal across the world. Linked tightly to that other center of American cultural production, Hollywood, yet with their own distinct spin and far more localized and domesticated articulations, the U.S. giant networks for more than eighty years bestrode the nation, telling Americans who they were and what the parameters of their culture might be at any given time, provoking debates and paroxysms of controversy about just such definitions, and representing the face of America to the world. By the 1990s they had begun to lose their central position as other venues eroded the domestic audience and new technologies of viewer choice turned the formerly mighty presences into just a few voices among many. Perhaps it is only now that we can see the networks for what they were and what they brought to twentieth-century culture.

What We Talk about When We Talk about Networks

How then to think about "the voice of the nation" in the dispersed world of American broadcasting? A network can be understood on a number of levels. On one level, it is a technological infrastructure—so many studios, control rooms, transmitters, receivers, towers, landlines, cameras, lights, and buildings to house them. On another it is an institution, meaning an organization with not only an economic but a social function, whose parameters can be seen in personnel, organizational structure, patterns of economic exchange, relationships with other social bodies (such as regulators, educators, politicians, and citizens), creative decision-making strategies, and presence in everyday life. A network can also be regarded as a matrix that brings a variety of forces into contact, each with an agenda that leaves a mark on the central product, the texts that are produced and disseminated, as well as the audiences assembled to view them. Thus the network mediates between advertisers, program producers, ratings organizations, regulators, and the public (among others) to produce not only texts but a scheduled flow of them, marked by characteristic patterns and practices.

Or a network can be seen in the images of itself that it produces: in logos, chimes, promos, screen markers, spokesmen and women, Web sites, and merchandise. A network might also be thought of (and sometimes promotes itself) as a kind of imaginary universe, populated with characters, stories, places, and celebrities, a world we enter into each Tuesday night or Saturday afternoon, often a more reassuringly familiar and comfortable world than the one we actually live in. And sometimes a network is just a corporation, a business with shares and assets that can be bought and sold by other corporations, as reported on the business pages. Networks can also function as semiofficial organs of the state, as they did in the United States during World War II, and as ambassadors of American culture around the globe, for better or worse. All of these definitions have come into play in the pages of this volume, and narratives that drive the stories they tell are predicated on the version that predominates.

But how do we as historians make the abstract concept of the network speak? Here today's historian encounters many of the same problems that beset Barnouw in defining the parameters for his own investigation. What resources are available for study, what sites of analysis are to be pursued? What, in short, is the nature of the archive? As corporate entities American networks have often served as producers of knowledge on their own behalf, issuing public reports and press releases, providing congressional testimony, and memorializing their own histories in documentaries and books. On the occasion of its seventy-fifth anniversary, NBC itself produced two volumes of retrospective history—self-promotional, to be sure, but full of information otherwise lost to today's historian (NBC 2002; O'Connell 1986). Nonetheless, to rely exclusively on the network to speak about its own past is to miss the fundamental characteristic that defines any network. While actively shaping broadcasting's forms of economic and cultural production, the network is by its very nature a diffuse formation, consolidating discourse but also dispersing it. Networks speak in places and in ways beyond what any official history can account for and provoke discourse within the larger social formation beyond what they can channel and control.

To view the network in this fashion is at once to facilitate and frustrate historical analysis: facilitate in that the resources for historical analysis are dramatically expanded; frustrate in that, like Barnouw, we move beyond the hagiography of any single official history and instead encounter a terrain riddled with contradictory accounts and competing claims to truth. Here, however, is where history begins: with the critical interrogation of existing accounts and the affirmation that there exists in the past that which has yet to be called to account. To conclude this volume, the remainder of this chapter offers a resource guide for researchers seeking to study NBC across diverse sites of historical analysis. While it is necessarily brief and incomplete, we hope that it will help bring to light new evidence and provoke new understandings of the network as a machine of economic and cultural production within the larger historical assemblage of American broadcasting.

Pathways through Time

Barnouw's history drew from a variety of published materials, and this class of resource remains valuable for today's historian. In addition to retrospectives such as NBC's that take the network itself as an object of study, a number of books have been devoted to the history of individual stations—perhaps most famous among them, William Banning's 1946 study of the Blue network's flagship station WEAF. Memoirs exist as far back as NBC radio announcer Graham McNamee's 1926 volume *You're on the Air*, and formal accounts of early network formations were published as early as Gleason Archer's detailed 1939 study *Big Business and Radio*.[2] Primary publications also provide a wealth of information. The National Association of Broadcasters' handbook, for example, guided operations at NBC and within the broadcast industry as a whole, while production manuals were published for radio as early as the 1930s and were in use by television screenwriters by the early 1950s.[3] Within the popular press, newspapers around the country and general entertainment magazines offered daily coverage of radio and television broadcasts, while dedicated journals such as *Radio Age* or *Television Age* and fan magazines like *Popular Radio*, *Radio Digest*, and *TV Guide* have provided the broadcast public with information on programming, broadcast personalities, and important network activities. Finally, trade publications such as *Variety*, *Broadcasting and Cable*, *Electronic Media*, *The Radio Dealer*, *Radio Merchandising*, *Radio Retailing*, *Printer's Ink*, *Sponsor*, *Advertising Age*, and *Billboard* served to both order and reflect practices of those within the broadcast industry and other professions with interests in broadcasting.[4]

A resource newly available to Barnouw, and one that he himself helped to expand, was Columbia University's Oral History Collection. Founded in 1948 by historian Alan Nevins, the Oral History Program began work in 1950, in conjunction with the present-day Broadcasting Pioneers Club (under the leadership of then-NBC executive William S. Hedges), to initiate its Radio Pioneers Project. Between 1950 and 1951, Columbia's Frank Ernest Hill, interviewer and director of the project, assembled "reminiscences" of about ninety individuals—from regulators Herbert Hoover (Department of Commerce) and Orestes Caldwell (Federal Radio Commission [FRC] chair), to NBC officer Mark Woods, program director Phillips Carlin, announcer Thomas Cowan, and news commentator H. V. Kaltenborn. In preparation for his own three-volume history, Barnouw conducted many additional interviews, dramatically expanding the collection's representation of television and of the creative side of the broadcast industry. Among those added during this second wave were reminiscences of Norman Corwin, Carleton Morse, Dorothy Parker, William Robson, Robert Lewis Shayon, Davidson Taylor, Jon Cassavetes, Betty Comden and Adolph Green, Fred Friendly, Philip Reisman, and Rod Steiger.[5]

In addition to oral histories, Barnouw also availed himself of official FRC and Federal Communications Commission (FCC) documents at the National Archives in Washington, D.C. Resources at federal repositories have expanded dramatically since Barnouw's time to include collections at the Smithsonian Institution's National Museum of American History (NMAH) and the Library of Congress. In addition to its collection of books and periodicals, the NMAH's Archives Center houses a number of advertising collections and perhaps most notably the George Herbert Clark "Radioana" Collection. The extensive personal collection of RCA's staff historian, this collection covers the period from 1900 to 1950 and contains not only documentation of RCA's involvement with early radio but numerous NBC-specific items: publicity stills of radio stations and personalities, articles and biographical information on company figures, speeches from network executives such as Sarnoff, and program schedules and press releases for Red and Blue network flagship stations WEAF and WJZ.[6]

Among Library of Congress holdings are most notably the NBC Radio and NBC Television Collections, although numerous smaller collections also exist. Consisting of files donated in 1992 from the company's corporate collection, the NBC Radio Collection is currently maintained by the Library of Congress's Recorded Sound Division and includes a variety of items from the network's beginnings in the 1920s through the Second World War—among them, information on network advertisers; activities of different departments, such as NBC's music and programming divisions; annual reports to stockholders; press releases; program cards and audio recordings; minutes of NBC Advisory Council meetings; records of NBC wartime activity; program logs and master books with scripts and schedules for daily programming; listener letters; and speeches by company officers, such as David Sarnoff and Sylvester (Pat) Weaver. The Recorded Sound Division also holds thousands of NBC radio recordings and features a separate Carlton E. Morse Script Collection.[7] The Television Collection, donated by NBC in 1986, is housed in the Motion Picture and Broadcasting Division and contains eighteen thousand programs produced by the company from 1948 to 1977, including a large kinescope collection and numerous musical and variety titles starting with *Dinah Shore* and *Ernie Kovacs* in the 1950s.[8] In addition, this division maintains the *Amateur Hour* Collection, donated by Lloyd Marx in 1970, and the *Meet the Press* Collection, donated by Lawrence E. Spivak. Other collections are available to researchers through the library's Manuscript Division, including scripts and related information for such broadcast personalities, scriptwriters, and program producers as Arthur Godfrey, Fred Allen, Johnny Carson, Edgar Kobak, Irving R. Levine, Paul Rhymer, Jane and Goodman Ace, H. V. Kaltenborn, Jessica Dragonette, Mary Margaret McBride, David Ogilvy, Raymond Rubicam, and the General Foods Corporation (Kraft). Finally, in addition to its copious collection of journals and books related to the history of broadcasting, the library maintains the National Union Catalog of Manuscript Collections database, for locating manuscript collections around the country, and co-sponsors (with the Association of Moving Image Archivists) the Moving Image Collections Union Catalog, which indexes collections of thousands of television programs as well as films.[9]

Repositories at state and municipal levels also offer valuable resources for contemporary scholars. At the state level, most notable is the Wisconsin Historical Society's Mass Communications Collection. H. V. Kaltenborn, a Wisconsin native, led the way by depositing his papers in the early 1950s. In 1958, just as Barnouw was beginning his research, NBC, at Kaltenborn's urging, donated over six hundred boxes of network reports, correspondence, publicity materials, scripts, and recordings dating from the 1920s through the 1960s. Beyond this NBC Collection, the Historical Society also maintains ancillary collections donated by historical notables such as NBC executives E. P. H. James, William S. Hedges, and Harry R.

Bannister; newscasters Chet Huntley, David Brinkley, Charles Collingwood, Edwin H. Newman, and Howard K. Smith; and creative personnel such as John Frankenheimer, Nat Hiken, Agnes Moorehead, Jane Cruisinberry, Paul Rhymer, Reginald Rose, Donald Sanford, Sidney Sheldon, and David Susskind. In addition, the Historical Society holds scripts and recordings for NBC programs such as *Kraft Television Theatre, Kaiser Aluminum Hour,* and *Philco Television Playhouse,* plus those created by production companies such as MTM Enterprises (co-founded by Mary Tyler Moore and former NBC officer Grant Tinker) and Ziv Television.[10]

Several municipal libraries also offer an impressive catalog of NBC-related items. The Thousand Oaks Library in California and the New York Public Library both hold numerous collections of scripts, papers, and recordings. In addition to a joint 2001 venture with the Pacific Pioneers Broadcasters to house over ten thousand scripts for programming produced for Pacific Coast stations, the Thousand Oaks Library boasts an American Radio Archive featuring collections donated by several significant figures in NBC radio and television programming. *The Jack Benny Program* is particularly well represented in the archive's Bob Crosby, Hilliard Marks, Sportsmen [Quartet], and Milt Josefsberg Collections, while other programs are documented within the Carlton E. Morse, Frank Bresee, John Pickard and Frank Provo, Marvin E. Miller, Milton and Barbara Merlin, Monty Masters, Morris Freedman, Rudy Vallee, Tom Koch, Tom Price, Robert Q. Lewis, and Arthur Wertheim Collections.[11] The New York Public Library also maintains a variety of scripts and in some cases recordings for NBC-originated radio and television programming, among them papers for writers Elaine Carrington, Edith Meiser, Phyllis Merrill, and Blanche Freedman, director James Elson, performers Wladimir Selinsky and John Tasker Howard, and sound engineer Charles Gray, as well as recordings of *The Bell Telephone Hour* from both its radio and its television runs.[12]

In the course of his own research, Barnouw consulted numerous corporate archives. While many of these corporations retain records for more recent decades, they have since divested themselves of substantial portions of their holdings. By the time Barnouw began his study, NBC had already made its donation to Wisconsin's collection, followed by its more recent Library of Congress donations. Its original parent company, RCA, donated many boxes of laboratory files and house organs through the mid-1900s to the David Sarnoff Library in Princeton, while additional records of its broadcasting activities may be found outside the company's own archives in personal collections of executives such as Edward J. Nally, at Princeton University, and Owen D. Young, at Saint Lawrence University, New York.[13] Current parent company General Electric has a long history of involvement in broadcasting, including operation of NBC affiliates WRGB and WGY. Many of its records through the mid-1900s, including station records, are now housed at the Schenectady Museum, New York.[14] While many other stations retain records of their own early broadcasting activities, many more, like Chicago's WENR and Philadelphia's KYW, donated significant holdings to the Library of American Broadcasting in College Park, Maryland, or to its predecessor, the Broadcast Pioneers Library, opened by its eponymous organization in Washington, D.C., in 1972.[15] Production companies have also made significant donations. In addition to those collections for advertising agencies and independent production houses already cited, the John W. Hartman Center for Sales, Advertising, and Marketing History at Duke University currently holds extensive records from the J. Walter Thompson company, including information on individual accounts, staff meetings, full radio and television scripts, and personal collections of those involved in program production.[16]

Since Barnouw first embarked upon his task, universities around the country have recognized the importance of documenting various aspects of broadcast history, including that of NBC. On the West Coast, UCLA's Film and Television Archive holds recordings of thousands of NBC television titles produced from 1949 to the mid-1980s, including an extensive collection of commercials. Its Archive Research and Study Center (ARSC) Audio Archive contains reference copies of re-broadcasts for many NBC radio titles originally aired from 1927 through the 1950s, including large runs of *Suspense, Dragnet, Jack Benny, Burns and Allen, Bing Crosby,* and *Amos 'n' Andy.* Meanwhile, the university's Special Collections Department maintains scripts and production materials for such shows as the *NBC Matinee Theatre, I Spy,* and *The Adventures of Ellery Queen.*[17] The University of Southern California in turn holds in its own Cinema-Television Library several radio and television collections that contain scripts, publicity materials, and in some cases production notes; among these are collections for Edgar Bergen, George Burns and Gracie Allen, Gosden and Correll, Jay Burton, Morton Fine, Fred Freiburger, Greg Garrison, Michael Gleason, Serge Krinzman, and Sidney Sheldon. The library also boasts the Bee Lavery Collection, with speeches and articles by Pat Weaver.[18]

Moving inland, the American Heritage Center (AHC) at the University of Wyoming maintains numerous collections for a variety of NBC creative staff and talent, among them news personalities Morgan Beatty, Irene Kuhn, Leonard Probst, Ronald Steinman, and William Sterne; writers and producers Andy White, Carroll Carroll, Barbara Searles, Edwin L. Dunham, Frank and Anne Hummert, Milt Josefsberg, Ozzie and Harriet Nelson, and Phillips H. Lord; and other on-air talent such as announcer Frank D. Barton and musician Hymie Shertzer.[19] These collections include valuable program scripts, personal correspondence, and fan mail. In the East, the University of Georgia houses the Walter J. Brown Peabody Awards Collection, with radio programs from the 1940s that include episodes of *Bob and Ray* and television programs from 1948 onward that include episodes of *Meet the Press, Omnibus, The Cosby Show,* and *Seinfeld.* In addition, the collection contains the African-American Television Project, with programs from national networks and local stations, beginning in 1949, that document African American history and culture.[20] Vanderbilt University in Nashville for its part boasts one of the most comprehensive collections of news programming in the country, with a Television News Archive containing recordings of the *NBC Evening News* from August 5, 1968, to the present, with searchable online abstracts of each story featured plus special network news coverage of political conventions, State of the Union addresses, presidential speeches and news conferences, the Iran hostage crisis, the Gulf Wars, the war in Afghanistan, and the September 11 attacks.[21]

Last but not least is the Library of American Broadcasting (LAB) at the University of Maryland. Among the most extensive collections in the country, the LAB houses the former Broadcast Pioneers History Project, begun under William Hedges's direction in the 1960s as an extension of Columbia's archive and including additional oral histories, official NAB publications, biographical files, and files on individual member stations.[22] The library also boasts over a thousand published and unpublished scripts for NBC radio and TV programs, from the 1920s through 1991; 288 NBC audio recordings and several dozen moving-image productions; hundreds of pertinent books and periodicals, including runs of NBC's house organs; hundreds more publicity stills and promotional pamphlets; and privately donated collections for creative staff such as Louis J. Hazam, Norman Sweetser, and Alois Havrilla, additional network personnel such as Herman Hettinger, Noran Kersta, and Hedges himself, and specific programs such as *Vox Pop* and *Wisdom*.[23]

In addition to university collections, museums devoted to radio and television have arisen around the country since Barnouw's time and play an important role as official repositories of knowledge. The David Sarnoff Library holds, in addition to its RCA Collection, a collection of Sarnoff's speeches, articles, government testimony, and correspondence, highlights of which have been published in the volume *Looking Ahead* (Sarnoff 1968). The Museum of Television and Radio, with branches in New York and Los Angeles, holds 7,200 NBC titles for radio programs produced as early as 1927 and 12,000 television assets dating as early as 1936, as well as collections of press releases, program cards, and files from the TV Information Office absorbed upon the closing of this office in 1989.[24] The Museum of Broadcasting in Chicago also holds titles for NBC-originated radio programming starting in the 1920s and television programming beginning in the late 1940s.[25]

Of critical importance to Barnouw and of continued value to researchers today have been, finally, ancillary organizations that do not always share the same institutional presence or authority as the press, broadcasting corporations and production houses, universities, or museums. Barnouw, as a man with industry experience, was familiar with a number of professional organizations. The Broadcast Pioneers still exist today, centered in Philadelphia, and have announced plans to begin a new collection, while the efforts of the Pacific Pioneers Broadcasters, founded in 1966 by announcer Art Gilmore and under the initial direction of performer Jim Jordan, have been noted above.[26] The Academy of Television Arts and Sciences in Los Angeles has for its part begun to compile an archive of Web-accessible interviews with television personalities, screenwriters, and producers.[27] Enthusiast clubs such as the Society to Preserve and Encourage Radio Drama, Variety, and Comedy (SPERDVAC) have also worked as preservers of knowledge about network programming and archivists of the programs themselves, boasting large libraries whose holdings are available to members.[28]

The Web has provided an expanded forum for such activities. Sites devoted to radio, such as otr.com and old-time.com, offer links to external pages with historical information on individual stations and complete program logs for various series, venues where programs themselves may be procured, and discussion boards for questions on programming or aspects of radio history. For television, in addition to detailed program information through sites like imdb.com and epguides.com, sites such as tv.com provide discussion forums, while other sites like fanforum.com provide not only boards devoted to current programming but archives of postings for many past shows. Amateur historians and individual fans may also, and often do, post information on stations, programs, producers, and stars on their personal Web sites and provide links to additional sites that might otherwise escape the researcher's notice.

Making Histories

The study of broadcasting as a cultural form is still in its early decades. While studies of broadcasting have been pursued by individual scholars since the 1930s, dedicated programs in media studies are a comparatively late addition to the American academy. Enjoying an initial period of growth after the Second World War, such programs have undergone a second period of expansion in recent decades with the turn in many disciplines to the study of popular culture. More and more PhDs are awarded in media studies every year, with serious scholarly consideration of mass media increasing along with course offerings for what has proven one of the most popular and rapidly growing majors around the world. Perhaps perversely, this renewed interest in broadcasting comes at a time when we are perched on the brink of digital transformations that may change our understanding of its most basic organizing principles, such as network, station, program, and audience. The present volume has provided examples of efforts to grapple with such concepts as these emerged and changed over the course of the past century. Specifically, these essays have been concerned to elaborate the role of the National Broadcasting Company, America's first network, in giving these concepts substance and shaping the forms of economic and cultural production that have defined the system of American broadcasting throughout its tumultuous history.

This chapter has worked to affirm the importance of the network as an object of historical analysis and has offered an overview of some of the major resources available to scholars within the ever-expanding field of media studies who wish to explore in more detail the history of the nation's first network. In this effort to compile resources for archival research, it is not entirely alone. Susan and David Siegel have recently published *A Resource Guide to the Golden Age of Radio*, which details numerous special collections, existing scholarship, and a vast number of Web resources for use by today's radio historian. A similar guide for television has yet to appear. However, we are fortunate to have broadcasting's history preserved in a small handful of compilations and reference works. Most notable in the latter category are the four-volume *Encyclopedia of Television*, edited by Horace Newcomb, now in its second edition (2004), and the three-volume *Encyclopedia of Radio* (2003), edited by Christopher H. Sterling. Both works extend the normal function of the encyclopedia—that of collecting and summarizing extant information—by contributing serious original scholarship to the field. In the category of more popular, but extremely useful, compilations, there are the guides by Alex McNeil (published in its fourth edition in 1996), and by Tim Brooks and Earle Marsh (published in its eighth edition in 2003). Radio is fortunate to possess, in addition, not only Harrison B. Summers's (1958/1971) groundbreaking study of national network schedules from 1926 to 1956, but also the program guides by John Dunning (1998) and Frank Buxton, Owen, and Morgan (1996), as well as Luther Sies's more recent *Encyclopedia of Radio* (2000), covering programs and performers from 1920 to 1960.

While this chapter has focused on resources relevant to the study of NBC, this network was ultimately but one of several to determine the historical trajectory of American broadcasting. Many of the issues raised with respect to NBC pertain equally to other, contemporary networks, including problems of archival research. Analysis of the nation's public broadcasting system benefits greatly from the National Public Broadcasting Archives at the University of Maryland, housed with the Library of Broadcasting in the Hornbake Library. A collaborative project of the Corporation for Public Broadcasting, the Public Broadcasting Service, and National Public Radio, it is a magnificent resource that assembles otherwise scattered historical materials on public radio and television's central organizations as well as many secondary ones, such as individual public broadcasting stations and groups such as the Children's Television Workshop. Resources for the study of NBC's commercial competitors lack any similarly centralized archive. While NBC's corporate records are well preserved through the 1970s within dedicated collections such as those of the Library of Congress and the Wisconsin Historical Society, no similar collections of corporate records for the remaining members of the Big Three networks, ABC and CBS, are available to historians at the time of this writing, leaving scholars to pick up what traces they can from evidence scattered throughout smaller collections across the country.

Of course, a comprehensive history of NBC itself has yet to be produced, much less one of its rival networks. Nor should efforts to advance our understanding of any network restrict themselves to corporate records. Rather, following the model set forth by Barnouw, this chapter and indeed this volume as a whole have advocated the study of NBC's history across multiple sites of analysis, in the interest of reclaiming details lost or otherwise distorted in official corporate histories and thus opening history to the play of competing accounts. However, in contrast to Barnouw's positioning of the network as but one institution among many through which to access that primary object of concern, American broadcasting, this chapter has argued for the importance of the network as an author of a vitally important aspect of American culture and as a primary architect of the "American system" of broadcasting, whose influence has been felt around the world.

Notes

1. Kristal Brent Zook's *Color by Fox* (1999) goes a long way toward charting a history of the Fox network's first decade, though focusing primarily on its groundbreaking black-oriented programs.

2. Archer's was by no means the first history of American broadcasting, however; it was predated by his own *History of Radio to 1926* (1938) and other works such as Schubert's *The Electric Word* (1928). For examples of other memoirs by early radio performers, see Harris (1937) and Husing (1935).

3. A useful source of NAB documents is the Library of American Broadcasting at the University of Maryland, College Park, discussed below. For a summary of radio production manuals from the 1930s, see Russo (2004b, 209–30). For examples of early screenwriting manuals for television, see Allan (1946), Heath (1950), Wiley (1950), and Campbell (1950).

4. While an adequate list of newspapers around the country would be impossible, a partial listing of additional radio and television journals includes *Popular Radio, Radio Age, The Dial, Radio Broadcast, Radio World, Proceedings of the Institute of Radio Engineers, Radio Television Journal, Television, Broadcasting,* and *Entertainment Weekly.*

5. For information on the Radio Pioneers Project and others within Columbia's Oral History Collection, follow the "Projects" link at www.columbia.edu/cu/lweb/indiv/oral. Thanks to Courtney Smith at the Oral History Research Office for providing a full list of reminiscences held within the collection. Truman State University's Pickler Memorial Library has microform copies for many of the Columbia interviews within its own archives; see http://library.truman.edu/microforms/columbia_oral_history.htm.

6. A list of advertising collections within the NMAH's holdings is available at the Archives Center Web site and includes records donated by the N. W. Ayer advertising agency. While no online search aid exists for the N. W. Ayer Records, a detailed search aid and a container list are available for the Clark Collection through the NMAH's Lemelson Center Web site; see http://invention.smithsonian.org/resources/fa_clark_index.aspx.

7. Search aids for both the NBC and Carlton Morse Collections may be accessed by following the "Guides and Reference Aids" link on the Recorded Sound home page, www.loc.gov/rr/record. The division's collection of radio recordings starts in the late 1920s but features programs mainly from the mid-1930s to mid-1950s. These may be located by searching the Library of Congress's SONIC database, also accessed from the Recorded Sound home page.

8. For an overview of the Motion Picture and Broadcasting Division's TV holdings, see www.loc.gov/rr/mopic/tvcoll.html#cata. Thanks to Mike Mashon for providing details on some of the programming within this collection.

9. For NUCMC, see http://loc.gov/coll/nucmc/. For the Moving Image Collections Union Catalog, see http://mic.imtc.gatech.edu/.

10. The Wisconsin Historical Society also holds numerous collections of related interest, such as those for the A. C. Nielsen and E. C. Hooper ratings companies and collections for federal regulators Newton Minow, Orestes H. Caldwell, and William Henry. To search for WHS holdings, use the "ArCat" and "Archival Finding Aids" links on the Society's Research Portal page, www.wisconsinhistory.org/research.asp. The MTM and Ziv Collections were acquired under the auspices of the University of Wisconsin's Center for Film and Theater Research. The Ziv Collection is housed within a larger collection for United Artists, which absorbed the company in 1960.

11. Information on both the American Radio Archive and Pacific Pioneer Broadcasters collections may be obtained by following the American Radio Archive link at www.toaks .org/library.

12. Online descriptions and search aids are available for many collections at the New York Public Library and are readily located at www.nypl.org/books/findingaids.html.

13. A brief overview of the David Sarnoff Library's holdings is available at www.david-sarnoff.org. An online guide to the Edward Julian Nally Papers is available through Princeton's Department of Rare Books and Special Collections; use the search aids link at www .princeton.edu/~rbsc/index.shtml. A two-hundred-page finding aid for the Owen D. Young Papers is available online through St. Lawrence University, at www.stlawu.edu/library/ libarc/young. Thanks to Alexander Magoun, director of the David Sarnoff Library, for his elaboration of its contents and for pointing out these additional collections.

14. For information on the Schenectady Museum's archives, click on the "Archives and Research" link at www.schenectadymuseum.org.

15. For a detailed description of the WENR-KYW Collection, select the appropriate link within the library's online collection index, at www.lib.umd.edu/LAB/collections.html.

16. For information on the J. Walter Thompson Collection, see the center's Web site, scriptorium.lib.duke.edu/hartman/jwt. Particularly relevant among the personal papers housed within the collection are those of Maury Holland, John F. Devine, and Dan Seymour. Thanks to the Hartman Center's Lynn Eaton for pointing these out and providing further details about the collection.

17. Profiles for collections of radio and television programs are available online through the Film and Television Archive Web site, www.cinema.ucla.edu. Thanks to Mark Quigley, Dan Einstein, and Mark Gens at UCLA for providing additional information about these collections. To locate manuscript collections, use the "Search Collections" link on the Department of Special Collections home page, www.library.ucla.edu/libraries/special/scweb.

18. For general information on the Cinema-Television Library, see www.usc.edu/isd/ libraries/collections. Thanks to Ned Comstock for providing details on pertinent collections within the library's holdings.

19. For general information on the AHC, see ahc.uwyo.edu. Brief descriptions of individual collections may be obtained by searching the center's catalog; see ahc.uwyo.edu/use archives/catalog.htm. The center's *Guide to Popular Culture Resources* also contains useful summaries of relevant collections, which are too numerous to list exhaustively in the space allotted. Thanks to AHC Reference Manager Carol Bowers for her help in determining pertinent collections and securing the appropriate finding aids.

20. For an overview of the Peabody Collection within the University of Georgia's Walter J. Brown Media Archives, see www.libs.uga.edu/media/collections/peabody/index.html.

21. For information on Vanderbilt's Television News Archive, see tvnews.vanderbilt.edu.

22. In a December 14, 1965, letter to E. P. H. James, Hedges described the collection that the Broadcast Pioneers had begun to assemble in the following terms: "The Broadcast Pioneers' History Project is a 'legitimate,' and I do emphasize that word, offspring of the Columbia University Oral History Project." Papers of William S. Hedges, Series 1, Box 1, Folder 2, Library of American Broadcasting, College Park, MD.

23. The Library of American Broadcasting has extensive information about its various collections on its Web page, www.lib.umd.edu/LAB. Thanks to Michael Henry for isolating items of particular relevance to study of NBC's history.

24. For the Museum of Television and Radio's home page, see www.mtr.org. The mu-

seum's radio collection is part of the same NBC divestiture through which the Library of Congress acquired its collection. Of the original 140,000 recordings within its possession, NBC still retains some within its own archives. Concerning the TV Information Office collection, since the original acquisition in 1989, museum staff have worked to keep the files current by adding to them on an annual basis. Thanks to Jane Klain and Doug Gibbons at the museum's New York branch for elaborating NBC-related holdings within their collections.

25. For online searches of the radio and television collections, follow the "Collection" link on the museum's home page, www.museum.tv/home.php.

26. Broadcast Pioneers, "The Broadcast Pioneers Archive," Broadcast Pioneers home page, www.broadcastpioneers.com, accessed March 1, 2006, and Pacific Pioneers Broadcasters, "About Us," www.pacificpioneerbroadcasters.org/about.html, accessed March 5, 2006.

27. See www.emmys.org/foundation/archive, and select the "Interviews" link for an index of all interviews within the academy's collection.

28. See SPERDVAC's Web site, www.sperdvac.org. For a useful guide of extant radio programming and other collectors clubs, see Hickerson (2005).

NBC Time Line

1919

RCA formed; David Sarnoff appointed general manager

1921

First radio broadcast licenses issued by Interstate Commerce Commission

Thirty stations go on air

1922

Class B licenses established

British Broadcasting Company (BBC) formed

First Radio Conference called by Secretary of Commerce Herbert Hoover

Westinghouse establishes station WJZ

AT&T establishes station WEAF

Bertha Brainard Broadcasting Broadway debuts on WJZ

1923

National Association of Broadcasters (NAB) organized

The Eveready Hour debuts on WEAF

1923 *continued*

RCA takes over operation of WJZ and introduces WJY

H. V. Kaltenborn begins weekly news commentary on WEAF

1924

AT&T experiments with first multiple-station hookup

1926

RCA purchases WEAF from AT&T; forms NBC

NBC Red network begins operations

Merlin Aylesworth named president of NBC

Bertha Brainard appointed director of commercial programming

WCFL, Chicago labor station, founded

1927

Radio Act of 1927 passed

Federal Radio Commission (FRC) created

NBC Blue network begins operations

1927 *continued*

United Independent Broadcasters, Inc. (UIB) formed; later renamed Columbia Broadcasting System (CBS)

NBC Pacific Coast network established

NBC Advisory Committee founded

1928

RCA buys RKO Pictures; General Order 40 established

William S. Paley purchases CBS

NBC begins regularly scheduled coast-to-coast programming

1929

Adolph Zukor of Paramount Pictures buys a 50 percent share in CBS

Amos 'n' Andy makes its network debut on NBC

1930

David Sarnoff appointed president of RCA

U.S. Census Bureau reports that 45 percent of U.S. households own radios

1931

John Royal named NBC vice president of programming

Metropolitan Opera broadcasts begin

NBC Public Service Department formed under direction of Margaret Cuthbert

1932

Paramount sells its shares back to CBS

American Society of Composers, Authors and Publishers (ASCAP) raises copyright fees by 300 percent

Presidential conventions broadcast by both NBC and CBS

GE and Westinghouse divest themselves of RCA shares

1932 *continued*

Canada makes sweeping reform of broadcasting system

1933

NBC's Radio City offices and studios open in Rockefeller Center

Press-radio war culminates in Biltmore Agreement

Educational radio groups lobby for radio reform

First "Fireside Chat" by President Roosevelt

1934

Communication Act of 1934 passed

Federal Communications Commission (FCC) replaces FRC

NBC Continuity Acceptance Department begins operations under Janet MacRorie

Mutual Broadcasting System organized by WOR, WLW, WGN, and WXYZ

1935

America's Town Meeting of the Air debuts

Biltmore Agreement breaks down

Wagner-Hatfield Amendment defeated

1936

NBC Hollywood studios open

NBC hires Arturo Toscanini to direct the NBC Symphony Orchestra

Lenox Lohr replaces Merlin Aylesworth as NBC president

First live Olympic Games broadcast from Berlin, aired on CBS and NBC

1937

CBS opens Hollywood studios

Irna Phillips's *The Guiding Light* begins its endless run

1937 *continued*

74 percent of U.S. households own a radio set

1938

FCC investigation of chain broadcasting begins

FCC sets aside channels in FM band for educational radio

World Broadcasting System (WBS) launches transcription network

War of the Worlds broadcast demonstrates power of radio

1939

NAB adopts broadcast code, bans Father Coughlin and Elliott Roosevelt from the air

Broadcast Music Inc. (BMI) forms as broadcaster-run alternative to ASCAP

RCA introduces television to public at New York World's Fair

1940

FCC chain broadcasting draft report released

NBC and CBS sell off talent bureaus (CBS's becomes Viacom)

Niles Trammell becomes president of NBC

FCC authorizes commercial stations in FM band

81 percent of U.S. households own radios

1941

FCC releases *Report on Chain Broadcasting*; NBC and CBS file lawsuits

North American Regional Broadcasting Agreement (NARBA) instituted between United States, Canada, Mexico, and Cuba

1941 *continued*

FCC approves commercial television on 525-line standard

NBC acquires first commercial TV license for station WNBT in New York City

United States enters World War II

1942

Office of War Information (OWI) created, with Elmer Davis as director

Armed Forces Radio Service begins operations

Labor for Victory premieres on NBC

1943

NBC sells Blue network to Edward R. Noble

FCC extends term of broadcast license to three years

The Second Battle of Warsaw airs on *Free World Theatre*, and *The Battle of the Warsaw Ghetto* airs for the first time

1944

OWI takes over operation of Radio Luxembourg

The Eternal Light debuts

1945

World War II comes to an end

Blue network renamed American Broadcasting Company (ABC)

TV frequencies established and FM band moved

1946

FCC issues "Blue Book," *Public Service Responsibility of Broadcast Licensees*

NBC begins regular television service

J. Walter Thompson produces *Hour Glass* on WNBT-TV

1946 *continued*

RCA demonstrates color TV

NBC links four television stations in network

DuMont television network begins broadcasting

1947

NBC premieres the *Kraft Television Theatre*, produced by JWT

First TV broadcast of World Series on NBC

1948

FCC institutes freeze on TV licenses

Thirty-seven stations now on air

Texaco Star Theater introduces Milton Berle

1949

Fortune article draws attention to the African American audience in "The Forgotten 15,000,000"

Sylvester "Pat" Weaver appointed NBC vice president for television programming

Jack Benny jumps from NBC to CBS radio network

1950

NBC hires consultant Joseph V. Baker to advise on racial issues

Red Channels published, blacklisting worsens

Sid Caesar's *Your Show of Shows* debuts to anchor Saturday night

9 percent of U.S. homes own television sets

1951

ABC and United Paramount Theaters announce merger (approved 1953)

NBC inaugurates first coast-to-coast live TV broadcast

1952

NBC debuts *Today*

CBS moves past NBC in television ratings ·

FCC lifts freeze on TV licenses

108 stations on air by end of year

1953

CBS takes *Amos 'n' Andy* television show off the air after NAACP protests

Pat Weaver becomes NBC president; Robert W. Sarnoff named vice president

NBC begins regular broadcasts in color

45 percent of U.S. homes own television sets

1954

Brown v. Board of Education decision launches civil rights movement

Joseph V. Baker resigns from NBC

ABC and Disney collaborate on *Disneyland*

1955

NBC launches weekend *Monitor* radio program

Robert W. Sarnoff appointed NBC president; Weaver becomes chairman of board

Demise of DuMont network

Independent Television (ITV) debuts in the United Kingdom as the first commercial television network in Europe

1956

Robert Kintner becomes executive vice president of NBC; Weaver resigns

Huntley-Brinkley Report debuts

1957

The *Tonight* show debuts with Jack Paar

Networks battle Pay TV

1957 *continued*

NBC brings in Lew Wasserman of MCA to revamp schedule

Videotape introduced to network news production

1958

Quiz show investigation begins

Robert Kintner becomes NBC president; Robert Sarnoff becomes chairman of the board

1959

Bonanza begins fourteen-year run at the top of the TV ratings

Number of licensed TV stations exceeds five hundred

TV set ownership in United States at 86 percent

1960

John F. Kennedy election launches New Frontier era

NBC White Paper documentary series begins

Networks control 80 percent of prime-time programming

Daytime serials end on network radio

Average time per day spent watching television is five hours and six minutes; radio listening is at one hour and fifty-three minutes

1961

FCC Chair Newton Minow makes his "vast wasteland" speech to the NAB

89 percent of U.S. households own TV sets; fewer than 1 percent have color TVs

1962

First commercial television satellite, Telstar, launched

1962 *continued*

COMSAT—Communications Satellite Corporation—formed

Ford Foundation gives $8.5 million to educational broadcasting

Wagon Train becomes first NBC top-ranked show in a decade

The Johnny Carson era begins on *Tonight*

1963

NBC and CBS begin half-hour nightly newscasts

President Kennedy assassinated

1964

Barbara Walters becomes *Today* host

1965

Walter D. Scott replaces Robert Kintner as NBC president

1966

NBC celebrates fortieth anniversary

Star Trek launches original series

93 percent of U.S. households own TV sets; 10 percent have color TVs

1967

Public Broadcasting Act signed, Corporation for Public Broadcasting forms

Dragnet returns for a new generation

1968

Children's Television Workshop founded

Rowan and Martin's Laugh-In debuts

PBS begins broadcasting

1969

Red Lion decision upholds Fairness Doctrine

1970

Prime Time Access Rule (PTAR) implemented

National Public Radio formed

Radio listening back up to three hours per day; TV watching at six

1971

Cigarette advertising banned from radio and television

FCC investigates children's programming

FCC introduces Financial Interest and Syndication Rules (Fin-Syn)

96 percent of U.S. homes own TV sets; 60 percent have color TVs

1972

FCC issues Third Report and Order, asserting jurisdiction over cable television

HBO debut initiates satellite-delivered pay cable television

1973

An American Family airs on PBS

U.S. withdraws from Vietnam

1974

Network audience share at 74 percent

1975

Saturday Night Live debuts

NBC Social Science Advisory Panel forms

70 percent of U.S. households own color television sets

1976

ABC moves into first place in network ratings

Paul Klein becomes vice president of programming at NBC

Barbara Walters leaves *Today* to co-anchor ABC evening newscast

1976 *continued*

Jane Pauley and Tom Brokaw take over *Today*

1977

Roots draws in an audience of thirty million on ABC

1978

NBC appoints Fred Silverman president of programming

Fin-Syn rules implemented after series of court battles

1979

C-Span introduced by founder Brian Lamb as cable public service

1980

CNN, BET, and ESPN launched

Big Three network audience share at 90 percent

1981

Mark Fowler appointed FCC chair

Hill Street Blues brings "quality" to the cop drama

Silverman resigns, Grant Tinker becomes NBC chair and CEO

Brandon Tartikoff promoted to NBC president of programming

1982

Courts rule against NAB Code on antitrust grounds

Cheers and *Family Ties* debut on NBC

Tom Brokaw replaces David Brinkley on *NBC Nightly News*

National Institute of Mental Health releases its reports on television and behavior

Late Night with David Letterman debuts to cap off NBC's schedule

1983

Phyllis Tucker Vinson becomes vice president of children's programming

Compact discs introduced

Final episode of *M*A*S*H* draws audience of 125 million to CBS

1984

Cable Communications Policy Act deregulates cable

WTBS becomes the first cable superstation

The Cosby Show begins

Color television in 90 percent of U.S. households

1985

General Electric announces plans to buy RCA/NBC

Murdoch purchases Metromedia and Fox Studios

1986

Robert C. Wright becomes NBC president and CEO, replacing Grant Tinker

Fox Network debuts

Cable penetration reaches 50 percent

Network ratings share down to 75 percent

1987

Star Trek: The Next Generation launched in syndication

FCC repeals Fairness Doctrine

1988

Ted Turner starts TNT network

1989

NBC launches CNBC cable channel

1989 *continued*

Dick Ebersol named head of NBC Sports

Time Inc. merges with Warner Communications, creating Time Warner Inc.

Sony purchases Columbia Pictures Corp.

1990

Children's Television Act of 1990 passed

Seinfeld debuts as a series on NBC (pilot in 1989)

Law & Order franchise begins on NBC

1991

Warren Littlefield becomes NBC president of programming

1992

Jay Leno replaces Johnny Carson on the *Tonight* show

NBC experiences sharp ratings decline

1993

Star Trek: Deep Space Nine debuts

NBC brands Thursday nights "Must-See TV"

Big Three audience share at 60 percent

1994

Viacom purchases Paramount Pictures

Fox drops most of its African American–oriented programs

ER and *Friends* debut

1995

NBC pays $3.5 billion for Olympic Games broadcast rights from 2000 to 2008

UPN and The WB both debut

Star Trek: Voyager launched on UPN

Time Warner becomes Time Warner Turner

ABC and Disney merge

1995 *continued*

Fin-Syn and PTAR rules expire

80 percent of U.S. homes own at least one VCR

1996

Telecommunications Act of 1996 passed

NBC airs Olympic Games in Atlanta

1997

V-chip ratings appear on television screens

Ellen comes out, marking a high point of gay-themed TV

1998

Big Three network audience share at 54 percent

Digital Millennium Copyright Act passed

Copyright Term Extension Act passed

70 percent of U.S. homes subscribe to cable

1999

Satellite Home Viewer Improvement Act passed

Who Wants to Be a Millionaire brings the quiz show back to prime time

2000

AOL merges with Time Warner Turner, creating AOL Time Warner

2001

Apple introduces original iPod

2002

NBC wins rights to Winter Olympics through 2012

NBC acquires the Telemundo and Bravo cable channels

2003

United States invades Iraq

American Idol captivates national audience

NBC pays $2 billion for exclusive media rights to 2010 and 2012 Olympic Games

2004

GE/NBC acquires Vivendi Universal Entertainment, creating NBC Universal

Friends and *Frasier* go off the air

95 percent of U.S. public libraries offer free Internet access

80 percent of U.S. homes own at least one DVD player

2005

UPN cancels *Star Trek: Enterprise*

Big Three network audience share down to 21 percent

2006

The WB and UPN merge, creating the CW network

Super Bowl XL on Fox gets $2.5 million per thirty-second spot

2007

Jeff Zucker replaces Bob Wright as NBC Universal president and CEO

Bibliography

Abzug, Ronald H. 1999. *America Views the Holocaust, 1933–1945: A Brief Documentary History.* Boston: St. Martin's Press.

Alexander, David. 1991. "Interview of Gene Roddenberry: Writer, Producer, Philosopher, Humanist." *Humanist* 52 (March/April): 5–38.

———. 1996. *Star Trek Creator: The Authorized Biography of Gene Roddenberry.* London: Boxtree.

Allan, Doug. 1946. *How to Write for Television.* New York: E. P. Dutton.

Anderson, Christopher. 1994. *Hollywood TV: The Studio System in the Fifties.* Austin: University of Texas Press.

———. 2004. "National Broadcasting Company." In *Encyclopedia of Television*, 2nd ed., edited by Horace Newcomb, 1606–10. New York: Fitzroy Dearborn.

Archer, Gleason L. 1938. *History of Radio to 1926.* New York: American Historical Society.

———. 1939. *Big Business and Radio.* New York: American Historical Company.

Bandura, Arthur. 1977. *Social Learning Theory.* New York: Prentice Hall.

Banning, William Peck. 1946. *Commercial Broadcasting Pioneer: The WEAF Experiment, 1922–1926.* Cambridge, MA: Harvard University Press.

Barnouw, Erik. 1945. *Radio Drama in Action: Twenty-Five Plays of a Changing World.* New York: Farrar and Rinehart.

———. 1966. *A History of Broadcasting in the United States.* Vol. 1. *A Tower in Babel; to 1933.* New York: Oxford University Press.

———. 1968. *A History of Broadcasting in the United States.* Vol. 2. *The Golden Web, 1933 to 1953.* New York: Oxford University Press.

———. 1978. *The Sponsor: Notes on a Modern Potentate.* New York: Oxford University Press.

———. 1983. *Documentary: A History of the Non-fiction Film.* New York: Oxford University Press.

———. 1990. *Tube of Plenty: The Evolution of American Television.* New York: Oxford University Press.

Battema, Douglas. 2002. "'The Picture Is Not Black . . .': Television Discourse in the African-American Press, 1948–52." Paper presented at the Society for Cinema Studies Conference, Denver, CO, May 24.

Becker, Ron. 2001. "Prime-Time Television in the Gay '90s: Network Television, Quality Audiences, and Gay Politics." *Velvet Light Trap* 42:36–47.

Bedell, Sally. 1981. *Up the Tube: Prime-Time TV and the Silverman Years.* New York: Viking Press.

Benjamin, Louise M. 1989. "Birth of a Network's 'Conscience': The NBC Advisory Council, 1927." *Journalism Quarterly* 66, no. 3:587–90.

Bensman, Marvin R. 1976. "Regulation of Broadcasting by the Department of Commerce, 1921–1927." In *American Broadcasting*, edited by Lawrence W. Lichty and Malachi C. Topping, 54–55. New York: Hastings House.

Bergreen, Laurence. 1980. *Look Now, Pay Later: The Rise of Network Broadcasting.* New York: Doubleday.

Berman, William C. 1970. *The Politics of Civil Rights in the Truman Administration.* Columbus: Ohio State University Press.

Bernardi, Daniel. 1998. *Star Trek and History: Race-ing toward a White Future.* New Brunswick: Rutgers University Press.

Bilby, Kenneth. 1986. *The General: David Sarnoff and the Rise of the Communications Industry.* New York: Harper and Row.

Bird, William L., Jr. 1999. *"Better Living": Advertising, Media, and the New Vocabulary of Business Leadership, 1935–1955.* Evanston, IL: Northwestern University Press.

Bliss, Edward. 1991. *Now the News.* New York: Columbia University Press.

Blue, Howard. 2002. *Words at War: World War II Era Radio Drama and the Postwar Broadcasting Industry Blacklist.* Lanham, MD: Scarecrow Press.

Boddy, William. 1990. *Fifties Television: The Industry and Its Critics.* Urbana: University of Illinois Press.

Bodroghkozy, Aniko. 2001. *Groove Tube: Sixties Television and the Youth Rebellion.* Durham: Duke University Press.

Bogle, Donald. 2001. *Primetime Blues: African Americans on Network Television.* New York: Farrar, Straus and Giroux.

Brauer, Ralph. 1975. *The Horse, the Gun and the Piece of Property: Changing Images of the TV Western.* Bowling Green, OH: Popular Press.

Breitman, Richard, and Alan Kraut. 1987. *American Refugee Policy and European Jewry, 1933–1945.* Bloomington: Indiana University Press.

Brindze, Ruth. 1937. *Not to Be Broadcast: The Truth about Radio.* New York: Vanguard.

Brooks, Tim, and Earle Marsh. 2003. *The Complete Directory to Prime Time Network and Cable TV Shows: 1946–Present.* 8th ed. New York: Ballantine.

Brown, Les. 1971. *Television: The Business behind the Box.* New York: Harcourt Brace Jovanovitch.

———. 1998. "The American Networks." In *Television: An International History*, edited by Anthony Smith, 147–61. Oxford: Oxford University Press.

Bruck, Connie. 2003. *When Hollywood Had a King.* New York: Random House.

Buxton, Frank, Bill Owen, and Henry Morgan. 1996. *The Big Broadcast, 1920 to 1950.* 2nd ed. Lanham, MD: Scarecrow Press.

Calvert, S. L., A. Stolkin, and J. Lee. 1997. "Gender and Ethnic Portrayals in Children's Saturday Morning Television Programs." Poster session presented at the biennial meeting of the Society for Research in Child Development, Washington, DC, April.

Campbell, Laurence. 1950. *A Guide to Radio-TV Writing.* Ames: Iowa State College Press.

Cantor, Eddie. 1957/2000. *My Life Is in Your Hands and Take My Life: The Autobiographies of Eddie Cantor.* With Jane Kesner Ardmore. New York: Cooper Square Press.

Carroll, Raymond L. 1989. "Economic Influences on Commercial Network Television Documentary Scheduling." *Journal of Broadcasting* 23, no. 4:411–25.

Cawelti, John. 1984. *The Six-Gun Mystique*. Bowling Green, OH: Popular Press.

Chase, Francis. 1942. *Sound and Fury: An Informal History of Broadcasting*. New York: Harper.

Chester, Giraud. 1947. "The Radio Commentaries of H. V. Kaltenborn: A Case Study in Persuasion." PhD diss., University of Wisconsin.

Clark, David Gillis. 1965. "The Dean of Commentators: A Biography of H. V. Kaltenborn." PhD diss., University of Wisconsin.

———. 1968. "H. V. Kaltenborn and His Sponsors: Controversial Broadcasting and the Sponsor's Role." *Journal of Broadcasting* 7:309–20.

Columbia Broadcasting System. 1941. *What the New Radio Rules Mean*. New York: CBS.

Committee on Civic Education by Radio. 1936. *Four Years of Network Broadcasting*. Chicago: University of Chicago Press.

Craig, Douglas B. 2000. *Fireside Politics*. Baltimore: Johns Hopkins University Press.

Croteau, David, and William Hoynes. 2001. *The Business of Media: Corporate Media and the Public Interest*. Thousand Oaks, CA: Pine Forge Press.

Culbert, David. 1976. *News for Everyman: Radio and Foreign Affairs in Thirties America*. Westport, CT: Greenwood Press.

———. 2002. "Erik Barnouw's War: An Interview Concerning the Armed Forces Radio Services' Educational Unit, 1944–1945." *Historical Journal of Film, Radio, and Television* 22 (October): 475–90.

Curtin, Michael. 1993. "Beyond the Vast Wasteland: The Policy Discourse of Global Television and the Politics of American Empire." *Journal of Broadcasting and Electronic Media* 37, no. 2:127–45.

———. 1995. *Redeeming the Wasteland: Documentary Television and Cold War Politics*. New Brunswick: Rutgers University Press.

Czitrom, Daniel J. 1982. *Media and the American Mind: From Morse to McLuhan*. Chapel Hill: University of North Carolina Press.

de Haas, Anton, ed. 1928/1974. *The Radio Industry: The Story of Its Development, as Told by Leaders of the Industry to the Students of the Graduate School of Business Administration, George F. Baker Foundation, Harvard University*. New York: Arno Press.

Denning, Michael. 1997. *The Cultural Front: The Laboring of American Culture in the Twentieth Century*. London: Verso.

Denny, George V., Jr. 1937. "Bring Back the Town Meeting!" In *Capitalizing Intelligence: Eight Essays on Adult Education*, edited by Warren C. Seyfert, 101–29. Cambridge, MA: Harvard University Press.

———. 1940. *Town Meeting Discussion Leader's Handbook*. New York: Town Hall Press.

Diamond, Sander. 1969. "The *Kristallnacht* and the Reaction in America." *Yivo Institute for Jewish Research* 14:198–203.

Diner, Hasia R. 2000. *Lower East Side Memories: A Jewish Place in America*. Princeton: Princeton University Press.

Dinnerstein, Leonard. 1994. *Anti-Semitism in America*. New York: Oxford University Press.

Dinnerstein, Leonard, and David M. Reimers. 1975. *Ethnic Americans: A History of Immigration and Assimilation*. New York: Dodd Mead.

Dizard, Wilson. 1964. "American Television's Foreign Markets." *Television Quarterly* 3 (Summer): 55–65.

Doherty, Thomas. 2003. *Cold War, Cool Medium: Television, McCarthyism, and American Culture.* New York: Columbia University Press.

Dorr, A., C. Doubleday, P. Kovaric, and D. Kunkel. 1981. *An Evaluation of NBC's 1980–81 Prosocial Children's Programming: Drawing Power, Play Alongs, How to Watch TV.* Los Angeles: University of Southern California, Annenberg School of Communications. (ERIC) Document Reproduction Service No. ED 216 796, May 13.

Douglas, George H. 1987. *The Early Days of Radio Broadcasting.* Jefferson, NC: McFarland.

Douglas, Susan J. 1987. *Inventing American Broadcasting.* Baltimore: Johns Hopkins University Press.

———. 1999. *Listening In.* New York: Times Books.

Downie, Leonard, Jr., and Robert G. Kaiser. 2002. *The News about the News: American Journalism in Peril.* New York: Knopf.

Dreher, Carl. 1977. *Sarnoff: An American Success.* New York: Quadrangle.

Dryer, Sherman H. 1942. *Radio in Wartime.* New York: Greenberg.

Dunning, John. 1998. *On the Air: The Encyclopedia of Old-Time Radio.* New York: Oxford University Press.

Ely, Mary L. 1937. *Why Forums?* New York: American Association for Adult Education.

Ely, Melvin Patrick. 1991. *The Adventures of Amos 'n' Andy: The Social History of an American Phenomenon.* New York: Free Press.

Entman, Robert, and S. Wildman. 1992. "Reconciling Economic and Non-economic Perspectives on Media Policy: Transcending the 'Marketplace of Ideas.'" *Journal of Communication* 42, no. 1:5–19.

Ettema, J. S. 1982. "The Organizational Context of Creativity: A Case Study from Public Television." In *Individuals in Mass Media Organizations: Creativity and Constraint,* edited by J. S. Ettema and D. C. Whitney, 91–106. Newbury Park, CA: Sage Publications.

Ewen, Stuart. 1996. *PR: A Social History of Spin.* New York: Basic Books.

Fein, Irving. 1977. *Jack Benny.* New York: Pocket Books.

Feuer, Jane, Paul Kerr, and Tise Vahimagi, eds. 1984. *MTM: "Quality Television."* London: British Film Institute.

Fine, Joyce. 1988. "American Radio Coverage of the Holocaust." *Simon Wiesenthal Center Annual* 5. http://motlc.wiesenthal.com/resources/books/annual5/chap08.html.

Fisher, James. 1997. *Eddie Cantor: A Bio-Bibliography.* Westport, CT: Greenwood.

Fones-Wolf, Elizabeth A. 2000. "Promoting a Labour Perspective in the American Mass Media: Unions and Radio in the CIO Era, 1936–1956." *Media, Culture and Society* 2:285–307.

———. 2006. *Waves of Opposition: The Struggle for Democratic Radio, 1933–58.* Urbana: University of Illinois Press.

Frappier, John. 1969. "U.S. Media Empire/Latin America." *North American Congress on Latin America* 2 (January): 2–10.

Gerstle, Gary. 2001. *American Crucible: Race and Nation in the Twentieth Century.* Princeton: Princeton University Press.

Gilbert, Douglas. 1940. *American Vaudeville: Its Life and Times.* New York: Dover.

Gitlin, Todd. 1985. *Inside Prime Time.* New York: Pantheon.

———. 1987. *The Sixties: Years of Hope, Days of Rage.* New York: Bantam.

Godfried, Nathan. 1993. "Legitimizing the Mass Media Structure: The Socialists and American Broadcasting, 1926–1932." In *Culture, Gender, Race and U.S. Labor History,* edited by Ronald C. Kent, Sara Markham, David R. Roediger, and Herbert Shapiro, 123–49. Westport, CT: Greenwood Press.

————. 1997. *WCFL: Chicago's Voice of Labor, 1926–78.* Urbana: University of Illinois Press.

Goldenson, Leonard H. 1991. *Beating the Odds.* New York: Charles Scribner's Sons.

Goldman, Herbert. 1997. *Banjo Eyes: Eddie Cantor and the Birth of Modern Stardom.* New York: Oxford University Press.

Goldsmith, Alfred N., and Austin C. Lescarboura. 1930. *This Thing Called Broadcasting.* New York: Henry Holt.

Gomery, Douglas. 2005. *The Hollywood Studio System: A History.* Berkeley: University of California Press.

Goodman, David. 2004. "Democracy and Public Discussion in the Progressive and New Deal Eras: From Civic Competence to the Expression of Opinion." *Studies in American Political Development* 18, no. 2:81–111.

Goodman, Mark, and David Gring. 2000. "The Radio Act of 1927: Progressive Ideology, Epistemology, and Praxis." *Rhetoric and Public Affairs* 3, no. 2:397–418.

Grobman, Alex. 1978. "What Did They Know? The American Jewish Press and the Holocaust, 1 September 1939–17 December 1942." *American Jewish Historical Quarterly* 68 (June): 327–52.

Habermas, Jurgen. 1991. *The Structural Transformation of the Public Sphere: An Inquiry into a Category of Bourgeois Society.* Cambridge, MA: MIT Press.

————. 1992. "Further Reflections on the Public Sphere." In *Habermas and the Public Sphere,* edited by Craig Calhoun, 421–61. Cambridge, MA: MIT Press.

Hangen, Tona. 2002. *Redeeming the Dial: Radio, Religion, and Popular Culture in America.* Chapel Hill: University of North Carolina Press.

Harris, Credo Fitch. 1937. *Microphone Memoirs: Of the Horse and Buggy Days of Radio.* Indianapolis, IN: Bobbs-Merrill.

Harrison, Taylor, Sarah Projansky, Kent A. Onon, and Elyce Rae Helford. 1996. *Enterprise Zones: Critical Positions on Star Trek.* Boulder, CO: Westview Press.

Hawes, William. 1986. *American Television Drama: The Experimental Years.* Tuscaloosa: University of Alabama Press.

Heath, Eric. 1950. *Writing for Television.* Los Angeles: Research Publishing.

Hickerson, Jay. 2005. *The Ultimate History of Network Radio Programming and Guide to All Circulating Shows.* 3rd ed. Hamden, CT: Presto.

Hill, Doug, and Jeff Weingrad. 1987. *Saturday Night: A Backstage History of Saturday Night Live.* New York: Vintage Books.

Hill-Scott, Karen H. 2000. "Industry Standards and Practices: Compliance with the Children's Television Act." In *Handbook of Children and the Media,* edited by Dorothy Singer and Jerome Singer, 605–20. Thousand Oaks, CA: Sage Publications.

Hilmes, Michele. 1990. *Hollywood and Broadcasting: From Radio to Cable.* Urbana: University of Illinois Press.

————. 1997. *Radio Voices: American Broadcasting, 1922 to 1952.* Minneapolis: University of Minnesota Press.

————. 2003. "Who We Are, Who We Are Not: Battle of the Global Paradigms." In *Planet TV: A Global Television Reader,* edited by Lisa Parks and Shanti Kumar, 53–73. New York: New York University Press.

————. 2006. *Only Connect: A Cultural History of Broadcasting in the United States.* 2nd ed. Belmont, CA: Wadsworth.

————. 2007. "*Front Line Family:* Women's Culture Comes to the BBC." *Media, Culture, and Society* 29 (January): 1–25.

Hilmes, Michele, and Jason Loviglio, eds. 2002. *Radio Reader: Essays in the Cultural History of Radio.* New York: Routledge.

Hollander, Ron. 2003. "We Knew: America's Newspapers Report the Holocaust," in *Why Didn't the Press Shout? American and International Journalism during the Holocaust,* edited by Robert Moses Shapiro, 41–50. Jersey City, NJ: Yeshiva University Press and KTAV Publishing House.

Holt, Jennifer. 2004. "Vertical Vision: Deregulation, Industrial Economy and Prime-Time Design." In *Quality Popular Television,* edited by Mark Jancovich and James Lyons, 11–31. London: British Film Institute.

Horten, Gerd. 2002. *Radio Goes to War: The Cultural Politics of Propaganda during World War II.* Berkeley: University of California Press.

Howe, Irving. 1976. *World of Our Fathers.* New York: Harcourt Brace Jovanovitch.

Husing, Ted. 1935. *Ten Years before the Mike.* New York: Farrar and Rinehart.

Jenkins, Henry. 1992. *What Made Pistachio Nuts? Early Sound Comedy and the Vaudeville Aesthetic.* New York: Columbia University Press.

Jordan, Amy. 1998. "Growing Pains: Children's Television in the New Regulatory Environment." In *Children and Television,* edited by Amy B. Jordan and Kathleen Hall Jamieson, 125–32. Thousand Oaks, CA: Sage Publications.

Kahn, F. J., ed. 1984. *Documents of American Broadcasting.* Englewood Cliffs, NJ: Prentice Hall.

Karnick, Kristine Brunovska. 1988. "NBC and the Innovation of Television News, 1945–1953." *Journalism History* 15:26–34.

Kavanagh, Jacqueline. 2004. "The BBC Written Archives." *Records Management Journal* 14 (August): 78–84.

Kelman, Ari. Forthcoming. *Station Identification: A Cultural History of Yiddish Radio in New York.* Berkeley: University of California Press.

Kepley, Vance, Jr. 1990a. "From 'Frontal Lobes' to the 'Bob-and-Bob Show': NBC Management and Programming Strategies, 1949–65." In *Hollywood in the Age of Television,* edited by Tino Balio, 41–62. Boston: Unwin Hyman.

———. 1990b. "The Weaver Years at NBC." *Wide Angle* 12, no. 2: 46–63.

Klein, Paul. 1979. "Programming." In *Inside the TV Business,* edited by Steve Morgenstern, 11–36. New York: Sterling.

Koch, Frederick H. 1945. "Drama in the South." In *Pioneering a People's Theatre,* edited by Archibald Henderson, 7–19. Chapel Hill: University of North Carolina Press.

Koseluk, Gregory. 1995. *Eddie Cantor: A Life in Show Business.* Jefferson, NC: McFarland.

Kramer, William M. 1992. "Eddie Cantor: Hollywood Jewish Activist." *Western States Jewish History* 24, no. 3:224–25.

Kunkel, Dale. 1998. "Policy Battles over Defining Children's Educational Television." *Annals of the American Academy of Political and Social Science* 557:39–53.

Kunkel, Dale, and J. Canepa. 1994. "Broadcasters' License Renewal Claims Regarding Children's Educational Programming." *Journal of Broadcasting and Electronic Media* 38:397–416.

Leff, Laurel. 2005. *Buried by The Times: The Holocaust and America's Most Important Newspaper.* New York: Cambridge University Press.

Lenthall, Bruce. 2002. "Critical Reception: Public Intellectuals Decry Depression-Era Radio, Mass Culture, and Modern America." In *Radio Reader,* edited by Michele Hilmes and Jason Loviglio, 41–62. New York: Routledge.

Lerner, Daniel. 1958. *The Passing of Traditional Society: Modernizing the Middle East.* New York: Free Press.

Levine, Elana. 2006. *Wallowing in Sex: American Television in the 1970s.* Durham: Duke University Press.

Lichty, Lawrence, and Thomas Bond. 2004. "March of Time: Docudrama Series." In *The Encyclopedia of Radio*, edited by Christopher H. Sterling, 897–900. New York: Dearborn.

Lichty, Lawrence W., and Malachi C. Topping. 1976. *American Broadcasting.* New York: Hastings House.

Lipstadt, Deborah E. 1986. *Beyond Belief: The American Press and the Coming of the Holocaust, 1933–1945.* New York: Free Press.

Loviglio, Jason. 2002. "Vox Pop: Network Radio and the Voice of the People." In *Radio Reader: Essays in the Cultural History of Radio*, edited by Michele Hilmes and Jason Loviglio, 89–111. New York: Routledge.

———. 2005. *Radio's Intimate Public: Network Broadcasting and Mass-Mediated Democracy.* Minneapolis: University of Minnesota Press.

Lyons, Eugene. 1966. *David Sarnoff.* New York: Harper and Row.

MacDonald, J. Fred. 1979. *Don't Touch That Dial! Radio Programming in American Life, 1920–1960.* Chicago: Nelson-Hall.

———. 1987. *Who Shot the Sheriff? The Rise and Fall of the Television Western.* New York: Praeger.

———. 1990. *One Nation under Television: The Rise and Decline of Network TV.* New York: Pantheon.

———. 1992. *Blacks and White TV: African-Americans in Television since 1948.* 2nd ed. Chicago: Nelson-Hall.

MacLatchy, Josephine H., ed. 1943. *Education on the Air: Fourteenth Yearbook of the Institute for Education by Radio.* Columbus: Ohio State University Press.

Mansfield, Irving. 1983. *Life with Jackie.* New York: Bantam Books.

Marc, David. 1996. *Demographic Vistas: Television in American Culture.* Philadelphia: University of Pennsylvania Press.

———. 1997. *Comic Visions: Television Comedy and American Culture.* Malden, MA: Blackwell.

———. 2003. "Roseanne." In *Entertaining America: Jews, Movies, and Broadcasting*, edited by J. Hoberman and Jeffrey Shandler, 199–200. New York: Jewish Museum.

Marchand, Roland. 1998. *Creating the Corporate Soul: The Rise of Public Relations and Corporate Imagery in American Big Business.* Berkeley: University of California Press.

McChesney, Robert W. 1993. *Telecommunications, Mass Media, and Democracy: The Battle for Control of U.S. Broadcasting, 1928 to 1935.* New York: Oxford University Press.

———. 2004. *The Problem of the Media: U.S. Communication Politics in the 21st Century.* New York: Monthly Review Press.

McCracken, Allison. 1999. "'God's Gift to Us Girls': Crooning, Gender, and the Re-creation of American Popular Song, 1928–1933." *American Music* 17, no. 4:365–95.

McDougal, Dennis. 1998. *The Last Mogul.* New York: Crown.

McGilligan, Pat. 1990. "The Ravetches." *Sight and Sound* 59, no. 3:187.

McLeland, Susan. 2004. "Grant Tinker." In *Encyclopedia of Television*, 2nd ed., edited by Horace Newcomb, 2340–41. Chicago: Fitzroy Dearborn.

McNamee, Graham. 1926. *You're on the Air.* New York: Harper and Bros.

McNeil, Alex. 1996. *Total Television: The Comprehensive Guide to Programming from 1948 to the Present.* 4th ed. New York: Penguin.

Medoff, Rafael. 1996. "New Perspectives on How America, and American Jewry, Responded to the Holocaust." *American Jewish History* 84, no. 3:253–66.

Milavsky, J. R., R. C. Kessler, H. H. Stipp, and W. S. Rubens. 1982. *Television and Aggression: A Panel Study.* New York: Academic Press.

Miller, Arthur. 1987/1995. *Timebends: A Life*. New York: Penguin.

Miller, Jeffrey. 2000. *Something Completely Different: British Television and American Culture*. Minneapolis: University of Minnesota Press.

Miller, Kathleen B. 2002. "The Red and The Blue: The NBC Collection at the Library of Congress." In *Performing Arts: Broadcasting*, edited by Iris Newson, 42–73. Washington, DC: Library of Congress.

Minow, Newton N. 1984. "Address to the International Radio and Television Society, 27 September 1962." In *Equal Time: The Private Broadcaster and the Public Interest*, edited by Newton N. Minow, 212–14. New York: Atheneum.

Morris, Dick. 2002. *Power Plays: Win or Lose—How History's Great Political Leaders Play the Game*. New York: Regan Books.

Murray, Susan. 2005. *Hitch Your Antenna to the Stars: Early Television and Broadcast Stardom*. New York: Routledge.

Murrow, Edward R. 1967. "13 December 1942." In *In Search of Light: The Broadcasts of Edward R. Murrow 1938–1961*, edited by Edward Bliss Jr., 57. New York: Alfred A. Knopf.

National Broadcasting Company. 1937. *The NBC 1937 Yearbook*. New York: NBC.

———. 1939. *Broadcasting in the Public Interest*. New York: NBC.

———. 1944a. *NBC and You*. New York: NBC.

———. 1944b. *NBC Program Policies and Working Manual*. New York: NBC.

———. 1945. *Annual Review, 1944–45*. New York: NBC.

———. 2002. *Brought to You in Living Color: 75 Years of Great Moments in Television and Radio from NBC*. New York: John Wiley.

Neale, Steve, and Frank Krutnik. 1991. *Popular Film and Television Comedy*. New York: Routledge.

Newcomb, Horace. 1994. *Television: The Critical View*. New York: Oxford University Press.

———, ed. 2004. *The Encyclopedia of Television*. 2nd ed. Chicago: Fitzroy Dearborn.

Newcomb, Horace, and Paul Hirsch. 2004. "Television as a Cultural Forum." In *The Encyclopedia of Television*, 2nd ed., edited by Horace Newcomb, 561–74. Chicago: Fitzroy Dearborn.

Newton, Gregory D. 2003. "Localism in Radio: US Regulatory Approach." In *The Encyclopedia of Radio*, edited by Christopher H. Sterling, 869–72. Chicago: Fitzroy Dearborn.

Nielsen Media Research. 2000. *2000 Report on Television: The First 50 Years*. New York: Nielsen Media Research.

Oboler, Arch, and Stephen Longstreet, eds. 1942. *This Freedom: Thirteen New Radio Plays*. New York: Random House.

———, eds. 1944. *Free World Theatre*. New York: Random House.

O'Connell, Mary C. 1986. *Connections: Reflections on Sixty Years of Broadcasting*. New York: NBC.

Overstreet, Harry A., and Bonaro W. Overstreet. 1938. *Town Meeting Comes to Town*. New York: Harper.

Paper, Lewis. 1987. *Empire: William S. Paley and the Making of CBS*. New York: St. Martin's Press.

Patinkin, Sheldon. 2000. *The Second City: Backstage at the World's Greatest Comedy Theater*. Naperville, IL: Sourcebooks.

Paul, Eugene. 1962. *The Hungry Eye*. New York: Ballantine.

Pearson, Roberta, and Máire Messenger Davies. Forthcoming. *Small Screen, Big Universe: Star Trek as Television*. Berkeley: University of California Press.

Perry, Jeb H. 1983. *Universal Television: The Studio and Its Programs*. Lanham, MD: Scarecrow Press.

Pleasants, Julian M. 2000. *Buncombe Bob: The Life and Times of Robert Rice Reynolds*. Chapel Hill: University of North Carolina Press.

Pondillo, Bob. 2005. "Racial Discourse and Censorship on NBC-TV, 1948–60." *Journal of Popular Film and Television* 33, no. 2:102–13.

Pounds, Michael C. 1999. *Race in Space: Ethnicity in Star Trek and Star Trek: The Next Generation.* Lanham, MD: Scarecrow Press.

Quigley, William J., ed. 2004. *International Television and Video Almanac.* La Jolla, CA: Quigley.

Quinlan, Sterling. 1979. *Inside ABC: American Broadcasting Company's Rise to Power.* New York: Hastings House.

Ravetch, Irving. 1944. "The Second Battle of Warsaw." In *Free World Theatre,* edited by Arch Oboler and Stephen Longstreet, 221–35. New York: Random House.

Razlogova, Elena. 2003. "The Voice of the Listener: Americans and the Radio Industry, 1920–1950." PhD diss., George Mason University.

Reeves-Stevens, Judith, and Garfield Reeves-Stevens. 1997. *Star Trek: The Next Generation. The Continuing Mission.* New York: Pocket Books.

Robinson, Thomas P. 1943/1989. *Radio Networks and the Federal Government.* New York: Arno Press.

Rosen, Phillip. 1980. *The Modern Stentors.* Westport, CT: Greenwood Press.

Russo, Alexander. 2004a. "Defensive Transcriptions: Radio Networks, Sound-on-Disc Recording, and the Meaning of Live Broadcasting." *Velvet Light Trap* 54:4–17.

———. 2004b. "Roots of Radio's Rebirth: Audiences, Aesthetics, Economics, and Technologies of American Broadcasting, 1926–1951." PhD diss., Brown University.

Sarnoff, David. 1939. *Principles and Practices of Network Radio Broadcasting: Testimony . . . before the Federal Communications Commission, November 14, 1938 and May 17, 1939.* New York: RCA Technical Institutes Press.

———. 1968. *Looking Ahead.* New York: McGraw-Hill.

Savage, Barbara Dianne. 1999. *Broadcasting Freedom: Radio, War and the Politics of Race, 1938–1948.* Chapel Hill: University of North Carolina Press.

———. 2002. "Radio and the Political Discourse of Racial Equality." In *Radio Reader: Essays in the Cultural History of Radio,* edited by Michele Hilmes and Jason Loviglio, 231–56. New York: Routledge.

Sayre, Jeanette. 1939. "Progress in Radio Fan-Mail Analysis." *Public Opinion Survey* 3 (January): 272–78.

Scannell, Paddy, and David Cardiff. 1991. *A Social History of British Broadcasting.* Vol. 1. *Serving the Nation.* Oxford: Blackwell.

Schlesinger, Philip. 1991. *Media, State and Nation: Political Violence and Collective Identities.* Newbury Park, CA: Sage Publications.

Schubert, Paul. 1928. *The Electric Word: The Rise of Radio.* New York: Macmillan.

Sethi, S. Prakash. 1977. *Advocacy Advertising and Large Corporations: Social Conflict, Big Business Image, the News Media, and Public Policy.* Lexington, MA: Lexington Books.

Shales, Tom, and Andrew James Miller. 2002. *Live from New York: An Uncensored History of Saturday Night Live.* Boston: Back Bay.

Shandler, Jeffrey. 1999. *While America Watches: Televising the Holocaust.* New York: Oxford University Press.

Shandler, Jeffrey, and Elihu Katz. 1997. "Broadcasting American Judaism." Jewish Theological Seminary of America. http://learn.jtsa.edu/topics/reading/bookexc/tradren/chap27c.shtml.

Siegel, Susan, and David S. Siegel. 2006. *A Resource Guide to the Golden Age of Radio: Special Collections, Bibliography, and the Internet.* New York: Book Hunter Press.

Sies, Luther F. 2000. *Encyclopedia of American Radio, 1920–1960*. Jefferson, NC: MacFarland.

Skornia, Harry. 1964. "American Broadcasters Abroad." *Quarterly Review of Economics and Business* 3 (1964): 10–23.

Slotten, Hugh Richard. 2000. *Radio and Television Regulation*. Baltimore: Johns Hopkins University Press.

Smith, Judith. 2002. "Radio's 'Cultural Front,' 1938–1948." In *Radio Reader*, edited by Michele Hilmes and Jason Loviglio, 209–30. New York: Routledge.

Smith, Sally Bedell. 1990. *In All His Glory*. New York: Simon and Schuster.

Smulyan, Susan. 1994. *Selling Radio: The Commercialization of American Broadcasting, 1922 to 1934*. Washington, DC: Smithsonian Institution Press.

Snyder, Robert W. 2000. *The Voice of the City: Vaudeville and Popular Culture in New York*. Chicago: Ivan R. Dee.

Sobel, Robert. 1986. *RCA*. New York: Stein and Day.

Solow, Herb, and Robert Justman.1996. *Star Trek: The Real Story*. New York: Pocket Books.

Steele, Richard W. 1985. *Propaganda in an Open Society: The Roosevelt Administration and the Media, 1933–1941*. Westport, CT: Greenwood Press.

Steichen, Edward. 1955. *The Family of Man: The Greatest Photographic Exhibition of All Time*. New York: Museum of Modern Art.

Steiner, Monica. 2005. "Primetime Update (Full Season)." *Media Insights: Magna Global* 27 (May): 1–8.

Sterling, Christopher H. 2003. *Encyclopedia of Radio*. Chicago: Fitzroy Dearborn.

Sterling, Christopher H., and John M. Kittross. 2001. *Stay Tuned: A History of American Broadcasting*. 3rd ed. Mahwah, NJ: Lawrence Erlbaum.

Stipp, Horst, Karen Hill-Scott, and Amy Dorr. 1987. "Using Social Science to Improve Children's Television: An NBC Case Study." *Journal of Broadcasting and Electronic Media*, 31, no. 4:461–73.

Stott, William. 1973. *Documentary Expression and Thirties America*. New York: Oxford University Press.

Summers, Harrison B. 1958/1971. *A Thirty-Year History of Radio Programs Carried on National Radio Networks in the United States, 1926–1956*. New York: Arno Press.

Tartikoff, Brandon, and Charles Leerhsen. 1992. *The Last Great Ride*. New York: Random House.

Taylor, Robert. 1989. *Fred Allen: His Life and Wit*. Boston: Little, Brown.

Tedlow, Richard S. 1979. *Keeping the Corporate Image: Public Relations and Business, 1900–1950*. Greenwich, CT: JAI Press.

Thomas, Dave. 1996. *SCTV: Behind the Scenes*. Toronto: McClelland and Stewart.

Tinker, Grant. 1994. *Tinker in Television: From General Sarnoff to General Electric*. New York: Simon and Schuster.

Tulloch, John, and Henry Jenkins. 1995. *Science Fiction Audiences*. New York: Routledge.

Warner, H. P. 1948. *Radio and Television Law*. New York: Matthew Bender.

Watson, Mary Ann. 1990. *The Expanding Vista: American Television in the Kennedy Years*. New York: Oxford University Press.

———. 1998. *Defining Vision: Television and the American Experience since 1945*. Fort Worth, TX: Harcourt Brace Jovanovitch.

Weaver, Pat. 1994. *The Best Seat in the House: The Golden Years of Radio and Television*. With Thomas M. Coffey. New York: Alfred A. Knopf.

Weber, Donald. 2003. "Goldberg Variations: The Achievements of Gertrude Berg." In *En-

tertaining America: Jews, Movies, and Broadcasting, edited by J. Hoberman and Jeffrey Shandler, 113–23. Princeton: Princeton University Press.

Weinstein, David. 2004. *The Forgotten Network: DuMont and the Birth of American Television.* Philadelphia: Temple University Press.

Westfahl, Gary. 1996. "Where No Market Has Gone Before: The Science Fiction Industry and the *Star Trek* Industry." *Extrapolation* 37, no. 4:291–301.

White, Llewellyn. 1947. *The American Radio.* Chicago: University of Chicago Press .

Whitfield, Stephen E., and Gene Roddenberry. 1968. *The Making of Star Trek.* New York: Ballantine Books.

Wiley, Max. 1950. *Radio and Television Writing.* New York: Rinehart.

Williams, Esther. 1999. *The Million Dollar Mermaid.* New York: Pocket Books.

Williams, Raymond. 1975. *Television: Technology and Cultural Form.* New York: Schocken Books.

Wishengrad, Morton. 1947. *The Eternal Light.* New York: Crown.

Woodard, E. H. 1999. *The 1999 State of Children's Television.* Report no. 28. Philadelphia: Annenberg Public Policy Center, University of Pennsylvania.

Wyler, Marjorie G. 1986–87. "*The Eternal Light:* Judaism on the Airwaves." *Conservative Judaism* 39, no. 2:18.

Wynn, Keenan. 1959. *Ed Wynn's Son.* Garden City, NY: Doubleday.

Yellin, David G. 1973. *Special: Fred Freed and the Television News Documentary.* New York: Macmillan.

Zahavy, Zev. 1959. "A History and Survey of Religious Broadcasting." PhD diss., Yeshiva University.

Zook, Kristal Brent. 1999. *Color by Fox: The Fox Network and the Revolution in Black Television.* New York: Oxford University Press.

Notes on Contributors

Christopher Anderson is Associate Professor in the Department of Communication and Culture at Indiana University. He is the author of *Hollywood TV: The Studio System in the Fifties* (University of Texas Press, 1994).

Michael Curtin is Professor of Media and Cultural Studies in the Department of Communication Arts at the University of Wisconsin-Madison and director of the UW Global Studies Program. His books include *Redeeming the Wasteland: Television Documentary and Cold War Politics* (Rutgers University Press, 1995), *Making and Selling Culture* (coeditor, Wesleyan University Press, 1996), *The Revolution Wasn't Televised: Sixties Television and Social Conflict* (coeditor, Routledge, 1997), and *Playing to the World's Biggest Audience: The Globalization of Chinese Film and TV* (University of California Press, 2007). With Paul McDonald, he is coeditor of the British Film Institute's International Screen Industries book series.

Elizabeth Fones-Wolf is Professor of History at West Virginia University. She is the author of *Selling Free Enterprise: The Business Assault on Labor and Liberalism* (University of Illinois Press, 1994) and *Waves of Opposition: Labor and the Struggle for Democratic Media* (University of Illinois Press, 2006). She also served as an editor of the first three volumes of the *Samuel Gompers Papers* (University of Illinois Press, 1986–2003) and has published articles dealing with business, labor, and broadcasting history in the late nineteenth and twentieth centuries.

Murray Forman is Assistant Professor of Communication Studies at Northeastern University. His publications on media and race include *The 'Hood Comes First: Race, Space, and Place in Rap and Hip-Hop* (Wesleyan University Press, 2002). He edited *That's the Joint! The Hip-Hop Studies Reader* (Routledge, 2004) with Mark Anthony Neal and is coeditor of the *Journal of Popular Music Studies*. He is currently writing a historical analysis of popular music on early television (1948–55), titled *One Night on TV Is Worth Weeks at the Paramount: Popular Music on Television before Elvis* (Duke University Press, forthcoming).

Nathan Godfried teaches history at the University of Maine. He is the author of *WCFL: Chicago's Voice of Labor, 1926–1978* (University of Illinois Press, 1997) and several articles on organized labor, radicals, minorities, and radio and television.

Douglas Gomery is Resident Scholar in the Library of American Broadcasting at the University of Maryland. His book *The Hollywood Studio System: A History* (University of California Press, 2005) covers in more detail how Lew Wasserman changed the film and television industries. His coauthored *Who Owns the Media?* (Lawrence Erlbaum, 2000) earned the Association for Education in Journalism and Mass Communication Picard Prize. His *Shared Pleasures* (University of Wisconsin Press, 1992) earned the Theatre Library Association prize. He has fifteen other books to his credit and more than a thousand articles.

David Goodman teaches American history at the University of Melbourne in Australia. He is the author of *Gold Seeking: Victoria and California in the 1850s* (Stanford University Press, 1994) and more recently of "Democracy and Public Discussion in the Progressive and New Deal Eras," in *Studies in American Political Development* (Fall 2004). He is completing a study of the civic role of American radio in the 1930s.

Michael Henry has been with the Library of American Broadcasting since 1994, serving a wide variety of researchers from all over the world as Research Specialist and Photo Archivist. He attended graduate school at George Washington University. He is a recipient of the Allen Rockford Award and the Stan Cawelti Award for his contributions to the vintage radio community.

Karen Hill-Scott, EdD, is one of the nation's foremost content consultants for children's media. She has been the chief consultant for the NBC children's schedule for the past ten years, and her clients have also included broadcasters Nickelodeon and Disney and content producers such as the Jim Henson Company. She is Adjunct Professor at the UCLA School of Public Policy, and she recently authored the chapter on broadcaster practices and compliance with the Children's Television Act for the *Handbook of Children and the Media*, edited by Jerome and Dorothy Singer (Sage Publications, 2001).

Michele Hilmes is Professor of Media and Cultural Studies and Director of the Wisconsin Center for Film and Theater Research at the University of Wisconsin-Madison. She is the author or editor of several books on broadcasting history, including *Radio Voices: American Broadcasting, 1922–1952* (University of Minnesota Press, 1997); *Only Connect: A Cultural History of Broadcasting in the United States* (Wadsworth/Thomson Learning, 2002); *The Radio Reader: Essays in the Cultural History of Radio* (co-edited with Jason Loviglio, Routledge, 2002); and *The Television History Book* (British Film Institute, 2003). She is currently at work on a history of the mutual influence and opposition between U.S. and British broadcasters during radio and television's formative years.

Elana Levine is Assistant Professor in the Department of Journalism and Mass Communication, University of Wisconsin-Milwaukee. She is the author of *Wallowing in Sex: American Television in the 1970s* (Duke University Press, 2007) and coeditor (with Lisa Parks) of *Undead TV: Essays on Buffy the Vampire Slayer* (Duke University Press, 2007). She has published articles on television history and criticism in *Critical Studies in Media Communication, Television and New Media, The Velvet Light Trap*, and *Studies in Latin American Popular Culture*.

Amanda D. Lotz is Assistant Professor in the Department of Communication Studies at the University of Michigan. Her book *Redesigning Women: Television after the Network Era* (University of Illinois Press, 2006) explores the rise of female-centered dramas and cable networks targeted toward women in the late 1990s as they relate to changes in the U.S. television industry. She is currently working on a book that explores the effects of the institutional redefinition of the U.S. television industry since the 1980s on the medium's role as a cultural institution.

Mike Mashon is Head of the Motion Picture, Broadcasting, and Recorded Sound Division at the Library of Congress. He holds a PhD from the University of Maryland and has written and lectured extensively on media history as well as issues in film and television preservation. He is Chair of the Television Studies Commission for the International Federation of Television Archives (FIAT).

Máire Messenger Davies is Professor of Media Studies and Director of the Centre for Media Research in the School of Media, Film and Journalism at the University of Ulster, Coleraine, Northern Ireland, UK. She was Associate Professor in Television Studies at Boston University in the United States from 1990 to 1994, and in 1993 she was one of the first recipients of an Annenberg Scholarship at the Annenberg School for Communication, University of Pennsylvania. Her research interests focus particularly on audience reception, including young audiences. She is the author of *Fake, Fact and Fantasy: Children's Interpretations of Television Reality* (Lawrence Erlbaum, 1997), *Television Is Good for Your Kids* (Hilary Shipman, 1989, 2001), and *Dear BBC: Children, Television Storytelling, and the Public Sphere* (Cambridge University Press, 2001). She is currently writing a book for the University of California Press on American television, using the series *Star Trek* as a case study, in collaboration with Professor Roberta Pearson of Nottingham University.

Jeffrey S. Miller is Associate Professor of English and Journalism at Augustana College in Sioux Falls, South Dakota. He is the author of *Something Completely Different: British Television and American Culture* (University of Minnesota Press, 2000). He is currently working on a project about "quality" media culture in the United States during the latter half of the twentieth century.

Roberta Pearson is Professor of Film and Television Studies and Director of the Institute of Film and Television at the University of Nottingham, UK. Together with Máire Messenger Davies she is writing a book on *Star Trek* called *Small Screen, Big Universe: Star Trek as Television*, to be published by the University of California Press. She is also the coeditor of *Cult Television* (University of Minnesota Press, 2004).

Kevin S. Sandler is Assistant Professor of Media Arts at the University of Arizona, specializing in U.S. popular media, censorship, and animation. He has published in a wide range of journals and anthologies, including *Cinema Journal, Animation Journal*, and most recently Heather Hendershot's *Nickelodeon Nation* (New York University Press, 2004). He is the editor of *Reading the Rabbit: Explorations in Warner Bros. Animation* (Rutgers University Press, 1998) and coeditor of *Titanic: Anatomy of a Blockbuster* (Rutgers University Press, 1999). His forthcoming books include *The Naked Truth: Why Hollywood Does Not Make NC-17 Films* (Rutgers University Press) and *Scooby Doo* (Duke University Press).

Michael J. Socolow is Assistant Professor in the Department of Communication and Journalism at the University of Maine. He previously taught at Georgetown University and Brandeis University, where he directed the Journalism Program. A former CNN Assignment Editor, his media commentary has appeared in the *Baltimore Sun*, the *Boston Globe*, and the *Chicago Tribune*. He is currently completing a manuscript on NBC and CBS in their first two decades.

Christopher H. Sterling has been Professor of Media and Public Affairs at George Washington University since 1982. He served as an FCC Commissioner's Assistant from 1980 to 1982 and was a member of the Temple University communications faculty during the 1970s. He has written or edited more than twenty books, including the *Encyclopedia of Radio* (3 vols., Dearborn, 2004) and *Stay Tuned: A History of American Broadcasting* (3rd ed., Lawrence Erlbaum, 2002), and has collected books and other printed material about radio history for nearly four decades. He has edited what is now *Communication Booknotes Quarterly* for almost as long (it began in 1969 as a monthly mimeo), and he served as the third editor (1972–76) of the *Journal of Broadcasting.*

Horst Stipp is Senior Vice President of Primary and Strategic Research at NBC in New York. He received his PhD in sociology from Columbia University and has been involved in media research for over thirty years. His publications, in English and German, cover a wide range of topics, including children and television and the impact of new media technologies. He is coauthor of a major study, *Television and Aggression: A Panel Study* (Academic Press, 1982), and of journal articles that are based on his work on NBC's self-regulatory process (Social Science Advisory Panel) designed to enhance the quality of the network's children's programming. He also teaches a seminar at Columbia University's Business School.

Shawn VanCour is a PhD candidate in the Department of Communication Arts at the University of Wisconsin-Madison, where he has served as a Lecturer in Media and Cultural Studies, and is a coordinating editor for *The Velvet Light Trap: A Critical Journal of Film and Television.* His dissertation examines efforts in 1920s American culture to establish the aesthetic parameters of radio production and radio reception and analyzes their role in the construction of American broadcasting.

David Weinstein is a Senior Program Officer in the Division of Public Programs at the National Endowment for the Humanities. He is the author of *The Forgotten Network: DuMont and the Birth of American Television* (Temple University Press, 2004) and has written essays on media history for several scholarly books and journals, including *Washington History,* the *Journal of Popular Film and Television,* and the *Quarterly Review of Film and Video.* He earned his PhD in American studies from the University of Maryland in 1997 and taught mass communication, media history, and television production at the University of Maryland and George Mason University before joining the NEH.

Index

Abbot, Bill, 299

ABC (American Broadcasting Company): *ATMA* and, 44, 50–51; creation of, 22, 74, 95; Disney and, 154; *Kraft Television Theatre* and, 147; ownership changes and, 276; programming in the 1970s and, 224, 225, 226–27, 228–31; programming in the 1980s and, 267; ratings in 2004 and, 292; scheduling strategies at, 297; sexual representation and, 228–31; VHF affiliates and, 182

academic consultants. *See* NBC Social Science Advisory Panel

Academy of Television Arts and Sciences (Los Angeles), 317

Ackenberg, William, 37

Ackerman, Harry, 155

Ackroyd, Dan, 202, 203

ACLU. *See* American Civil Liberties Union (ACLU)

action/adventure formula, 182, 183

Adams, David, 157

advertising agencies: development of broadcast genres and, 17–21; program production by, 4, 13, 17–21, 137–42, 146, 150; program scheduling and, 143, 145; shift to network control of programming and, 143–49. *See also* Thompson, J. Walter (advertising agency)

advertising-based economics: digital era and, 284–85, 286, 293, 299–302, 303; radio programming policies and, 61, 62–63, 66–68. *See also* American System; sponsors

"advertorials," 295

affiliate stations: American localism and, 12; CBS and NBC rivalry and, 34–35, 37–38; CBS business model and, 30; early NBC dominance and, 83, 88, 89; licensing rules and, 11–12, 89–90; NBC-Blue and, 36; network competition for, 34–35, 86, 89, 182; network control over, 17, 22, 86, 88; programming discretion and, 16–17, 34, 64–65. *See also* chain broadcasting; local stations

AFL. *See* American Federation of Labor (AFL)

African Americans: early programming content and, 117–18; Joseph Baker as liaison with, 124–30, 132; network blue penciling and, 121–24; postwar racial initiatives and, 120–21. *See also* black press; minority audiences; racial representation

age representation, 268

AHC. *See* American Heritage Center (AHC)

AJC. *See* American Jewish Committee (AJC)

Alexander (show), 234–36, 237

Allen, Steve, 193

All in the Family, 224, 226

Amateur Hour Collection, 314

amateur radio operators: Class B licenses and, 11; early experimentation and, 8–10

American Broadcasting Company. *See* ABC (American Broadcasting Company)

American Civil Liberties Union (ACLU), 64, 64, 74

American cultural history. *See* historical analysis of broadcasting; resource materials for historical analysis

272–73; network strategies and, 261, 263, 271–73; programming challenges and, 292–93, 296–98; revenue streams in, 293, 298–302; viewer options in, 262–63. *See also* audience fragmentation; cable networks; digital age (1985 to present); media conglomeration

preemption, 12, 252. *See also* chain broadcasting

Preston, Walter, 50

Prime Time Access Rules (PTAR), 173, 259

prime-time television: 1970s programming and, 227–28; 1980s programming and, 283; cross-polination in, 295; independent producers and, 304; multiple vs. single sponsors and, 159; NBC dominance in, 159, 263

Prince, Charles, 144

Prince, Jonathan, 302

Prism Award, 254

Procter & Gamble, 18, 302

production companies: historical materials from, 316; package shows and, 83, 154–56, 159–60, 165; program development process and, 242–43

product placement, 300–302, 304

profitability: 1960s revenues and, 83; 2004 revenues and, 303; Aylesworth and, 29; early television and, 145, 148; early years of networks and, 29; mid-1930s, 39, 50; Sarnoff and, 50, 156–58. *See also* revenue streams

program production, control of, 83; early television and, 135–37; network assumption of, 143–49, 171; philosophy of scheduling and, 142–43; in radio networks, 17–20; Thompson agency involvement and, 137–42, 150. *See also* television programming

program scheduling: coherence and, 266–67; early philosophy for, 142–43; multiple vs. single sponsors and, 159; NBC success in nonprime hours and, 263; postnetwork era and, 292–93, 296–98; *Star Trek* and, 218–19; *TW₃* and, 198. *See also* children's programming; late-night television; prime-time television; Thursday night schedule

propaganda: antilabor, 68–69, 70–71; business self-promotion and, 66–68, 69; unions as agents of, 63

"propaganda" stations, 15

prosocial program content, 245, 246, 249–51

prostitution, representation of, 234–36

Pryor, Richard, 202

PTAR. *See* Prime Time Access Rules (PTAR)

public service programming: at 1937 NBC radio, 23; airtime for unions and, 61–62, 64–65; American concept of, 15–16, 22, 23; *America's Town Meeting of the Air (ATMA)*, 20, 44–60; children's programming and, 251–52; FCC network rules and, 91, 94–95; on NBC-Blue, 91, 94–95; network production of, 20–21, 22; regulatory oversight and, 4, 15–16; during World War II, 68. *See also* documentary programming; sustaining programs

public sphere, 4, 46, 48, 54, 58. *See also America's Town Meeting of the Air (ATMA)*

Pure Oil Company, 70, 72

"quality" identity, 261–62, 272–73. *See also* "must-see TV"

quality standard in radio: Class B licensing and, 11; network radio program production and, 17, 20; sustaining programs and, 20. *See also* taste, standards of

Queen for a Day (show), 162

Quinn, Stanley, 140

Quinn, T. K., 68

quiz shows, 161

quiz show scandals, 165, 171, 172, 300

Quroga, Alex, 217

racial representation, 81, 117–34; African American Television Project and, 316; *ATMA* and, 56–57; "blue pencil" specialists and, 121–24; casting of *Star Trek* and, 213, 214, 216; children's programming and, 243, 247–49; civil rights documentaries and, 188–89; DJ format and, 82; early radio programming and, 117–20; Integration without Identification Policy and, 117, 129–30; Joseph Baker at NBC and, 124–30, 132; mid-1980s programming and, 268; postwar social context and, 120–21. *See also* Jewish people; women, representation of

Radio Act of *1912*, 14

Radio Act of *1927*, 12, 15–17, 27, 85

radio broadcasting industry (1919–38), 3–5; business and labor relations and, 61–77; emergence of the "American System" and, 7–24; public interest programming and, 44–60; rivalry between CBS and NBC and, 25–43. *See also* American System; business and labor relations; CBS (Columbia Broadcasting System); public service programming

Radio Broadcast (journal), 28

Text:	10/12 Baskerville
Display:	Baskerville
Compositor:	Integrated Composition Systems
Indexer:	Marcia Carlson
Printer and Binder:	Sheridan Books, Inc.